DOSTOYEVSKY

Dostoyevsky:

A HUMAN PORTRAIT

by Robert Payne

NEW YORK

ALFRED · A · KNOPF

1971

L. C. catalog card number: 60–53443

THIS IS A BORZOI BOOK,
PUBLISHED BY ALFRED A. KNOPF, INC.

Copyright © 1958, 1961 by ROBERT PAYNE.
All rights reserved under International and Pan-
American Copyright Conventions. Published in
the United States by Alfred A. Knopf, Inc.,
New York, and in Canada by Random House
of Canada Limited, Toronto. Manufactured in
the United States and distributed by Random
House, Inc., New York.
PUBLISHED APRIL, 1961
SECOND PRINTING, MARCH 1967
THIRD PRINTING, SEPTEMBER 1971
*The chapter entitled "LAST DAYS" originally
appeared in NEW WORLD WRITING #14 in
slightly different form as "DOSTOEVSKI: THE
LAST DAYS."*

for

P A T R I C I A   J A N E

with love

Man is a mystery. This mystery

must be solved, and even if you

pass your entire life solving it,

do not say you have wasted your

time. I occupy myself with this

mystery, because I want to be a

man.

FOREWORD

THIS IS A STUDY of Fyodor Dostoyevsky, who came to birth in the same miraculous year which saw the birth of Flaubert and Baudelaire.

I have been more concerned to portray the living man than to use him as a peg for a variety of theories. I wanted to see him plain, with his warts and his strange shuffling walk, so that it would be possible to recognize him if he entered a room. His presence, his voice, his hesitations, his acts of charity, all those things which help us to understand his way of grappling with the problems of his time, which are very largely the problems of our own time—all these seemed more important than the intellectual systems which generations of psychologists and Soviet scholars have visited upon him in an effort to explain his life and work. He defies system. To the end he remains the most inconsistent of men, shifting direction and emphasis according to the deep-seated changes in the weather of his soul. Freud saw him as a man suffering from a classic Œdipus complex. Soviet scholars see him alternatively as an enemy of the Bolsheviks or as one of their precursors. I have preferred to see him as a very human person, suffering more than most men, and content to record what he saw within himself and in the world outside, as variable as Shakespeare, and like Shakespeare rarely taking sides.

ix

Inevitably in a work of this kind there are personal prejudices. Thirty-five years ago, when I first read *The Idiot*, I was struck by the extraordinary human strength displayed by Prince Myshkin in his long-fought duel with the satanic Rogozhin, and I suspected that the author must have been at least as strong as the Prince to have described him with so much understanding. Since then I have found nothing to change this view. There was a time when students in German universities would use the initials K.M. when speaking of Beethoven. For them he was *die königliche Majestät*—"the kingly majesty." So I feel of Dostoyevsky that he belongs to those who still order and rule our lives; and some part of this feeling has inevitably colored these pages.

For the most part I have let Dostoyevsky speak for himself, quoting at some length from the four volumes of his collected letters. I suspect there is more autobiography in his novels than we have ever guessed, and I have quoted some of the passages which seem to reflect his personal beliefs and obsessions. I was interested in his novels only as they helped to build up the portrait of the man. Those who believe that he raped young girls, suffered from an unconscious desire to murder his father, and gambled like a maniac will find little comfort here.

For the rest, it is only necessary to add that the background has been sketched in lightly, because to do otherwise would involve a book of at least a thousand pages. Dostoyevsky's relations with his contemporaries are known, and form the subject of an increasing number of monographs, but they add little to the portrait of the man, who deliberately chose to think his own thoughts. He was a man of desperate passions, but few friendships; and I have therefore discussed his passions more often than his friends.

I owe a special debt of gratitude to Prince Alexis Scherbatov, who carefully read through my manuscript and gave me the benefit of his scholarly knowledge of nineteenth century Russia, and to Count Alexis Bobrinskoy, who told me some of the stories about Dostoyevsky which were current in St. Petersburg during his childhood. I am also deeply indebted to Dr. Clarence Decker, who obtained for me in Moscow many of the photographs included in this book, and to Miss G. B. Ponomareva, the Director of the Dostoyevsky Museum, who kindly made the photographs available.

CHRONOLOGY

All dates are given in the Russian "old style," twelve days earlier than ours. The Russians adopted the Western calendar in February 1918.

1789	Mikhail Dostoyevsky, father of Fyodor, born
1800	Marya Nechayeva, mother of Fyodor, born
1819	Marriage of Mikhail and Marya Dostoyevsky
October 30, 1821	Fyodor Dostoyevsky, born in Moscow
January 29, 1837	Death of the poet Alexander Pushkin
February 27, 1837	Death of Dostoyevsky's mother
January 16, 1838	Dostoyevsky enters Military Engineering College, St. Petersburg
June 24, 1839	Murder of Dostoyevsky's father
August 12, 1843	Dostoyevsky graduates from Engineering College with rank of sublieutenant
June–July 1844	He publishes his translation of *Eugénie Grandet*
October 19, 1844	He retires from the army
1846	Gogol publishes *Selected Passages from Correspondence with my Friends*
January 15, 1846	Dostoyevsky publishes *Poor Folk*

February 1846	Publishes *The Double*
April 23, 1847	Belinsky attacks Gogol
May 26, 1848	Death of Belinsky
December 1848	Dostoyevsky publishes *White Nights*
April 23, 1849	Petrashevsky conspirators, including Dostoyevsky, arrested
December 22, 1849	Public degradation and "execution" on Semyonov Square
January 23, 1850– February 15, 1854	Dostoyevsky serves prison sentence at Omsk
November 1854	Meets Baron Wrangel
1854–6	Crimean War
March 2, 1854	Dostoyevsky enrolled as private
1855	Writes first drafts of *The Village of Stepanchikovo, The House of the Dead,* and *The Insulted and Injured*
February 18, 1855	Death of Tzar Nicholas I
December 1855	Baron Wrangel leaves Semipalatinsk
October 1, 1856	Dostoyevsky promoted to ensign
February 6, 1857	Marries Marya Issayeva at Kuznetsk
March 18, 1859	Permitted to leave the army
March 1859	Publishes *My Uncle's Dream*
November 1859	Settles in St. Petersburg
November–December 1859	Publishes *The Village of Stepanchikovo*
February 19, 1861	Abolition of serfdom in Russia
January–July 1861	Publishes *The Insulted and Injured*
1861	Publishes *The House of the Dead*
June–September 1862	Travels abroad
February–March 1863	*Winter Notes on Summer Impressions*
August–October 1863	Travels abroad with Polina Suslova
April 15, 1864	Death of his wife

July 10, 1864	Death of his brother Mikhail
1864	*Notes from Underground*
January 1865	Korvin-Krukovsky family arrives in St. Petersburg
June 1865	Signs contract with publisher Stellovsky
July–October 1865	Travels abroad
January 1866	First installment of *Crime and Punishment*
April 4, 1866	Karokozov attacks Tzar Alexander II
October 4, 1866	Dostoyevsky engages Anna Snitkina as stenographer
February 15, 1867	Marries Anna Snitkina
April 14, 1867	Travels abroad with Anna
Summer, 1867	Suffers from gambling fever
September 14, 1867	Makes first notes for *The Idiot*
February 22, 1868	His daughter Sonya born in Geneva
May 12, 1868	Sonya dies
September 14, 1869	His daughter Luba born in Moscow
November 21, 1869	Nechayev kills Ivanov
July 16, 1871	Dostoyevsky's son Fyodor born
August 14, 1872	Nechayev arrested in Switzerland
December 1872	Dostoyevsky appointed editor of *Grazhdanin*
August 10, 1875	His son Alexey born
July–August 1876	Visits Ems for the cure
1876–1877	Publishes *The Diary of a Writer*
May 16, 1878	Death of Alexey
June 23, 1878	With Solovyov visits Optina Pustyn
January 1879	*The Brothers Karamazov* begins to appear
June 8, 1880	Delivers speech at Pushkin Festival in Moscow

November 9, 1880   Finishes *The Brothers Karamazov*
January 28, 1881   Dies in St. Petersburg
January 31, 1881   His body removed to Alexander
                   Nevsky monastery
February 1, 1881   Funeral at Tikhvin cemetery of the
                   Alexander Nevsky monastery

CONTENTS

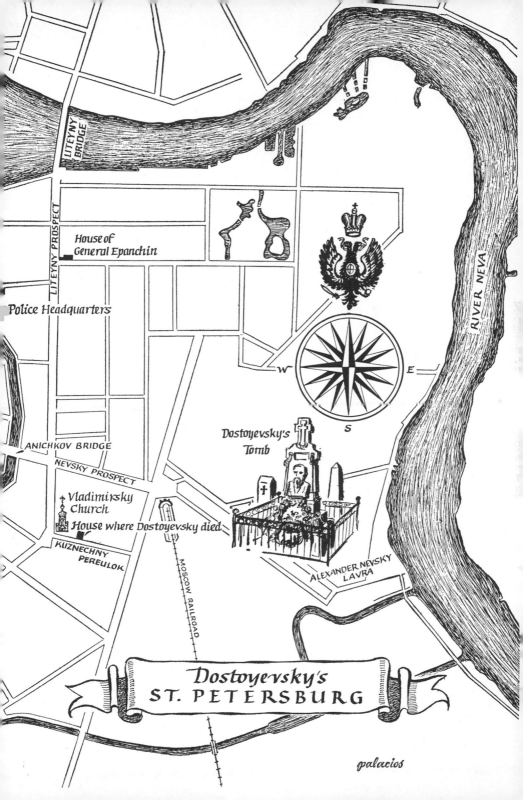

LITEYNY BRIDGE

LITEYNY PROSPECT

House of
General Epanchin

Police Headquarters

W E

S

RIVER NEVA

Dostoyevsky's
Tomb

ANICHKOV BRIDGE

NEVSKY PROSPECT

Vladimirsky
Church

House where Dostoyevsky died

KUZNECHNY
PEREULOK

MOSCOW RAILROAD

ALEXANDER NEVSKY
LAVRA

Dostoyevsky's
ST. PETERSBURG

palacios

DOSTOYEVSKY

THE MURDER

IT WOULD SEEM to be a law of nature that when a man is murdered all those who are in any way connected with the crime are haunted. The last cries of the dead man are heard long after his death, and sometimes they are heard many generations after his death.

On Midsummer's Day, 1839, there occurred in the remote village of Chermashnya in the province of Tula, about a hundred miles from Moscow, the murder of an obscure doctor who claimed descent from the Tartars of the Golden Horde and from a long line of court dignitaries, robber barons, magistrates, landowners and priests. The doctor had been intended for the priesthood, but for some reason which he never explained he turned against the Church and entered the School of Medicine in Moscow, where he spent most of his life. During the campaign of 1812 he helped the wounded. For nine years he was in private practice, and he continued to see private patients when he was installed as attending physician at the Maryinsky Hospital of the Poor. His tasks were largely administrative, and he bore the title of government assessor. His name was listed in the register of the hereditary nobility.

On the whole the doctor was a kindly man, strict in his management of the hospital, careful in his finances, and attentive to the needs of his children, who were never whipped and rarely scolded. He had a low forehead, high cheekbones and a heavy, pointed chin, but there was an expression of tenderness in his

3

dark eyes, and though he held himself stiffly, he would always unbend when his children were present. In his full uniform, with his white stock and high collar embroidered with gold laurel leaves, he looked like any middle-aged government official. There was even a hint of aristocratic delicacy in his manner. He could never forget that he was descended from conquerors.

In the summer of 1839 the doctor was a widower spending the summer months with two of his daughters on his estate at Darovoye. The death of his wife had driven him nearly mad with grief and loneliness, and sometimes at night he was heard conversing in a strange, vehement voice with the wife who had died two years before in his arms. He drank heavily, took a peasant girl, Katerina Alexandrovna, for a mistress, and sometimes spoke of marrying the daughter of a neighboring landowner. All his life he had been a man of strict morality. Now in his grief he kicked over the traces.

The estate at Darovoye consisted of a country house, farm lands and a village of a hundred "souls"—a hundred male serfs who according to the fashion of the time were his property, to do with as he pleased. There were perhaps four hundred people in the village, and another forty or fifty in the tiny village of Chermashnya, which could be reached across the field through an avenue of oak trees.[1]

In the past the doctor had been an understanding master, but now he raged through the village like a madman. He was drunk from morning to night, and no woman was safe from him. For the slightest offense he gave out harsh punishments. One day the peasant Fedot Petrov was working in the fields when the doctor suddenly appeared by his side. The peasant was too surprised to salute. The doctor, almost incoherent with anger, shouted at him that he had failed to salute on purpose, it was a monstrous crime,

[1] The following account is based on two documents given in Leonid Grossman, *Dostoyevsky na zhiznennom puty,* page 81 ff. Village tradition is quite extraordinarily strong in Russia, and some part of the story was uncovered by V. C. Nechayeva as recently as July 1925.

and he must be punished. "Come to the stable!" he shouted. "I'll have you whipped!" Fedot Petrov was flogged, and with that flogging the doctor signed his own death warrant.

No one knows any longer whether there was a deliberate conspiracy to murder the doctor, or whether it came about as the result of inevitable forces working among the peasants, spontaneously. There were rumors that Ephim Maximov, the uncle of Katerina Alexandrovna, had prepared everything beforehand, but it was generally agreed that such preparations were unnecessary. Only a spark was needed to fire the concentrated hatred of the peasants.

The spark was provided by the doctor that morning when, after having flogged Fedot Petrov, he summoned his workmen around him and saw that four of them were missing. All four came from the pathetic little village of Chermashnya.

"What the devil has happened to them?" the doctor demanded.

"They are ill," someone replied.

"If they are ill, I know how to cure them!" the doctor roared, shaking his stick, and he gave orders for his horses to be harnessed.

He drove to Chermashnya, and was not particularly surprised when he found the four wandering down the street as though they had no cares in the world. He knew them well. Their names were Melikhov, Issayev, Ephimov and Nikitin. Waving his stick, he jumped down from the carriage and chased them into a courtyard, thinking he would give them a punishment they would never forget. Instead, the peasants turned on him. Vasily Nikitin, a strapping, ruddy-faced youth, slipped behind the doctor and imprisoned his arms. For a moment the others were too bewildered to do anything, and then Nikitin shouted: "What are you standing there for? Haven't we agreed on what we have to do?"

The peasants took courage. They threw themselves on the doctor, pulled him to the ground, tied him up, and then to punish

5

him for his drinking and wenching they poured vodka down his throat until he could no longer breathe, and one of them, probably Vasily Nikitin, took the doctor's genitals in his hands and crushed them. They had decided beforehand that if the doctor ever fell into their power, they would kill him in a way which would leave no trace. They had also decided to permit him the last rites of the Church. They summoned the priest of Chermashnya after taking him a little way out of the village and propping him up at the foot of an oak tree.

He was still breathing when the priest arrived, but he was evidently dying and could not speak.

"What happened?" the priest asked.

"A sudden stroke," someone said, and the priest asked no more questions.

For two days the body was left to rot near the oak tree; then it was buried.

When the police came to inquire about the incident, the peasants remained silent. There was no trial, for there was no evidence. No one in the family pursued the affair, for it was known that nothing would be gained by an inquiry. A garbled account of the murder was handed down through the family, and it was believed that the doctor was suffocated to death under the cushions of his carriage.

Most of the doctor's children grew up normally and died normally. One of his daughters, Varvara, married into great wealth, but when her husband died, she became a miser, living on crusts. It was rumored that she concealed a great treasure under her bed. In 1893 thieves broke in, searched for the treasure, and not finding it, they stabbed her to death and set fire to her body.

Fyodor Mikhailovich Dostoyevsky was the son of the doctor who was murdered in Chermashnya.

THE CHILDREN
OF THE DOCTOR

IN THE CHILDHOOD of Fyodor Mikhailovich Dostoyevsky there was nothing in the least unusual. It was a family like many other families of the Russian gentry, following established customs and warmed by the affection of the parents and a host of servants.

The children of the doctor were brought up to obey their father, to adore their mother, to work hard at their lessons, and to attend church regularly. Family life followed a pattern of unchanging decorum, and everyone knew exactly what was expected of him. It was a very quiet and sheltered existence, behind high walls. The children worshipped their mother, who was beautiful and gentle and capable of acts of astonishing self-abnegation; she lived for her children and her husband. A portrait of her in a copy made by one of her children has survived: it shows a face of grave delicacy, and quiet purposeful authority, with enormous eyes under wide arching brows and lips which suggest a passionate nature. She wears her hair in ringlets, and she is dressed in a modish costume with a high collar which sets off her dark beauty. She was the daughter of a rich Moscow merchant called Nechayev.

To Marya Dostoyevskaya there were born eight children, and since she was never a strong woman, she wore herself out in childbearing, and died young. Her first child was a boy, Mikhail, born in 1820. There followed Fyodor, who was born on October 30,

1821, and in the next year came Varvara. There was a three-year pause, and then came her third son Andrey, and then again there was a long pause before the birth in quick succession of twin daughters, one of whom died in infancy, and two more children. Not very long after the birth of the last child she died.

The four children who came between the years 1820 and 1825 were inseparable. They grew up together, learned from one another, and sometimes regarded themselves as the indisputable rulers of the family. Mikhail was slow and gentle, never very sure of himself. Varvara was impulsive, and something of a tomboy. Andrey, who was called "Little Tail," because he came last, was quick, eager and energetic. But it was Fyodor who possessed the spirit of mischief and led them into wild escapades—those escapades which children play even in small furnished apartments where they are compelled to rely on their imaginations to discover reasons for excitement. In these adventures they were aided by an extraordinary woman, Alyona Frolovna, who was continually bubbling with laughter and who was so enormous that her stomach reached to her knees. She was continually telling the children stories, and whenever any question of discipline arose she always took their side. Marya Dostoyevskaya was one of those women who are quite incapable of running a family; that task was given to Alyona Frolovna, who had no hesitation in taking the family under her wing. She was a peasant, but she always spoke to the doctor as to an equal; and the stern doctor rarely objected.

The family lived in four small rooms which looked over a neighboring park called Mary's Woods. The rooms were on the first story of a building given over to the families of doctors and interns, and like many of these buildings made no claim to elegance. There was a parlor painted cobalt blue, and a living room painted canary yellow. Part of the vestibule was boarded off to make a bedroom for the boys, while Varvara slept in her parents' bedroom. The ceilings were high, and that perhaps was the best thing about those rooms filled with ugly furniture and continually crowded with children and servants—sometimes there were eight servants attached to the household. The furniture sometimes puzzled the children. There was a card table set between two windows in the living room, but no one was allowed to play cards.

It was a happy family, plagued only by poverty, for the doctor tried to live on his official salary, and it was sometimes difficult to make ends meet, with a growing family and eight servants to feed. The doctor held the purse-strings, but does not seem to have been unusually parsimonious. He like to say: "Poverty is no sin." He gave his children little or no pocket money, but in this he did not differ from the custom of the time. He saw that their needs were satisfied. They were always well-dressed, and never went hungry. Two or three times a year there were feasts. These took place when the wealthy relatives of Marya Dostoyevskaya suddenly descended on the family in carriages loaded with gifts of food and toys; and to the end of his life Fyodor remembered the sudden blaze of excitement when wealthy and fashionably dressed women appeared in the cobalt-blue parlor, dispensing presents to the children.

There was of course one dark shadow over the lives of the growing children. The father was attached to the Maryinsky Hospital for the Poor, and something of the atmosphere and the smells of the hospital penetrated the small official apartment where they lived. They could see the patients wrapped in shapeless white gowns walking beyond the fence at the bottom of the garden. From the time when he was able to reason, Fyodor was aware of the fatality which commands that some people should live abundantly and others should be cut down by ill-health. There was no explanation for these things. It was something he observed from the days of his childhood.

Whenever Fyodor spoke about his family, he always remembered that it was "typically Russian and very pious." Both his father and mother were deeply religious. Every year there were visits to a nearby monastery. The church with its brilliant rituals

9

and sonorous chants formed an important part of their lives. Fyodor's earliest recollection was of being taken to some place in the country, where there were huge lime trees and flower gardens, and suddenly he was taken into a church, and held up to receive the sacrament and to kiss the chalice. In the bright summer air Fyodor distinctly caught sight of a dove flying in through one window of the cupola and darting out of the other; with the chalice just in front of him, he cried out: "A dove! A dove!" He saw the dove only for an instant, but he was haunted for the rest of his life by its inexplicable beauty.

There were many other memories of childhood. He remembered how during the hot summer months his father would take a siesta after stationing one or more of his sons around him, giving them orders to brush away with a linden branch any flies that dared to settle on his face. Sometimes the children would crowd round the father, watching the approach of the flies with fearful expectancy. "Woe to him who let a fly pass!" Andrey Dostoyevsky wrote in his memoirs, but he did not suggest there was anything very tyrannical about the doctor's desire to sleep in peace.

He was a man of habit, whose life moved according to a precise ritual. The family rose at six. At eight o'clock the doctor went to make his rounds at the hospital. He returned an hour later, and a coach would be waiting for him to take him on his rounds through the city. At twelve or a little later he returned, and lunch was usually on the table at one o'clock. After lunch it was his habit to lock himself in the blue parlor for a nap. At four o'clock there was afternoon tea with the whole family gathered round the samovar, and then the doctor would visit the wards of the hospital again. During the evenings there were walks, and afterward perhaps the doctor would read from the books in his small but comprehensive library, or he would correct the children's lessons. He was a good teacher, and made sure that they all learned French, German and Latin. It was remembered that when the children were called upon to recite, they had to stand bolt upright beside their father, but this too was the accepted practice of the time. The doctor suffered from rare bouts of melancholia, and at such times he became remote and forbidding, but he was nearly always gentle with his children, and he had a special affection for Varvara.

The doctor was not quite so gentle with Alyona Frolovna, who sometimes exasperated him. That mountainous woman, who took snuff and was constantly being visited at night by a disreputable tobacco merchant, had her own homemade theories about everything on earth. She was like an elemental force introduced into the calm backwaters of the doctor's apartment. She had theories about food, about God, about the proper behavior of doctors. She insisted that one should eat a mouthful of bread between every bite of fish or vegetables. She believed in mystic marriages, and when the doctor taunted her about the visits of the tobacco merchant, she drew herself up to her full height and answered: "Heaven have pity on you, am I not married to the Lord?" The children were a little in awe of her, but she told stories so well, making them up on the spur of the moment from the inexhaustible fountains of her imagination, and so they loved her. They loved her even when indigestion or nightmares made her bellow like a wild bull at night. The doctor, awakened from his precarious sleep, would leap from his bed, run to the little cubbyhole where she slept, shake her until she awoke, and then threaten her with a bloodletting if she persisted in waking everyone up. It was one of her fancies that if she went to sleep on an empty stomach she would dream of gypsies; and she lived in fear of gypsies.

Sometimes another elemental force penetrated the apartment. This was Lukerya, who had been the wet nurse of all the children born after Mikhail. She was a swarthy woman, who walked with the slow sure-footed tread of a peasant who rarely came to Moscow. She arrived twice a year, and her visits were events to be remembered for weeks afterward. She came into the parlor with ribbons on her head, wearing linden bark shoes, and after she had made the sign of the cross and prayed before the icon, she would be greeted warmly by Marya Dostoyevskaya and then she would embrace the children one by one, giving them the homemade whey cakes she carried in her colored kerchief. She always arrived in the morning, when the children did their lessons, and so she would vanish into the kitchen until lunch was served. At night she stole into the children's room and told them even better stories than they heard from Alyona, about Prince Ivan, Bluebeard, and the Firebird. There were stories, too, about Alyosha Popovich, the half-crazy son of a priest, who always succeeded in getting what he wanted. She spoke with the brogue of a peasant, in a warm racy voice, and in her presence the children were delirious with pleasure.

They soon learned to tell stories themselves; they read whatever they could lay their hands on; and they were taught a great respect for literature. When he was seven or eight, Fyodor read Karamzin's *History of Russia,* and the influence of that violently nationalistic work remained with him throughout his life. Karamzin's eight-volume history celebrates the power and glory of the Russian empire, and he never tires of reminding his audience that it covered an area far greater than the Roman empire. "You have only to take a glance at the map of our empire, and you are staggered!" Karamzin wrote. "Rome in all her majesty was never the equal of this!" It was an opinion which Fyodor found particularly consoling.

About the time he was reveling in Karamzin's *History* and the same author's sentimental stories, Fyodor was suddenly thrust into an uneasy awareness of the futility of man compared with the power and majesty of God. The Russian empire might be the greatest that had ever existed on earth, but the individual Russian was plagued with a sense of human insecurity. On the Monday of Passion Week, when he was attending mass with his mother, an acolyte placed on the lectern an enormous Bible, opened it at the book of *Job* and read: "There was a man in the land of Uz, whose name was Job; and that man was perfect and upright, and one that feared God, and eschewed evil." The boy was shaken to the core by the recital of Job's adventures; and just as his mind never moved very far from the knowledge that Russia was "the chosen one," the nation with the greatest spiritual and moral power, destined to conquer the world, so he remained throughout his life devoted to Job, who dared to rebel against God.

There was no time in his life when he did not believe in God, but there were many times when he believed in rebellion against God.

It was, of course, an age of rebellion, of formal protest against orthodoxy concealed in the massive colors of romanticism. Karamzin pointed to the eternal verities of the Russian state, but Schiller in *The Robbers* had painted the rewards of revolutionaries. Pushkin and Lermontov had in their different ways blessed the revolutionary fervor of the Russian middle classes, who had not yet dared to raise their voices in protest, although the sense of the need for revolution was fermenting among them. At the age of ten Fyodor read *The Robbers*. It made his hair stand on end, and he could not sleep for many nights afterward. *Job* was one side of the coin; *The Robbers* was the other. In Fyodor's mind, Job and Karl Moor were brothers.

We should not be surprised that the doctor's children were so precocious. They were educated relentlessly by their father, who read aloud to them every night, continually cross-examined them on their knowledge, and continued to teach them when he took them for walks. Fyodor was still very young when he delighted his godfather by quoting long passages of Voltaire's *Henriade* in accurate French.

There was also much lighter reading. The children reveled in Walter Scott and *The Arabian Nights*, and they had a profound knowledge of *Robinson Crusoe*. When they passed the summer months on their father's country estate at Darovoye, two days drive from Moscow, they liked to pretend they were on a desert island, or else they were Red Indians from the pages of *The Last of the Mohicans,* which had been translated into Russian shortly after it appeared in America. Fyodor particularly enjoyed the visits to the estate. His brother reports how for days previously he would be like a whippet straining at the leash, and on the day when they actually drove out of Moscow, there was a kind of wild, intoxicated look about him, as of one who rejoiced in freedom above all things.

The children and their mother would sometimes spend the entire summer at the country estate. Then at last they were free from the severe, organized lectures, the cluttered house, the sight of the patients in the hospital. They played games with the village children, among them a game called *troika,* where the children took the part of horses, a strong young peasant boy in the middle with small girls as mares on either side. Fyodor, Mikhail or Andrey would be the drivers, and in this fashion they would gallop through the village and into the birch forests. They also played a game called *horse fair,* and pretend to be buyers of horseflesh, the horses as usual being the children of the village serfs. Similar games were played by the children of most landed proprietors, and there is no reason to believe that cruelty was involved in them.

Sometimes Fyodor would go off alone to the woods, to brood, to collect mushrooms and wild berries, to watch the small quick red lizards, and to break off switches from the hazel trees. Years later, in St. Petersburg, he would remember vividly the fragrance of the birch woods in the south and the smell of damp, rotted leaves. He was very close to the earth in those days; and all his later works are colored with a peculiar attitude towards the earth as a kind of mysteriously regal presence, so beautiful that she contained all beauty within herself. So we find Father Zossima saying in one of his homilies: "God took seed from different worlds and sowed them in the earth, and made his garden grow, and everything that could come up came up, but what grows, lives, and is alive only through the feeling of contact with other mysterious worlds." And throughout the novels, at moments of great crisis, his heroes bow down and kiss the earth. "Kiss the earth and love it with an unceasing, consuming love. Love all men, love everything, seek that rapture and ecstasy." The words are placed in the mouth of Father Zossima, but they seem to come directly from Dostoyevsky's heart.

But while Dostoyevsky found his greatest happiness as a boy in Darovoye, it was also there that he suffered moments of awful fear. In one of the autobiographical fragments which appear in *The Diary of a Writer* he described how, as a boy of nine, he was wandering through thick shrubbery on a dry, windy August day when amid the silence he heard the sharp cry of "Wolf! Wolf!" Hearing the cry, he screamed in panic and raced in the direction of an old peasant who was plowing along a slope nearby. The peasant, who was called Marei, was thickset and tall, with much grey in his heavy flaxen beard. As soon as he heard the cry, the peasant stopped his mare and looked around. Fyodor came running breathlessly up to him, clutching at him, saying there was a wolf in the woods.

"Eh, what's that? A wolf, eh?" the old peasant said.

"Yes, someone shouted," Fyodor shouted in panic, holding on to the plowshare and the peasant's smock.

"Well, there are no wolves around here," the peasant said, stroking the boy's cheek. "Don't be afraid! Christ be with you, just cross yourself!"

The boy's mouth was moving convulsively, and he could not cross himself. Seeing that he was helpless and in need of comfort, the peasant touched the boy's lips with his fingers black with earth, and afterwards made the sign of the cross over him. No longer afraid, but still perplexed and anxious, the boy walked away.

When Dostoyevsky thought about this incident afterwards, he remembered that he had received the benediction of the earth before he received the benediction of Christ. To the end of his life he was to remain aware of those two sources of morality. To the end the Russian earth and the Russian Christ were at war within him.

But though he admired the peasants and loved them this side idolatry, he was not blind to their faults. He knew their appalling drunkenness and cruelty. In *Crime and Punishment,* Raskolnikov dreams of a terrible incident in his childhood. In a village street some drunken peasants are beating an old grey-brown mare. They are incensed because every time they hurl the mare to the ground, she rises again. At last an old peasant decides to put an end to the mare, and equips himself with a bar of iron. She is clubbed to death in full view of a small boy who runs up and throws his arms round the dead, bloodstained muzzle, and kisses her on the eyes and on the lips. Afterwards, he attacks with his puny fists the peasant who killed the mare.

When his father arrives to rescue him from the crowd, the boy asks: "Why did they have to murder the mare?"

"They're drunk," the father says, leading him away. "They are playing the fool. It is not our business!"

For Dostoyevsky, the peasants, in spite of their lapses into bestiality and drunkenness, were the soul of Russia. They were overwhelmingly humble before Christ, and this was their greatest virtue. In *The House of the Dead,* he tells how the peasants would stand at the church doors, humbly making way for some nobleman with a huge paunch or an important lady dressed in the height of fashion, and it occurred to him that it was only the peasants who knew how to pray with real fervor and humility.

One evening in Moscow, when Fyodor was nine, the whole family was sitting round the table in the living room, drinking tea. The conversation turned to the small estate in the south, and how they would all spend the summer there. It was Easter week, and they were all caught up in the excitement of the religious ceremonies. Suddenly the door burst open, and an old peasant wearing an old cloak and with bast shoes on his feet stood on the threshold. The man looked very tired, as though he had walked for many miles, and there was despair written on his face.

The children immediately recognized the man. He was Grigory Vasilyev, the manager of the estate.

"What happened?" the doctor shouted in alarm.

"The estate is all burned!" Grigory Vasilyev said in his deep voice.

Since the estate was the delight of the children, and the doctor's only possession, everyone was immediately thrown into panic. They learned that the peasants' huts, the granary, the cattle-shed, all the spring seed, some of the cattle, and a peasant called Arkhip had all been burned. They fell to their knees, and prayed. The doctor's wife was weeping, and the doctor shouted that ruin had come upon him. Only Alyona Frolovna, who had raised the children from birth, seemed to be immune from the panic which had descended upon all of them. She was a serf, and had earned very little money over the years, but she had saved 500 rubles against her old age. She went straight up to the children's mother and said: "Please take my money—I have no use for it. . . ." The offer was refused, because the doctor was able to rebuild the huts and granaries and the cattleshed out of his own money, but the children never forgot the peasant who had walked all the way from Darovoye or Alyona's gesture.

When Fyodor was twelve or thirteen, his mother began to spit blood. She was already dying of tuberculosis. The doctor believed she would recover her health better in Darovoye than in Moscow, and so she went to live on the estate with the younger children, leaving Mikhail and Fyodor with their father. The apartment seemed suddenly empty. Now instead of the tumultuous family there was only the stern and overworked father, and the two tutors who gave the boys their lessons. The earliest of Fyodor's surviving letters was written to his mother.

Dear Maminka,

I was very unhappy, dear Maminka, when you left us, and now too, dear Maminka, whenever I think of you, I am overcome with sadness. If only you knew how much I want to see you, how impatient I am for the happy moment when we shall meet again. Every time I think of you, I pray God for your health. Tell us, dear Maminka, whether you arrived safely, and embrace Andrey and Vera for me. I kiss your hands and remain your obedient son,

F. DOSTOYEVSKY [2]

The letter was written in the spring of 1834, when she was already doomed. About the same time Alyona Frolovna, the good servant who had been looking after the family in the mother's absence, began to spit blood. A wall of sickness descended on the family.

While the doctor brooded, Mikhail and Fyodor were sent to a private school owned by a certain Chermak, a little fat man almost without education, though he took care to surround himself with young teachers from the University. It was an expensive school, one of the best in Moscow. The children boarded there during the week, returning at weekends to face their father's interrogations. Because he was spending money he could ill afford on their educations, he wanted to know exactly how they were progressing; and by dint of repeating at weekends the lessons they had learned during the week, they became good scholars, earning high marks. Only one thing disturbed the doctor—a curious wildness and explosiveness in Fyodor's character. Once he remarked prophetically: "Mark my words! You'll wear the red cap yet!" He meant the red caps worn by the soldiers in Siberia who were recruited from the prisons.

Most of the year the mother remained in Darovoye, a stran-

[2] *F. M. Dostoyevsky: Pisma 1.* Edited by A. C. Dolinin. Moscow-Leningrad, 1928–59. Subsequently referred to as *Letters.*

ger to the children who were left in Moscow. She grew so weak
that she was unable to comb her hair, of which she was especially
proud, and she had her hair cut off. The doctor was beside himself with worry. In his loneliness and despair, he wrote off a letter
accusing her bluntly of unchastity. She replied: "I swear by God,
by heaven and earth, that I have never betrayed you and will
never betray the sacred oath I made at the altar." Her letter is
dated May 1836. A few weeks later she returned to Moscow to
die. She lingered through the summer and fall, growing increasingly weaker, living in a pavilion in the hospital grounds, attended
by her husband and by all the other doctors he could summon to
her bedside. She died on February 27, 1837. She was only thirty-
six years old.

With her death, a vast change came over the family. It was
as though they had all aged with grief. The doctor grew sullen and
morose, and seemed to be moving in a nightmare of his own.
Mikhail found solace in poetry, reading and writing poems
interminably. Fyodor never recovered from her death. Suddenly
his voice, which had been strong and vibrant, became hoarse;
and he spoke with that strangely ugly voice for the rest of his
life.

A month earlier the great poet Pushkin had died in a duel.
Both brothers adored Pushkin, and when the news of Pushkin's
death came to them while their mother was dying, they felt they
were attending a double funeral. The doctor urged them to select
the inscription for the tomb, and they settled upon an epitaph
from Karamzin: "Lie here, beloved dust, until the joyful dawn."
In later years Fyodor seems to have been appalled by the choice,
for he pilloried the epitaph mercilessly in a short story describing
the conversations of the dead in a waterlogged cemetery and
again in *The Idiot,* where a man solemnly buries his own leg and
raises the same inscription over it.

His love for his mother was the guiding force in Fyodor's
life. Without her he felt lost. He was sixteen, with a thin, nerv-

ous, handsome face, a little girlish, but with his mother's death his features grew harder, sterner, haunted by death.

For a few more weeks the brothers remained in Moscow. There were long discussions with the doctor about their future, and it was decided to enter them in the Imperial Engineering College at St. Petersburg. The brothers had never been to the Russian capital, and were eager to go; and neither seems to have been appalled at the prospect of being trained in engineering. They were good at mathematics; they were happy to escape from Moscow; and they regarded St. Petersburg as a holy place, for had not Pushkin died there? They promised themselves that as soon as they reached the city they would seek out the rooms where Pushkin had written his poems and they would stand on the place where he had fallen in the duel.

Among the treasures which Fyodor took with him on the journey was a small medallion given to him by his mother. It bore the figure of an angel, and the words:

J'ai le cœur tout plein d'amour,
Quand l'aurez-vous à votre tour?

The words were like a challenge. They demanded from him the utmost love and the utmost dedication. These words were graven on his heart, and he could no more escape from them than he could escape from the memory of his mother. He carried the medallion for the rest of his life.

THE FORTRESS

O<small>N THAT DAY</small> in May when the brothers set out for St. Petersburg with their father, they were in good heart. There was a solemn leave-taking, with the hospital chaplain presiding over a private mass; there were presentations and speeches about how the boys would uphold the honor of the family. At last they entered the hired *kibitka* for the long slow journey across the northern plains, staying the night at verminous inns, spending the days watching the swamps and farmland vanishing in smoky mist, and at every relay the coachman would find an excuse for wasting several hours.

As Fyodor remembered the journey years later, they were almost delirious with joy. They both yearned to escape from Moscow; they were both dedicated to serving "the great and the beautiful"; and they quivered in anticipation of the prospects in store. Mikhail wrote three poems every day, and Fyodor meditated on a long novel with a Venetian background. The slow pace of the horses annoyed them—for most of the time they went at a walking pace—but nothing disturbed their uneventful progress until they came to a village in the province of Tver. They were sitting in an inn, waiting for the horses to be changed, when Fyodor looked out of the window and saw something which shocked him almost out of his wits.

What he saw was an example of cruelty which somehow symbolized all official cruelty. He remembered it all his life, and sometimes he would try to puzzle some meaning out of it. The ugly incident is mentioned twice in *The Diary of a Writer* and twice more in his novels.

There was nothing to suggest that pure horror was about to descend on the street. Opposite the inn was the post station, and when a *troika* drove up with a courier and a postboy he seemed to be watching something completely normal and ordinary. The courier disappeared into the post-station for a glass of vodka, and a new postboy made ready to jump into the driving seat. Fyodor observed that the courier was a tall thickset man with a livid red face, wearing full uniform and an imposing three-cornered hat with white, yellow and green plumes. Three fresh spirited horses were put into the traces.

> Then quite suddenly the courier came running down the stairs, and took his seat in the *troika*. The postboy flicked his whip, but they had moved only a few feet when the courier stood up and silently brought his huge fist down on the back of the boy's head. The boy jerked forward, lifted his whip high, and then with all his strength he began to lash at the wheel horse. The horses were now dashing forward, but the courier showed no signs that he was pleased.
>
> There was method in what he was doing; it was not mere anger. It was a method which had been developed and tested through long years of experience. The terrible fist rose and fell, always striking at the back of the boy's head, up and down, again and again, and so it continued until the *troika* was out of sight. Of course the postboy could hardly keep his balance. Incessantly, every second, like a madman, he lashed at the horses, until finally he had whipped them so hard that they were racing ahead furiously, as though possessed.
>
> I asked our coachman about this, and he told me that all couriers behave in roughly the same way, but this particular courier was notoriously brutal, and everyone recognized the fact. As soon as he jumps into the *troika,* he starts beating the boy, and it is always "in precisely

and exactly the same fashion", unreasonably, regularly, his fists swinging up and down.

"His trick," the coachman told me, "is to hold the postboy at his mercy for a mile or two, hitting out at him with his fists, and then he stops. If he wearies of the progress they are making, he will resume the beating midway in the journey, but God may prevent it. But when they are coming to another post station, he always gets up on his feet and for a mile he will keep swinging his fists up and down until they reach the station, so that everyone in the village will gaze at them in amazement." [1]

So that everyone in the village will gaze at them in amazement . . . Fyodor seems to have been deeply impressed by the coachman's interpretation of the act as one stemming from perverted pride. "That courier," he wrote at another time, "found greater pleasure in his polished Petersburg boots and the feathers in his hat than in any Russian peasant, and I suspect that he loved them more than he loved Russia herself, though he had crossed the country from end to end."

Fyodor himself had already entered upon that love affair with Russia which would last all his life. Determined to serve "the great and the beautiful," he would serve Russia and the Tzar. He would become a good officer in the Tzar's army, and obey the imperial purposes of the dynasty to the end.

First, however, it was necessary to go to a cramming school kept by a certain Koronad Philipovich Kostomarov, an elderly ex-officer of engineers with a bushy black mustache and piercing eyes. Kostomarov was the best type of teacher, eager, knowledgeable, hard-working. He boarded his pupils, watched over them, and encouraged them all through the spring and summer, preparing them for the examinations in September. In June the brothers wrote a joint letter to their father, who had by this time abandoned

[1] *The Diary of a Writer,* entry of January 1876, III, i.

his practice in St. Petersburg and had settled with his remaining children at Darovoye:

> Our affairs are progressing properly. We are study-ing geometry and algebra, we draw plans of fortresses: redoubts, bastions, etc., and sometimes we trace the mountains in ink. Koronad Philipovich is happy with our progress, and exceptionally kind to us. He has brought us 30 rubles worth of fine instruments and 12 rubles worth of paints. It was simply impossible to do without them, because the plans have to be colored, and the other pupils are too miserly to lend us theirs. We have no other expenses except for letter paper and the paper used for making plans . . .[2]

Meanwhile the doctor was doing his best. He sent them books, used his influence in government circles, and encouraged them with long sermons on the necessity of invoking divine aid, and they replied in kind, invoking divine aid on their father, a troubled man burdened with the upkeep of eight children. Their letters to him breathe a quiet confidence; there were no clouds on the horizon.

Though they worked hard, they did not work all the time. Occasionally, and especially on Sundays, they would roam round St. Petersburg with a young man called Ivan Shidlovsky, who was handsome, intelligent, and ferociously romantic. Shidlovsky looked a little like a Byronic hero, thin and pale, in love with Pushkin and Schiller. He was always writing verses and always falling in love. Once he wrote in a letter to Mikhail: "This is the true sign of the great poet, the man of eminence—trample him in the mud, cover him with ashes, drag him along the earth, crush him and torture him, but still his soul will remain strong, true to itself, and the angel of inspiration will lead him safely out of the darkness of this life into the world of immortality on the wings of eternal glory."

The pale, romantic Shidlovsky was six years older than Fyo-

[2] *Letters:* 6, July 3, 1837.

dor, but they spoke to one another like people of the same age. For the first time Fyodor enjoyed the intoxication of talking to a man who was singularly free of disguises. He was rich, charming, elegant, well-dressed, but he accounted none of these things as worthy. For him the only virtue was to be drunk with poetry. He suffered from the passion of unrequited love, and rejoiced in his anguish. "The waters of the canal," he wrote, "lure me with the same passion as the bridal bed lures the beloved." In Shidlovsky's company the brothers visited the cathedrals and stood before the golden icons, caught up in an extraordinary enthusiasm for the beauty of the world around them.

Shidlovsky's influence on Fyodor was all-pervading and decisive. From the moment of their encounter in a St. Petersburg inn, Fyodor seems to have fallen under his spell. When they met, they were inseparable; and Fyodor lived only for the next meeting. For three or four years Shidlovsky, who had come to the capital to enter the Ministry of Finance and later abandoned all ideas of a government career, served as Fyodor's confidant and mentor; and when he vanished from St. Petersburg to return to his country estate, Fyodor was heartbroken.

The subsequent career of this extraordinary man shows him to have been one of those rare men who carry enthusiasm to its logical conclusion. Poetic exaltation was transformed into religious mysticism, and then to fanaticism. He abandoned his immense work on the history of the Russian church, lived a life of monkish isolation on his estate, went on pilgrimage to the Lavra at Kiev, learned from the lips of an old *starets* that God required him to seek salvation in the world, and still wearing his cassock he retired to his estate, where he gave himself up to occasional drunken orgies, but afterwards he would take to the road, preaching the Gospels. For the rest of his life—he died in 1872 at the age of fifty-eight—he continued to live "the life of enthusiasm," alternately preaching and getting drunk. The local bishop forbade him to enter the monasteries for fear he would corrupt the monks.

Without Shidlovsky there might have been no Prince Myshkin and no Alyosha Karamazov.

Meanwhile the work at the cramming school went on, with the brothers spending all their waking hours preparing for the examination which would take place on September 15th. They felt they had good prospects. Kostomarov was highly regarded by the directors of the engineering college; there were forty-three candidates for twenty-five places, but Kostomarov's pupils were usually among the top ten. "Time itself can't keep pace with us," the brothers wrote in another joint letter to their father. "We are always working. So much work to be done after writing this letter. I must tell you that we had to buy new hats for the examination. That cost us fourteen rubles. There has been no news for a long time from Shidlovsky."

So they worked themselves to a state of exhaustion, and Mikhail's health seems to have suffered, for when the time came for the physical examination, he was rejected on the grounds of physical weakness. Fyodor came through with flying colors; he claimed that he obtained first place in the examination, but was placed twelfth because other students had bribed the examiners. Mikhail was allowed to enter the Engineering Academy at Reval, an inferior college.

In January 1838, Fyodor officially entered the Engineering College with the rank of *conductor*. The college was housed in a building called "The Fortress of Engineers," formerly the Mikhailovsky Palace, built by the mad Tzar Paul I at a cost of eighteen million rubles. With its massive Ionic columns and granite staircases it represented the utmost extent of imperial splendor; and only a mad Tzar would have dared to build it. There were secret passageways, earthworks, moats, drawbridges, enormous porticoes, a throne room, a church, a vast courtyard so designed by the architects that it gave an impression of being even vaster than it was. At the main entrance stood a towering equestrian statue of Peter the Great. Across the length of the main building, in enormous letters, were the words: "May the holiness of God decorate thy house all the length of thy days." Paul I made this forbidding palace-fortress his headquarters, but enjoyed it for only forty days. In one of its rooms the mad Tzar was strangled on March 24, 1801. By order of Alexander II, this room was transformed into a memorial chapel.

Fyodor entered the college with high hopes. Discipline was strict, but he had been accustomed to strict discipline all his life. Not all his time was spent in studying maps and fortifications: there were lessons in singing, dancing, fencing, and French. There were interminable drills, which he hated, but since everyone else hated them, he was in good company. When they drilled facing the sun and their bayonets quivered, the drill sergeant roared at the top of his voice: "Pay no attention to the sun! The sun is not on parade!" The Tzar and the Grand Duke Mikhail inspected the cadets, and sometimes the entire imperial family was present to watch them on parade.

In February, 1838, Fyodor wrote to his father saying that he was proud to enter the Tzar's service, but he could find little good to say about the other pupils. He disliked their rough ribaldry, and their lack of refinement, but they were not unfriendly to him. A small group gathered around him, surprised by the fervor of his hoarse and strangely articulated voice whenever he discussed poetry or novels; they were spell-bound by his fanatical faith in whatever god presided over literature. One of his fellow students remembered him as a pale thickset boy with a snub nose, freckles, a high forehead, and grey eyes which had a fierce light in them. He wore his uniform badly. He was given the nickname of Photius, after the great ninth century patriarch of Constantinople, the most learned man of his time, who excommunicated the entire Western Church.

Fyodor was an unusually good student, proficient in all subjects except mechanical drawing, which he detested. He spent most of his spare time reading, and often late at night he would be found sitting at a worktable, barefoot, with a blanket round his shoulder, writing by the light of a candle stuck in a tin candlestick. No one knows what he wrote—poems, novels, essays, dramas? Sometimes in the midst of one of his letters to his brother the tone abruptly changes, and we seem to be reading from one of those long essays on the nature of man which he wrote late at night when all the other students were sleeping. He writes to his brother in the summer of 1838:

> It's absolutely true that I am lazy, terribly lazy. But what can I do, when the only thing left for me is to abandon myself to a perpetual *far niente*. I do not know whether I shall ever escape from these melancholy thoughts.
>
> One single condition is given to man. The weather of his soul is formed by the union of earth and heaven, and man is therefore a child beyond all laws. The law of spiritual nature has been violated. It seems to me that our universe is a purgatory inhabited by heavenly spirits imbued with evil thoughts. I think the world has taken a negative direction, and what was once a high and beautiful spirituality has become a caricature. And should there enter into this world someone who shares neither the appearance nor the thoughts of the rest, someone who is altogether foreign to them—what happens? The world is destroyed and cannot continue as before.
>
> To know that the whole universe languishes under a dark cloud, to know that it needs only an effort of the will to shatter the cloud and enter into eternity, to know all this and to remain the least of creatures—that is what is so terrible. How cowardly is man! Hamlet! Hamlet! When I think of those stormy ones, of those savage speeches resounding with the groans of a numbed world, then no reproaches and no complaints have power to move my heart. My heart is so crushed by anguish that it dreads the knowledge of its own suffering, and of being torn to pieces by it. Pascal said once: Whoever rises against philosophy is himself a

philosopher. Pathetic philosophy! But I am going on too long.

I have only received two letters from you, not to speak of the last. You complain of your poverty, my brother. But I am not rich either, as you know. Will you believe that during the entire period of the maneuvers I had not a single copeck. It rained continually and we were always out in the open, and I caught cold and was ill from hunger, for I had not enough money to buy some hot tea. Then I somehow got well, but until I received the money from Papinka I was the unhappiest person in the camp. I paid my debts and spent the rest of the money . . .[3]

The maneuvers at Peterhof cannot have been wholly unrewarding, for Fyodor goes on to say that he read everything written by the German romantic novelist E. T. A. Hoffmann, and nearly everything written by Balzac. "Balzac is wonderful! His characters are the creation of universal intelligence." He read Goethe's *Faust,* many of Goethe's shorter pieces, all of Victor Hugo except *Cromwell* and *Hernani,* and a number of miscellaneous books. It is not surprising that after such an attack of acute bibliomania he should have added the postscript: "I have a plan: to go insane."

Fyodor's letter to his brother marks the emergence of the man. In it for the first time he stated the beliefs which were to accompany him to his death. The ghosts of Hoffmann and Schiller crowd at his elbow as he writes, and these too were to accompany him all his life. For the first time we catch a glimpse of Prince Myshkin, the man "who is altogether foreign," who enters the world only to shatter it by the power of his beauty and goodness. Nearly all the familiar preoccupations which fill the novels and more than nine hundred surviving letters are present in this letter either directly or by implication. It is the letter of a seventeen-year-old boy confronting the mysteries of the universe head-on,

[3] *Letters:* 9, August 9, 1838.

determined to solve them, using as weapons only his naked passion and his naked intellect. In the following year, in another letter to his brother, he announced his vocation. "I am sure of myself," he wrote. "Man is a mystery. This mystery must be solved, and even if you pass your entire life solving it, do not say you have wasted your time. I occupy myself with this mystery, since I want to be a man."

Almost casually Fyodor was announcing that he had assumed the greatest of imaginable burdens, and that he would spend his whole life weighed down with that terrible responsibility.

But while he was contending with great mysteries, he was also contending with the masters in the engineering college. He knew he was brilliant and made sure that some of the masters knew it, with the result that the teacher of algebra decided to punish him, removing him from the class, so that he was compelled to waste a whole year's work. In a letter to his father he claimed that he was at the top of his class—his marks were: Algebra 11/15, Fortifications 12/15, Artillery 8/10, Geometry 10/10, History 10/10, Geography 10/10, Russian 10/10, French 10/10, German 10/10, Catechism 10/10—but the other students were always able to bribe the teachers, and the decision to remove him from the class was irrevocable. He wrote like a man shuddering from a terrible blow, but still determined to continue. He had to borrow money for the stamps on the letter, and he begged his father "to send something as soon as possible, to get me out of this Hell." The proud young cadet was beginning to wonder whether it was possible to serve the Tzar and still retain his dignity as a man; and when his father answered with one of those interminable letters full of complaints of poverty, Fyodor may have remembered a recent letter to his brother in which he described his father at some length:

> How I pity our poor father! What a strange character! What sufferings he has borne! It makes me want to

cry to think I can do nothing to console him. But do you know, our father knows nothing at all about life. He has lived in the world for fifty years, and he retains the same opinion of people as he had at thirty. Happy ignorance! How wrong he is, but I believe it is the same with everyone in our family.[4]

On May 10th, 1839, Fyodor wrote his last letter to his father, begging for help and pointing out that he was in service and therefore completely dependent on outside sources for everything except bare necessities. He needed two pairs of boots—sixteen rubles. He needed a chest in which to put his papers, pens, books, all his private possessions—the government insisted that all students buy their own chests. He needed a minimum of twenty-five rubles to pay off old debts and expenses before the maneuvers which began in June. "So please send me the money by June 1st, if you want to help your son in his terrible plight. I am not demanding; I am not asking for too much; and my gratitude will be boundless." The doctor wrote a rambling letter, complaining about the failure of the wheat crop and how they had to sacrifice the thatch on the roofs to keep the cattle from starving. Himself, he had not a penny in his pocket, he had not been able to afford a new suit for four years, and the one he was wearing was falling off his back. Nevertheless he sent thirty-five rubles, which was ten more then Fyodor had asked for, and he pointed out that at the Moscow rates these rubles in notes were worth forty-three rubles and seventy-five copecks. He was being as generous as he could be.

The news of the doctor's death reached Fyodor while he was on maneuvers. He seems not to have known for many months or years exactly how his father was murdered: he knew only that his father was dead, and there were a lot of young children to care for. On August 16th he wrote to his brother:

I have wept many tears over the death of our father, but now our situation is still more terrible. I am not

[4] *Letters:* 10, October 31, 1838.

speaking of myself, but of our family. I am sending this letter to Reval without any assurance that it will reach you. I imagine it will never reach you. God willing, you are now in Moscow. If you are, I shall be happier for our family. Tell me, can there be any greater misfortune for our brothers and sisters? The thought of them being raised by strangers kills me.[5]

With the death of his father, his future was bleaker than ever. There might be a little money from his father's estate, but for many months there would be no one to appeal to for help. He went on working. His sister Varvara married a Government official in Moscow, Pyotr Karepin, a wealthy widower who offered to take charge of the remaining children. Varvara, then an attractive girl of seventeen with a pert face, seems to have entered upon the marriage deliberately for the sake of her brothers and sisters; and though Fyodor was shocked by the marriage, and never completely accepted Karepin as a member of the family, he was always profoundly grateful to his sister.

More and more Fyodor was turning to literature as an escape from the mechanical tasks of the engineering college. In August, 1841, he was promoted to ensign, and permitted to take up lodgings outside "The Fortress of Engineers." He reveled in his newfound freedom, and continued to work on the two immensely long poetic dramas, *Marie Stuart* and *Boris Godunov,* which he regarded as his passports to fame. He had recited speeches from the two plays to Mikhail, who came to St. Petersburg earlier in the year to attend his examinations; and Mikhail, who also regarded himself as a poet, seems to have regarded his brother's poetic dramas with less than enthusiasm. They were interminably quarreling about poetry. Fyodor's passion for Schiller had given way to a passion for Corneille and Racine, and when Mikhail remarked that both these poets were of little account because they were lacking in form, Fyodor raged with indignation in a wonder-

[5] *Letters:* 13, August 16, 1839.

ful letter filled with tumultuous fire and an accurate knowledge of French poetry:

> Miserable wretch that you are! And then you add with such effrontery: "Surely you agree they are both bad poets?" Racine no poet! Racine, who is so ardent and passionate and truly idealistic, no poet? Do you dare to say such a thing? Have you read *Andromaque* —eh? Have you read *Iphigénie?* Can you say it is not completely charming? And isn't Racine's Achilles worthy of Homer? I grant that Racine stole from Homer, but what a thief! How marvelous his women are! Try to understand him! And then—Racine not a genius? incapable of writing drama? a mere copyist of Corneille? How can you think these things? And then there is *Phèdre.* My brother, I don't know what I shall think of you unless you admit that *Phèdre* is the highest, the most natural, the greatest and the purest poetry. Why, it is all truly Shakespearian, even though made of plaster and not of marble.
>
> Now about Corneille . . . You haven't read him, and that's why you dare to laugh at him. Don't you know that with his titanic figures and romantic spirit, he is almost on the level of Shakespeare? Miserable wretch that you are! To all questions you have only one reply: "Classic form." Poor fool, don't you know that it was not until fifty years later that the pathetic, inept and miserable Jodelle (author of the pitiable *Cléopâtre*) that Corneille appeared, and that was fifty years after Ronsard, who is a foretaste of our own Trediakovsky, and Corneille was almost a contemporary of that insipid poetaster Malherbe. How can you demand form from him? Happily he derived his form from Seneca. Have you read his *Cinna?* And after the divine figure of Octavius, what becomes of Karl Moor, of Fiesco, of Wilhelm Tell, of Don Carlos? That work would have done honor to Shakespeare. Wretched person, if you haven't read it, read it at once—read especially the conversation between Augustus and Cinna in which the Emperor pardons him

for his treason, and how wonderfully he pardons him!
Only the fallen angels could speak in this way . . .[6]

Fyodor's knowledge of French literature was astounding: he
seems to have read all the heroic poets, even the minor ones, and
his judgment on the romanticism of Corneille is curiously modern.
He had not, of course, abandoned Schiller. He had rejoiced in
Schiller as a child; he had read the plays with Shidlovsky; and he
still worshipped Schiller above all the poets. "Schiller is my
brother," he wrote in the same letter to his brother. "I shall say
nothing more about him, because the very sound of his name
fills me with tears."

The years in the engineering college passed slowly. The
drudgery choked him, but there was always freedom at the end
of the day. He still hated mechanical drawing, and thirty-five
years later, when he was writing *The Diary of a Writer,* he
would remember vividly those hours spent in shading maps and
plans of fortifications with India ink, the gradations of monochrome from the darkest black to a colorless white. He worked
well, being proficient in all his studies, and he was especially
proficient in the art of laying mines. He was still poor, desperately
poor. Occasionally remittances would come from the Karepins,
but as often as not the money would be spent in a huge celebration. He would give immense dinner parties or gamble it away on
billiards. Mikhail married a girl called Emily Ditmar. Fyodor sent
him a gift of 150 rubles, and a few weeks later he was writing
in despair: "In heaven's name send me five rubles, or even one.
For three days I haven't had a single copeck." Even in those days
he was completely incapable of managing money. It has been calculated that his income from his father's estate together with his
stipend from the engineering college amounted to 5,000 rubles a
year, roughly corresponding to $5,000 in our money, a consider-

[6] *Letters:* 15, January 1, 1840.

able sum for a young engineering student. In those days people could live for a whole year on a thousand rubles.

Some demon drove him. He was determined to be in the front rank among the engineering students, but he was also determined to devote himself to literature. When Balzac arrived in St. Petersburg in the summer of 1843, on a visit to Countess Evelina Hanska, he was fired by the ambition to translate the works of the master and set about preparing a translation of *Eugénie Grandet.* He was soon deeply immersed in a flock of translations. Eugène Sue's novel *Mathilde* had been appearing as a *feuilleton* in a translation by a certain Serchevsky, but was later abandoned. Fyodor determined to continue the translation with the help of his brother and another engineering student who was a friend of the chief censor. Fyodor planned to print and sell the finished work. He made inquiries among printers and booksellers, and came to the conclusion that on a sale of 7,500 copies there would be a profit to each of the translators of 4,000 rubles. This heady mathematics was characteristic of him, and nothing came of the translation.

He was luckier with his translation of *Eugénie Grandet,* which he made while simultaneously completing a long verse play called *The Jew Yankel,* the third of his poetic dramas. He wrote to his brother in January, 1844:

> Did you know that I finished Balzac's *Eugénie Grandet* during the holidays? (O marvel, marvel!) My translation is wonderful! I shall receive at least 350 rubles for it. I have a burning desire to sell the work, but though I am evidently a future millionaire I have neither the time nor the money to have it copied. In the name of the heavenly angels send me 35 rubles (cost of copying it). I swear to you by Olympus and by my Jew Yankel, which is a play I have just finished, and by what else? Well, by my mustache

which will grow one day, I hope. I swear to you that half of what I get for *Eugénie* will go to you. *Dixi.*[7]

Nothing is known of the fate of *The Jew Yankel,* but Fyodor's translation—it was very loosely translated, and was in fact an adaptation—appeared in the magazine *Repertory and Pantheon.* It was well received, although the editor cut it by a third. Fyodor went on to translate George Sand and to embark on an extraordinary plan of translating all Schiller's plays, with his brother as his collaborator. By the fall he hoped to publish *The Robbers, Fiesco, Don Carlos* and *Marie Stuart.* Once again he marshaled costs and prices in long imaginative letters to his brother—5,000 sheets of the best paper would cost 100 rubles, printing would cost 150 rubles, a salmon pink or green jacket would cost another 280 rubles. Printing would begin in June, and soon enough they would be in possession of a small fortune. He was in a rage to become a publisher and translator, and mortally weary of being a sublieutenant of engineers. "Bored with my profession," he wrote to Mikhail in April, and on the next line he added: "Bored to death."

Mikhail fell in with his brother's plans and translated Schiller's *The Robbers* with commendable speed. Fyodor was impressed. "You translated the lyrics excellently: the songs alone are worth their weight in gold, and the prose too is done to complete perfection." There were, he noted, a few minor errors, and whole sentences which appeared to have been translated in a fit of negligence, but all this could be tidied up. To his other burdens Fyodor proposed to add the not inconsiderable burden of being an editor.

Meanwhile his literary affairs were still progressing unfavorably. He was writing a novel, or two novels; he had almost completed a translation of George Sand's *La Dernière Albini* when he learned to his horror that it had already been translated seven

[7] *Letters:* 21, January 1844.

years previously; and there was already a translation of *Don Carlos* in existence by a certain Obodovsky, but mercifully it had not yet been printed. Mikhail must hurry. It was absolutely necessary to produce a complete edition of Schiller by the fall, in order to capture the market. Then there would be a great firework display of Schiller; the plays would be performed in the theaters; surely everything was to be gained by hurrying forward on the great and holy tide of Schiller's works in the inestimable translations by the Dostoyevsky brothers.

So Fyodor wrote in the happy delirium of a man embarking on a literary career, while the debts mounted and publishers looked at him askance and the mortal weariness of being a sublieutenant drove him almost to madness. As usual, he had passed his examinations with honors, and late in the summer of 1844 he learned that he was to be posted to the provinces. He rebelled, sent in his resignation, and walked out of "The Fortress of Engineers" for the last time. "I couldn't stand it any more," he wrote to his brother. "It disgusted me to waste the best years of my life in this way. They wanted to send me into the provinces. For heaven's sake, what would happen to me without St. Petersburg?"

The love affair with St. Petersburg lasted all his life. He was to know that beautiful city in all its moods, in its poverty and its splendor, in terrifying misery and at the height of success. He was to conquer it and make it his own, and in the end he was to die there. For the sake of St. Petersburg and literature he abandoned a well-paid army career and descended into the depths from which only the strong emerge. He knew exactly what he was doing, and he had counted the cost.

By instinct he was a gambler, but this was the greatest gamble of all. He would storm the fortress of literature, or perish in the attempt.

POOR FOLK

S T. PETERSBURG in the forties of the last century was a city of marble palaces and terrible wooden slums, dank and evil-smelling in winter, outrageously hot in summer when the hot dust spilled through the narrow streets. Disease was rampant, for there was almost no sanitation, and rats were everywhere. Except in the great boulevards radiating from the Winter Palace, there were no pavements: wooden boards were floated on the mud, and one walked as best one could through streets piled with refuse. It was an evil city on the edge of the marshlands, smelling of rotten wood and damp cloth, of fish and vodka and the sweating bodies of poor wretches who lived in the tenements. The characteristic sounds of the place were the crack of whips, the rumbling of carriages and horse carts, and the sudden barking shouts of drunks emerging from the inns. Walking along those fog-laden streets at night, a traveler would soon grow accustomed to the sudden cries of anguish and despair coming from dark interiors.

It was a city of immense wealth and of a vast brooding poverty, ruled by an underpaid bureaucracy. The police were everywhere; so too were the moneylenders, who charged extravagant interest. Those who succumbed met the full terror of life, and died like dogs; and there were some days when thirty bodies were dragged out of the Neva. Dominating the city was the golden spire of the Peter and Paul Fortress, where the Tzars were buried and held their most solemn celebrations and kept their most dangerous political prisoners. Moscow was a small city in the provinces.

In all of St. Petersburg there was no palace so sumptuous as "The Fortress of Engineers," or so comfortable for an aspiring officer. An army officer possessed rank and privilege; he was a law to himself, with many of the cherished immunities of the aristocracy. While in service he lived under the protection of the Tzar. Those who chose to live outside the Tzar's patronage lived in the jungle.

When Fyodor Dostoyevsky left "The Fortress of Engineers" in the summer of 1844, at the age of twenty-three, he was without prospects, and heavily in debt. All his plans for publishing a complete edition of Schiller proved abortive. Six weeks after his resignation he was at the end of his resources: most of his clothes were at the pawnbroker's, and he was in danger of being sent to prison for debt. "I am in a hellish situation," he wrote to his brother. "For God's sake tell them to send me something. The worst is that I shall soon have no clothes." He raged against Karepin, the executor of his father's estate. He must have been in a state of almost complete nervous prostration when he wrote in the same letter: "Karepin drinks, fucks, shits, drinks vodka, pulls rank, believes in God, and has arrived at this all by himself." Then he went on to speak of the novel he was writing. "I am absolutely happy with my novel, and never stop rejoicing over it. I am sure it will bring me money, and then—"

He had begun the novel many months before. It was a somber novel, quite short, written in an extraordinary sensuous and lapidary style, consisting of an exchange of letters between Makar Devushkin, a poor overworked copying clerk, and Varvara Dobroselova, a young woman of twenty-five, who suffers from ill-health and whose checkered life fills the copying clerk with an overwhelming pity. There is nothing he will not do for her. He confides his dreams and aspirations to her; runs errands for her; shyly presents her with flowers; weaves around her a web of intimacy which is almost terrifying in its secret nakedness. In his letters to her he talks to himself as much as he talks to his beloved. She lives in a rented room on the other side of the courtyard, and sometimes he catches glimpses of her. For him she is a vision of incomparable grace and beauty, and he is prepared to lay down his life for her. He knows he looks "like something a fly could overturn with his wing," but he knows too that he possesses an inner serenity and great depths of soul. He likes telling her about all the strange and extraordinary things that happen in the office. One day he misses a whole line when copying an important document. He is confronted by His Excellency, who glares at him, "and at that moment a button hanging by a single thread broke loose, and hopped and skipped and jingled and rolled right up to His Excellency's feet." There is a terrible silence. Devushkin stoops down to pick up the button. Of course he should have remained perfectly still with his hands clapped to his sides, but His Excellency has pity on him, removes a hundred ruble note from his wallet, and suddenly offers it to the confused copying clerk: "Here, my dear fellow, regard it as a loan. I would like to do something for you."

Devushkin writes on the edge of sentimentality, but he is a completely credible and rounded figure. He lives in the present; Varvara lives in the past, absorbed in her memories of a childhood spent happily in the country. Her memories are evidently Dostoyevsky's own memories. September has come, and she finds herself dreaming of September evenings on the estate:

> I preferred the autumn evenings to the mornings. There was a lake beyond the hill, a short distance from the house—I can almost see it now. It was very broad and bright, a great sheet of crystal. And if the evening was quiet, the lake lay very still, and there was no murmur from the overhanging trees. The air would be cool and bracing. The dew would settle on the grass, and there would be lights in the windows

below the thatched roofs, and the herds would be returning home.

Those were the hours when I loved to slip away to
my lake, forgetting everything, watching the rays of the
sun running along the water from the fires lit by the
fishermen on the shore, and then the cool blue of the
sky touched with fading red until the moon rose; and
the limpid air would carry all sounds like a silver bell:
a bird's wing, the slightest whisper of rushes, the splash
of a fish.

Afterwards the mists rose, so thin and transparent
over the darkening surface, and in the distance all
things would grow vague and disappear. But close at
hand everything lay clear, as if carved: the boats, the
water's edge, the islets: or a barrel forgotten in the
water, or a twig of yellow broom caught in the rushes.
A late-flying gull would dive into the cold depths and
flurry off again. I would stand there looking and listening and feeling wonderfully strange. I was a child then.[1]

The writer was already a conscious artist, shaping his memories into visions. This particular vision haunted Dostoyevsky all
his life, and we shall see it again, subtly changed, in Stavrogin's
dream in *The Devils,* written nearly thirty years later. It was as
though he were announcing in his first book that mysterious attachment to the earth, from which he drew his strength.

Poor Folk is a richly contrived work, written with quite
extraordinary self-consciousness. The artist is in full command.
There is no hurry, no bristling nerve-ends, only the sense of im-
pending disaster half-humorously accepted. Occasionally there are
flashes of *grotesquerie,* which Dostoyevsky derived as much from
Gogol as from his own sense of the ridiculous. He is describing a
funeral:

At last the coffin was closed, screwed down, placed
upon a cart and carried away. I followed it to the end
of the street. The driver set the horse at a trot, and

[1] *Poor Folk.* Letter of September 3.

the old man came running behind, sobbing breathlessly. He had lost his hat, but he had no time to pick it up. His hair was wet with the rain, and the sharp wind was lashing his face. He seemed to notice nothing, and kept darting from one side of the cart to the other, the tails of his old coat flapping. Books protruded from all his pockets; he clutched the largest one to his breast.

While the passers-by uncovered their heads, and some even stopped to gaze at the poor old man, the books kept tumbling from his pocket into the mud.[2]

It is perhaps a kind of self-portrait, and we shall see that grotesque old man in many of the later novels. Devushkin's last despairing letter betrays the authentic voice of the author: "Write to me. My style is just taking shape now. What style? I hardly know what I am saying or what I am writing about, and it doesn't matter so long as I keep on writing and writing. . . . Farewell, little dove, my only one, my darling!"

All through the fall and winter Dostoyevsky worked on *Poor Folk,* writing painfully and slowly, continually revising and correcting the manuscript. When his brother hinted he should write more quickly, he answered that Chateaubriand had written *Atala* seventeen times, and out of a thousand scattered pages Laurence Sterne had put together the slender volume of *A Sentimental Journey.*

During that winter he shared a small apartment with his half-French friend Grigorovich, who had some money and helped to support him, though they were often reduced to living on bread-rolls and barley coffee. They both thirsted for literary fame, but sometimes doubts crept in. Dostoyevsky was horrified when he read in a magazine article about the German poets, many of them astonishingly famous, who had died of cold or starvation or in madhouses. "I am still trembling," he wrote, and added mysteriously: "One must be a charlatan."

Grigorovich was one of those charming and unassuming men

[2] *Poor Folk.* Letter of June 1.

who take on the burdens of others. He was always trying to help his friend. When Dostoyevsky grew pale and ill, Grigorovich would insist that he go for a walk or take a long rest from his work. Then they would go out into the open air, and as often as not Dostoyevsky would fall into a faint and have to be carried home.

Once during one of these walks they came on a funeral procession: the black horses, the priests with the softly waving banners, the choristers, and the open coffin. The coffin was open to show the sickly rubber-colored face of the dead man who wore a paper crown inscribed with ritualistic formulas, and there was a small crucifix in his hands. Dostoyevsky took one look, turned, began running, and suddenly collapsed on the sidewalk. He was carried into a milkshop and it was some minutes before he could be revived.

There were many similar incidents. Dostoyevsky was working himself into a breakdown. He had hoped to publish the novel himself, but his money had run out and he decided to offer it to the magazine called *Fatherland Notes,* which had a circulation of 2,500 copies. "If I don't publish my novel, then there is nothing left except to jump into the Neva," he wrote to his brother. "What else can I do? I have thought of everything. I shall not survive my *idée fixe.*"

One day in May, Grigorovich, who was about to leave St. Petersburg for his summer estate, suggested that the manuscript should be offered to Nikolay Nekrasov, then better known as an editor than as a poet. There was a brief meeting between the young writer and the established editor, and Dostoyevsky went off to spend the evening with a friend, leaving Grigorovich alone with Nekrasov. He was in a mood of profound uneasiness, afraid the short novel would meet only with ridicule. Was it possible, he asked himself, that all those hours of relentless work had produced a mirage, something that had no relation to life?

He returned to his apartment at four o'clock in the morning. He could not sleep. He kept wondering about the fate of his

manuscript. He paced restlessly about the room, and then opened
the window and gazed into the warm, brilliant radiance of
the night. It occurred to him that the best thing he could do was
to drown himself. Suddenly he heard the bell ringing. When he
opened the door Nekrasov and Grigorovich were standing there,
and without a word they embraced him.

For a wild moment Dostoyevsky thought they had gone mad.
Then he learned they had read the manuscript together. At first
Nekrasov had said: "It will be quite easy to judge the work after
reading ten pages." They had read ten pages, and then ten more,
and they were still reading late into the night. When Nekrasov read
about the student's death and the father running after the coffin,
he struck the manuscript with his hand and exclaimed: "He's a
devil—that's what he is!" It was Nekrasov's highest form of
compliment. Finally, when they had read the entire manuscript,
which amounted to 112 pages, Grigorovich said: "We shouldn't
put off the good deed. If he is sleeping, we ought to wake him.
It can't be helped; it is more important than all the sleep in the
world!"

Nekrasov, who was usually reserved, cautious and uncom-
municative, fell in with the plan and accompanied Grigorovich
to the apartment. He was in great good humor. He kept shaking
Dostoyevsky by the shoulders and saying: "Belinsky must see it!
I will give him your novel today! What a man he is! You will
come to know him, and realize the great depths of his soul!" The
visitors stayed for half an hour. There was a good deal of talk
about poetry and truth and "the circumstances of the present time,"
and they quoted Gogol to each other. "Go to sleep now," Nekrasov said at last. "We are leaving, but tomorrow come to my
office!"

Dostoyevsky could not sleep. He was in that state of pure
bliss which comes to an author perhaps once in a lifetime. He
never knew how he lived through that day. During the morning
Nekrasov took the manuscript to Belinsky, the most acute of liv-

44

ing critics, a man whose word was law. "A new Gogol has appeared!" Nekrasov said, and Belinsky answered: "Gogols grow like mushrooms wherever you are!" But he took the manuscript, read it, and by evening he was declaring that it was a work of genius. "Bring him to me as soon as you can!" Belinsky said, and the next day Dostoyevsky went to call on the critic, who was famous for his savagery.

"My heroes are the destroyers of the old—Luther, Voltaire, the Encyclopedists, the Terrorists, Byron," Belinsky had written. "I prefer the blasphemies of Voltaire to acknowledging the authority of religion, society, or anything on earth!"

He was that kind of man: harsh, opinionated, determined to smash the windows and let the new fresh air from Europe pour into Russia. He spoke bitterly against Christianity, and he was outspokenly in favor of Christ. He hated cruelty, the government, serfdom, and bad literature so vehemently that he had a reputation for rudeness, but he was astonishingly gentle in appearance with a small pale face, a curiously crooked mouth and brilliant blue eyes flecked with gold. He always wore a padded grey frockcoat and was continually tapping with small, delicate fingers on the top of his snuffbox.

Such was the man before whom Dostoyevsky trembled— "the dreadful and terrible" Vissarion Belinsky, who was at the height of his fame, capable of making and unmaking authors with a stroke of the pen.

Dostoyevsky was struck by his unexpected appearance and still more by his gravity and the piercing light in his eyes.

"Tell me," said Belinsky, "do you yourself really understand what you have done?"

Dostoyevsky was too taken aback to reply.

"No, it is impossible for you to understand," Belinsky went on. "The moment when that poor functionary of yours, who is crushed and annihilated and has nothing left to live for, when he speaks of 'their excellency'—not 'your excellency,' but 'their ex-

cellency,' and then the torn-off button, and then other things—
the moment when he kisses the general's hand—this is not compassion, but the purest horror! Yes, in that very gratitude there
is horror! You have touched upon the heart of things. With one
stroke you have accomplished the most important thing of all. We
critics try to explain it in words, but you—the artist—you explain
it in a single image so tangible that it can almost be held in the
hand, and so the least of your readers can grasp it at once! This
is the mystery of art! This is the truth of art, and the artist's
service to truth! Treasure your gift, be faithful to it, and you will
become a great writer!"

The magnificent tirade seemed endless, and Dostoyevsky sat
there with a look of wild astonishment, wondering whether "the
dreadful and terrible" Belinsky was talking about him or about
someone else altogether.

At last, dazed and enraptured, he left the apartment and
halted at the street corner, and it seemed to him that he had
never known such a moment of triumph, though in fact he had
known another triumph almost as great the day before. Twenty-
two years later he could still remember the exhilaration that swept
over him:

> I looked up at the heavens, at the bright day, at the
> people passing, and I felt with my whole being that
> a solemn moment had occurred in my life, changing
> it forever; that something entirely new had begun in
> me, something I had not anticipated even in my most
> passionate dreams (I was then a passionate dreamer).
> "Can it be," I asked myself, "that I am so great?" I
> spoke these words shyly, in a kind of timid ecstasy.
> Oh, do not laugh, for later I never thought I was
> great; but then, was it possible to resist it? "Oh, I
> shall prove worthy of this praise," I told myself. "What
> men there are! What men! It is here that one finds
> them! I shall earn this praise! I shall endeavor to be-

come as beautiful as they are! I shall remain faithful! I am going out of my wits! Yes, indeed, if only Belinsky knew the deceitful, shameful thoughts dwelling within me . . .

I recall this moment with complete lucidity. And never could I forget it. It was the most wonderful moment in my whole life. When I was in prison, it strengthened my spirit every time I recalled it. Even now I always recall it with rapture.[3]

As he stood there near the Anichkov Bridge, looking at the four colossal groups of statues representing the mastery of men over all animal creation, he knew that his exaltation would be short-lived. He still had no money, and slight prospects. He was heavily in debt, with nowhere to go. He spent a confused summer, much of it alone. For a few weeks he stayed with his brother Mikhail at Reval, and since Mikhail was doing well and in addition was happily married, he felt lonelier than ever. He was violently seasick on the ship returning him to St. Petersburg at the end of August. It was a night of storm and fog and misery, and he was overwhelmed by a weariness of the spirit. He speaks of sitting huddled on deck, succumbing to strange, unhappy presentiments of the future, all of them tragic. Neither Grigorovich nor Nekrasov had returned to St. Petersburg, and so, when he came home, he sat down to complete his second novel, *The Double,* which he had begun earlier in the year, but he had no heart for it.

As autumn came and his friends returned to the city, his spirits revived. Nekrasov returned at the beginning of October and paid him 150 rubles for *Poor Folk,* promising a further 100 rubles on publication. Meanwhile the novel was still at the censor's, and there was no indication when it would be released. "They drag on, they drag on," Dostoyevsky wrote helplessly, "and who knows where it will end?" He was afraid the novel would never be pub-

[3] *The Diary of a Writer,* 1877, II, 3.

lished, but he was beginning to enjoy the seductions of success, for Belinsky had already informed St. Petersburg about the arrival of a new and unexpected star in the firmament.

By mid-October, Dostoyevsky was once more in a state of manic exaltation. He was meeting everyone of importance, and being invited to the most select houses. *Poor Folk* was being read in manuscript, and he was receiving praises from every side. In a delirium of happiness he wrote to his brother:

> My brother, my glory can never be greater than it is now. Everywhere I go, I arouse unheard-of respect and terrible curiosity. I have met dozens of people from the most fashionable circles. Prince Odoevsky begged me to honor him with a visit, and Count Sologub is tearing his hair over me. Panayev told him that I am the possessor of a talent which will soon put other writers underground. So Sologub ran to everyone and at last, in the home of Kraevsky, he asked point-blank: "Who is this fellow Dostoyevsky? Where can I get hold of this Dostoyevsky?" Kraevsky, who is not the kind of man to be disconcerted by anything, told him bluntly that Dostoyevsky would certainly not honor him with a visit.
>
> All this is true, of course. That miserable aristocrat climbs on his high horse and imagines he will annihilate me with the majesty of his caresses. Everyone thinks of me as a marvel. I have barely opened my mouth when people in all corners are saying: 'Dostoyevsky said said that; Dostoyevsky wants to do this.' Belinsky could not show me greater signs of affection.
>
> Recently the poet Turgenev (I am sure you have heard of him) has returned from Paris, and from the very first moment he has attached himself to me, demonstrating so much affection that Belinsky says he must be in love with me. What a man, my brother! I myself am almost in love with him. A talented poet, aristocrat, handsome, rich, intelligent, cultivated, twenty-five years old—nature has refused him nothing . . . I am crammed with ideas, and have only to mention them to someone like Turgenev and the next day all St. Peters-

burg knows that Dostoyevsky is writing something. If I were to try to make a list of all my successes, there would not be enough paper in the world.[4]

It is such a letter as a young man might write when he is very unsure of himself and is still baffled by the course of events. His successes, however, were real. Nekrasov had offered to make him editor of a humorous magazine; Belinsky had reaffirmed his faith in his young protégé. He could tell himself that he had triumphed with his first masterpiece. Seventeen years were to pass before he published another.

In the intervals of being lionized he was writing continually. *Poor Folk* was a brilliant excursion into sentiment with hardly a grain of satire. He decided to follow it with a bitter satirical novel directed at all the hopeless confusion of the bureaucracy. Inevitably it became a kind of self-portrait, for his own confusions when he was an officer of engineers and a prospective publisher, one side of him at odds with the other, are clearly involved in the strange Hoffmannesque figure of Yakov Petrovich Golyadkin.

The Double, which describes Golyadkin's adventures when he meets himself in his office and continually confronts himself in unexpected places, is overwritten and often hysterical. Dostoyevsky regarded it as a masterpiece. "It is ten times better than *Poor Folk*," he wrote to his brother early in 1846. "Our friends say that nothing like it has been written in our holy Russia since *Dead Souls;* it is a work of genius; and they say a thousand other things. I have great hopes for it." He was continually revising it, continually changing its direction. It is at once a psychological study of a split personality, an experiment in hysteria, a disguised autobiography, and a daring attack on the bureaucracy. Belinsky praised and denounced it, saying the author displayed immense powers of creative genius and his hero was "one of the most profound and daring conceptions that Russian literature can boast of," but the work suffered from a shocking lack of restraint. There

[4] *Letters:* 30, November 16, 1845.

49

was no balance, no sense of proportion. Everything was thrown to-gether. Belinsky was equally trenchant in his condemnation of Dostoyevsky's next story, *Mr. Prokharchin,* about the death of a miser. As soon as he is dead, people rush in to discover the hoard of gold coins hidden under the mattress. In the confusion, the body topples over the foot of the bed. "He fell head downward, showing only two thin blue legs waving in the air like the branches of a burned tree."

Belinsky was unimpressed by this excursion into the world of the grotesque. "We see the brightly glowing sparks of a great talent," he wrote, "but they glow in such a dense gloom that their light is of little help to the reader." It was evident to Belinsky that Dostoyevsky had lost his way, and only with the greatest humility would he be able to find his way back again.

Dostoyevsky was in fact in an extraordinary state of mind. Flattery had gone to his head. He had fallen madly in love. He was still desperately poor, living in a cheap rented room where the only articles of furniture were a bed and a broken-down chair. He was suffering from nervous exhaustion and lack of food. He was ferociously proud of his success, and he was making a host of enemies. Even Nekrasov, who claimed to be his friend, found pleasure in lampooning him in a poem:

> *Oh Knight of the Sorrowful Countenance,*
> *Dostoyevsky, dear braggart,*
> *On the nose of literature*
> *You blossom like an over-ripe pimple.*

The critics of the period, alarmed by Dostoyevsky's frenzied claims to greatness, added more verses at their leisure.

Only a few people seem to have observed that he was desperately sick and in danger of losing his mind. Turgenev, who despised him, engaged him in conversation only for the ex-press purpose of torturing him. The fashionable *littérateurs* circu-lated compromising stories about him. He was invited to *soirées* where he was praised so fulsomely that he fled in terror, realizing at last that he was being baited; and once when a young girl praised him, he fainted at her feet.

Even more troubling was his unrequited love for the beautiful Avdotia Panayeva, the wife of a successful publisher. She was one of the leaders of St. Petersburg society. With her dark hair, deepset black eyes, and astonishingly graceful figure, she presided over a salon attended by all the St. Petersburg notables; and inevitably Dostoyevsky was invited to meet her. Madame Panayeva found him unprepossessing and impressionable. Many years later she described him in her *Memoirs:* "He was thin and small with hair like flax, with a sickly complexion. His small grey eyes kept shifting restlessly from one object to another. His pale lips were continually twitching." Dostoyevsky fell in love with her at first sight. On February 1, 1846, two months after meeting her, he wrote to his brother: "I fell hopelessly in love with Panayeva, I'm over it now, but I'm not sure. My health is terribly disturbed; my nerves are affected, and I am afraid of fever resulting from nervous exhaustion." He added that the best cure would be sea-bathing, and he hoped shortly to take a holiday, probably in Reval with his brother. He did not take the holiday. He went on writing.

In those days he was like a man whose imagination lashes out in all directions in the hope of gaining a sure foothold. He was attempting everything at once. He was writing a long novel, *Netochka Nezvanova,* planning a *feuilleton,* preparing short sketches for newspapers, and contemplating innumerable short stories. He started two stories, *The Shaved Whiskers* and *The Abolished Chancelleries,* and then abandoned them. He finished *The Mistress of the House,* which describes the infatuation of a young man for a woman held in the power of a mysterious priest. The young man comes to live in the old priest's house. He is in the delirium of fever when the young woman appears and throws herself on the bed beside him, only to rise a moment later to hurl herself at the foot of the icons on the wall, accusing herself of murder. The story clearly derives from Dostoyevsky's infatuation with Madame Panayeva, but it is as unformed and hysterical as such stories usually are. Belinsky attacked the story ferociously as incomprehensible nonsense. He wrote to a friend: "Every new work of his is a miserable failure. I was a fool to be taken in by him."

In his slow painful fashion, Dostoyevsky went on writing, living as miserably as ever, borrowing money from his brother, basking in the confidence of his few remaining friends. He noted that though he was disliked, he was being read. He kept up friendly relations with Belinsky, explaining that Belinsky was a man "who changed his ideas as often as he changed his shirt."

As a conscious artist Dostoyevsky knew exactly how he must go about perfecting his art. He must refine himself, seek those levels in himself where he could move with the greatest clarity, and continually explore human nature. He must hold his wild, leaping fantasy in check, and strike a balance between the outer and inner worlds. The holy task must be accomplished with perfect simplicity of heart. There must be a moral rebirth, but a physical rebirth was equally necessary. So he wrote in those letters to his brother, which often read as though they were letters to himself, with their occasional blandishments of self-praise and their cautious admonishments.

The painful apprenticeship was rewarded, not with a masterpiece like *Poor Folk,* but with a whole series of short stories which show him to be the master of his craft. All these stories appeared in 1848. They are without savagery; their strength lies in irony, in gentleness, and compassion.

The Honest Thief is hardly a story at all. A poor drunkard steals a pair of riding breeches from his only benefactor, an old tailor, spends the money on drink and dies confessing his sin, a little mortified by the ruse he has played on the tailor. In a few deft strokes Dostoyevsky has painted the whole scene, giving his characters the same human grandeur which appears in a Rembrandt drawing.

Poor Folk

A Christmas Tree and a Wedding describes a children's New Year's Eve party attended by the middle-aged Yulian Mastakovich, "a pink-cheeked, potbellied little man with plump thighs, as round as a nut." The eleven-year-old daughter of the wealthy host is known to have a dowry of 500,000 rubles. Yulian Mastakovich ingratiates himself with the family, makes careful calculations on the value of the dowry at an interest of four per cent, waits five years and marries the girl. Dostoyevsky does not accuse. He is content to present his villain and heroine in the light of their formidable humanity.

White Nights is a variant of *Poor Folk*. The lovers meet for a few brief moments, disclose their loneliness to one another, and then separate for ever. There is no attempt to prove anything; nor is there any sorrow. In the end the hero is left alone to rejoice in the happiness they have given each other. "Dear Lord! A whole moment of bliss! Isn't such a moment enough for a whole lifetime!"

The Faint Heart is a story of another gentle creature confronting the massive indifference of Yulian Mastakovich, and this too is told with irony and compassion. So it is with all the other stories written during that prodigious year which saw Dostoyevsky emerging at last from the feverish compulsions of his early fame.

He was still writing his novel, *Netochka Nezvanova*, which he described in a letter to his brother as "a confession, like Golyadkin, only in an entirely different sytle." That huge, sprawling torso of a novel, which he never completed, is the product of fantasy rather than imagination. It moves like a flood carrying in its wake the detritus of many incomplete experiences and many disturbed memories. Netochka herself is the daughter of a poor musician, who goes mad; she is then brought up in the house of Prince X with every imaginable luxury, and falls in love with the young Princess Katya, only to be delivered into another house where she is friendless. It is a mysterious fragment, full of heavy and overstrung tension. The poor musician is evidently Dostoyevsky's father; the house of Prince X is "The Fortress of Engineers"; Princess Katya is Shidlovsky; and the friendless house of the last chapters is clearly St. Petersburg seen through the eyes of the poverty-stricken Dostoyevsky. We need not be surprised that Dostoyevsky presents himself in this fantasy as a woman, for many of his own secret thoughts were uttered by Varvara Dobroselova in *Poor Folk,* and such transformations are common among young writers. What is more disturbing is to see Dostoyevsky at a loss to control the flights of his fancy. It is an adolescent novel, propelled by the heat of adolescent memories, with more than a hint of homosexual tendencies, for Dostoyevsky never wrote a better love scene than the one describing the passing affections of Netochka for Princess Katya. While the adolescent in him was writing this novel, the adult in him wrote *The Honest Thief.* The mastery was in his hands, but it was many years before he was able to write a good novel.

Always poor and often ill, suffering from strange fevers and sudden convulsions, always changing his apartment, at odds with his former friends and continually quarreling with his editors and publishers, Dostoyevsky presented a strange spectacle in the literary world of St. Petersburg. There was something about him which suggested that he had come to stay, but there were many who laughed outright at his unmanageable pride. He wrote to his brother: "A host of new writers are arising. Some are my rivals, and the best among them are Herzen and Goncharov. The first has already published something, the other not yet. They are praised enthusiastically. But I still have the advantage over them, and I hope I shall hold it for ever."

It was one of his more remarkable and accurate prophecies, but when he made it, he had little grounds for believing that he would survive. He looked like a dying man, his heartbeats were irregular, and his pulse was uneven. Inexplicably, for no reason at all, he would suddenly turn white as a sheet and disappear into a remote ice-cold world of his own. The attacks of epilepsy were to come later, but long before he became an epileptic he suffered from strange fevers which left him so exhausted that he could neither work nor think nor recognize where he was.

He was attended by an intelligent and cultured doctor who left a record of his meetings with Dostoyevsky.

Dr. Stepan Yanovsky was a bachelor, very earnest, deeply interested in current literature, with a happy knack of putting his patients at their ease. They met for the first time in May, 1846. The doctor had never seen him before, and was surprised by his appearance: he was quite short, big-boned, with heavy shoulders and powerful hands. His grey eyes were unusually small, and his lips were compressed, as though with pain. His hair, then flaxen, was to acquire an orange tint as he grew older, and the doctor observed that it was of an extreme fineness. There was nothing of the officer in his stance; he slouched like a divinity student.

Dr. Yanovsky saw him often. One day in July, 1847, the doctor was crossing St. Isaac's Square, haunted like Prince Myshkin in *The Idiot* with the sense that someone was in desperate need of him. He found Dostoyevsky there, glassy-eyed, staggering, leaning on the arm of a soldier. He was hatless, and his collar was undone. The doctor brought him home in a carriage and bled him; the blood came out thick and black like tar. In the throes of his convulsions, he could be heard muttering: "I am saved! I am saved!"

But it was not in this way that salvation came to him. He was still lost, a derelict thrown up on the shores of St. Petersburg, in need of rest and sunshine. He said once: "I am wriggling like a fish under the ice." He spoke of the need of some shock which would somehow bring him to his senses.

In the end he applied his own shock-treatment. He joined a conspiracy against the Tzar and became one of its leading members.

THE CONSPIRATORS

D URING 1848 a wave of revolutionary feeling spread over Europe, but there were no revolutions in Russia. The Tzar's government held the reins tight. With unwavering diligence Nicholas I succeeded in placing his spies in every corner of the land where rebellion might emerge. He was determined that there should be no repetition of the uprising which came to be known as the Decembrist Revolt, led largely by the nobility. The revolt broke out on December 14, 1825. It was quashed easily. More than a thousand arrests were made, and a hundred and twenty sentences were passed by the supreme criminal court, including five death sentences. Some of the most famous and talented Russians, including the poet Pushkin, were implicated in the revolt. The throne was shaken, and the Tzar lived in an uneasy truce with his people.

The stern, handsome Tzar regarded his people as though they were soldiers, to be ordered about at his bidding. He had no understanding of social forces, and no liking for intellectual pursuits. Once driving past Moscow University, he pointed to the main building and said grimly: "There's the wolf's lair." He thought the university and especially the philosophy department threatened his throne; and he abolished the chair of philosophy. He was incapable of sharing his power even with his ministers, and attempted to rule every department of state, and meticulously examined thousands of documents every week. He was especially interested in the department of justice, and he enjoyed making exact calculations on the proper forms and gradations of punishment. After the Decembrists were put on trial and found guilty, the Tzar himself drew up the sentences; there survives a document in which he carefully graduated the approved punishment. He ordered five of the most important conspirators to be drawn and quartered, thirty-one to be guillotined, and the rest to be deported to Siberia. Later he commuted many of the sentences, and in the end only five were sentenced to death by hanging. All through his life the Tzar showed the same careful attention to detail.

Under such an emperor there could be no peace. Outwardly Russia seemed to have escaped the social revolution which swept across Europe, but under the surface she was seething with discontent. The Tzar expected trouble from the nobility and from the universities. In fact it came from the minor officials in his government and from the small coteries of literary figures in St. Petersburg and Moscow.

Among those who plotted against the Tzar was a minor official in the Ministry of Foreign Affairs called Mikhail Vasilievich Petrashevsky, a follower of Fourier and St. Simon. This extraordinary man affected the appearance and manners of a revolutionary to such an extent that he appeared to be almost a caricature. He gazed at the world with profoundest melancholy, but there was a mad gleam in his eyes. Nearly everyone who met him spoke of some indefinable quality of menace in him. He wore a full black beard, let his hair grow long, and was always seen in a Spanish cape and a dark broad-brimmed hat. At school he was the terror of his teachers, but he surprised them on his last day with a superb speech written in their honor, enumerating all their good qualities. The teachers were so pleased with the speech that they had it published.

Brilliant, intolerant, delighting in his own eccentricities and the rare eccentricities he detected in others, he joined the

Ministry of Foreign Affairs as a translator. He liked to play practical jokes on his superiors. One day he was ordered to have his hair cut. He returned the next day with hair which looked longer and streamed down his back. His superior was shocked until Petrashevsky removed the wig and showed that he had obeyed the ministerial command. When he was asked to draw up a memorandum on improving the form of government, he replied with a long treatise hilariously attacking all the accepted forms of government. Included in the treatise were discussions on: (a) The advantage of civilizing apes by shaving them; (b) An examination of the guilt of the Russian people who permitted the Moscow fire of 1812; (c) The need to transform monasteries into charitable institutions; (d) An exposition of the true principles of Christian philosophy; and (e) The advantage of introducing the English jury system into Russia. The horrified officials of the ministry quietly locked the treatise away.

Petrashevsky was not a charlatan. He was attempting to change the climate of official Russia by a series of well-calculated shocks. Under the pseudonym of Kirillov—Dostoyevsky remembered this name when he came to write *The Devils,** giving it to the superb rebel against God who flaunted his own self-will in front of the revolutionaries—Petrashevsky published *A Dictionary of Foreign Terminology* which was in fact a political encyclopedia discussing a vast number of social ideas. There were articles on socialism, communism, Fourierism, the constitution, the nature of absolutism, and so on. Most of these articles contained undisguised attacks on the Russian autocracy, but Petrashevsky had taken care to obtain the permission of the Grand Duke Mikhail, the Tzar's brother, to dedicate it to him, and the censor, assuming the book was being published by royal privilege, made no effort to prevent publication. Some time passed before the explosive quality of the book was noticed in high circles. It was then withdrawn from sale and burned, and the censor was punished.

* Also known as *The Possessed.*

The Conspirators

Petrashevsky was a rich man, the owner of a number of villages, and he was perfectly capable of putting his ideas into practice. He would steal out at night and read to beggars and the watchmen in the street his own translation of Fourier's works, and to those who said they understood perfectly what he was saying he would give twenty copecks. Then on another day he would read the works again to the same beggars, giving them only five copecks. He would explain that it was easier for them the second time, because they had heard it all before and had no need to exert their brains so much. "No, master," they answered. "We should be paid more, for we have been in your service longer." Petrashevsky gave up his street-corner readings.

When one of his villages burned to the ground, he decided it was time to put Fourierism into practice. He would build a communal village. Everything was to be in common—common dormitories, dining rooms, coach houses, stables and cowsheds. There were forty families in the village, and at first, as they watched the magnificent new buildings rising, they were pleased. Petrashevsky went off to St. Petersburg and invited his close friends to attend the official opening of the Fourierist "phalanstery." When Petrashevsky reached the village he found the whole "phalanstery" burned to the ground.

Quietly and methodically, keeping just within the law, Petrashevsky was attempting to destroy the state. He had friends in high places. In 1848 he wrote a memorandum with the attractive title of *Ways of Raising the Value of Land,* dedicating it to the nobility of the Petersburg province: the noblemen who read it casually regarded him as a benefactor to their cause. Those who read it more carefully observed that he was recommending a general sale of land to the merchant classes, who by law were not permitted to own land at all, nor were they permitted to own serfs. If, following Petrashevsky's proposal, land was sold to the merchants, the emancipation of the serfs would follow inevitably.

From about 1844 onward he began to invite various friends

59

to his Friday evening soirées in the upstairs drawing room of his small house on Pokrov Square. Though rich, he lived in happy squalor. Visitors climbed the rickety wooden stairway lit by an evil-smelling rapeseed oil lamp and found themselves in a large plainly furnished room, where the two most prominent objects were a piano and a large samovar. Petrashevsky himself, very short, with piercing black eyes and a thick beard, usually sat on a dingy cretonne-covered sofa. He talked continually, and rarely troubled to introduce his guests to one another.

Like the engineer Kirillov in *The Devils*, Petrashevsky regarded himself as "an engineer of ideas." He was the ideal moderator, always keeping the subject of the conversation in mind and getting the best out of his guests. Sometimes, if the arguments grew too heated, he would open the piano. The air would become green with cigarette smoke as the visitors discussed such vast and important subjects as "Is Greek religion at variance with Fourier's ideals?" and "Can the execution of spies and traitors be reconciled with the principle of loving one's fellow man?" Most of the debates dealt with various aspects of Fourier's socialism or the new books, usually French, concerned to demonstrate that Christ spoke in favor of the social contract, like Cabet's *Le Vrai Christianisme suivant Jésus Christ,* a book which was later found in Dostoyevsky's possession. The accent was on the intellectual revolution, but such revolutions nearly always lead to bloodshed. Petrashevsky was playing with fire.

In later years, Dostoyevsky said there was no conspiracy, and no one ever spoke of attempting the Tzar's life, or of coming out in open rebellion. No doubt this was true. They spoke more often of the aims of the revolution than about how it would be brought about. They were visionaries wrapped in green cigarette smoke, but they were the precursors of the Nihilists of the seventies, and therefore of the Bolsheviks.

Dostoyevsky began to attend the Friday evening meetings in the winter of 1846. He came as an observer, took little part in the discussions, and was always borrowing books from the library of Petrashevsky, who as an official in the Foreign Ministry had access to banned books and loaned them out regularly. He was not very impressed by Petrashevsky; there was something a little too theatrical about this man who affected an air of settled gloom and wore his large Spanish cloak and broad-brimmed hat like a professional conspirator. He was more impressed by some of the visitors who talked quietly and amusingly about the mistakes of the government. There was the gentle satirist Saltykov-Shchedrin, who later became a provincial governor; the young poets Alexey Pleshcheyev and Sergey Durov; the writer Apollon Maikov who became one of his closest friends; and a number of guards officers who were often more outspoken than the others. One of them, Nikolay Mombelli, had written an essay suggesting that the Tzar should be forced to eat the same food as the peasants of Vitebsk, who ate bread which scarcely differed from horse dung.

Such were the people who gathered in Petrashevsky's living room, drank tea, smoked innumerable cigarettes, and looked forward with considerable detachment to the time when Russia would be caught in a wave of European liberalism.

Not that they were always detached. Sometimes tempers rose, and there were outbursts of anger. Once Dostoyevsky recounted in tones of ferocious anger how an officer of the Finland regiment had been made to run the gantlet. He had a horror of all forms of cruelty. "When anything touches him deeply," wrote Semyonov Tian-Shanski, "he is capable of descending into the street with a red flag in his hand."

The Friday evening conversations were leading nowhere, and inevitably there were disagreements. There were different shades of Fourierism as there are different shades of socialism. The more determined and forthright members of the Petrashevsky group began to meet in the house of the poet Durov and came to be known as the "Durov circle," though in fact the leader of the group was a certain Nikolay Speshnev, an immensely wealthy landowner who was blessed with superb good looks, a quick ironical mind, and a gift for satanic mischief.

Speshnev was one of those rare men who are genuinely intoxicated with thoughts of destruction. He despised the abstract intellectual discussions of the Petrashevsky group. He wanted a violent upheaval, a lethal blow at the heart of the government. Speaking very calmly and coldly, he announced that they would be better occupied in preparing an insurrection against the government.

There was an air of mystery about Speshnev, which he deliberately cultivated. It was believed that he had eloped to Switzerland with a young woman who committed suicide, leaving him inconsolable. In that melancholy period in his life he came under the influence of Bakunin, then attempting to bring about an anarchist revolution from his headquarters in a dingy hotel room in Geneva. Speshnev returned to Russia determined to place his gifts at the service of the revolution.

Speshnev's greatest asset was his power to charm. He was astonishingly handsome in a Russian way, with a delicate almost feminine profile, with full lips, large deepset eyes and thick curly hair. Years later, when Dostoyevsky was writing *The Devils,* he described Speshnev accurately under the name of Stavrogin:

> He did not talk very much, and was elegant without any exaggeration, strangely modest and at the same time very willful and determined, unlike the rest of us. The dandies among us gazed at him enviously, and were all outclassed by him. I was particularly struck by his face. His hair was a curiously intense black, his light-colored eyes were peculiarly limpid and calm, his complexion was unusually soft and white, and the color in his cheeks was a little too bright and clear. Then, too, his teeth were like pearls, and his lips like coral— one would have said he was a paragon of beauty, but there was a hint of something strange and repellent about him. There were people who said his face was a

mask; but they were always saying such things about him; and some spoke of his extraordinary physical strength.[1]

Such was the man who ruled over the Durov circle by employing all the arts of seduction. He had an uncanny instinct for selecting the weaker ones and making slaves of them: Durov, who was pious, intelligent and curiously colorless, the young poet Pleshcheyev, who lived his life by a code of unbounded generosity, and Dostoyevsky, who was for a while closer to Pleshcheyev than to anyone on earth, dedicating to him two of his stories. The Durov group was always small, and probably never amounted to more than eight persons. How deeply the group was implicated in revolutionary activity we can guess from the draft of the revolutionary oath found among Speshnev's papers after his arrest. It read: "I, the undersigned, do hereby undertake to pledge myself unreservedly to a full and complete participation in the rebellion and the subsequent fighting at such time as the Committee decides to come out in open rebellion, and I further undertake to provide myself with firearms and other weapons . . ."

Speshnev explained to the police that the revolutionary oath was nothing more than romantic nonsense, written for his own amusement. He explained that no one had signed it, and he had never asked anyone to sign it. Yet there is no doubt that he intended to form a revolutionary group. He was not just playing with fire. He was determined, if possible, to set all Russia aflame.

For this purpose he needed willing servants bound to him by a common purpose, by oath, or by blackmail. Among these servants was Dostoyevsky, who borrowed 500 rubles from Speshnev and then found himself hopelessly at the mercy of the handsome revolutionary. About this time Dr. Stepan Yanovsky, who was Dostoyevsky's lifelong friend, began to wonder why the young writer was becoming so strangely irritable. "I saw that he was growing fantastically nervous and irritable," Dr. Yanovsky wrote

[1] *The Devils,* Part I, Chapter ii.

in his *Memoirs.* "He would begin to quarrel on the slightest pretext, and he was complaining more and more about a pain over his heart. According to Dostoyevsky himself, the cause of all this was his connection with Speshnev, or more exactly the fact that he had borrowed money from him."

The doctor suggested that the depression would soon pass.

"No," said Dostoyevsky, "it will never pass, and it will always torment me. I have borrowed money from him. I am with him, and belong to him. I can never return his money, and he will never let me return it. That is the kind of man he is. So you see, I have my own Mephistopheles now!"

Dostoyevsky was committed to revolutionary activity, and he could no longer escape even if he wanted to. "I am with him, and belong to him." He was heart and soul in the enterprise.

Very little is known about the intimate workings of the Durov circle. We know that Speshnev ordered all the members to write subversive articles which he promised to have printed abroad and smuggled into Russia. At the very first meeting we hear of the guard's officer Nikolay Mombelli urging a close association of people with advanced views, while a young student called Philippov proposed that all the members should co-operate in a systematic survey of conditions in Russia, and write essays on various aspects of the revolutionary struggle. He invited Dostoyevsky to write the paper on socialism. Philippov was something of a fire-eater, known for his reckless bravery. When he suggested they should acquire a lithographic stone and distribute hand-printed revolutionary pamphlets throughout the country, Dostoyevsky was silent and Durov muttered into his black beard. No one was quite prepared for such a drastic step at the time, and soon the piano was opened, and the conspirators gathered round it and sang for the rest of the evening. At the end of the meeting there was a collection to pay for the refreshments and the rent of the piano. Everyone paid three rubles.

Count Orlov, the chief of the Gendarmerie, was already

aware that some subversive statements were being made at the Friday meetings at Petrashevsky's house. The problem was to find a spy who could penetrate the closed group and talk on equal terms with the conspirators. The task of finding a suitable spy was given to Liprandi, an official in the Ministry of the Interior. He was of Italian descent, and he finally discovered a former student of St. Petersburg University, also of Italian descent, who was prepared to report on the meetings.

The police-spy was the son of a well-known painter called Antonelli. He had a long nose, blond hair and charming manners, and he had already achieved some sort of fame from his habit of wearing scarlet waistcoats. He talked easily and well about the errors of the government and the stupidities of the church—a little too well, for some of the revolutionaries became suspicious, and Speshnev in particular refused to have anything to do with him and made sure that he came to know little or nothing about the Durov circle. Antonelli first attended the Petrashevsky meetings in March, 1849. After each meeting he wrote out a full report for Liprandi, who sent a copy to Count Orlov. Finally these reports came to the attention of the Tzar.

Meanwhile the Durov circle was busily preparing to lay the foundations for a rebellion. It needed recruits, and one night in January, 1849, Dostoyevsky called on his old friend Apollon Maikov and spent the whole night begging him to join the conspiracy. According to Maikov, there were at that time only six members in the Durov circle, and they were even then in process of obtaining a printing press. Dostoyevsky explained that the circle was entirely independent of Petrashevsky, who was "an idiot, a mountebank and a man who talked for the sake of talking, and therefore nothing can be hoped from him."

Maikov was alarmed, and counseled caution. He explained to Dostoyevsky that certain death would be the punishment for anyone found operating a subversive printing press. "You and I," he said, "are poets, we have no practical sense at all, and therefore we should have nothing to do with these clandestine affairs." Dostoyevsky continued to argue, insisting that it was a question of pure patriotism. "I remember Dostoyevsky in his nightshirt with the collar open at the neck," Maikov wrote in a letter discovered in 1922. "I remember him sitting up, like a dying Socrates among his friends, enlarging with all his eloquence on the sacredness of the undertaking, and how it was our absolute duty to save the country, etc. etc., and when he had come to the end of his harangue I burst out laughing and began to joke with him, and then he said: 'You won't join us?' 'No,' I said, 'I will never join, never!' "

The next morning Dostoyevsky left Maikov's house after begging him not to breathe a word about the revolutionary circle or the printing press.

According to Maikov, the printing press was not a fiction of Dostoyevsky's imagination, but actually existed. It had been designed by Philippov in such a way that the various pieces could be easily concealed and assembled when needed. It was in fact assembled in the house of "one of the associates called M . . ." (presumably Mombelli), and though the house was searched and the police even set eyes on it as it stood among a great confusion of scientific instruments, they paid no attention to it. The door was sealed by the police, but friends were able to lift the door by the hinges and remove the press without breaking the seal. The press was assembled only a day or two before the arrests.

The police never proved the existence of the printing press. If they had, the fate of the members of the Durov circle might have been very different. Many years later Dostoyevsky revealed to his wife that he had known all about the printing press. "The Socialists sprang from the Petrashevsky conspirators," he told her. "They sowed many seeds, and among them was everything that was used in succeeding conspiracies, among them lithography and secret printing presses, but our press was never used."

Time was running out for the conspirators. Dostoyevsky was still attending the meetings of the Petrashevsky circle, and he was

present at a strange dinner given on the evening of April 7, 1849,
in honor of the birthday of Fourier. Nearly all the conspirators
were present. Antonelli, as charming as ever, was filling his
capacious memory with impressions of the meeting. There were
many speeches and many toasts. One of the speakers raised his
glass and spoke of the coming of the Golden Age in words which
seem to breathe the ageless preoccupations of the human soul as it
manifests itself in Russia:

> Restore the image of man in all its splendor and
> beauty, for which he has lived so long. Liberate and
> organize his deep harmonious passions, which are now
> oppressed and stifled. Tear down the cities and the
> towns, and use the bricks for building new cities and
> towns. Let the shame and grief and beggary and misery
> all vanish, and be utterly transformed into perfect joy
> and riches and harmony. That all the earth shall be
> covered with palaces and fruit trees and adorned with
> flowers—this is our high aim, and there is no greater
> aim on earth! [2]

This typically Russian dream was almost as old as Russia;
variants of it can be found among the writings of the Russian
theologians. Out of that dream came the famous *Revolutionary
Catechism* of the archconspirator Nechayev, and it was never very
far from the thoughts of Lenin. "Tear down the cities and the
towns . . ." "*Razrushit stolitsi, goroda . . .*" In Russian the
words have a terrible beauty.

A week after the dinner in honor of Fourier, Dostoyevsky
again attended a meeting of the Petrashevsky circle, this time
taking an active part. His task was a very simple one. He was to
read two letters obtained from an unknown source by Pleshcheyev
in Moscow. These letters were perhaps the most significant letters
written in nineteenth century Russia, for they were written by
geniuses and they stated in simple and passionate tones two
opposing views of the nature of the Russian mind, and therefore

[2] Leonid Grossman, *Put Dostoyevskovo,* page 76.

of the two opposing paths opening into the future. One letter was written by Belinsky, the other by the great novelist Gogol. To the end of his life Dostoyevsky was to be haunted by these letters. It was as though the ideas expressed by these letters were the positive and negative poles of his existence, and his own thoughts were continually leaping from one pole to the other in fierce, erratic explosions of electricity.

The exchange of correspondence between Gogol and Belinsky owed its origin to the publication of Gogol's book called *Selected Passages from Correspondence with my Friends.* The book consisted of thirty-one letters written in a tone of quite extraordinary unctuosity by Gogol to his friends, some named and others anonymous. They were the letters of a sick man pleading with his friends to put wickedness away, to devote themselves to the truth of God, and to obey immediately, instantly, the sacred words falling from Gogol's lips. Occasionally there are gleams of genius, a brilliant phrase, a sudden marshaling of images, but those moments are rare. Gogol saw himself simultaneously as a prophet and a sinner close to damnation; and most of the time he was too ill to know what he was saying.

Selected Passages was the work of a man in the last stages of exhaustion, from which he rallied only long enough to write the wonderfully precise and limpid *Meditations on the Divine Liturgy.* He could think only of spiritual things; when he wrote about the government or the lives of ordinary thinking people, he was like a presumptuous, headstrong, and stupid child.

The book was published on January 1, 1847, and Belinsky wrote a cautious review in *The Contemporary,* in which he warned Gogol the artist against Gogol "the false prophet." In the summer, dying of consumption, Belinsky went abroad for the first time. He was in Salzbrunn, a watering-place in Austria, when he received a letter from Gogol gently reproving him for criticizing *Selected Passages.* The tone of the letter, unctuous, earnest, schoolmasterish, threw Belinsky into a ferocious temper. On July 3, 1847, he answered it, determined to punish Gogol for his temerity. This most merciless of letters, written in savage indignation, was a masterpiece of ruthless and passionate vituperation, but in so far as it was an attack on Gogol, it was unworthy of Belinsky. He was bringing up a twenty-ton sledge hammer to punish an erring child.

The letter has deservedly become a classic for many reasons which have little to do with Gogol. It was easy to destroy Gogol; it was much more difficult to destroy the Tzarist state. For twenty pages Belinsky poured out his determined hatred of the government, which was "only a vast corporation of official robbers and thieves," and of the Church, which was "the champion of inequality, the enemy and persecutor of the brotherhood of man." In words that were addressed to the Tzar as well as to Gogol, he wrote:

> You have failed to understand that Russia sees her salvation not in mysticism, nor asceticism, nor pietism, but in the successes of civilization, enlightenment and humanity. What she needs is not sermons (she has heard enough of them!) nor prayers (she has repeated them too many times!), but the awakening of the people to the sense of their human dignity lost for so many centuries amid the dirt and the refuse; she needs rights and laws conforming not with the preaching of the Church, but with common sense and justice, and their strictest possible observance.
>
> Instead of this, Russia today presents the dire spectacle of a country where men traffic in men, without even having the excuse so insidiously exploited by the plantation owners in America, who claim that the Negro is not a man. Russia is a country where no one has a name; instead there are only nicknames like Vanka, Vaska, Steshka, Palashka. It is a country where there are no guarantees of individual freedom, honor and property, where there is no law obeyed by the police, and the government is only a vast corporation of official robbers and thieves. The most vital na-

69

tional problem in Russia today is the abolition of serfdom and of corporal punishment, and the strictest possible observance of the laws that have already been passed. This is even realized by the government itself, which is well aware of how the landowners treat their peasants, and of how many landowners are annually killed by the peasants, and all this is proved by the timid and abortive half-measures for the relief of the white Negroes and the amusing substitution of the knout for the cat-o'-three-tails . . .

The Church has always served as the defender of the knout and the servant of despotism, but why have you mixed Christ up in this? What have you found in common between Him and any Church, least of all the Orthodox Church?

Christ was the first to bring to people the teaching of freedom, equality and brotherhood, and He set the seal of truth to that teaching by His martyrdom. And this teaching was men's *salvation* until it became organized in the Church and took the principle of Orthodoxy for its foundation. The Church became a hierarchy, and therefore the champion of inequality, the flatterer of authority, the enemy and persecutor of the brotherhood of man—and so it has remained to this day.

The meaning of Christ's message, however, has been revealed by the philosophical movement of the preceding century. That is why a man like Voltaire who stamped out the fires of fanaticism and ignorance in Europe by ridicule is all the more the son of Christ, flesh of His flesh and bone of His bone, and much more the son of Christ than all your priests, bishops, metropolitans and patriarchs, Eastern or Western . . .

According to you the Russian people are the most religious in the world. This is a lie! The basis of religious feeling lies in piety, reverence, and the fear of God. But the Russian utters the name of the Lord only when scratching himself somewhere. He says of the icon: *If it isn't good for praying, it is good for covering the pot.*

Take a closer look, and you will see that by nature

the Russians are a profoundly atheistic people, who still retain a good deal of superstition, but not a trace of religious feeling. Superstition passes with the advance of civilization, but religious feeling often survives for a while. We have living examples of this in France, where even today there are many sincere Catholics among enlightened and educated men, and where many who have rejected Christianity still cling to some kind of God. But the Russian people are quite different. Mystic exaltation is not in their nature. They have too much common sense, their minds are too positive and lucid, and therein lies the vastness of their historic destiny.

The truth is that religious feeling does not even exist among the clergy, and certainly the example of a few people given to coldly ascetic meditations proves nothing. The majority of our clergy are distinguished only by their round paunches, their scholastic pedantry and their savage ignorance. It would be pathetic to accuse them of religious intolerance and fanaticism; they should be praised for their exemplary indifference to matters of faith . . .

I shall not speak of your panegyric on the love of the Russian people for their lords and masters. I shall only remark that the panegyric has not met with agreement from anyone and has lowered you in the eyes of those people who would otherwise find themselves very close to your ideas. As far as I am concerned, I leave it to your conscience to admire the divine beauty of the autocracy.

I will add this: When a European, especially a Catholic, is seized with religious ardor, he becomes a denouncer of iniquitous authority, similar to the Hebrew prophets who denounced the iniquities of the great ones of the earth. With us it is different: no sooner is a person (even a reputable person) afflicted with the malady known to psychologists as *religiosa mania* than he begins to burn more incense to the earthly god than to heavenly one, and he so overshoots the mark that the earthly god hesitates before rewarding him for his slavish zeal, because he realizes he would compromise himself in the eyes of society. What roguish fellows our Russians are! . . .[3]

Belinsky's letter is worth reading carefully, if only because he demonstrates an acute and vigorous mind grappling with problems which were very close to the hearts of the young revolutionaries. He was saying what many thought and did not dare to express, and he was laying the foundations for the Bolshevik revolution which took place seventy years later. To him the Russian Communists owe a debt they have often recognized.

The Tzar and his ministers were perfectly aware of the explosive power of that letter if it was widely disseminated.

For making hand-written copies of the letter and for preparing to print it in thousands of copies, Dostoyevsky was sentenced to death.

[3] Letter to Gogol, July 3, 1847.

THE PRISONER

IN THE OFFICES of the Third Division of the Imperial Gendarmerie the police were working overtime. From Antonelli they had obtained the names and addresses of nearly all the revolutionaries, and Count Orlov had presented a massive dossier to the Tzar, Nicholas I, who wrote on the margin: "I have read everything. The affair is serious. Even if it is only foolish talk, it is nevertheless criminal and intolerable. They must be arrested, as you recommend."

Count Orlov prepared the ground carefully. High officers were placed in charge of the arrests, and a certain Major Chudinov received from the Count a warrant to arrest Dostoyevsky on the night of April 22/23. The warrant, which has been preserved, read:

BY HIGHEST ORDER

You are commanded to arrest former lieutenant of engineers and author Fyodor Mikhailovoch Dostoyevsky tomorrow, at four o'clock in the morning, at his lodging at the corner of the Malaya Morskaya and the Voznesensky Prospect. He is to be found in the house belonging to Shill, on the third floor, in the apartment belonging to Breyer. All his books, papers and effects to be sealed and delivered into the safekeeping of the Third Division of the Imperial Chancellery.[1]

[1] Leonid Grossman, *Dostoyevsky na zhiznennom puty,* page 172.

7 3

None of the conspirators knew that he was in danger. Dostoyevsky was going about his normal affairs. April 22 was a Friday, and he had decided to pay his usual visit to Petrashevsky to discuss a standing project: the publication of a newspaper. It was an unusually warm evening. He looked forward to an enjoyable meeting, but Petrashevsky's house was a considerable distance from his apartment, and he was caught in a sudden shower. Drenched, he decided to call on his friend, Dr. Stepan Yanovsky, to change his clothes and borrow some money for a *droshky*. Dr. Yanovsky had no money on him, and broke open his alms box. Dostoyevsky went off to the meeting in a borrowed suit, with thirty copecks, which he promised to return. The doctor never saw the money again, and it was many years before he set eyes on Dostoyevsky, who returned to his own apartment in another shower just before four o'clock in the morning. He undressed, went to bed, and was soon asleep. Many years later he described how he became aware of the presence of the police:

I was still sleeping when I became obscurely aware that some strangers had somehow entered my room. I heard a sabre rattling, knocking against something. It seemed to me very queer, but what exactly was happening? With an effort I opened my eyes, and heard a soft and very gentle voice saying: "Get up!"

I saw a police officer or perhaps a police commissioner with a beautiful beard. He did not speak. Someone else, wearing a blue uniform with the epaulettes of a lieutenant colonel, was speaking.

"What is happening?" I asked, rising from the bed.

"Orders."

I looked, and saw it really was "orders." By the door stood a soldier, also in blue. It was his sabre which was rattling.

"What on earth is happening?" I thought, and then I said: "Excuse me, what—"

"It doesn't matter, it doesn't matter," the lieutenant

colonel was saying, and his voice seemed more beautiful than ever. "Get up! We can wait!"

While I was dressing they rummaged through all
my books and papers and tied them together with
string. With my pipe stem the officer began to rake
over the dead ashes in my small stove, and he ordered
a lieutenant of the gendarmerie to stand on a chair and
examine the top of the stove, but in reaching out for a
cornice his grip failed, he fell heavily on the chair and
then from the chair to the floor. This was how these
intelligent gentlemen came to learn there was nothing
in the stove.

On the table there was a five copeck piece, old and
bent. The officer studied it carefully, and after a while
he nodded in the direction of the lieutenant colonel.

"Is it counterfeit?" I asked.

"Hm, well, we'll find out about that," the officer
grumbled, and added the coin to the other evidence.

Then we left. At the door the landlady and her servant Ivan said good-by. Ivan was especially frightened,
but he looked grave, as befitted the seriousness of the
occasion; certainly it was not a very festive ceremony.

We drove off to the Fontanka prison by way of the
chain bridge and the Summer Garden.[2]

In the Fontanka prison there was a famous "white room"
for the reception of prisoners, and here the sleepy prisoners were
briefly interrogated by Count Orlov, the head of the Third
Division, and General Dubelt, his assistant. One by one the
prisoners arrived from all over St. Petersburg. Among them were
a number of guards officers, and it was perhaps for the benefit
of the officers that the prince ordered that a meal with hors
d'œuvres and wine be sent in. The presence of the prince suggested
that the government regarded the matter very seriously indeed.

There were altogether thirty-four prisoners, and the strangest
of all was Dostoyevsky's brother, Andrey, who had obviously

[2] *Letters:* 933. Written in the album of Olga Miliukova on May 24,
1860, and first published in March 1881.

been arrested in error, for he had never attended the meetings in Petrashevsky's apartment. He had clearly been mistaken for Mikhail. Dostoyevsky begged him to remain silent and accept his punishment, at least for a few days, since Mikhail's wife had just given birth to a child and was not yet fully recovered. If Andrey remained silent there would be time for Mikhail to make arrangements before he too was committed to prison. Andrey agreed to the ruse, and his brothers were everlastingly grateful to him.

At one moment during the preliminary interrogation Dostoyevsky was able to see some words penciled on the top of the charge sheet. They read: *Antonelli, agent.* He knew now the name of the police spy responsible for his arrest. Many years later when the police archives were opened, it was learned that Antonelli had agreed to act for the police only on condition that his name should never be recorded in any documents connected with the case.

The prisoners remained at the Fontanka prison for the rest of the day, and at eleven o'clock at night they were removed to the Peter and Paul Fortress. They were lodged in the special cells called the Alexis Ravelin built by Peter the Great for the conspirators who assembled around his own son Alexey; and in one of those cells Prince Alexey himself had been tortured to death.

This prison was reserved for great prisoners of state, and few who entered it came out alive. The stone dungeons were always damp, lapped by the waters of the Neva. There was almost no light. A small window, smeared with chalk, heavily barred and standing eight feet from the ground, let in the faint gleam of watery sunlight. There was room to move in, for the cells were fourteen feet by eleven, but the prison architects designed them so that they seemed much smaller, and they were grotesquely uncomfortable with their ugly iron beds, iron tables, and commodes. There were paper-thin blankets, pillows stuffed with straw, and straw mattresses; and the straw soon became damp and evil-smelling. The door was opened five times a day: at seven o'clock for tea, at ten for inspection, at noon for lunch—the meal rarely consisted of much more than a bowl of soup with some meat floating in it—and in the evening there was dinner. Finally a guard came in to light the candle or kerosene lamp, which permitted the prisoners to watch their shadows moving across the grey walls, which were lumpy and resembled the mottlings and corruscations on a decaying corpse.

The Peter and Paul Fortress was not a fortress; it was a prison, a city of the dead, a monument to the ancient vengeance of long-dead Tzars. Very early the Tzars had learned that the most terrible punishment was silence. No one was allowed to speak; the guards wore felt boots and moved noiselessly about. There was only the sound of the Neva lapping the casemates. The walls absorbed the screams of dying men.

The silence of the Peter and Paul Fortress was broken at intervals by the chimes of the fortress cathedral playing the liturgical response "Have mercy, O Lord" every quarter of an hour and the canticle "How glorious is our Lord in Zion" every hour. At midnight they chimed "God save the Tzar." The bells broke the silence, but after the echo of the last chime had faded the silence was greater than before.

One of the revolutionaries who was later imprisoned in the fortress was Vera Figner, who related in her memoirs that after several months of silence her vocal chords weakened and her sense of time became hopelessly distorted. When she was released, if anyone dropped a silver teaspoon, she had to exert all her will to prevent herself from screaming, so great was the strain on her nervous system. Silence bred silence, and there came a time when she had no desire to speak.

Dostoyevsky was a model prisoner. He seems to have known he was in grave danger of going mad in prison, and he deliberately kept his mind occupied with thoughts of the novels and stories he would write when he was free. Nearly all the other prisoners suffered from prison fever, sudden bouts of near-madness, fits of terrible depression. Katenev went mad and was removed to the prison hospital, where he soon died. Yastrzhembsky wrote in his memoirs: "I remained in the Ravelin from April 23 to December 23, and if I had stayed there a day longer I would have gone insane." Aksharumov tore a nail out of his bed and kept sharpening it. Petrashevsky wrote to the prison commandant a strange letter in which he spoke of "whispers trying to destroy me"; he would like to have the whispers officially removed. There are no recorded incidents of Dostoyevsky giving way to any form of hysteria while in prison. Without pen and paper, without books, without visitors, he remained extraordinarily calm. He was determined to survive. He learned to send messages in code by tapping on the wall. He learned that his brother Andrey had been released; for a while Mikhail was under arrest, but in June he too was released, and the official announcement of his release says he committed no crime against the government, adding mysteriously: "He even tried to prevent it." No one has yet been able to discover how he prevented anyone from taking part in the conspiracy.

Three weeks later, on July 11, Dostoyevsky received his first letter from his brother. He was wildly happy, but did not trust himself to reply until a week later. He wrote:

> You tell me, beloved, not to lose courage, and I have not lost my courage. Of course I am bored and disgusted, but what can I do? Time passes very irregularly—sometimes too fast, sometimes terribly slowly, and there are days when I even feel I have become acustomed to this life and nothing matters any more. I do my best to drive away the temptations of my imagination, but sometimes my imagination is stronger than me, and my soul is assailed by memories of the past and former sensations; they all come back to me. But this in the nature of things.
>
> Nowadays the days are beautiful, or at least most of them are, and this delights me. Even when the weather is bad, it is bearable: the prison seems only to become more austere. I have things to do. I am not wasting my

time. I have planned three short stories and two novels.
I am writing one of them now, but I dare not work very
hard.

Especially when I am writing with all sails flying (I
have never worked so *con amore* as I do now), I become easily exhausted and at the mercy of my nerves.
When I was free I was always getting up from my work
and pottering around and wasting time, but here I
write steadily with the full power of my emotions. My
health is good except for my hemorrhoids and the nervous spasms which keep getting worse. Spasms in the
throat, like those I had before, hardly any appetite, and
I sleep only for a little while, and there are terrible
nightmares. I sleep only about five hours, and I wake
up four times each night. That is what is so hard . . .
All I desire is to keep well, for all these troubles will
pass; and then too it depends on me whether I am
cheerful or not. Men have a surprising vitality and unfathomable powers of resistance. I would not have believed it if I did not know it from experience.[3]

His astonishing calm suggests an unexpected strength, a
calculated determination to survive. He was in good heart, especially after being given permission to write. Of the three short
stories and two novels he mentions in his letter only the story
called *The Little Hero* survived, being published eight years later,
in September, 1857.

The Little Hero is a strange and wonderful story, among the
most perfect things he ever wrote. It is about many things, about
Petrashevsky, about being sentenced to death, about a wild horse,
about an eleven-year-old boy's awakening knowledge of sexuality,
about the sunlit calm of a country estate. Death and Petrashevsky
are present by implication. To the reader who does not know the
circumstances under which the story was written, their presence
would pass unobserved.

The Little Hero, which is written in the first person, begins

[3] *Letters:* 55, July 18, 1849.

with the unnamed hero, evidently Dostoyevsky himself, staying on the vast country estate near Moscow belonging to his relatives. The fifty guests amuse themselves with picnics and riding horseback through the woods. Everything sparkles—the flowers, the faces of the girls, the music and the dancing. Plays are performed in a small theater, and the boy watches the performance of a play with a sense of extraordinary involvement, while standing beside a beautiful girl. When the girl suggests that he should sit on her lap, he slips away, burning with shame. Her presence haunts him, and he is haunted too by the girl's close friend, a married woman with a pale, intense, Madonna-like face, whose arrogant husband is continually slipping away for brief and mysterious visits to Moscow.

Dostoyevsky describes the husband at length. He is one of those men "who have a lump of fat instead of a heart." He has beautiful teeth, a ruddy face, sideburns, a distinguished manner. He scoffs at everything, is always using other people to advance his purposes, and continually admires himself. He is delightfully witty according to the fashion of the time, but in fact he never says anything of importance. It is a mordant caricature of Petrashevsky, the amateur revolutionary who was responsible for a conspiracy doomed to failure from the beginning.

One day all the guests on the estate prepare for a ride through the neighboring countryside. They are all on horseback or in carriages. An untamed stallion called Tancred is led out by the grooms, and the owner of the estate dares an officer of Hussars to ride it, but the officer quails before the horse, which is champing at the bit and pawing the ground, rearing on its hind legs and terrifying everyone in sight. At this moment, the lady with the face of a Madonna allows her gaze to fall on the boy, who sees himself as a medieval knight in her service. He immediately springs on the wild horse, which rushes like a tornado down the road and he is saved only because some horsemen ride up just in time. He has shown his courage and returns a hero. The young women make a fuss over him, kissing and caressing him, so that once more he is shamefaced and confused.

On another day the boy is wandering on the edge of the woods and watching the mowers at work, "the sharp scythes flashing in the sun, streaking up like little tongues of flame." The idyllic picture is interrupted by the appearance of a young man on horseback who is talking with the Madonna. The horseman is her lover, on his way to the south. They embrace and kiss passionately, and before the horseman rides away he hands her a sealed envelope. She drops the envelope while wandering distractedly through the woods. The boy finds it in the reddish sand, and follows her, but cannot give it to her because she is close to the house and might be observed. When she realizes she has lost the envelope, she is unnerved, for her whole life depends upon recovering it.

The boy is searching for an opportunity to give her the envelope, but none comes. He gazes at her with longing and utter helplessness, and suddenly we are made aware that the focus has shifted, and the letter represents all Dostoyevsky's despairing hopes as he lies in prison. He is describing the lady as she stands on the terrace surrounded by all the other guests, hoping for a miracle.

> I can still remember every detail of her face; it was a face which had gone beyond all suffering. She felt, she knew, she was certain that at any moment, or perhaps in a quarter of an hour, everything would be revealed, and she was waiting for this moment as the condemned man waits for his execution. Perhaps someone had found the envelope and picked it up. There was no name written on it, and anyone could rip it open, and then. . . Then the executioner's knife would fall on her.
> So she moved among those who would sit in judgment over her. Their flattering, smiling faces would

soon grow heavy and inexorable. She would see mockery, malice and disdain written on those faces, and then the night would fall, an eternal night without hope of any dawn.

I could not then have understood all this in the way I now understand it. But I remember my suspicions and misgivings and the pain in my heart because so much danger threatened her, even though I did not understand the nature of the danger. But whatever her secret, much of her guilt was atoned for, if there was need of atonement, in those grief-laden moments which I witnessed and shall never forget.

At last it occurs to her that she may have dropped the envelope in the woods and she hurries back along the path, and the boy hurries after her. He is wild with excitement. He plans to offer her a bouquet with the envelope concealed inside it. He gathers sweetbriars and wild jasmine, runs into the cornfield for cornflowers, finds a whole nest of forget-me-nots, hurries down to the river for water lilies, adds bright green maple leaves and violets, twines the bouquet together with blades of grass, and shyly presents it to her. She pays no attention to the bouquet until a large golden bee buzzes round her and to protect herself she waves the bouquet, and the envelope falls out. The amazed woman devours the letter, her eyes alight and her cheeks flaming; only then does she observe the boy watching her.

Then she came towards me and bent over me, and I could feel she was looking straight at my face. My eyelashes quivered, but I controlled myself and did not open my eyes. I tried to breathe even more tranquilly, but my heart was choking me with its ferocious beating. Her hot breath scorched my cheeks. She bent very close to me, as though to make sure. Then she kissed me and a tear fell on my hand—the hand that lay on my breast. And twice she kissed it.

"Natalie! Natalie! Where are you?" the voices sounded again from the distance.

The boy raises his eyes and watches her vanishing along the path. When, two hours later, he returns to the house, he learns that she has already left for Moscow with her husband.

It is worth while to ponder the story, for quite clearly Dostoyevsky was living on many levels of consciousness while in the Peter and Paul Fortress. The tender account of the boy's awakening into life is also a desperate plea for freedom. The mysterious letter was simultaneously a letter to a woman from her lover, the letter of Belinsky, and an order signed by the Tzar releasing him from prison. In the story everything depended upon the letter; in life everything depended upon two letters—the one which was the presumptive cause of his imprisonment, and the other which would mysteriously release him. At no time does Dostoyevsky tell us what was written in the letter, but we are made aware that a terrible light beats down on it.

He lived for letters—the occasional letters he sent out, the rare letters he received, and those more mysterious letters which were never sent and therefore never answered. At the end of August he wrote to Mikhail: "I am still in ignorance about my case. My life is monotonous as ever, but I have been given permission to walk in the garden where there are seventeen trees." He asked for books on history and the Bible in French, and complained of his hemorrhoids, which he was attempting to cure with castor oil, and of pains in his chest, and of a strange excitement which overcame him in the evening. In the past he would employ that excitement and direct it into his writing, for he seemed to write best in those hours when his whole body was quivering with some inexplicable frenzy, but he dared not attempt the feat in prison. "Meanwhile one lives, and I hope one day to be cured."

So the weeks passed, and soon it was autumn, the skies darkening and the fortress growing damp and there were always the guards pacing outside the cells in their felt boots. What he hated most of all was the thought that soon there would be no more blue sky to be seen through the little square of window. He felt like a man in an air chamber, from which the air was slowly being expelled. He was a nerve, a brain, a sponge for soaking up ideas; and in this way he kept his health. "For the moment my health remains," he wrote to his brother in September. "I had expected it would be worse, but I realize now that I have reserves of vitality which can never be consumed." In later days he was to say: "I have the vitality of a cat." He was remarkably sturdy, and stood the pressures of prison life better than most of the other prisoners.

Meanwhile the investigation dragged on. There were endless interrogations. From time to time the prisoners would be taken to face the interrogating commission, which consisted of five members—Prince Gagarin, Prince Dolgoruky, and the three generals Dubelt, Rostovtsev, and Nabokov, who was the chairman of the commission and the commander of the Peter and Paul Fortress. The Princes were courteous, and Dostoyevsky remembered them in later days with something approaching affection. Dubelt was the most dangerous member of the commission. Known as "the fox," he had a long, lean face, drooping mustaches, and cheeks covered with a spider-web of wrinkles. He was the chief of the gendarmerie, and famous for his cruelty.

The whole of Dostoyevsky's testimony has survived. He did not deny the accusations; he simply attempted to place the conspirators in their proper historic context and lectured his interrogators on the subject of Fourierism. He admitted readily that he had been in possession of Belinsky's letter, but he denied that he had ever believed in it. He had read it to his friends "inadvertently," without realizing its implications, as one might read some interesting article in a newspaper. "We would all be guilty," he told the commissioners, "if our intimate thoughts were investigated, if we were held accountable for every word we said to our intimate friends." He insisted that he had never acted with malice against the Tzar or the government, and had never been a socialist, but he reserved the right to read and study every kind of book and docu-

84

ment concerned with social problems. About the printing press he was quietly evasive.

From time to time they made attempts to trap him. Rostovtsev offered him a full pardon if he would tell the whole story of the conspiracy. Dostoyevsky remained silent. He had already told what he knew about the conspiracy, and there was nothing more to add. Suddenly Rostovtsev jumped up from the table, shouted: "I cannot look at Dostoyevsky any more!" and marched out of the room.

The commissioners failed to find evidence of an organized secret conspiracy, but they found enough evidence to suggest that a conspiracy would inevitably have evolved out of the discussions in Petrashevsky's house. They were standing in judgment over a *potential* crime, one which had not yet taken place. Speshnev and Philippov had confessed to possessing an illegal printing press, but no trace of it was found; yet the commissioners never doubted its existence. When they drew up their final verdicts, they pointed especially to that mysterious press which haunted them throughout the long months of the investigation.

At last, eight months after the prisoners were arrested, the judgments were handed down. Dostoyevsky was condemned for "taking part in criminal designs, for circulating the letter of the journalist Belinsky full of insolent expressions against the Orthodox Church and the Supreme Power, and for having attempted in collusion with others to circulate certain writings against the government on a lithographic press."

Dostoyevsky did not know he had been condemned. On the morning of December 22, 1849, he was escorted out of the Peter and Paul Fortress to receive his punishment.

THE EXECUTION

O N THAT DAY which was the last of his youth and the beginning of his premature old age, Dostoyevsky was lying on his narrow cot when he heard steps in the corridor, whispers, the clanking of swords, sudden commands followed by the creaking of the key in the rusty lock. It was about half-past five in the morning, and still dark. The door opened. In the light of a lantern Dostoyevsky saw an unknown officer standing there, and suddenly the officer announced that by the orders of the Tzar the prisoner had been sentenced to death by shooting. The officer stepped back, the door was closed, and once more there was darkness in the cell.

Afterward, when Dostoyevsky had recovered from the shock, he remembered that nothing had been said about when the sentence would be carried out.

About half an hour later one of the prison guards entered the cell, bringing with him a small package containing the clothes worn by the prisoner when he entered the prison eight months before. There was a thin overcoat, coat, trousers, shirt, cravat, socks, heavy-soled boots. Dostoyevsky put them on, and was then led out into the courtyard. The first light was coming through the fog.

He shivered in the cold winter air. There was deep snow on the ground.

"What is happening?" he asked one of the guards.

"We are forbidden to tell you," the guard answered, and

about this time Dostoyevsky made out the shapes of five carriages. Mounted gendarmes in light blue uniforms, with naked swords in their hands, came wheeling across the prison courtyard.

Gradually the courtyard was filling with prisoners. He could make out Petrashevsky and Durov and many of the others whom he now saw for the first time since his arrest. They were not allowed to talk. Someone shouted that the prisoners were to get into the carriages—four to each carriage. A soldier jumped in after them. There was the crack of a whip, and soon all the carriages were rolling out of the courtyard, and Dostoyevsky said: "What are they going to do to us?"

"We have been told to tell you nothing," the soldier answered.

The glass in the carriage window was covered with a film of frost, and when Dostoyevsky began to rub the frost away, the soldier rebuked him, "Please don't do that," he said. "They'll have me flogged, if you do."

So the prisoners huddled together in silence, gazing straight in front of them or throwing furtive glances at the window. They knew they were crossing the bridge over the Neva by the sound of the horses' hooves on the wooden blocks, and they knew they were going along the Liteiny by the sound of the hooves on cobblestones, but afterwards they soon lost their sense of direction. Time hung heavy on them. It seemed an interminable journey, but was in fact only three miles. At last the carriages came to a halt on the Semyonov Square, overlooked by the Church of the Holy Virgin of Vladimir with its five golden domes, which could be seen dimly through the floating mist.

When Dostoyevsky stepped out of the carriage he realized he had come to the place of execution.

Already the crowds had gathered—the police report mentions 3,000 people in the square, not including a massive detachment of guards from the Moscow Infantry Regiment. In the middle of the square a small sturdy platform had been built during the night. It was covered with black cloth, which sparkled with snow. There were steps leading up to the platform. In front, a little to one side, were three thick oak stakes stripped of bark: to these the condemned men would be tied before they were shot.

Because the steps were narrow the prisoners were led up to the platform in two's. Dostoyevsky was gradually coming out of the fit of torpor which gripped him in the carriage. He recognized the enigmatic Speshnev, and Palm, who wore the close-fitting uniform of a guard's officer. He wanted to embrace them and exchange words of comfort, but there was no time, and besides, as soon as they left the carriages they were marched to the scaffold, a priest in heavy vestments running before them, holding a Cross and the Gospels.

At last there were twenty-one men standing on the platform, formed into two rows. Dostoyevsky was made to stand on the extreme left of the first row, with Petrashevsky on the extreme right. Next to Dostoyevsky was Mombelli, and while the lines were being formed and the bemedaled generals rushed about importantly in front of the platform, Dostoyevsky found himself telling Mombelli the theme of the novel he had conceived in prison. He was very calm, in the strange state of exaltation and exhaustion which comes to those who are condemned to die, and at the same time he could not believe he was about to be executed.

The deliberate purpose of the Tzar was to instill fear in his prisoners and to torture them in such a way that they would become aware of the enormity of their crimes. Therefore he prolonged the punishment.

Frozen, their faces turning blue, wearing only the clothes they were wearing on the spring day when they were arrested, they stood on the platform while an official with a curiously harsh voice proceeded to proclaim their names, their crimes, and the punishments which the Tzar in his infinite mercy had chosen for them, paying due regard to the recommendations of the commission of enquiry. For half an hour the official continued to recite a litany of the dead. First Petrashevsky was condemned to death by shooting, then Mombelli, then Grigoryev and Aksharumov. At last came the name of Dostoyevsky. He could not believe he was going to die. He had the curious feeling that it was all a nightmare, and very soon he would wake up. Just at the moment when he heard the words: ". . . condemned to death by shooting" after his own name had been pronounced, the sun came out through the mist and illumined the beautiful golden cupolas of the Church of the Holy Virgin of Vladimir. It occurred to him that this was a sign that he would not die, and none of the others would die. He whispered to Durov: "After all they are not going to kill us." Without saying a word Durov nodded in the direction of the cart, drawn up only a little way away, which was covered with matting and seemed to contain coffins.

Strange things were happening on the platform. All the prisoners seemed to be caught in a spell. Only Kashkin, who was standing in the second row, began to cry. Seeing him crying, General Golovachev rode up to the platform and said quickly: *"Vous serez graciés tous, tous!"* It was odd behavior for a commanding general who had sworn to uphold the Tzar's order to leave the prisoners in ignorance of their fate. He may have excused himself with the thought that he was not violating discipline, inasmuch as he spoke in French and was speaking privately, as man to man, to one of his former officers.

The official finished reading the imperial rescript. Long afterward Dostoyevsky remembered how the officer carefully folded the sheet of paper and put it in his pocket, behaving throughout with a strange awkwardness, like a marionette.

By this time, Dostoyevsky had lost all hope. In a bemused way he observed a wart on the cheek of one of the gendarmes, and then he saw a copper button shining in the sun. The fog was clearing. There was a blinding radiance from the five cupolas, and he could make out the yellow façade of the barracks and the crowds of people jostling silently to see the executions.

89

The official was replaced by a priest who invited the prisoners to make their confessions. Only one man, a certain Shaposhnikov, confessed, but when the priest offered them the crucifix to kiss, they all knelt and kissed it. The priest went on to deliver a short sermon on the text: "The wages of sin is death." He spoke in a weak strangled voice of the joys of Heaven, and the eternal bliss which awaited them in the life to come. When he had finished, two men in brilliant kaftans climbed onto the platform and broke swords over the heads of all those who belonged to the nobility, so testifying that they no longer possessed any rights or privileges. This was the last act before the execution. In a sense, the breaking of the swords was the ultimate punishment, removing them from the world of honor; the actual shooting would be almost an anticlimax.

For a very long time the prisoners had remained on the platform, numbed and shivering, but the tempo was quickening. The men in the brilliant kaftans left the platform, but the priest remained, muttering prayers. Another general rode up and shouted: "Father, you have done your work! There is no need to stay up there!" The priest walked down the steps.

Then it was the turn of some soldiers to mount the platform carrying with them the white vestments in which the condemned were always clothed when they were led to their deaths. These vestments took the form of white hooded shrouds with long sleeves trailing to the ground. Petrashevsky, Grigoryev and Mombelli, who were thought to be the ringleaders of the conspiracy and therefore the most guilty, were the first to be clothed in their shrouds. Suddenly there was heard the mocking voice of Petrashevsky: "What absurd clothes they are giving us! Really, they don't know how to dress a man!" Swords flashed, a trumpet sounded, and there was a roll of drums as the three men were led down the steps and marched to the stakes, where they were bound with ropes, the long white flapping sleeves drawn behind them. A platoon of fifteen soldiers took up position. The command rang out: "Take aim!" and the soldiers lifted their rifles to their shoulders. In a moment the commanding general would shout: "Fire!" and then there would be wet bloodstains on the white shrouds.

Dostoyevsky no longer had any hope that his life would be spared. He believed he had at most five minutes to live, and he decided to devote those precious five minutes to the best possible advantage. He would divide them into three parts: two minutes to say farewell to his friends, two minutes for meditation on the whole course of his life and his approaching death, and one minute for a last desperate glance at the world.

In his agony he tried to imagine himself dead. It astonished him that a man could be full of life and consciousness one moment, and the next moment nothing at all. The cupolas of the church were still glinting. He kept gazing at their blinding radiance, and he was seized with the fancy that this radiance was the new world which he would soon be entering. He was horribly frightened. He did not want to die, and felt a physical aversion from death.

It seemed to him that his death was advancing towards him from somewhere in the square. There was a strange stir on the platform. Everyone was craning and looking in the direction of an officer riding full-tilt across the square, waving a white handkerchief. The rider rode straight up to General Rostovtsev, who was in command of the executions, and handed him a sealed letter. The soldiers still had their rifles at their shoulders.

The general read the letter carefully and glanced up to see that Petrashevsky had somehow torn the hood from his face. Though very pale, he was smiling.

"Lower arms!" the general shouted, and then, standing only a few paces from Petrashevsky, he began to read the letter he had just received, signed by the Tzar in his own hand.

The letter was immensely long, and the general suffered from a pronounced stutter. Dostoyevsky listened, but he heard very little of it. Just as when he was told for the first time that he was condemned to death by shooting, and could not believe it, so now, learning that he was about to be pardoned or at least to suffer a punishment less than death, he could not believe that he would be spared.

All letters from the Tzar began with the recital of his innumerable titles.

"By the grace of God, We, Emperor and Autocrat of all the Russias, Tzar of Moscow, Kiev, Vladimir, Novgorod, Tzar of Kazan, Tzar of Astrakhan, Tzar of Poland, Tzar of the Taurian Chersonese, Tzar of Georgia, Lord of Pskov and Grand Duke of Smolensk . . ."

By this time everyone knew that the sentences of death had been commuted and that the Tzar had deliberately arranged this strange charade to punish and torture the prisoners. Rostovtsev continued reading. His voice dropped. He held the paper close to his face as he announced that Petrashevsky had, by the grace of the all-powerful Tzar, received a sentence of penal servitude for life, while Mombelli and Grigoryev were to be punished with a sentence of fifteen years hard labor. Dostoyevsky, who was tenth on the list, was sentenced to four years hard labor and degradation from the ranks of the nobility. Palm alone received a full pardon. He fell to his knees and began praying, and once he exclaimed: "How good the Tzar is! Oh, how grateful I am to the Tzar!" Only Ippolit among the conspirators spoke bitterly. He shouted: "It would have been better if they had shot us!" but no one paid any attention to him.

Dostoyevsky was shortsighted, and he was unable to see everything that happened on the parade ground. He was numb with shock, with cold, with the ferocious excitement which overcame him at the prospect of his approaching death. He was shivering with cold, but not aware that he was shivering. For twenty minutes he had stood without coat or overcoat on the platform—these had all been removed shortly after they climbed the steps. Some were already suffering from frostbite. All in their different ways were suffering from the fever of exhilaration now that the death penalty had been lifted from them. They embraced one another and wept. Some like Grigoriev seemed indifferent, but he had in fact gone mad while he was being tied to the stake.

The Tzar had insisted that exemplary punishment should be meted out to the ringleaders, who were sent back to their places on the platform and then shackled. Petrashevsky watched the soldiers shackling him with the amused and scornful air of a man who tolerates the services of unimportant people, and because the soldiers were nervous and having difficulty fastening the shackles round his ankles, he snatched the hammer from their hands and finished the work himself. No one made any move to prevent him.

For a few more minutes the prisoners remained on the platform, while Petrashevsky, Mombelli and Grigoryev were helped down the steps and put in a waiting carriage, to be sent immediately to Siberia. They were lucky. None of the others knew what was going to happen to them. Someone started the rumor that they were to be sent to Orenburg in the Urals, but there were a few who thought they would continue to be imprisoned in the Peter and Paul Fortress. Meanwhile they waited, and at last some clothes were given to them. These clothes were in the cart covered with matting. Having reduced them to quivering fear and shown his power over them, it pleased the Tzar to demonstrate his clemency and generosity; and he gave them new felt boots, new sheepskin overcoats, and new fur hats. Soon the prisoners were being ordered off the platform to the waiting carriages. They walked through the snow like men walking through a nightmare.

None of the prisoners recovered from the experience; they all bore the scars to the end of their days. Again and again in conversation and in his writings Dostoyevsky returned to this most terrible moment in his life—a life which knew many terrible moments—and there can hardly have been a single day when he was not fascinated and troubled by the memory of the conspirators standing in the Semyonov parade ground within an inch of death. His horror was a naked horror of death, but it was also much more. It was a horror which included gratitude, for he felt abundantly grateful to the Tzar for permitting him an experience which seared his soul and at the same time gave him a sense of ultimate community with his fellow men. Twenty-four years later, remembering the scene, he wrote: "There came to me then the realization that I had become even as they were, and I was equal to them, even on the lowest level of being."

But the overwhelming feeling was one of the sanctity of life and of how life under any conditions at all is preferable to the insane horror of death. "Someone condemned to death," says Raskolnikov in *Crime and Punishment,* "says or thinks an hour before his death that if he had to live on a steep pinnacle or on a rock or on a cliff-edge so narrow that there was only room to stand, and around him there were abysses, the ocean, and everlasting darkness, eternal solitude, eternal tempests—if he had to remain standing on a few square inches of space for a thousand years or for all eternity, it would be better to live than to die! Only to live, to live, to live, no matter how!" To this belief in the grace of life under any conditions Dostoyevsky clung through all the remaining years of his life.

For the rest of the day, after he had been returned to the Peter and Paul Fortress Dostoyevsky paced his cell, singing loudly and uninterruptedly, as people will when they are overcome with an unexpected joy, so happy was he that life had been given back to him. He seemed to be exhibiting all the signs of a religious conversion—a conversion to life.

That afternoon he wrote a long letter to his brother Mikhail, telling him briefly what had happened on Semyonov Square, and making arrangements for the future. He believed he was strong enough to face all eventualities, and wrote in a mood of sustained joy and tranquillity:

94

The Execution

My brother, I am not dejected, I have not lost courage. Life is life everywhere, life is in ourselves, not in the world that surrounds us. There will be people around me, and to be a *man* among men, and to remain one forever, under whatever circumstances, not to weaken, not to fall, that is what life is, that is the real meaning of life. I understand all this at last. The idea has entered into my flesh and my blood! Yes, it is true, that head which created and lived in the high realm of art, which came to know the gravest demands of the spirit and was familiar with them, that head has already fallen from my shoulders. There remain only my memories and the characters I have created which have not yet assumed flesh! It is true, of course, that they will tear me apart! But I still have my heart, and this flesh and blood which will always be capable of loving and suffering and lamenting and remembering, and, after all, I shall be alive. *On voit le soleil!* . . .

So embrace your wife and the children. Tell them to remember me, and never to forget me. Perhaps we shall see one another one day. My brother, look after yourself and your family, live peacefully and always be very careful. Think of the future of your children, and look forward always. Never have I known, as now, such an abundant and healthy reserve of spirtual energy rising within me. I do not know whether my body will hold out, I am ill, but my dear brother, I have suffered so much in life that there are very few things that can make me frightened now . . .

Perhaps one day we shall be able to embrace each other and remember the beautiful days of the past, the golden times of our youth and those hopes which I must now tear out of my heart with my blood and bury away. Shall I ever take up the pen again? Perhaps in four years I shall be able to write. And if I should work at writing, then I shall let you see everything that comes from my pen. My God, how many characters invented by me must now perish, go out like lights going out in my mind, or continuing to live only like a poison in my blood! If I am forbidden to write, I shall die! Fifteen years in prison were preferable, assuming I could have a pen in my hand! . . .

If anyone has any bad memories of me, if I have quarreled with anyone, if I have made an unfavorable impression on anyone, tell them when you meet them to forgive me. There is no malice or anger in me. At this moment I would like nothing more than to love and hold close to me someone from those other days. Today, too, that consolation was known to me, when I embraced my friends before dying. I remember thinking how you would die when you heard about my execution. And now there is nothing more to worry about. I am still alive, and I shall live for the time when we shall embrace one another.[1]

Again and again in that long letter Dostoyevsky begged his brother to be careful, to look after his family, and not to worry too much about the long years of imprisonment ahead. On the contrary, this new life was for the best, prison held no horrors for him, he had received the gift of an almost intolerable happiness, and only those who have been sentenced to death know that every minute is an eternity of the purest joy. He had spoken in his letter of embracing his friends "before dying." This was not a slip of the pen. He had died, and been reborn. He felt an overwhelming sense of compassion for all creatures, the good and the bad equally. He loved all men, and only one thing disturbed him— that he might never see his brother again.

He did in fact see his brother two days later, a few hours before leaving for Siberia.

The meeting took place on Christmas Eve, during the late evening, in a bare room lit by a single lamp, in the house of the governor of the Peter and Paul Fortress. Mikhail and a writer called Miliukov had obtained the governor's permission to say farewell. They were kept waiting for half an hour, and then Dostoyevsky and Durov were led in. They were both smiling, very

[1] *Letters:* 58, December 22, 1849.

calm, very sure of themselves. Mikhail was trembling, and had difficulty in speaking. His mouth twitched convulsively. Dostoyevsky put his arm over his brother's shoulders.

"You mustn't weep," he said. "There is no reason for it—I am not descending into my grave, and this is not a funeral. Believe me, the people I shall live among in prison are not beasts, they are human beings, and perhaps they are better human beings than I am. And then of course I shall resume writing one day. I have experienced so much in prison, and I shall experience much more out there. I will have something to write about."

Mikhail was still weeping and shuddering. In the half-darkness of the unfurnished room a guard watched them from the shadows.

"You mustn't weep, dear brother," Dostoyevsky went on. "You know me well. We shall see one another again, I am sure of it. I confidently hope for it, and I have no doubt that we shall meet again."

Those words spoken to his brother on the eve of his exile were remembered in the last months of his life, for they appear almost unchanged on the very last page of *The Brothers Karamazov*. It was as though the wheel had turned full circle, and in the last days of his earthly life he remembered the words he had spoken at the beginning of the new life which opened out for him when he left the Peter and Paul Fortress for Siberia. All his life he was aware of the protecting presence of his brother, and he was all the more aware of it when Mikhail was dead.

Mikhail kept sobbing throughout the interview, unable to shake off his gloom. Anyone who watched the behavior of the two brothers would have said it was Mikhail who was being sent to Siberia. It was a brief interview. Half an hour later the prisoners were returned to their cells. Exactly at midnight, when the bells in the spire of the Fortress cathedral were pealing to announce the coming of Christmas Day, Dostoyevsky's feet were shackled with ten-pound irons and then he was led into the courtyard where three open sleighs and a coach were standing in the snow. There were three prisoners in this convoy to Siberia—Dostoyevsky, Durov and Yastrzhembsky, one of Petrashevsky's most active supporters, who had been sentenced to six years hard labor. There was a sleigh for each prisoner, and in each sleigh there was a gendarme. In the closed coach sat the ministerial courier who would accompany them to Tobolsk.

At the moment of leaving the Fortress, Dostoyevsky felt a profound depression. While the sleighs glided through the deserted streets of St. Petersburg, his heart groaned at the thought of all he was leaving behind; but soon the freshness of the air gave him strength and a kind of exhilaration, and he was calm again. They passed the house of the publisher Kraevsky, who had invited Mikhail to spend the evening with him. The house was brilliantly lit, and Dostoyevsky remembered that Mikhail's children would probably be sitting round the Christmas tree, and then once again he felt as though he had been stabbed with a knife. All that night they drove through the snow, and towards morning they arrived sleepless and famished at Schlüsselburg, the small fortress town on Lake Ladoga.

In the tavern, where they took breakfast, Dostoyevsky and Durov were in high spirits, but Yastrzhembsky was overwhelmed with misery and kept talking about the hideous fate in store for them. Dostoyevsky paid no attention to him, and instead engaged the imperial courier in conversation. He was an old man, long in the service of the Tzar, and he proved to be surprisingly gentle and kind. They had been driving in open sleighs; the courier gave orders that the sleighs should be covered. His name was Kuzma Prokofievich Prokofiev; he had traveled widely all over Europe; and he had a fund of stories about his travels. It pleased him to pay part of the prisoners' expenses out of his own pocket. Yet the journey was a nightmare, with a slashing wind coming from the north; it penetrated their thick clothes, and after ten hours hard driving they were all frozen to the bone. When, at the end of each day, Dostoyevsky tumbled out of his sleigh and tried to warm himself over a tavern fire, he wondered despairingly whether he would ever feel warm again.

The snow fell mercilessly, and they were mercilessly cheated by the tavern keepers. The worst moment came when they were crossing the Urals. It was bitterly cold. A snowstorm was raging, and suddenly the horses and sleighs sank deep in the snow. It was night. They got out and waited until the horses and then the sleighs could be extricated, and the storm wheeled round them, and they were lost in it. "We were standing on the frontiers of Europe and Asia," Dostoyevsky wrote later. "Before us lay Siberia and the mysterious future; behind us lay all the past. It was such a bitter thing to be standing there that tears came to my eyes."

There were to be many more tears before he traveled that road again, but when he reached Tobolsk on January 11th there were encouraging signs. The local police captain permitted the prisoners to talk with the members of a local charitable society. These were the wives of the exiled Decembrist revolutionaries, saintly women who had elected to share their husbands' punishments. For twenty-five years they had been at Tobolsk; many of them were old and grey, and few of them had any wealth, but they always made it their duty to help prisoners traveling through the town. They gave the prisoners money, clothing, the New Testament. They showered them with affection and encouragement. It was a relief to receive sympathy after passing through countless villages where the peasants stared with hard and steely eyes.

But though there was good news, there was bad news as well. They heard that the Commandant of the Omsk prison was a man of honor, but the warden, Krivtzov, was an unspeakable bully. Then, too, they were forced to suffer the humiliation of branding. On their forearms they were branded with the letters KAT (from *katorga,* hard labor), and their heads were shaved. They were already suffering from exposure. Dostoyevsky complained of abscesses in the mouth, Durov's hands and feet were curiously white, and Yastrzhembsky's nose was frostbitten. Speshnev and the other conspirators who had already arrived at Tobolsk were in no better plight.

Then the order came for them to make the three-day journey to Omsk. For some reason Yastrzhembsky was left behind; Dostoyevsky and Durov went on ahead. Worn out by the long journey across Russia, they were filled with the strange fever which attacks all prisoners on their way to prison, a fever which grows until the very moment when the prison doors close on them. The Governor of Western Siberia had sent off a dispatch: "Treat them without favor." The old and gentle Kuzma Prokofiev no longer accompanied them. There was only the horrible taste in the mouth, the birch trees, the clanking of irons and the eternal spaces of snow.

Two saintly women had decided to take a final leave of the prisoners some miles from the town. Natalya Fonvizina, the wife of one of the exiled Decembrists, had bribed the guards. She was related to the Governor of Western Siberia. Once beautiful, she was exceptionally gracious and understanding, and she was determined to pay a last tribute to the two prisoners.

With a friend she hid in a birch copse at the turning of the road, and when the sleigh bringing the prisoners came in sight, the two women ran out and embraced them. "We have written to Omsk," Natalya Fonvizina said. "We believe there are influential people there who will take care of you and lighten your burdens." The meeting lasted no more than a few minutes. She made the sign of the cross over the heads of the prisoners, smiled, said: "May Christ hold you in His keeping," and then she stepped back.

The guards whipped up the horses, and soon the two women were lost to sight. In front of them on the snow-covered plain, the prisoners saw only the gusts of whirling snow.

On the afternoon of the third day they came to the House of the Dead.

THE HOUSE
OF THE DEAD

IN THE BOOK which Dostoyevsky wrote many years later describing his prison life in Siberia, he said: "It occurred to me once that if it were desired to reduce a man to nothing—to punish him atrociously so that even the most hardened murderer would tremble before the punishment, it would only be necessary to give his work a character of complete uselessness and absurdity."

For four years Dostoyevsky lived a life of "complete uselessness and absurdity." He lived in a kind of relentless vacuum, in a senseless round of tasks which filled him with disgust because they were deprived of meaning, suffering an unappeasable boredom which reduced him to a lump of quivering jelly. He hated every moment of his life in prison, and at the same time he was supremely grateful for it. Never before or afterwards was he to come in such close contact with humanity. Prison life was his university and his training ground; without it he might have been a novelist of the level of Goncharov or Pisemsky. With it he was able to fashion those instruments of perception which made him a great novelist. His work in prison—the work of watching, understanding, penetrating into the souls of the prisoners—was never-ending, and never assumed a character of "complete uselessness and absurdity."

It is possible that he never worked harder in his life than

when he was sitting on his plank bed and watching the other prisoners in the dark and evil-smelling hut.

Dostoyevsky was not a good prisoner, nor a bad one; he had no affection for his guards, and very little for his fellow prisoners. He was hardly aware of the passing of the seasons; showed only a perfunctory interest in the strange animals and fauna of Siberia; was often boorish and contemptuous; and was always fiercely reserved and touchy. He reminded himself continually that he was an aristocrat who had no reason to consort with his inferiors. As an aristocrat he must submit in honorable silence to his punishment, whether or not it was deserved; and he seems to have believed that he had received a comparatively light punishment for the sins he had committed. This aristocratic reserve helped him to survive. In a strange way he separated himself from the prisoners and became an observer, an innocent eye patiently recording the agonies of others until his own agonies were forgotten or shorn of their sharp thorns.

Outwardly he was an unpleasant, shabby, thinly bearded man who limped about the prison alone whenever it was possible for him to be alone. He had an air of authority about him, and was usually addressed respectfully by the guards and by the other prisoners. Friends and relatives sent him enough money to pay for two servants, who mended his clothes and did his errands. He was often ill, and then for days he would escape to the prison hospital, where he would watch with fearful fascination the arrival of prisoners who had been flogged within an inch of their lives, their backs dripping with blood. He was not allowed to write, and the only book he was permitted to read was the Bible; but long after he left the prison he was to say that these two privations were in fact advantages which helped him to regain his sanity. In a letter to his friend, Dr. Yanovsky, he wrote: "You loved me, cared for me, and I was then *sick in mind* (I realize it now) before my journey to Siberia, where I was cured."

The cure was a prodigiously long one, and very nearly killed the patient. But when he left the prison he could claim that he had been tempered in the fiercest of all flames and he had suffered the utmost human degradation. He had walked through the flames of Hell and magically survived.

Hell was an area of no more than five or six acres surrounded by a stockade of oaken posts, not far from the Irtysh river, and about three miles from Omsk on a flat plain. The ruler of Hell was a small, squat, satanic man with a crimson face covered with pimples, called Vasily Grigoryevich Krivtzov, who suffered from ungovernable rages and whose only amusements seem to have been walking his dog and superintending the flogging of prisoners. He could always think of excuses for punishing a prisoner. If a prisoner slept on his right side, he would receive a flogging, and if he cried out in his sleep he would receive another. He ordered an old Polish professor to receive a hundred blows with a stick for declaring on his arrival: "We are not bandits, we are political prisoners." He had power of life and death over everyone within the stockade.

The terror inspired by this little man was such that people panicked, became speechless, and even vomited just at the sight of him. He was always dirty, always drunk, and his dark-blue uniform was always stained and unpressed, except when some high official visited the prison. He wore a dirty orange cap-band, his silver epaulettes were tarnished, and there was something indescribably outrageous in such a man parading in his uniform, capable of ordering the death of anyone who displeased him. Quite early Dostoyevsky realized that Krivtzov's power came from that shabby uniform. "I am a major, by the grace of God," the prison commander would say, but it was not true. He was a major by the grace of a uniform.

When Dostoyevsky saw him first, immediately after arriving in the prison, he was struck by the major's resemblance to a spider about to hurl himself on a fly. He looked stupid, dangerous and insane. He barked at Durov: "What's your name?" When Durov answered him, he turned to Dostoyevsky, asked the same question, and in a sharp voice, speaking very rapidly, he gave orders for them to have their heads shaved, and then seeing their long yellow cloaks with yellow circles sewn on the backs, which had been given to them in Tobolsk, he said sarcastically: "It must be some new uniform they are wearing—something new from St. Petersburg. Well, have they brought anything else with them?"

The escort who had accompanied them from Tobolsk said they had brought their own clothes with them, and for some reason this infuriated the major.

"Take off their clothes!" he shouted. "They can keep their white underwear, that's all! If they have any colored underwear, have it sold at auction and give them a receipt. A prisoner has no property. Remember to behave yourselves. Don't let me have any complaints, otherwise there will be corporal punishment. For the slightest transgression, a whipping!"

Then the major turned on his heels and vanished, having established in the minds of his new prisoners a curious sense of the importance of clothes.

To reduce the prisoners to insignificance, all that needed to be done was to destroy their human dignity by making them look ridiculous. That same afternoon Dostoyevsky's head was shaved "in the civilian style," which meant that only one half of it was shaved. Half of his mustache was removed, and all his beard. His clothes also were ridiculous, for he was made to wear grey canvas trousers, and a coat half black and half gray with a yellow circle on the back. He was also permitted to wear a short sheepskin jacket and a kind of sailor cap without brim or visor. The sheepskin jacket did not prevent him from nearly freezing to death.

When he was shaved and given his prison clothes, he was taken to the log hut where he spent most of the next four years. He described the hut, which contained thirty prisoners, in a letter written to his brother Mikhail after his release:

The House of the Dead

Imagine an old dilapidated wooden hut, which should long ago have been broken up as useless. In summer it is unbearably hot, in winter unbearably cold. All the floor boards are rotten; on the ground filth lies half an inch thick; every instant you are in danger of slipping and falling. The small windows are so frozen over that there is no time in the day when it is possible to read. There is another half inch of ice on the panes. The ceilings drip, there are draughts everywhere. We are packed like herrings in a barrel. The stove is heated with six logs of wood, no heat, the ice scarcely melts in the room —and so it goes on all through the winter.

In the same room the prisoners wash their clothes, and everything is drenched. No way to move. From dawn to dusk we are forbidden to leave the hut to satisfy our needs, for the doors are bolted. A large wooden trough is placed at the entrance, and the stench is intolerable. All the prisoners stink like pigs; they say it is impossible not to behave like pigs, since "we are living beings."

We slept upon bare boards; each man was allowed one pillow only. We covered ourselves with short sheepskins, and our feet were outside the covering all the time. So we froze night after night. Fleas, lice and all kinds of vermin by the bushel. In the winter we were given thin sheepskins to wear, usually mangy, but they did not keep out the cold, and boots with short uppers; in these we had to go out into the Siberian frost!

For food we got bread and cabbage soup. By regulations, the soup was supposed to contain a quarter pound of meat per person, but they put in flakes and dribbles of meat, and I could never find a piece of genuine meat. On feast days there was gruel, but with scarcely any butter. On fast days cabbage, water and scarcely anything else. My stomach went to pieces, and I was often ill.

From all this you can understand that it was impossible to live without money; if I had not had some money, I would assuredly have died; no one could endure such a life. But all the prisoners do some sort of work, sell it, and acquire a few copecks. I drank tea and sometimes bought myself some meat, and this saved my life. It was impossible to do without smoking, for otherwise I would have choked in the stench. All this was done behind the backs of the officials.

I was often ill in the hospital. My nerves were so shattered that I suffered from some epileptic attacks, but this did not happen often. I have rheumatism in my legs now. Except for that, I feel well enough. Add to all these discomforts the near impossibility of getting any books, and that when I did finally get one, I always had to read in secret. And always around me the eternal hostility, the sounds of quarreling, cursing, shouts, noise, never alone, always being watched, and all this without any modification throughout four years, and you will realize how hard it is! And then, too, there was the ever-present dread of some punishment, the irons, the utter oppression of spirit—and you have the picture of my daily life.

I won't even try to explain to you what became of my soul, my faith, my mind, and my heart, in those four years—it would take too long. Yet the eternal concentration, the escape into myself from bitter reality, has borne fruit. There exist in me now many needs and hopes which I never thought I possessed. But all this must be a mystery to you . . .[1]

The eternal concentration, the escape into myself from bitter reality . . . So Dostoyevsky described that curious leap backwards into himself which was always disconcerting to the other prisoners. He seemed inhuman. There was no warmth in him. Again and again in *The House of the Dead,* he divides the sheep from the goats, the handful of prisoners of aristocratic descent and the "common vermin," who were in his judgment filled with envy, malice and hatred against the aristocrats, their oppressors. According to Dostoyevsky there was war between them, with hardly a moment of the day when peace descended. "We of the nobility," he wrote, "were the never-ceasing objects of their malicious envy.

[1] *Letters:* 59, February 22, 1854.

They continually picked quarrels with us, and every moment they tried to put us in the wrong, and they were eternally throwing at us looks of menacing hatred." He spoke of the changed atmosphere in the hospital, where there seemed to be no distinction between the aristocrats and their inferiors, and "there was something like comradeship."

Dostoyevsky's curiously unpleasant attitude toward his fellow prisoners has ample confirmation. The Polish revolutionary Szymon Tokarzewski wrote a long account of his own prison experiences at Omsk, and described his meetings with Dostoyevsky at considerable length. Many things puzzled him. He was especially puzzled by Dostoyevsky's ferocious nationalism. The Russians were the greatest nation on earth, and though the French "at least to some extent resembled men," there was nothing to be said in favor of the English, Germans, and Spaniards, who were no more than "caricatures of human beings." In prison Dostoyevsky seemed to be overwhelmed with the desire to smash and annihilate everything foreign in order to prove paradoxically the superiority of the Russians over every other nation on earth. For the Russians *en masse* Dostoyevsky seemed to have only disdain; the only true virtue lay among the aristocrats, who possessed the exclusive right to national leadership. To them belonged the Ukraine and Poland and the vast reaches of Siberia. Had they not conquered the Baltic provinces? By right of the holy sword the Russian Tzar had received the allegiance of the conquered people. Then why should the Poles dare to resist the civilization granted to them by the great mercy of the Tzar?

Tokarzewski was an unusually intelligent man, accustomed to search into the origins of things. He was deeply perturbed by Dostoyevsky's attitude, and in his book *Seven Years of Hard Labor,* he described his meetings with Dostoyevsky at considerable length. He wrote:

> Fyodor Mikhailovich Dostoyevsky, the famous novelist, the author of *Poor Folk,* and the glory of the

Northern capital, appeared to us as a man who had not grown to a stature equal to his fame. No doubt he had talent as a novelist, but I shall not concern myself with his novels. How did this man become a conspirator? How was it possible for a man who was immeasurably proud of belonging to a privileged class ever to have taken part in a democratic movement?

Whenever he spoke to the Poles, he always used words like 'nobility,' 'noblemen,' 'I am a nobleman,' and 'we, the nobility.' At such times I always interrupted him.

"Excuse me, sir," I would say, "it seems to me that there are no aristocrats in this prison, there are only men who are being deprived of their rights, only prisoners."

Dostoyevsky would foam with anger.

"Well then," he would say, "it evidently pleases you that you are a convict."

He always shouted the words in anger, sarcastically.

"Yes, it pleases me that I am a prisoner," I would answer quietly.[2]

The Pole, arrested for stirring up rebellion against Russia, regarded his imprisonment as a badge of honor, while Dostoyevsky, arrested for his small and obscure part in a conspiracy he conceived as one which would add to the greater glory of Russia, regarded his imprisonment as an atrocious trial that had to be endured. There could be no common ground between them.

Dostoyevsky's attitude towards the Poles and other prisoners cannot easily be excused, but it can perhaps be explained. Brought up on Karamzin's *History of Russia,* he was to remain a fervent nationalist to the end of his days. He paraded his dubious aristocratic descent only when in prison in an effort to assist the progress of his "escape into myself from bitter reality." He needed respect, however artificially contrived. He needed a wall of silence round him. He needed above all some artifice which would remind him that he was destined for greater things than an eternity of

[2] Quoted in Waclaw Lednicki, *Russia, Poland and the West* (New York: Roy Publishers; 1954), page 274.

misery in prison. In much the same way the poet Rainer Maria Rilke found solace in the contemplation of his imaginary descent from medieval barons.

Throughout his years in prison Dostoyevsky was fighting for his life. More terrible than epilepsy was the prospect of madness. Like many short, thin men, he was wiry and possessed vast reserves of physical strength; he had shown by his behavior in the Peter and Paul Fortress that he possessed considerable mental stamina; but his spiritual resources were far from being inexhaustible. In Siberia he was always walking a tightrope. Below the tightrope was a sheer drop into unfathomable blackness.

For him the greatest suffering came from the absolute lack of privacy. He was continually being watched by the guards, by the other prisoners, by invisible presences. "To be alone," he wrote, "is a necessity of normal existence, like eating or drinking; otherwise in this forced communal life you become a hater of mankind. The society of people acts like a poison or an infection. There have been moments when I hated everyone who crossed my path, whether they were blameless or guilty, and I regarded them as thieves who were stealing my life with impunity." The worst was the forced proximity, the absolute impossibility of getting away from them except during occasional lonely walks beside the palisades.

From the beginning he waged a constant warfare against his fellow men. To survive, he could hardly do otherwise, for most of them were in a state of hopeless degradation, and he was desperately afraid of being swallowed up in the morass. He hated their bickering, their querulousness, their cynical laughter, their continual obscenity; so he removed himself from them by an act of will, and continued to study them as a surgeon will study on the pain-racked body of another the disease from which he is himself suffering.

Inevitably he came to identify himself with those rare prisoners who had not buried their hopes, who were determined to survive *at any cost*. These were "the resolute ones," who would murder or set the whole prison on fire in order to escape. There were men like the prisoner Orlov, "who despised punishment and feared nothing in the world," being dominated by an inflexible will and a superb thirst to exact vengeance from his adversaries. Dostoyevsky met him first during the summer of 1850, when he was in the prison hospital. He was being carried back from a flogging.

> It was late afternoon when they brought him in. It was already dark, and the candles had been lit. Orlov was terribly pale, almost unconscious, and his thick curly jet-black hair was disheveled. His swollen back was blue, dripping blood. The prisoners nursed him through the night, changed his poultices, turned him from one side to the other, applied the lotions ordered by the doctor, all the time behaving as though they were his kin or benefactors.
>
> The next day he recovered consciousness, and even took one or two turns round the ward. This was amazing, because he looked so broken and powerless when he was brought in. He had received no less than half the number of blows demanded by his sentence. The doctor intervened only when it became clear that his life was in danger.
>
> Orlov was below average height. He was not a strong man, and his constitution had been undermined by long imprisonment. Those who have seen prisoners after they have been flogged will remember their haggard features and feverish looks. In spite of this Orlov soon recovered his powerful energy; some inner spiritual energy seemed to be assisting him. He was surely no ordinary man. Curiosity prompted me to make his acquaintance, and I was able to study him at leisure for a whole week. Never in my life have I met a man with more iron in his character.
>
> He was a brilliant example of the triumph of the mind over the flesh. He was perfectly in command of himself. He despised punishment and feared nothing in the world.

His dominant characteristic was a boundless energy, a thirst for vengeance, and an inflexible will. He also possessed a strange arrogance, looking down on us from the height of his grandeur. He did not pose. His pride was natural to him, innate in him. I am sure that no one could have the least influence over him. He regarded everything that happened with calm composure, as though nothing in the world could astonish him. He knew the other prisoners looked up to him, but he never took advantage of this to give himself airs.

Nevertheless, vanity is a common trait among prisoners. He was intelligent and strangely frank, without being talkative. He answered my questions openly, and told me he was waiting impatiently for his full recovery, so that he could be finished with the remainder of his punishment. He had feared he might not survive the first flogging.

"Now it's all right," he said, winking. "I'll get the rest of the flogging over, and then I'll get myself sent to Nerchinsk with a convoy of prisoners, and then—you'll see—I'll make my escape! If only my back heals quickly!" [3]

Seven days later, when he thought his wounds had healed sufficiently, Orlov took the rest of his punishment. He had overestimated his strength, and he died a few hours later on the same bed where he had lain during his brief convalescence.

Dostoyevsky could not forget him. For him Orlov was the type of the proud hero, to be distinguished from the Petrashevskys and the Speshnevs of this world by their relentless determination to shape their own lives. They were enviable because they were free, no matter what touched them.

There were the proud, and there were the humble. He found few who were truly proud, and perhaps there were fewer still who were truly humble. Occasionally he came across a prisoner who lived his life quietly and uncomplainingly, with a strange joy and

[3] *The House of the Dead,* Part I, Chapter v.

humility. Such a prisoner was Alei, a young Tartar from Daghestan, who with his two brothers had waylaid the caravan of a rich Armenian merchant and decamped with the plunder after murdering the merchant. All the brigands were captured, tried, flogged and sent to Siberia.

Alei was twenty-two and looked younger. He slept beside Dostoyevsky. He had one of those calm, gentle, aristocratic faces which are to be found sometimes among the Tartars of central Asia. He was always smiling with a kind of childish gaiety. It was an artless smile, very trusting, very friendly, and Dostoyevsky was immediately taken with him, and he was especially attracted by the large, dark, soft eyes of the boy. "When I was filled with anguish and grief," he wrote, "I would find myself looking at him, and then all my misery would vanish."

There was something about the appearance of the boy which suggested a visitor from another world. He possessed all the virtues. The long years of imprisonment had not corrupted him. He was gentle, quick, intelligent, brave, chaste, curiously untouched. He could be insulted with impunity, but there was never the slightest suggestion of cowardice. He avoided quarrels, preserved his dignity, and was loved and caressed by everyone.

Sometimes the boy spoke of his life in Daghestan: his mother, his sister, the foothills of the Caucasus, Mohammedan feasts. He did not speak about these things often, for he, more than any of the others, was aware of a lost paradise. He would fall into long reveries, lying on his plank bed with his hands clasped behind his head. Then quite suddenly he would awake from his reveries and smile—it was a smile "which would have filled the first beauty of the world with envy."

Dostoyevsky taught him to read Russian with the help of a Bible, the only book permitted in prison. He was an apt pupil, and within a few months could read perfectly. One day they were reading the Sermon on the Mount together, and the boy's face lit up with joy.

"Yes, yes, Jesus is a holy prophet!" the boy exclaimed. "He speaks the words of God! How beautiful!"

"What are the words that particularly please you?"

"When He says: Forgive, love, and do not offend, love your enemies, too. Ah, how divinely He speaks!"

Then the boy turned to talk with his two brothers about the mystery of the Sermon on the Mount, and they smiled and nodded gravely, and said that Jesus was a prophet also among the Mohammedans, and according to the *Koran* had breathed life into a dead bird so that it flew away.

Alei was released during Dostoyevsky's term of imprisonment, and there was an affecting farewell. They went outside the hut and suddenly the boy threw himself on Dostoyevsky's neck and broke into sobs. "He had never embraced me before, and never before had he wept in my presence," Dostoyevsky wrote. "Where is my good, kind, beloved Alei now?"

We have the advantage over Dostoyevsky, for we know what happened to Alei. The simple, quiet, saintly and entirely charming Alei became Alyosha Karamazov, on whom in the last years of his life Dostoyevsky expended his greatest art and his greatest affection. By one of the most superb paradoxes of Russian literature, Dostoyevsky found the model of a Christian saint in a deeply religious Mohammedan from the wild valleys of Daghestan.

Orlov and Alei were the exceptions. On the whole, Dostoyevsky found little to admire in the other prisoners. Their whining and toadying, their constant quarrels, their gift for intrigue, their lack of good manners, and their evident dislike of the nobility, all these things disgusted him. In Dostoyevsky's eyes they were nearly all peasants, and therefore they were deprived of very little in prison; they lived the same coarse, unenlightened life in prison they had lived outside. He studied them carefully—those who were weighed down with melancholy, those who were depraved, those who had "handed in their tickets" and simply waited patiently for release, and many of them appeared later in his novels.

In prison, too, he continued his study of the people he called "the executioners." He had begun to study them on the Semyonov- sky parade ground, and they were to be his familiar study through- out the rest of his life. He paid them the tribute of careful analysis, and some of his most brilliant and terrible psychological discoveries were concerned with the nature of "the executioner."

Unlike Baudelaire and De Maistre, who both regarded "the executioner" as the essential representatives of kingly power, being the very arm by which the king dispenses power, aesthetically and historically justified, Dostoyevsky saw him as the embodiment of human error and degradation. He represented all that was corrupt in the human animal, the one from whom all grace is absent, the most terrible of the creations of man because he is the most useless and absurd, inspiring fear and mystical horror only because he is given the power which is given to all men—to act treacherously against life.

Dostoyevsky knew "the executioners" well, talked with them and seems to have watched them at work, though he never gave a description of an execution he had seen. There were the little maniacs like Major Krivtzov, with his steel-rimmed spectacles and his passion for dogs; there was the ineffable Lieutenant Zherebyat- nikov, a heavy fat man who roared with laughter when his victims were presented to him and who continued to roar with laughter throughout the whipping which nearly always led to the victim's death. He was so good-humored that he seemed to have added another, and more terrible, dimension to the task of snuffing out men's lives. There was Lieutenant Smekalov, who somehow con- trived to introduce an element of quiet dignity and even "homeli- ness" into the game for which he had very little liking. All were sadists, but they were sadists of different kinds. All were damned, but it was a damnation they shared with the rest of humanity. "The instincts of the executioner are in germ in nearly every one of us," Dostoyevsky wrote, meaning that only a few people, like the boy

Alei, were immune from the contagion. The desire to execute others is a nearly universal disease.

Dostoyevsky pondered deeply on the nature of "the executioner," and there is an extraordinary passage in *The House of the Dead,* which is written in a style of intense deliberation, with the horror of the thing seen or heard still on him. It is a discursive book; he relates his reminiscences disjointedly, as though he were trying to avoid coming to grips with his memories. But in this passage he speaks with crystalline character about the nature of the beast who once haunted Europe and now haunts the whole world:

> There are people who are greedy for blood like tigers. Those who have once tasted this unlimited power over the blood, the body and the souls of their fellow men, being brethren according to the law of Christ—those who have tasted this power and have taken possession of the boundless opportunity to humiliate most bitterly another made in the image of God—such men become the servants and not the masters of their insatiable desires.
>
> Tyranny is a habit which is capable of being developed into a disease. I declare that the best of men may grow hardened and degraded to the level of a beast by nothing more than force of habit. Blood and power intoxicate; from them comes the most exquisite brutality and lust. The greatest perversions finally become acceptable and even delightful to the mind and heart. The man and the citizen disappear for ever in the tyrant. The return to human dignity, repentance and the resurrection of the spirit become scarcely possible.[4]

For the rest of his life Dostoyevsky was to explore the tyranny in man. He seems to have known, as few others knew, that the hopes of the French revolutionaries were doomed. Not reason, but tyranny, was to extend its empire over mankind. The prison he

[4] *The House of the Dead,* Part II, Chapter iii.

knew was a small bud, which was to grow in time into a poisonous tree covering the whole land.

Dostoyevsky wrote his memoirs of prison life seven years after leaving Omsk, when his memories were already fading. He forgot faces and names. The chronology of the stories is curiously at odds, and he seems to have remembered most vividly the events which happened during the first year of his imprisonment when, as he says, he could never settle down and his nerves were raw and everything seemed strange and unendurable and hostile. Sometimes the gears slip in his mind. He will begin to relate an incident, and then if the development of the story is too painful he will suddenly drop it, and resume it for no apparent reason a hundred pages later. When he wrote, he remembered Orlov and Alei and perhaps ten others vividly, but the rest were already fading into the background.

There were, however, memories which never faded, which he was to carry with him throughout his life. There was for example the memory of the small bathhouse with a hundred naked men still wearing chains round their feet, screaming and pummeling one another while the steam scalded them:

> The steam grew thicker and thicker every moment, until the whole place gave an impression of being boiled in blazing pitch, and all the time the prisoners were shouting and howling, to the accompaniment of the clanking chains on the floor. Those who tried to move found their chains inextricably entangled with the chains of others; they swore, slipped, and knocked against the heads of the men crouching below. The dirt flowed past in streams. They seemed to have gone wild, shrieking and crying out in exaltation.
>
> They jostled and crowded at the window of the antechamber through which the hot water was delivered, and much of it was spilled on the heads of the crouching ones. We seemed to be free and unobserved, but from time to time the mustached face of a soldier would peer

round the door, a musket at his feet, to see that there was no serious disorder.

The shaved heads of the prisoners, and their reddened bodies, which the steam made the color of blood, seemed more monstrous than ever. The scars left by whips and rods stood out on their backs, as though they were about to bleed again. Terrible scars! A shudder passed through me when I saw them. And when more steam came, and the thick scalding clouds filled the room, there were fresh shouts, fresh laughter. Here and there through the clouds there flashed a back cut to ribbons, or a shaved head, or a foot dragging chains.[5]

It is, of course, the most famous passage in *The House of the Dead,* and was included in young ladies' almanacs, but in its context it is a disturbing passage. Quite suddenly, without warning, after a long and not very convincing picture of the religious observances of a Jew called Isaiah Fomich Bumstein, we are introduced to the bathhouse. The lens opens wide. The horror is seen sharply, in focus, with every detail carefully arranged, so that we are almost conscious of the presence of a stage director. "Terrible scars," he says. "A shudder passed through me when I saw them." One has the feeling that the scene has been arranged a little too deliberately, with an eye for effect, as though he wanted to capture a single moment of horror which would symbolize all the other moments and therefore he was reduced to injecting an element of artificiality into the scene. The description of physical horror was never his *forte.*

His *forte* lay in his descriptions of the human soul at moments of crisis, of the strange and dangerous movements of the soul in its perturbations, whenever it was confronted with something greater then itself. *The House of the Dead* is usually regarded as a work of amazingly accurate reportage, curiously impassionate, deliberately photographic. So, to a very large extent, it is. But Dostoyevsky's relentlessly theoretical mind was concerned with more

[5] *The House of the Dead,* Part I, Chapter x.

than a photographic record of his experiences in prison. He was living among murderers; most of the prisoners were murderers, and many of the guards had murdered prisoners. He had to ask himself why a man would kill, what happens to him at the moment of the murder, whether murder breeds murder, and how and in what state of mind a murderer lives with himself until the moment he is arrested. When he speaks of the psychology of murder, he speaks with the authentic voice of a man who has pondered the subject over a long period of time and is perfectly capable of developing an entire theory of murder. Here is his sketch for a theory of murder:

> A man is living quite calmly and peacefully. He has a hard life, but he is resigned to his fate. He may be a peasant, a domestic serf, a townsman or a soldier. Suddenly something gives way within him, and he plunges his knife into his oppressor or his enemy, and from that moment begins the strange part of the affair. Suddenly he goes beyond all measure. The first victim is his oppressor, the enemy, and the crime is perfectly understandable, because there is a demonstrable cause. But afterwards he goes on to kill others who are not his oppressors or his enemies, killing them indiscriminately for the pure pleasure of killing—for an abusive word or an unpleasant look, or simply to make the number of his victims equal, or merely because someone is standing in his way.
>
> He is now behaving like a drunken man, like someone in delirium. It was as though he had passed some fatal line, and was elated to discover that nothing was sacred for him any more. Some inner urge causes him to break all laws, defy all powers, and enjoy the sensation of boundless freedom. He enjoys the turmoil of his own heart and the terror he inspires. He knows, too, that a dreadful punishment lies in store for him. His sensations are like those of a man on a high tower as he stares at the abyss yawning below, and would be happy to hurl himself headlong if only to hasten his end. Such things

happen to the most quiet and inconspicuous people. There are some, of course, who dramatize themselves in their delirium, and the more they were downtrodden before, the more they bluster and put on airs. They glory in the fear and revulsion they inspire. They affect *desperation* to the point where *punishment* comes as a relief from the strain of keeping up the game. The curious thing is that the excitement only lasts until the moment when they are punished, as though some unknown law measured the extent of their exaltation. After that, the thread is cut, and they become suddenly calm, limp, drained of courage, and they implore pardon from the people.[6]

This is not reportage; this is the plot of *Crime and Punishment*. Out of these two paragraphs came the four great novels of his maturity.

Dostoyevsky had, of course, more than the common man's interest in murder. His father had been murdered, and he had himself been so close to execution that he knew the sensations of a victim up to the very moment when the knife descends. He spoke with the authority of a man who had explored murder until he knew its deepest recesses, its most mysterious hiding places. The strange calm of *The House of the Dead* is the calm of a man watching a perpetual execution, who is accustomed to it and even a little bored by it. He knew only too well that murder is in the air we all breathe.

Yet there were moments when he could forget the murderous prison and all who were in it. There was the moment when the prisoners heard that Major Krivtzov had been dismissed from his post, not for the crimes he had committed in prison but for his errors of judgment when he was police superintendent at Tobolsk. The blow fell suddenly. The major wept like an old woman and proclaimed his innocence, but his superiors refused to listen, and he was obliged to sell his two horses and vanish into obscurity. The prisoners celebrated that day with an exquisite joy.

[6] *The House of the Dead,* Part I, Chapter viii.

Quite inexplicably, animals made their way into the prison. Snow-white geese quacked and paraded through the grounds, to the huge delight of the prisoners. Then there was a white kid, so well-fed that it could hardly stand upright, the owner of a superb pair of horns. The prisoners were in ecstasies. It became the mascot of those who worked by the river. Dostoyevsky fell in love with it, and wanted to have the horns gilded, but it was decided that the gold paint would flake away. Instead, the prisoners adorned the horns with leaves and flowers, and they liked to march behind the kid like conquerors following a triumphal chariot. In the end, the kid fell a victim to the major's passion for murder.

Then there was the eagle which dropped out of the sky with a wounded wing, and the prisoners nursed it. Dostoyevsky loved it, as he loved the kid, with a strange and tender passion. For him the eagle was like "a wounded king," and like those desperate and unyielding prisoners whom he especially admired, he praised it for its defiance. "Lonely and implacable, the eagle waited for death, refusing to be reconciled with anyone or anything." The prisoners decided to carry it out of the prison, even though its wounds had not healed. They wanted it to die in freedom. So they carried it to the ramparts on a cold autumn day when the wind was whistling on the bare steppe and the yellow grass was crackling, and they watched it until it vanished into the distance, dragging its broken wing.

Exactly four years after he had been admitted into the prison, Dostoyevsky himself was free. With Durov, who had grown ill in prison, he went to the smithy where his chains were knocked off by one of the prisoners. It was strange to see them lying on the ground, and he picked them up in a gesture of valediction. Then without any guards beside him he simply walked through the prison gates.

THE EXILE

WHEN THE POET Rainer Maria Rilke read *The House of the Dead,* he found in it the exaltation of Slav passivity. "There exists in the Slav soul," he wrote, "an almost perfect degree of submission: even when oppressed by the most immediate pressure, the soul creates a secret place, a further dimension of existence where true freedom can be found, however painful the outward circumstances." It is a judgment with which Dostoyevsky would have profoundly disagreed.

In after years, whenever he discussed his imprisonment, he spoke of it as a nauseating and terrifying experience, but it had probably saved his life, and it had certainly given him an advantage which distinguished him from all other writers. In prison he learned to know the Russian people; he had also learned to be hard, to endure, to possess a pitiless will. He had modeled himself on "the resolute ones," and he had miraculously survived. Contrary to some newspaper reports of the time, he had never been flogged.[1] He had suffered in prison, and his health was affected,

---

[1] Various stories about a flogging suffered by Dostoyevsky were circulated. George Kennan relates an interview with a former prisoner, Rozhnovsky, who said:

> Dostoyevsky was flogged the first time for making complaint, in behalf of the other prisoners, of a lump of filth found in their soup. His second punishment was for saving a fellow prisoner from drowning when the major in command of the *ostrog* had ordered him not to do so. The flogging in each case was so brutally severe that the sufferer had to be

but he had never had to perform any acts of total submission. For weeks and perhaps months he had retired into the secret places of the soul and from those high palisades he had looked haughtily down at the prisoners who did not belong to the aristocracy, but in the end he had identified himself with the prisoners. He had learned, not submissiveness, but how to fight.

In the years before his arrest and imprisonment he had been very ill indeed. How ill he was, and exactly what dread disease he was suffering from, we can only guess. One day in the last year of his life he met a priest who suffered from the same disease, and he immediately recognized the symptoms—a certain lassitude, a certain inability to make rational statements, a kind of neurotic incapacity to grasp reality; and reporting on the priest to the Procurator of the Holy Synod, Dostoyevsky wrote: "His illness is a strange one, but luckily familiar to me, for I myself suffered from the same illness in the years 1847, '8, and '9. The paroxysms of this illness bring on moral derangement of the soul." He was perhaps even more explicit when he wrote in 1848 the terrible short story *The Faint Heart*, where under the disguise of Vasya Shumkov, a humble copying clerk, he portrays himself. Vasya has fallen in love and needs extra money; his employers give him extra work for which he will be paid, and he goes insane, unable to bear the weight of his sense of gratitude. One day his friend Arkady comes upon him working hard, "but there was no ink in the pen, and the pages he was turning over were perfectly clean, and he was hurrying, hurrying to cover the pages as though he were performing the

---

taken to hospital, and after a second "execution," Rozhnovsky says, the convicts generally regarded Dostoyevsky as dead. When he reappeared among them after lying for six weeks in hospital, they gave him the nickname of *pokoinik* (the dead). George Kennan: *Siberia and the Exile System* (New York: The Century Company; 1891), I, 143.

The story seems to have been invented by Rozhnovsky. Dostoyevsky denied that he was ever flogged, and both Baron Wrangel and Dr. Yanovsky deliberately questioned him about the flogging and were told it had never taken place.

task with the utmost efficiency and success." Vasya has gone insane. Arkady rushes to the superior's office with Vasya, hoping that in some way there may be found an explanation for the insanity, and perhaps a cure, but there is none.

"What on earth made you go out of your mind?" the superior asks kindly.

"Gratitude," Vasya answers haltingly.

A moment later a strange change comes over Vasya's features. His eyes suddenly gleam with hope, and he marches three paces forward, pauses, clicks his heels, and turns to his superior.

"I have a physical defect, Your Excellency," he says. "I am short and weak, and not fit for military service."

Saying this, he squares his shoulders like a guardsman, and marches out of the room. He is quite mad, and there is no hope for him.

Dostoyevsky had never had any desire to be a soldier, and was temperamentally unfitted for the role. Like Vasya, he was short and weak, and suffered from a physical defect, the epilepsy which first revealed itself in prison. He also suffered from rheumatism. He was in need of a long rest, preferably beside the sea in a warm climate. When he was released from prison, he was ordered to present himself to the commander of the garrison at Semipalatinsk, 480 miles south of Omsk, and to serve there as a common soldier.

Happily he was not ordered to leave for the south immediately. For a few weeks he was allowed to recover his health among friends in Omsk and to begin the long process of catching up with his reading. Officially he was allowed to read only the Bible in prison, but during the last months a kindly doctor in the hospital had slipped into his hands translations of *The Pickwick Papers* and *David Copperfield*. As soon as he was free, he wrote to his brother, begging for "books, books, and still more books." For him they were food and lodging and comfort, and after recounting his prison experiences in six graphic pages, he immediately launches into a peremptory command for the books he needs almost as much as he needs life itself. It is a curious and even frightening list. He wants the Fathers of the Church, a Church history, Kant's *Critique of Pure Reason,* Hegel's *Philosophy of History,* and the Koran. A few days later he asks for a German dictionary and all the ancient writers available in French—Diodorus Siculus, Plutarch, Josephus, Herodotus, Thucydides, Pliny, and Tacitus. It is clear that he is thinking in terms of history, and perhaps—for there is no clue to this sudden awakening of the historical sense in him—he was contemplating a history of the spirit of man, in the hope that he would somehow be able to explain and justify his own sufferings. He was bitterly hurt when the books failed to arrive.

But there were other matters, too, which demanded his attention. At various times he felt the necessity to state in the clearest terms the development of his religious beliefs. So now he wrote an account of his spiritual progress to Natalya Fonvizina, the woman who had arranged to stop the sleigh taking him to prison, and who had pressed on him a Bible in a last gesture of affection from the outside world.

It is one of the most astonishing of his letters. Clearly, firmly, without hesitation, he proclaims his faith in Christ while remaining a child of doubt. He believes, and does not believe. There is the glory of Christ, and there is also the darkness surrounding Christ. He will cleave to Christ with all his strength, and at the same time he knows that he does not belong to Christ. He writes:

> I have heard many people say you are deeply religious, but it is not because of your beliefs that I am telling you this, but because I myself have experienced and felt it keenly; there are moments when one thirsts after faith like the "dry grasses" and then quite simply the truth is revealed shining forth in our misery. I will say of myself that I am a child of the age, a child of unbelief and of doubt, and so I am now, and so, I know, I shall be to the grave. I have paid for this thirst to believe by terrible tortures, and I am still paying for it: this thirst which becomes all the stronger in my soul as I

bring up more and more powerful arguments against
faith.

Yet it happens that God sometimes sends me moments
of perfect peace; at these moments I love and I feel I
am loved by others, and in these moments, too, I have
formed within myself a confession of faith in which everything is clear and holy for me. This confession is very
simple. Here it is: to believe that there is nothing more
beautiful, more profound, more sympathetic, more reasonable, more manly, and more perfect than Christ;
and not only is there nothing, but, so I tell myself with
jealous love, there can be nothing.

Furthermore, if anyone should prove to me that Christ
lay outside the truth, and it *really* was so that He lay
outside the truth, I would prefer to be with Christ than
to be with the truth.[2]

I would prefer to be with Christ than to be with the truth . . .
Dostoyevsky was saying what many believers have said at moments of great agony of soul. He was saying very simply and very
humbly that the truth was not in him, that it was in Christ, and he
was unworthy; and to this belief he was to cling throughout the remaining years of his life.

The letter to Natalya Fonvizina has a cardinal importance in
the understanding of Dostoyevsky's beliefs. Twenty years later he
put almost the same words in the mouth of Shatov in *The Devils,*
in that terrible chapter called *Night,* and he will repeat phrases
very like these in many of his letters and many of his novels. When
he came to write *The Legend of the Grand Inquisitor,* he was saying no more than he said to Natalya Fonvizina, but the statement
was embroidered and orchestrated with a vast richness of spiritual
experience.

For the moment, however, he belonged to the world. He
crossed the long plains which separate Omsk from Semipalatinsk
in the last weeks of February 1854. Most of the journey was made

[2] *Letters:* 60, February 20, 1854.

on foot, though once he was lucky enough to ride for a few miles in a cart. Perched on a coil of rope, he gazed at the vast and empty spaces of the Kirghiz plain, at the black tents of the nomads, and the occasional camel caravans which darkened the horizon. He was blissfully happy, enjoying the new-found sense of freedom to the uttermost, for he knew it would not last. Soon he was to become a common soldier in the first section of the 7th battalion of Siberian Infantry.

Omsk was a miserable huddle of buildings, but at least it was the capital of Western Siberia: there were straight roads, imposing government buildings, a sense of order. Semipalatinsk was smaller, dirtier, and completely unlike any town he had ever seen. The name, which means "Seven Halls," apparently derives from the seven deserted courtyards where the Tunguz priests once attempted to convert the inhabitants to Buddhism. In Dostoyevsky's time the greater part of the inhabitants were Mohammedans. There were seven or eight mosques, a stone church, a pharmacy, and a general store to provide for the needs of the Tartars, Bokharians, Jews, and Kirghiz. There were no paved streets, no trees, while packs of hungry dogs ran wild through the town. In autumn the streets were knee-deep in mud, and in summer they were thick with dust. Semipalatinsk was a desert surrounded by a desert. Somewhere beyond the horizon the Kirghiz warriors were sharpening their swords.

When Dostoyevsky reached Semipalatinsk the town was in a state of alert; it was feared that the tribesmen were about to mount an attack. In official documents they were referred to as the Kara-Kirghiz, meaning the Black Kirghiz. They were a handsome people, dark-faced, with aquiline noses, and they feared no one. They had attacked the town before, and would attack again.

With all his dislike of soldiering, Dostoyevsky made a passable soldier. He drilled, went on guard duty, took part in rifle practice, and attended parades. His company commander, a certain Captain Vedenyaev, nicknamed "The Blizzard," was stern with him, and once remarked to the sergeant: "He's been in prison. Don't give him any leeway." Occasionally the sergeant would try to make life miserable for him, and once, when he refused to obey an order quickly enough, he received a heavy blow on the head, which was not calculated to improve the headaches from which he constantly suffered.

Still, his health was improving, and he enjoyed the physical exercise: to walk without chains was a luxury. He especially enjoyed the night watches on the edge of the steppes. He was happy too in the company of a young Jew, Nikolay Katz, who slept in the bunker beside his. The boy was seventeen years old, quick and intelligent. They kept their money in common and went on errands for one another and brushed each other's uniform. Katz bought a samovar with his savings, and was continually pouring out glasses of tea for his friend, who had developed that insatiable thirst for tea which was to last throughout his life. Many years later, Katz recalled those summer months when his companion in the barracks was a strange unsmiling man who rarely spoke, and then always in a surprisingly deep, hoarse voice. He remembered, too, that Dostoyevsky spent nearly every moment of his spare time poring over the most precious of his possessions, the New Testament.

Letters came rarely, and Dostoyevsky complained bitterly about the slowness of the mail and the curious hesitations of his brothers and sisters, who seemed to have forgotten him. He saw himself doomed to perpetual exile; only a miracle, he wrote to his sister, would permit them to meet again in this life. Yet it pleased him that he was as good a soldier as the next man. He wrote to his brother Mikhail in July: "When I came here, I knew nothing about army life, but this month I took part in a review with all the others, and I did my job as well as any man. How much it cost me in sheer fatigue is another question." Apparently he did not feel very close to Katz, for he spoke in his letters of living in strict solitude, saying he had spent five years in prison, continually watched by his guards, and was therefore happiest alone. And very briefly he mentioned his recurring attacks of "a strange disease which resembles epilepsy, but is not epilepsy, and I will tell you more about it later."

Lieutenant Colonel Belikov, the officer commanding the garrison, was one of those not very rare army officers who find reading to themselves a strain on the nerves. Learning that "an exceedingly gifted writer," one, moreover, who had until recently belonged to the hereditary ranks of the nobility, was in his service, he ordered the man to present himself. Dostoyevsky appeared, and learned to his amazement that he was required to read aloud to his commanding officer. He read the newspapers aloud, and went on to read from some of the more fashionable magazines. Belikov was taken with his new recruit and introduced him to the society of Semipalatinsk, which consisted of bored officers and their still more bored wives. Friendship with Belikov led to one outstanding improvement in Dostoyevsky's life. He was permitted to live outside the barracks, in a log hut belonging to the widow of one of the soldiers. The hut was built on sand, and was beginning to capsize. There was only one room. Dostoyevsky occupied a dark vermin-infested corner separated from the rest by a cloth curtain. In this corner there was only a bed, a table, a chair, a chest and a stove. There were thousands of fleas and cockroaches.

For this dark, miserable room, and for his board and laundry, he paid five rubles a month. The widow, however, was one of the wealthiest people in the town, for she acted as procuress for her two daughters, one of them being a sixteen-year-old beauty. She preferred that officials and officers should sleep with her daughters. "Ah, *barin*," she would say, "if it comes to that, they would have slept with army clerks or sergeants for two loaves of gingerbread or a handful of nuts. But when gentlemen come here, it is good business for them and a great honor for me."

Dostoyevsky detested his dark corner, but it was better than living in barracks. In later years he always liked to have space.

The Exile

"I had the feeling," his second wife wrote, "that he would do any-thing—anything on earth—just to have two large rooms."

He was to have space, as much space as he could ever want, a few months later, when the young Baron Alexander Wrangel arrived in Semipalatinsk, bought a house with a ravishing view over the river, and invited Dostoyevsky to stay with him.

Baron Wrangel was the unlikeliest of all visitors to Semi-palatinsk. He was twenty-one, handsome and cultivated, very ele-gant and very rich. He was filled with the desire to serve his coun-try and to explore the unknown regions of the Kirghiz steppes, and had deliberately exiled himself to Semipalatinsk, where he held the post of Public Prosecutor. By an extraordinary coincidence he had been present at the ceremony on Semyonovsky Square at which the Petrashevsky conspirators had been condemned to death. He was then a young cadet, related both to the adjutant general on the military tribunal and the officer in charge of the execution squad. Even at that time he had been particularly dis-turbed by the fate of Dostoyevsky.

The news that Baron Wrangel was leaving for Semipalatinsk reached Mikhail Dostoyevsky, who hurriedly prepared a parcel of books and clean linen for his brother. With the parcel went letters from Mikhail and Apollon Maikov, and fifty rubles. As soon as the baron arrived, he sent a servant to summon Dostoyevsky into his presence. Quite naturally Dostoyevsky was appalled to receive a message summoning him into the presence of the Public Prosecutor.

He need not have been appalled. Baron Wrangel could not have been kinder, though he was disconcerted by the appearance of the shabby private, whose chief occupation was to stand guard duty over the felt store. The private was wearing a grey military cloak with a high red collar and red epaulettes; his face was deathly pale, and he wore an expression of grave melancholy; only the deep-sunken eyes were vividly alive and watchful. Baron Wrangel explained quickly why he had been summoned, and gave him the letters and the other presents from St. Petersburg; and when Dostoyevsky asked permission to read them at once, Baron Wrangel nodded and calmly cut the envelopes of some of his own letters.

A moment later an extraordinary thing happened. Overcome by the thought that he had left his family and had no idea what prospects were in store for him, the Public Prosecutor began to sob uncontrollably, and fell on the neck of the lowly private. Dostoyevsky comforted him and kept pressing his hand. A few minutes later they were vowing to meet at every possible opportunity.

Almost immediately there was a great change in Dostoyevsky's fortunes, though he continued to live in the verminous lodgings with the procuress and the two girls. Baron Wrangel wrote to his parents, begging them to use all their influence on behalf of Dostoyevsky. He introduced Dostoyevsky to General Spiridonov, the military governor, a pleasant jovial man, who was soon inviting him to come to the governor's house "whenever he pleased." Baron Wrangel made it clear that he regarded Dostoyevsky as his closest friend, and would not be separated from him; society hostesses became accustomed to seeing them arrive together in a carriage, the Baron wearing full uniform, the private in drab grey. "I love him like a brother," Baron Wrangel wrote to his parents, "and respect him like a father."

When summer came, Baron Wrangel leased a summer house, which he called "Cossack Gardens," overlooking the river. It was the only country house in the neighborhood, and though it had a leaky roof and rotting floor boards, it was large and wonderfully situated in an immense park filled with ponds and living springs. Here he kept a small zoo, and a stable of four saddle horses, and he experimented with flowers imported from St. Petersburg. In his *Memoirs* he draws an unforgettable portrait of Dostoyevsky wandering among the flowerbeds in a pink shift which had faded from many visits to the laundry, and wearing round his neck a chain of blue glass beads, from which dangled an immense silver onion watch. The two girls from his lodgings were there, barefoot and wearing only chemises.

It was perhaps the only completely happy time in Dostoyevsky's life. With Wrangel and the girls, he bathed in the river, read old newspapers and went riding—he was a poor rider, and sometimes wondered why his friend rode so elegantly, while he always produced an impression of clumsiness. There were grass snakes all over the estate, and they would amuse themselves by trying to tame the snakes by giving them milk; and they deliberately arranged for the presence of a large number of snakes when some society ladies arrived. Thereafter they were left in peace.

But though there were moments of almost unbearable happiness, there were other moments of fierce depression. Dostoyevsky had fallen in love with a married woman, Maria Issayeva, the daughter of a certain Dmitry Constant, chief of quarantine at Astrakhan; it is just possible that he was the son of a French aristocrat who fled to Russia during the Terror. Maria was about thirty, quick and effervescent, with a small appealing face and very sensual lips. She was already suffering from consumption, and at the least opportunity there would appear a hectic flush on her cheeks. Wrangel describes her as "a rather handsome blonde, very thin and hysterical and *exaltée*." She was certainly hysterical, and the one surviving photograph shows her to have had handsome features; the photograph also suggests that she had a wild temper.

It was rumored, and believed, that she beat her husband unmercifully. She certainly ill-treated and humiliated him in public. Her husband, Alexander Issayev, was a former teacher who had been dismissed from his post; he was now an inspector of taverns, a coarse, brutal man in his cups, but gentle and kindly when sober. The town people disliked him because he was always making drunken speeches; his wife disliked him because he was a spendthrift and without ambition. She was looking for someone to replace her husband, but she seems to have had no profound affection for Dostoyevsky, who was poor and without prospects, and

131

suffered every three months or so from violent attacks of epilepsy. The doctors now had no doubt at all about the nature of his disease. In their eyes he was a doomed man, with only a few years to live.

Baron Wrangel had no high opinion of Maria Issayeva, but since Dostoyevsky was obviously in love with her, he was not a man to stand in the way. In his aristocratic way he described her as "an extraordinary woman unlike anyone else." Dostoyevsky reported these words to the woman he loved, and felt that an accolade had been bestowed on her. But when her husband was removed from his post, and friends arranged an appointment for him as court assistant at Kuznetsk, a town some seven hundred versts from Semipalatinsk, Dostoyevsky was inconsolable, so inconsolable indeed that Baron Wrangel took pity on him and arranged that he should travel part of the way with his beloved.

On that May day Baron Wrangel appointed himself master of ceremonies. He arranged everything to the last detail, paid off the Issayevs' debts, bribed the coachmen, saw that Alexander Issayev got hopelessly drunk on champagne, and then put him into the carriage after arranging that the lovers should travel together in the diligence. Alexander Issayev fell asleep with his head on the baron's shoulder, while Dostoyevsky promised eternal love to Maria. He was heartbroken by the separation and tried to delay the final leave-taking as long as possible. It was night and the moon was shining when they alighted, and while Alexander Issayev slep off his drunkenness in the diligence, the lovers made their farewell under a fir tree. Dostoyevsky cut a commemorative notch in the tree, promised he would love no one else, and wept uncontrollably when the diligence at last set off across the plains in a cloud of dust. The sound of the bells died away in the distance, and all the time Dostoyevsky gazed after it, standing "rigid and silent, with the tears streaming down his cheeks." "An unforgettable day," commented the baron, writing fifty years later.

Dostoyevsky was in despair. He had begun to write the story

of his years in prison, which he later published under the title *The House of the Dead,* but he now abandoned it. Maria's letters only exasperated his wounds. She complained of loneliness and despair, of ill-health and the ordeal of being married to a drunken husband, and she hinted that she would kill herself or take a lover. If Dostoyevsky was heartbroken before, he was now dangerously close to madness; and Baron Wrangel, acting out the role of master of ceremonies, arranged a liaison between his friend and a pretty seventeen-year-old Polish girl, Marina O., in the hope that Dostoyevsky would forget Maria. It was a very brief liaison, and nothing came of it. Dostoyevsky still yearned for Maria, still hoped that in some mysterious way they could be brought together, and talked about her endlessly. Once more Baron Wrangel exerted himself on behalf of his friend. To bring about a secret meeting, he arranged that Dostoyevsky should pretend to be ill in bed, with a doctor's certificate forbidding him to go on guard duty. He was not in bed. He was racing across the plains to the town of Zmiev, a hundred and ten miles away, for a secret rendez-vous with Maria; but when he reached the town he learned to his horror that she was still in Kuznetsk. She had sent a message, explaining that there were "changed circumstances," which unfortunately prevented her from joining him. Dostoyevsky immediately set off for Semipalatinsk.

He soon learned what these "changed circumstances" were: Alexander Issayev was dying. He died a few weeks later, in great agony, conscious to the last, calling upon God to keep her, and in the same breath cursing himself for leaving her in such dire poverty. Maria described the deathbed scene in great detail. She was prostrate with grief except in the moments when she was wildly hysterical.

Dostoyevsky was still helplessly in love with her, and kept urging her to join him. He made another secret visit to Kuznetsk and found her curiously composed, grateful for his help—he had sent all the money he could spare, and prevailed upon Baron Wrangel to send her more—but not yet ready to marry him. She was in fact thinking of marrying a young schoolteacher called Vergunov, although Dostoyevsky, who heard the rumors about the schoolteacher, believed he was a figment of her imagination. He could not tolerate the thought that she preferred anyone else, and at the same time he was overwhelmed by the realization that she did not love him, however often she protested her love in her letters. His letters to his brother and to Baron Wrangel, who had left Semipalatinsk for St. Petersburg, are full of despairing cries for help. "My decision is taken," he wrote to his brother, "and even if the earth falls on me, I shall marry her." To Baron Wrangel he wrote: "I shall die if I lose my angel; or else I shall go mad, or else the river Irtysh." He had hopes for a pardon, which would permit him to return to St. Petersburg; and he knew that his chances of marrying Maria would be all the greater if he could show her he had prospects in the capital. He spoke of becoming a functionary, to support her and her son Pasha. He wrote a frenzied letter to Baron Wrangel in which, under thirteen separate headings, he begged and demanded help in thirteen separate ways. He accused his brother, who was married with six children and therefore unable to send large sums of money, of being coldhearted, because in seven months he had written only one brief letter and sent only one small sum of money. "I don't want any help if you are not my brother," he raged. "Don't destroy me! I am so unhappy, so miserably unhappy! I am crushed, torn to pieces! My soul is sick unto death! In these last seven years I have suffered agonies beyond belief, but there must be an end to them!"

He was like a wild beast trapped in a cage. He must leap out of the cage, hurry to Maria, marry her, return to his beloved St. Petersburg, somehow acquire money, somehow re-establish himself as a writer. He would write another *Poor Folk,* and be famous again. All St. Petersburg would bow at the feet of the returning hero!

There were intervals when he could think clearly and sensibly. At the engineering college he had been friendly with the brother of Eduard Totleben, who gained great renown as the builder of the fortifications of Sebastopol during the Crimean War. Counting on his friendship with the brother, Dostoyevsky appealed to the general for permission to leave the army and become a minor official in the government. The letter is an important document in establishing whether he was or was not guilty of taking part in a serious conspiracy against the Tzar. He wrote:

> I was guilty, and I acknowledge my guilt fully. I was convicted of the intention (but only the intention) of acting against the Government; I was lawfully and justly condemned; the hard, painful, and tortured experiences of these last years have sobered me, and changed my views on many subjects. But in those days, when I was still blind, I believed in these theories and utopias. When I was sent to Siberia, I had at least the comfort of having borne myself honestly before the tribunal; I did not try to shift my guilt onto others; I even sacrificed my own interests in order to save others. I had not completely lost faith in myself or in my ideas, and so it happened that I did not confess everything, and so I was punished all the more sternly.
>
> Previously I had suffered for two years from a strange moral disease. I was a hypochondriac. There came a time when I completely lost my reason. I was exaggeratedly irritable, had a morbidly developed sensibility. The very simplest facts would become distorted in my mind, and I would transform them into totally unrelated things. This sickness had a powerful and evil influence on my destiny, but to put this sickness forward as an excuse seemed to me laughable and humiliating. Nevertheless, at the time, I was scarcely conscious of all this. Forgive me for sending you these details.[3]

The letter rings true; and everything we know about his examination by the military tribunal dovetails into the pattern of his admitted guilt. The letter forms a *mea culpa* written with remarkable honesty. He does not commiserate with himself. He describes

[3] *Letters:* 77, March 24, 1856.

plainly what happened—he had surrendered to dreams and theories when a more sensible person would have surrendered to facts; and he was being punished for having dreamed. Now above everything else he wanted to be useful to the state, to serve the Tzar loyally, not as a soldier, but as an official and writer. "I believe writers belong to the most noble and useful profession of all," he wrote to the soldier, who believed that commanding armies and building defense works was the height of all human achievement. He compared his own fate with that of the victorious general, and in the style of a suppliant praised him for the defense of Sebastopol. Totleben was not a men who normally gave way to flattery, but he was impressed by the letter. He ordered that Dostoyevsky should receive the rank of ensign in the regiment of the Second Army Corps, and gave him permission to write "as long as his works have a lawful tendency."

Dostoyevsky's desire to serve the Tzar was perfectly genuine. He believed in the divine mission of Russia to save Europe, with the Tzar as the instrument of salvation. He believed Nicholas I had been just in punishing him, and he would describe this Tzar's successor, Alexander II, as "the Angel Emperor" without in the least feeling that such an ascription was ridiculous. When Nicholas I died, Dostoyevsky was overwhelmed with grief and wrote a long poem to the widowed Tzaritsa Alexandra Fyodorovna:

> *I dare not pronounce his name with my sinful lips;*
> *The evidence lies before us in his immortal works.*
> *Like an orphaned land Russia burst into tears,*
> *And petrified she succumbed to terror and fear.*
> *Oh, but you, you yourself, lost more than the others!*
> *Still I know that in this anxious hour*
> *When there came to us the awful news of his death,*
> *Your gentle and mournful image came to our minds,*
> *Came to us on the wings of melancholy vision,*
> *Like a shape of gentleness, like holy humility.*

The very bathos of the poem, which continues for some 99 lines, only testifies to Dostoyevsky's grief. He wrote poems in honor of the Crimean War and for the coronation of the new Tzar, all equally heavy-footed, with no good lines to redeem the intolerable flow.

There was perhaps some method in his poetry. He was writing verses acceptable to the Tzar, and through Baron Wrangel it was very likely they would come to the Tzar's attention. He still hoped for a direct pardon from the Tzar.

Meanwhile he was gradually warming himself back into literature. In November 1856 he wrote to Mikhail about a long comic novel he was writing, and spoke of publishing the completed portions in a magazine. It would, he thought, bring him fame and money, but was there a magazine anywhere which published extracts from a long novel? He was on fire to write again, and complained that he was overwhelmed by the thought of how much remained to be written, and there was so little time, and he worked so slowly even when he was in good health. Still, the novel was progressing. It was called *The Village of Stepanchikovo,* and rather surprisingly it took the form of a farce, the chief part being played by Foma Opiskin, a writer who wrote nothing at all. Foma seems to have stepped straight out of the *commedia dell' arte.* As Dostoyevsky describes him, he is abut fifty, with grizzled hair and a hooked nose, little wrinkles all over his face and a huge wart on his chin. He walks with measured steps, his eyes downcast. He was the family buffoon until the head of the family died, whereupon he took complete charge, dominated the entire family, demanded that everyone call him 'Your Excellency,' and behave with furious tyranny. The worm had turned, and from being one of the oppressed, he became the oppressor, until those he oppressed in turn rebelled and threw him out of the house during a storm. Then for a little while he wandered like Lear on the blasted heath, but the household took pity on him, and Colonel Rostanev jumped on his horse and brought him back in triumph.

Commentators have busied themselves with finding the original of Foma Opiskin. It has been suggested that he was modelled on Gogol, on Belinsky, and on Dostoyevsky himself. With just as much assurance one could prove that "the Dong with the luminous nose" was modeled on Gladstone. *The Village of Stepanchikovo* is a lighthearted frolic written by a man in need of relaxation. Foma is a kind of Punchinello, and like the figures of the *commedia dell' arte* he will sometimes forsake reality and enter a world of sheer lunacy. Nothing disturbs him more than the peasant boy Falalay who is everlastingly dreaming about white bulls; he absolutely refuses to dream about ladies disporting themselves in elegant gardens. Foma rages against a world which produces Falalays:

> "Where are those days when I had faith in love and rejoiced in mankind, when I embraced man, and wept upon his bosom. Where am I? Who are about me? There are only the bulls turning their horns against me! Life, what art thou? I tell you, to live is to be dishonored, disgraced, humbled, crushed to the ground; and when at last the earth is poured on my coffin, only then will I be remembered, only then will there be a monument erected over my poor bones!"
>
> "Holy saints," whispered Yezhevikin, joining his hands. "He is talking about monuments."
>
> "Oh, do not put up a monument for me," Foma exclaimed. "I beg you to desist! I do not need a monument! Raise up a monument for me in your hearts! That will be enough!" [4]

In the same style of rodomontade Foma rages against all tyrants, against ingratitude, and against the curious behavior of young ladies. Rage devours him, and he is perfectly content to be devoured. He knows that posterity will have nothing to do with him in spite of his prolonged labors at three immense works—the historical novel laid in seventh century Novgorod, the epic poem in blank verse called "The Anchorite in the Churchyard," and the vast novel on the aristocracy called "The Countess Vronsky." These works, of course, were never finished, or even begun. It is

[4] *The Village of Stepanchikovo,* Part II, Chapter v.

just possible that at such moments Dostoyevsky was amusing himself with a brief sidelong parody of his own lack of creativity.

In the course of the novel there is only one paragraph which seems to have the flavor of autobiography. The Colonel is taking his young nephew, Seriozha, through the garden. "Why is it that man is wicked?" the Colonel asks. "Look at the trees—how wise they are! They seem to know everything!" And having delivered himself of many more romantic utterances, the Colonel continues:

> Marvelous, marvelous is the Creator! You must remember this garden well, Seriozha, for I remember you used to play in it and run about in it when you were young. I remember you were not allowed to go to the pond alone. But do you remember there was one evening when Katya called to you and began fondling you. . . . You had been running in the garden, and you were very flushed, and your hair was so fair and curly, and she kept playing with it. It was evening, and you were both bathed in the glow of the sunset . . .[5]

Suddenly, reading these words, we find ourselves in the familiar atmosphere of Dostoyevsky's continuing dream of the Golden Age: a lake in the sunset, Claude Lorrain's painting of a bay in the Greek archipelago with the lovers fondling one another in the foreground, the sense of the earth's fruition and of all time stilled in a moment of exquisite vision. Dostoyevsky will put this vision into the mouths of Stavrogin and Maria Timofeyevna. To the end of his life he was to remain haunted by a dream which may have come to him first on the estate at Darovoye when he saw the forbidden pond in the red flare of the sunset.

Before finishing *The Village of Stepanchikovo*, Dostoyevsky embarked on still another comic novel called *My Uncle's Dream*. Once more there is a farcical central character, Count K, a kind of mechanical doll put together out of a wig, false teeth, false whiskers, a corset, powder and rouge. He is more than half mad,

---

[5] *The Village of Stepanchikovo*, Part II, Chapter vi.

very courtly, always dressed in the height of fashion, with dazzling white linen. He wears a monocle over a glass eye, and speaks in an elaborate St. Petersburg accent. Maria Moskaleva is determined to marry off her daughter Zina to this extraordinary creature, but Zina will have none of it until her mother suggests that there are advantages in the marriage: she will be rich, and able to send her consumptive lover to Switzerland, and the Count will die soon. So the Count proposes to Zina when he is in his cups, and she accepts him, to the horror of the young gallants contending for her hand, who succeed in convincing the Count that he only dreamed of the proposal.

The Village of Stepanchikovo and *My Uncle's Dream* overlap. Comic scenes in one could be transferred bodily to the other. The Count also dreams of white bulls, but unlike Foma Opiskin he commiserates with the fate of tyrants:

> "Do you know, my friend, I'm really quite sorry that the English treated Napoleon so badly. Of course, if they hadn't chained him up, he would have begun attacking people again. He was such a desperate fellow! Still, it is a pity! I would never have done it myself. I would have put him on a desert island!"
>
> "Why a desert island?" asked Mozglyabov absently.
>
> "Well, then, on a populated island, but only one with reasonable people living on it. I would have got up all kinds of entertainments for him—theater, music, ballet, all paid for out of state funds. I would have let him walk about—under surveillance, of course, or he would have run away. He was very fond of pies. I would have seen that he had pies every day. I would have been like a father to him, you know, and I'm quite sure he would have repented." [6]

There are many scenes like that, so gay and inconsequential that Dostoyevsky must have laughed aloud when writing them. Perhaps he owed this gaiety to the knowledge that Maria Issayeva

[6] *My Uncle's Dream,* Chapter xi.

had consented to marry him. The wedding took place in Kuznetsk in February 1857, with the local chief of police giving the bride away. Dostoyevsky was overjoyed, and sent off a long rambling letter to his brother describing the event. For a few hours he was as happy as he had ever been, but at Barnaul, on the journey to Semipalatinsk, he suffered a severe epileptic attack. He went to see a doctor, who said that such attacks were especially dangerous at the time of the full moon and warned him that he would probably die of asphyxiation brought on by a throat spasm. There is a story that when Maria saw him in his convulsions, she screamed at him: "You cursed convict!"

So began the ill-starred marriage, which lasted for a little more than seven years. Maria proved to be a virago. He endured her tantrums, cared for her when she was ill, adopted her son Pasha as his own, and sometimes, when he could endure her no longer, he abandoned her for long periods while he sought the company of other women. He loved her and hated her, and long after her death he continued to speak of her with a special veneration. She was "my angel," "a being of immaculate sweetness," "the most perfect creature in the world."

In *Poor Folk* Varvara writes in one of her letters: "Unhappiness is contagious. Unhappy people should stay away from each other." Dostoyevsky did not follow this advice when he married Maria Issayeva.

A SENTIMENTAL JOURNEY

THERE ARE PEOPLE who live out their lives like the characters of Arabian tales to whom everything is granted except escape. There is a sense in which Dostoyevsky never succeeded in breaking the habits of servitude, never left his prison, never wandered free in the sunlight. One could imagine *The Brothers Karamazov* being written in a prison or in a monk's cell, for the ordinary air of the world never penetrates the novel and the creatures of his imagination seem to move with the faltering steps of prisoners, always looking over their shoulders to see whether they are being followed, and they suffer from prison pallor and that strange secret excitement which affects prisoners who have been confined for many years. Prsion and military service, which was for him only another form of imprisonment, left their mark on him. He was always fighting against the jailers and the menacing shadows on the walls.

Now that he was married, he fought more vigorously than ever. He was determined to leave Siberia and take his place among the writers of St. Petersburg. He was continually plotting and planning. There were encouraging signs. He was no longer a soldier of the line, but a *praporshchik,* an ensign, an officer of the lowest rank, but nevertheless an officer. In May 1857, he was restored to his official status as a member of the hereditary nobility. Then, at the end of the year, the doctor attached to the troops at Semipalatinsk issued a medical certificate, which was in fact a petition to permit Dostoyevsky's resignation, and a month later he officially transmitted his resignation to St. Petersburg, where it seems to have been pigeon-holed and forgotten for months. A whole year passed, and there was still no news from St. Petersburg. At last in the spring of 1859 he learned from Mikhail that his resignation had been accepted in an imperial decree of March 18th; in the same decree he was ordered to spend the next two years in Tver, a town 120 miles north of Moscow on the Moscow–St. Petersburg railroad. Official confirmation of the decree reached Semipalatinsk at the beginning of May, but it was two months before all the formalities could be completed. On July 2, 1859, in a *tarantass* he had bought for the occasion, he set out for European Russia. Ten years had passed since his arrest, but he still hoped to make up for lost time.

He hated Tver, which was the capital of a province, crowded with churches and government establishments. The local gentry made much of him, and the Governor invited him to the Governor's palace. "I am anchored here," he wrote to Mikhail, "but all the same nothing can prevent me from being a wanderer." To Baron Wrangel he wrote: "Tver is a thousand times worse then Semipalatinsk—cold, somber, the houses all stone, no movement, nothing interesting, not even a good library. It's an absolute prison." Fighting for survival, he believed he could survive only in St. Petersburg. It was intolerable that he should be so far and yet so near. He pulled strings. Baron Wrangel and Mikhail were both commandeered to effect a rescue. He wrote another appeal to General Totleben, pointing out that many of the Petrashevsky conspirators had been permitted to return to the capital. He was contemplating a complete edition of his works, but they could not be published without his presence in St. Petersburg. "I have placed all my faith in your endeavors on my behalf," he wrote. "Forgive a sick and miserable man for importuning you." With more daring he wrote a long and reasoned appeal to the Tzar, calling upon "the revered being who rules over us" to restore him to life by giving him the opportunity to earn his living in St. Petersburg, "and thus permitting me to be useful to my family and perhaps to my country."

It is an abject appeal, but there is not the least doubt that it was written with the utmost sincerity. He fawns; he importunes; he presents himself in the light of a reclaimed sinner; but over the whole of this long petition there shines the light of a redeeming humility. He concludes the appeal with a characteristic eulogy of the Tzar's majesty:

> Your Majesty is like the sun which shines on the just and the unjust alike. You have already given happiness to millions of Your people. May You now give happiness to a poor orphan and to his mother and to this unfortunate sick man, who still suffers under a curse, and who is prepared, at this moment, to give his life for his EMPEROR, the benefactor of His people.[1]

Dostoyevsky put this appeal into the hands of the Governor of Tver, Count Baranov, who then sent it through carefully selected hands to the Tzar. Without knowing it, Dostoyevsky had defeated his own object, for Prince Dolgoruky, the Minister of War, had already signed an order permitting him to live in St. Petersburg when this latest appeal was received. A new examination of the documents concerning the former conspirator was therefore ordered, while bureaucracy marked time and Dostoyevsky continued to send imploring messages in all directions. At last, on November 25, he received the long-wished-for permit to stay in St. Petersburg. There were still more infuriating delays before he was able to leave Tver late in December, to spend Christmas Eve with Mikhail. A new life had begun.

To those who attended the parties given in honor of the returned convict, it was as though a ghost from the past had assumed flesh after springing from a forgotten grave. At one of these parties the table was decorated with chains. When one of the

[1] *Letters:* 120, October 1859.

A Sentimental Journey

guests exclaimed that it was in bad taste to remind Dostoyevsky of his punishment, the guest of honor replied that on the contrary he welcomed the gesture, for he had been imprisoned justly and his punishment had preserved him from a worse fate. Then, characteristically, he bent down and kissed the chains.

His temper was now conservative, monarchical, deeply religious, and at the same time there was a vast residue of liberal feeling to color his beliefs. In order to make a living he edited with his brother Mikhail a new magazine, *Time,* which mirrored his curious mingling of advanced liberalism with devotion to the Tzar. They were times of feverish change, with all Russia in the throes of political experiment as preparations were made for liberating the serfs.

Dostoyevsky threw himself into the role of editor with all his feverish pent-up energy. He wrote editorials, art criticism, *reportages.* He advised contributors and strenuously criticized them. With the help of the young philosopher Nikolay Strakhov and the brilliant Apollon Grigoryev he was able to produce a magazine which quickly became a popular success and rivaled all the old-established magazines in the capital. *Time* became the vehicle for a carefully thought-out policy of conservative liberalism, against both the Westerners and the Slavophils, preaching "the middle road." The magazine was so popular that for some years Dostoyevsky was in easy financial circumstances, with sufficient money to keep two establishments—his own lodgings in St. Petersburg, and his wife's in Vladimir, where she had gone to escape the rigors of the northern weather—and to travel extensively. Photographs taken at the time show the unmistakable marks of success. The heavy military mustache he wore at Semipalatinsk was gone. He allowed his beard to grow. His hair was receding; he looked older than his forty years and comported himself with dignity. He bought his clothes at the best tailor, wore flowered waistcoats and silk ties. With his wife away, he engaged in a series of extramarital adventures. He was riding a precarious wave.

145

Among the letters which have survived from this time are three addressed to the young and beautiful Alexandra Schubert, a noted actress, who insisted on returning to the stage after her marriage to Dr. Yanovsky, who had attended Dostoyevsky in earlier days. Dostoyevsky acted as an intermediary, hoping to effect a reconciliation. The interview was stormy. At one point Dr. Yanovsky observed Dostoyevsky staring at a portrait of his wife, and immediately turned the portrait to the wall. Dostoyevsky was more than half in love with her, and took the opportunity of declaring his affections in a long letter describing the interview. He wrote:

> I am so happy that you have demonstrated so much loyal and affectionate confidence in me. That is being a friend! I tell you frankly: I love you warmly and deeply, to the extent of being able to say that I am not in love with you. For above all I want to be in your good graces, and dear God, how I suffered when I thought you had lost confidence in me! I accused myself for a long time! What a terrible misfortune that would have been. But in your letter you have completely set my doubts aside, dear, sweet, infinitely kind friend! May God shower on you all His blessings! I am so happy to be so sure of myself, to know that I am not in love with you! In this way I can be even more devoted to you than before . . .[2]

It is, of course, a very cavalier and calculating letter. He declares his love, withdraws his declaration, declares it again, and retreats in a cloud of happy mystification. Most of Dostoyevsky's surviving letters consist of urgent pleas for help, or frenzied commentaries on approaching disaster; these three letters to Alexandra Schubert show him employing a tone of amused courtly bewilderment, which is rare among his correspondence.

Still rarer are the letters describing his dreams and visionary experiences. The draft of one such letter, addressed to an unknown

[2] *Letters:* 136, June 12, 1860.

correspondent about the year 1860, has survived. It describes an extraordinary dream, and seems to be connected in some way with his vision of the Golden Age:

> Please explain my dream to me. I have asked everyone, and no one understands it. In the East I saw the full moon, which divided into three parts, which moved away from one another and three times they joined one another.
>
> Then there came a shield from the moon: the shield bore the letters DA DA in ancient Slavonic characters:

> and these swept across the whole heavens, from east to west, and vanished at last over the horizon. The shield and the letters were surrounded with halos.
>
> DOSTOYEVSKY
>
> Ask everyone, everyone without exception. This is something which enormously interests me.[3]

Though Dostoyevsky took particular care to record his dreams, and still suffered from epileptic attacks which sometimes had the effect of producing visions, he was living the sober life of a successful editor. Not that he had stopped writing or planning novels. His reminiscences of prison life, called *The House of the Dead,* had appeared in the columns of *Time. The Little Hero,* which he wrote in the Peter and Paul Fortress long ago, had appeared in *Fatherland Notes* while he was still living in Semipalatinsk, while *My Uncle's Dream* appeared in *The Russian Messen-*

---

[3] "DA" means "yes" in Russian. *Letters:* 133, *circa* 1860.

ger, and so too did *The Village of Stephanchikovo.* He still regarded himself above all as a novelist. For him the novel was the highest form of creative endeavor, and accordingly he prepared himself to write a novel which would have the same impact as *Poor Folk.* He was keenly aware that none of his works had reached so large a public as that short novel which was the first fruits of his apprenticeship to literature.

The Insulted and Injured which appeared in installments in the pages of *Time* was intended to be a work of lasting importance. "It will be my *chef d'œuvre,*" he wrote. "It will bring me into fashion." It did not bring him into fashion; it was not a *chef d'œuvre,* and gave signs of having been written in great weariness of spirit. He had written his two farces with considerable warmth, but he had not yet prepared himself for the more massive task of composing a long novel which would describe his own times. He was still a stranger to the life growing around him in St. Petersburg. He was still restless and uncomprehending.

The Insulted and Injured is not to be dismissed lightly. There are whole chapters which resemble parodies of Dickens. It is a book which one reads with difficulty, amazed that Dostoyevsky could write with so little discipline and control. Yet here and there the old flame burns brightly. The hero is a young writer, Vanya, who falls in love with his Natasha and like Devushkin in *Poor Folk,* surrenders her to another. He is desperately poor: Natasha is desperately noble, yet strangely treacherous. In a characteristic passage Dostoyevsky says of her that "she anticipated the ecstasy of loving passionately and torturing the one she loved simply because she loved him, and that perhaps was why she was anxious to let herself be his victim." She belongs to the category of passionate and treacherous heroines, oppressed by destiny and glorying in defeat, who appear in so many of his later novels. Her rival is the innocent and childlike Katya, who also seeks the love of Alyosha Valkonsky, a rich and silly youth who seems to be scarcely worth the trouble of pursuing. Alyosha is a nonentity, and Katya a marionette, but Natasha lives, and so, too, does the diabolic Price Valkonsky, the father of Alyosha.

Prince Valkonsky seems to have been an afterthought, but whenever he appears he dominates the novel with his relentless cynicism, his unbounded brutality and selfishness. He has no illusions about life. Like the Count in *My Uncle's Dream* he is a man of artifice; everything about his appearance was "somehow not his own, but always borrowed, artificial, deliberate"; and through this aristocratic mask there blazed a pair of beautiful grey eyes "which seemed unable to submit entirely to his will." There was a strange youthfulness about him, and there were times when he looked like the elder brother of the witless Alyosha.

Towards the end of the novel the Prince lures Vanya into an inn and proceeds to amuse himself by confessing his sins. Vanya compares him with Punchinello, and he roars with pleasure. He has committed every sin known to man. He had pursued a peasant girl on his estate, and had her husband thrashed to death —the peasant died in the superbly equipped hospital the Prince had built on the estate. He has deliberately seduced a woman given to good works and mysticism to the point that "in the most fiery ecstasies she would suddenly laugh like one possessed, and I understood it thoroughly." He confesses his credo:

> Personality, I, myself—that is what makes sense. All is for me. The whole world has been created for me. Listen, my friend, I still believe that it is possible to live happily on earth, and that's the best faith, for without it one cannot even live unhappily; there's nothing left but to poison oneself. . . . I, for one, have long since freed myself from all shackles, and even obligations. I recognize obligations only when I have something to gain from them. . . . Love yourself—that is the only rule I recognize. Life is a commercial transaction, don't waste your money, but kindly pay for your entertainment, and you will be doing your whole duty to your neighbor. These are my morals, if you really want to know them.

. . . I have no ideals, and don't want to have them. I've never felt the need for them. . . . I love consequence, rank, a mansion, a huge stake at cards (I am awfully fond of cards). But best of all women—women of all kinds. I'm all in favor of hidden, secretive vices, the more strange and original the better, and if there's some filth in them—well, that's for variety! [4]

Prince Valkonsky is like a sketch for the ferociously evil characters of the later novels; he saves the novel from total failure. But the novel remains incomplete. Dostoyevsky tells us that in order to meet a deadline he once wrote three and a half signatures —56 pages—in two days and nights. It is not difficult to recognize the pages written hurriedly. Having finished *The Insulted and Injured,* and seen the publication of *The House of the Dead* in book form, he decided to realize his long-cherished ambition to travel to Europe.

Whenever Dostoyevsky traveled abroad, he surrounded himself with a purely Russian atmosphere. He had no feeling for Europe, and very little understanding of it. He did not like Europeans, had no European friends, and was content to regard all those he encountered with mingled mistrust and resentment. He was like a man traveling on a safe-conduct through enemy territory.

He was forty when he set out for Europe for the first time. He had reached the age when most men have formed the convictions they will carry for the rest of their lives. He was prepared, however, to be generous and understanding. "I'll go everywhere, and see everything," he wrote. "I'll take a bird's eye view of the entire land of sacred wonders, like someone looking at the Promised Land from the mountaintop, and no doubt the result will be some new, powerful and wonderful impressions." But in fact he derived very few impressions from his visit to Europe. He hated, or was indifferent to nearly everything he saw. Most of the time

[4] *The Insulted and Injured,* Part III, Chapter x.

he was miserable and dying to be back in Russia. He complained continually about the weather, the people, the art galleries.

The journey started inauspiciously with the long two-day train journey from St. Petersburg to Berlin. There was something wrong with his liver. The rain and the fog accompanied him the whole way. When he got out of the train at Berlin, thoroughly exhausted, he was in no mood to be generous or understanding. To his disgust Berlin looked like St. Petersburg. There were the same straight and colorless streets, the same smells. Everything annoyed him—even the linden trees. He went off to Dresden and took an instant dislike to the Dresden women, until it occurred to him that he might be suffering from jaundice, and so he returned to his hotel room and examined himself in a mirror, sticking out his tongue and learning without too much surprise that his liver was completely out of order. He was to remain liverish until the end of the journey.

Cologne fared hardly better than Dresden. In his happy, snarling, liverish way he took a dislike to the Cathedral—"fripperies of lace." He disliked the merchants of *Eau de Cologne,* who seemed to be everywhere. For some reason he disliked the pride of the people of Cologne over their new and magnificent bridge, and he hated paying the toll, and he was sure they were all saying: "You miserable Russians don't have bridges like this." He spent one day in Berlin, another in Dresden, and perhaps two in Cologne, and he was evidently enjoying himself in a sardonic way.

He arrived in Paris towards the middle of June, knowing no one and apparently with no desire to know anyone, and still liverish. He hated Paris on sight. It occurred to him that Paris was simply a magnified German university town, a vast and well-regimented Heidelberg. "I have found the epithet which most completely characterizes Paris," he wrote. "It is the most *moral,* the most *virtuous* city in the entire world. What order! What prudence! What comfort!" He raged against the proclamations of

liberté, egalité, fraternité, as others have raged against them before and since, coming to very much the same conclusions. What
is liberty? The liberty to do as one pleases. When can one do as
one pleases? When one has a million. These not very illuminating
remarks are recorded in *Winter Notes on Summer Impressions*
written hurriedly on his return to St. Petersburg, when the misery
of the journey was still with him.

Dostoyevsky's love affair with France had been of long dura-
tion. French was the first language he learned after Russian; he
read French well and easily, and wrote it accurately; his first
published work was a translation of Balzac; and the French socialists, Fourier and Sebastien Cabet, were the heroes of his revolutionary adolescence. But when he came to Paris, he saw no
revolutionaries, and no great writers. He saw the well-contented
husbands strolling arm in arm with their well-contented wives in
the garden of the Palais Royal, where the fountains babbled
pleasantly, and once more he was reminded of the peace and
serenity of Heidelberg. "There are many similar fountains in
Paris," he went on, "and they make the heart rejoice."

Not that his heart rejoiced. On the contrary he loathed everything he saw with a stern, unappeasable loathing. There was no
spirit in France. It was a country given over to the *bourgeoisie.*
The workers, the farmers, the socialists—they had all fallen under
the spell of the *bourgeoisie* and desired only to imitate their masters. As for the vaunted self-sacrifice of the French, he saw no
sign of it. They were all individualists, utterly incapable of surrendering themselves for the good of the whole, each man looking
out for his own immediate advantage. He was in a mood to make
wild generalizations. "All Frenchmen," he wrote, "are really Pa-
risians." Or again: "In France marriage for love is considered
indecent." It was, he thought, a very remarkable fact that everything in France dated from the time of Louis XIV. So he continued to rage against the *bourgeoisie,* which put on such in-

tolerable, haughty airs, and measured everything by the state of your bank balance.

Dostoyevsky raging against Paris is not a pleasant spectacle. He was obviously lonely, ill, disgruntled, and out of his depth. Having very little money, he was outraged by the spectacle of so much money changing hands; and he came to the conclusion that there was hardly a Frenchman who would not sell his father for half a ruble, and he would do this with an air of becoming nobility. They were all extortionists, "stealing for the sake of virtue, and therefore everything is forgiven them." They were all vulgarians. They had a few ready-made ideas which they kept in reserve, like firewood for the winter, and they proposed to live by these ideas for the next thousand years. "Yet how indifferent they are to everything," Dostoyevsky sighs. "How ephemeral and empty their interests are!"

He was more amusing, and more revealing, when he visited the Pantheon in the company of a venerable and decrepit guide who made declamatory speeches before the tombs of the heroes. *"Ci-gît Voltaire,"* lisped the guide through his missing teeth. "Voltaire, the great genius of *la belle France,* who eradicated prejudices, annihilated ignorance, wrestled with the angel of darkness, and raised on high the torch of enlightenment. *Ci-gît Jean-Jacques Rousseau, l'homme de la nature et de la verité. . . .*"

Dostoyevsky roared with laughter, and took it upon himself to point out to the ignorant guide that Voltaire called Rousseau a liar, and Rousseau in turn called Voltaire an imbecile. There they were, lying side by side! It was extraordinary! The old guide was muttering away, having learned his patter by rote, and Dostoyevsky was struck by the incongruities of the Pantheon, where the dead seemed to be gathered up in the prevailing atmosphere of gentility and *bourgeois* servility, and the guide's eloquence was constantly being interrupted by the rude Russian, who showed no mercy at all, so that at last the guide paused, shook his grey head sadly, and said reproachfully: "Monsieur, I am sure you know all this better than I do, but since you took me for your guide, let me say it in my own words." Dostoyevsky was pleased when the guide airily dismissed the last tombs with the words: *"Quelques sénateurs . . ."* Then it was over and he went out into the sunlight, still fuming against the poor guide who loved eloquence for the sake of eloquence—the besetting sin of the French.

Dostoyevsky was almost at the breaking-point. He wrote to his friend Strakhov after ten days of Paris: "You cannot imagine the agony of solitude here! A sensation of utter misery and melancholy! If only we were together; we would see Naples and wander through Rome and then, God willing, we might amuse ourselves with a Venetian girl in a gondola, eh, Nikolay Nikolayevich? Meanwhile—'nothing, nothing, only silence,' as Poprishchin would say." Poprishchin was the leading character in Gogol's *Diary of a Madman,* and Dostoyevsky seems to have been on the edge of madness nearly all the time he was in Paris.

In London he fared better. He was not completely alone, for he could call on the famous expatriate Alexander Herzen who was then editing his socialist newspaper under the protection of the British government. Herzen was intelligent, affable, and always happy to receive Russians. Dostoyevsky came for tea, stayed throughout an afternoon, and according to Herzen "he showed an enthusiastic faith in the Russian people." It would seem that Dostoyevsky launched into a monologue on the superiority of the Russians over the French and the English. "He is naive, but somewhat confused, and quite amiable," Herzen reported to his friend Ogaryov.

Dostoyevsky was appalled by London, but he was also fascinated. Judging by his own account, Paris was known territory, a place where he had lived in his imagination and where, though he raged against the people, he was perfectly at home. London was unknown territory, producing a violent shock on the exposed nerves of the wanderer who felt that he had entered a new universe where entirely new laws were obeyed, and where everything was larger, darker, more satanic and more certain of damnation than anywhere else. London was Baal, a place given over to the horror of progress, the deadly sinfulness of industry. It was possessed by a fiendish spirit of pride. It lacked the profound humility of the Russian spirit. It boasted audaciously of its triumphs, and therefore there was reserved for it a terrible fate. "In the presence of such majesty, of the far-ranging pride of that sovereign spirit, of the triumphant perfection of the creations brought into being by that spirit, even the thirsting soul must find itself terrified: it humbles itself, and submits, and seeks salvation in gin and debauchery, and believes that everything is for the best." It is perhaps the oddest tribute ever made to the power and splendor of the city of London.

Dostoyevsky saw many odd things in London, and some of the things he believed he saw may have taken place in his imagination. He saw Englishwomen so beautiful that he caught his breath, and announced unequivocally that they were the most beautiful in the world. He was puzzled at the sight of beautiful and elegantly dressed women walking through crowded streets cheek-by-jowl with beggars in rags. There was something evidently wrong with the English who permitted the dregs of society to live in such close proximity to their betters. Dostoyevsky had very little sympathy with the English lower classes. "You cannot regard them as people," he reported with aristocratic disdain. "No, they should be regarded as a clot of systematic, submissive, calculated mindlessness."

So he fumed, awestruck by a city which gave an impression of fierce, unrestrained power. It was altogether larger and more splendid than Paris, and no one could accuse the Londoners of suffering from the disease of self-satisfaction prevalent in France. Some devilish spirit moved them. They were restless, not servile; drunkards by instinct; hardfisted and callous; and they beat their wives with pokers as a matter of habit, having nothing better to do on Saturday nights. As for the Anglican clergy, these rich and cultivated gentlemen were immune from the temptation of serving the poor, and considered that a life spent in the calm discussion of theological problems was a sufficient passport to Paradise. "The rich Englishmen," he wrote, "are extremely religious, gloomily, morosely, and peculiarly religious." It puzzled him that they were forever sending missionaries to Africa, while it never occurred to them to convert the savages in London.

London however stirred him deeply. It possessed a kind of satanic majesty, impressive in the sheer effrontery of its vastness and energy. He wrote:

> How different it is from Paris in all outward respects!
> A city as unfathomable as the seas, never-resting by day
> and night; the roar and pandemonium of machines; the
> railroads running above the houses (and soon they will
> be running under them); that spirit of bold enterprise;
> the apparent disorder which is actually the highest kind
> of bourgeois order; the polluted Thames; the air satu-
> rated with coal dust; the splendid gardens and parks;
> those sinister places like Whitechapel with its half-naked,
> savage and hungry people; a city populated by millions
> with a commerce stretching across the world; the Crystal
> Palace. . . .[5]

He did not approve of the Crystal Palace, which reminded him of a soulless machine, the monstrous Baal to which the world of industry and socialism was approaching. Hundreds of thousands congregated at this palace as to an altar. Under the glass roof lay a permanent exhibition of modern inventions, dark, emphatic, wholly without scruple. It was the purgatory announced by the nineteenth century, and Dostoyevsky found himself at a loss to understand why people applauded the achievements of material-ism. It was like seeing a prophecy from the Apocalypse coming true before your eyes. In words which are like a preliminary echo

[5] *Winter Notes on Summer Impressions,* Chapter V.

of *The Legend of the Great Inquisitor,* Dostoyevsky declares: "You feel that it would need a great and everlasting spiritual denial for a man to resist such a place. Only those who possess great fortitude could avoid submitting to it or capitulating before its power, not bowing to it nor in any way deifying it. One must be strong not to accept the material world as one's ideal."

One Saturday night he wandered through the streets and found himself in a gas-lit purgatory which seemed more terrible than the purgatory of St. Petersburg. The Londoners went about their pleasures without joy, in a spirit of somber and heavy brooding. They drank in the pubs like people racing against time; and the pubs were full of women and children. By five o'clock on Sunday morning most of these workmen had spent their week's wages. On that Saturday night Dostoyevsky lost his way and succeeded in returning to his own lodgings only after a hair-raising journey among morose and silent drunkards who finally understood his strange sign language—he did not speak a single word of English—and helped him on his way. For three days afterward Dostoyevsky trembled whenever he remembered that experience.

It must have been on that same Saturday night that he was accosted in the Haymarket by mothers intent on selling their daughters' favors. It was not in itself an unusual experience. The same thing might be observed in the Haymarket in St. Petersburg called the *Sennaya,* and when Dostoyevsky spoke of his encounter with a six-year-old girl, it is not clear whether he is speaking about something which happened in London or in St. Petersburg. He wrote in *Winter Notes on Summer Impressions:*

> I remember once seeing a six-year-old girl in a crowded street. She was dressed in rags, filthy, barefoot, terribly thin, with hollow cheeks. Through the rags you could see her little body all covered with black and blue sores. Yet she walked like someone unconscious of her surroundings, unhurriedly, and heaven knows what she was doing in the crowd. Nobody was paying any atten-

tion to her. I was impressed by her face which expressed so much sorrow, so much hopeless despair, and there was something strange in seeing this little thing crushed by such an evil fate. On her, despair seemed somehow unnatural and terribly pitiful.

She was continually rocking her tousled head from side to side as though she was discussing something with herself, and she would throw out her arms, gesticulating, and then suddenly bring them together, pressing them to her feeble, naked little chest. I went over to her and handed her a half shilling. She seized the silver coin, gazed momentarily into my eyes in sudden bewilderment, and then she was running off as fast as her legs would carry her, as though she was afraid I would take the money back. It was such a happy sight. . . .[6]

It was not, of course, a happy sight at all: Dostoyevsky was speaking with bitter irony. He was speaking about something very close to his heart, for the young defenseless waif lost in the dark city, infinitely pitiable because she is at the mercy of anyone who passes by, returns again and again to haunt his novels. He spoke about such children so often and so convincingly, describing the outrages they suffered and imagining so many brilliant details, that some people believed he had himself raped one of these defenseless children. After his death one of his very closest friends, Nikolay Strakhov, hinted as much in a letter to Tolstoy. Strakhov seems to have been unbelievably ignorant of the novelist's task, which is to know all the triumphs and all the degradations of the human spirit by means of a perpetual act of sympathy. Rémy de Gourmont once described the great artist as *chaste de cœur et libertin d'esprit*. Dostoyevsky was a spiritual libertine, but he was also unusually chaste for his time.

This same Strakhov became his traveling companion when he left London for Switzerland. Disliking Switzerland, the two friends went on to Genoa and Florence, which Dostoyevsky visited for the first time, apparently without being impressed by any of the works

[6] *Winter Notes on Summer Impressions,* Chapter V.

of art except Raphael's *Madonna della Sedia* in the Pitti gallery. Strakhov was puzzled. Dostoyevsky possessed the gift of blindness whenever he entered a gallery; paintings, sculptures, mosaics left him unmoved. Michelangelo's *David* and Cellini's *Perseus* he seems not to have noticed; he was more interested in watching the people in the streets and he was continually leading Strakhov into the busiest quarters of Florence, extolling the virtues of ordinary Italians over the paintings of princes and saints in the museums. "All his attention," said Strakhov later, "was concentrated on watching the faces of the people in the streets."

He was happy in Florence. Every evening he sat with Strakhov in a sidewalk cafe over a carafe of red wine, and watched the people passing. He was doing no work. He stayed in Florence for a week, made plans to journey to Rome, cancelled the plans, and then quite suddenly decided to return home. Strakhov returned to Paris, and Dostoyevsky took the train for St. Petersburg.

Dostoyevsky returned to Russia with none of his illusions shattered. Those steady grey eyes which saw everything in perspective in Russia were curiously blinkered in Europe; he had seen only what he wanted to see. "In Europe it was I, and I alone with my yearning for Russia, who was free," he said; and it was not true. In his loneliness and misery he had seen the world colored by his own darkness. Those few carefree days spent in the company of Strakhov were the only ones he remembered with pleasure.

That winter, in St. Petersburg, he wrote *Winter Notes on Summer Impressions*. It is a cold humorless work, mercifully short, written in haste. It was a bad winter. His epileptic attacks came with increasing frequency. He complained that his memory was failing, and the periods of intense melancholy after the attacks left him with little energy for work. He needed sunlight, and there was none. He needed good doctors, and the best of them were in Europe; he made plans to visit doctors in Paris and Berlin, but nothing came of them. He wrote a short story called *An Un-*

pleasant Predicament about a high official who decides to attend
the wedding celebration of one of his clerks who earns ten rubles
a month. The clerk has scraped up just enough money to hold
the celebration, and is on edge. The high official arrives at the
miserable apartment, and the clerk almost faints with surprise.
The party comes to an end. Everyone feels obliged to attend to
the needs of the official, who reminds everyone that he has come
out of the magnanimity of his heart to share their joy. Drunk on
vodka and champagne, the official delivers a speech on the regeneration of Russia. One of the more headstrong revelers explains that when high officials attend wedding parties it is only
because they are interested in the wives of the clerks. Suddenly
the official, disheartened and angry, screams that he has come
only with the best of intentions, and then falls unconscious, his
head dropping into a plate of blancmange.

It is a good story, and belongs to that famous series of comic
interludes he wrote while taking part in the Petrashevsky conspiracy, but it was not a work which suggested that he was reaching out into new territory. He was standing still. He published
the story in his magazine, *Time,* and it was among the last con-
tributions to that ill-fated magazine, which was promptly banned
when the Tzar convinced himself that an article by Strakhov on
the Polish question lent aid and comfort to the Polish rebels.
Strakhov had not intended to lend aid and comfort to the rebels;
he had in fact intended the reverse; but the Tzar's *fiat* was irrevocable. *Time* disappeared, to be revived later under another
name. Mikhail and Fyodor Dostoyevsky lost their jobs, and
found themselves saddled with a mountain of debts.

All through the spring and early summer of 1863 there were
these mounting crises. Maria was dying, and he visited her occasionally, remembering the days when they enjoyed secret trysts
in Semipalatinsk, but there was no longer any real affection between them. He came to her like a visitor from another planet,
determined to provide for her to the best of his ability, but other-

wise indifferent to her. Almost immediately after the marriage he realized it had been a mistake.

That winter he had been living in St. Petersburg with a wild, dark-haired beauty called Polina Suslova. In the summer he traveled with her across Europe. It was the most rewarding, and the most exasperating, of all his love affairs.

POLINA SUSLOVA

O F ALL THE WOMEN whom Dostoyevsky met, none was so imperious and demanding as Polina Suslova, who seems to have modeled herself on the Natasha of *The Insulted and Injured*. She possessed a seductive manner and a brazen desire for mastery; and she was determined to draw Dostoyevsky into her toils. No other woman ever came so close to destroying him.

We do not know how they came together. She may have met him in the second year of his return to St. Petersburg from Siberia, for she contributed a story to the magazine *Time* in 1861, and it is possible that they met about that time. Dostoyevsky's daughter Luba, who is always an unreliable witness, declares that Polina sent him a passionate declaration of love and immediately became his mistress. She describes Polina as a rebellious student at St. Petersburg University, always inciting her follow students against the government, leading their processions against the Cossacks, and continually singing the *Marseillaise*. Of her life at the University very little is known. She was the daughter of a former serf on the estate of Count Sheremetev, and by all acoounts she was a high-spirited and voluptuous woman with a talent for intrigue. Photographs only hint at the beauty of her long aristocratic face, which was unusually mobile and graced with very dark and beautiful eyes.

Very little is known about the beginnings of the affair. She seems to have been an occasional mistress, angry because Dostoyevsky would not divorce his ailing wife and marry her, and determined to win him by stragegy. In the spring of 1863 she abruptly left St. Petersburg for Paris, hoping he would follow immediately. Business matters kept him in the capital until the summer, and he did not reach Paris until August. By this time she was having an affair with a handsome young Spaniard called Salvador, a medical student at the University. On August 19, Salvador told her he was intending to leave for America. She wrote in her journal:

> Although I had expected it, I was shaken by the news; the emotions of fear and suffering must have appeared plainly on my face. He kissed me. I bit my lips and made an incredible effort not to burst into tears. He kissed me and said he would not be gone for long, and perhaps he might never go—he said this after I had composed myself and was no longer close to tears. . . . Today I received a letter from F. M. He is coming in a few days. I wanted to see him so that I could tell him everything, but I have decided to write.[1]

She was trapped between her desire for Salvador and her desire for Dostoyevsky. Salvador was playing a cat-and-mouse game, and she was afraid that Dostoyevsky might do the same. To forestall the advances of Dostoyevsky, she decided to confront him with her surrender to Salvador, and later that day she wrote him an extraordinary letter admitting she had surrendered to her Spanish lover "at the first call, without struggle, without assurance, almost without hope." She wrote:

> You are a trifle late. Only a short while ago I was dreaming of going with you to Italy, and I even began learning Italian. But everything has changed in these few days. You once told me I was not a person to surrender my heart quickly. I gave it within a week at the first call, without struggle, without assurance, almost without hope. I was right to be angry with you when you first went into ecstasies over me. Do not think I am

[1] A. P. Suslova: *Gody Blizosti s Dostoyevskim,* page 47.

condemning you. I am only trying to say that you do not know me, and I did not know myself. Farewell, my dear.

I wanted to see you, but where would it lead to? I wanted so much to *speak* with you about Russia.[2]

Polina copied out the letter into her journal, adding: "Now I am so very unhappy! How magnanimous and noble he is! What mind! What heart!" But thoughts of Dostoyevsky, on his way to Paris from St. Petersburg, gave place to still more troubled thoughts of Salvador, who remained silent, never visiting her in her apartment on the rue Soufflot, and never answering her letters. She did however see him briefly on the Sunday following his declaration that he was leaving for America. It was a stormy meeting. He accused her of keeping secrets from him. Polina solemnly entered the details of the meeting in her diary. "This time," she wrote, "it appeared to me that he did not love me, and there arose a strong desire to make him love me. This is possible; only it is necessary to act coldbloodedly. I know his weak traits; he is very vain."

Meanwhile Dostoyevsky was making his way to Paris, having paused for a few days at Baden, where he played roulette, won a large sum, lost half of it, and succeeded in leaving the tables with about 5,000 francs on hand. He earmarked part of the money for his wife; the rest was to be spent on travel with Polina. He arrived in Paris on the 27th and sent her a letter announcing his arrival. Polina dutifully noted in her journal: "In his letter he says he is so happy to see me. I sent him the very short note I prepared earlier. I am so very sorry for him."

That evening he appeared at her apartment, apparently with no idea there had been a change in their relationship. Polina describes their conversation at length in her journal:

"How are you?" I said in a trembling voice, and then he asked me whether there was anything wrong, and this only made me more agitated, while at the same time his

[2] *Ibid.,* pages 47–8.

own uneasiness increased. "I thought you were not coming," I said, "after that letter I wrote to you."

"What letter?"

"To tell you not to come."

"It is too late."

His head sank down.

"I must know everything. Let us go somewhere, and you must tell me, or I shall die."

I suggested we should go to his lodging. The whole way we were silent. *I did not look at him. From time to time* he would shout at the coachman in a desperate and impatient voice: *"Vite! Vite!"* The coachman would turn round and look at us like someone bewildered. I tried not to look at F. M. He, too, tried to avoid looking at me, but he held my hand, and sometimes he would *squeeze* it and make curious convulsive movements. I said: "Calm yourself, I am with you!"

When we reached his room, he fell at my feet and clasped my knees, sobbing loudly and saying: "I've lost you! I knew it!" And then growing calm, he began to question me about the man. "He may be young and handsome and a fine fellow with words, *but you will never find another heart like mine.*"

For a long time I did not want to answer him.

"Did you give yourself to him completely?"

"Don't talk. It's not right," I said.

"Polya, I don't know what is right or wrong. Is he a Russian? A Frenchman?"

"No. No."

I told him I was very much in love with the man.

"You are happy?"

"No."

"You are in love and not happy! How can that be?"

"He does not love me."

"Does not love you!" he shouted, clutching his head in despair. "But you don't love him like a slave, tell me that! I must know! Would you follow him to the ends of the earth?"

"No, I . . . I'm going to the country," I said, and burst into tears.

"Oh, Polya, why are you so unhappy? It was bound to happen that you would love another. I knew it. You made a mistake in loving me, because you have a big heart. You waited until you were twenty-three; you are the only woman who demands no commitments of any kind, but think of the cost: men and women are not the same—the man takes, the woman gives."

When I told him about the man, he said that at that moment he had experienced a nasty sensation—he felt relieved because this was not a man worthy in any respect, he was no Lermontov. Then we went on to talk about other matters. He told me he was happy because he had found a person like me in the world. He begged me to remain his friend and he especially asked me to write to him when I was unusually happy or unhappy. Then he suggested that I should go to Italy with him— he would be like a brother to me. When I reminded him that he would be at work on his novel, he said: 'What do you take me for? Do you think all this will leave no impression on me?' I promised to come the next day. I felt relieved after talking to him.[3]

She was in an exalted mood, simultaneously in love with Dostoyevsky and Salvador, almost completely sure that Dostoyevsky loved her in return, but baffled by the silence of Salvador. She immediately sat down to write Dostoyevsky a strange taunting letter, which was also a confession of failure. She wrote:

All the people who have ever loved me have made me suffer, even my father and mother. My friends are all good people, but weak and poor in spirit, rich in words and poor in deeds. Among them I have not met one who was not afraid of the truth, and did not retreat before the generally accepted laws of life. So they condemn me, but I cannot respect them. It seems to me a crime to say one thing and do another. I fear only my conscience. And if it should ever happen that I should sin against it, then I would confess it only to myself. I do not in the least regard myself with exceptional leniency, but I have

[3] *Ibid.,* pp. 50–2.

no liking for weak and timorous people. I flee from those people who deceive themselves, even unconsciously, because I do not want to be dependent on them. I am thinking of burying myself in the country among the peasants. . . .[4]

Polina had of course no intention of burying herself among the peasants. In her mind's eye she was a beautiful woman being eagerly pursued by a famous author and a strikingly handsome young Spaniard. She would play one against the other, and see what happened.

After her visit with Dostoyevsky she returned to her own apartment and spent a sleepless night, thinking about Salvador. She felt she had betrayed him until she found on her table a letter from a friend of Salvador, informing her that he was ill with typhoid fever and asking her to refrain from visiting him. She was sure he was dying, for it was well-known that typhoid was especially dangerous to young people. She hurried off to Dostoyevsky, who cheered her a little by telling her that the Paris air was good, and the French doctors were excellent, and there was no danger.

Salvador was not in fact suffering from typhoid fever, for Polina met him in the street near the Sorbonne the next day. She caught up with him. He was in perfect health, and plainly enjoying himself.

"Where are you going?" he asked innocently.

"I'm just taking a walk," she answered, and showed him the letter she had received from his friend.

He seemed uninterested in the letter, and turned into a house where he said he was expected, leaving her alone on the street.

When she reached her own apartment, she was close to hysteria. She became feverish, and, according to Dostoyevsky's daughter, she armed herself with a long knife with the intention

[4] *Ibid.,* p. 52.

of killing her lover that day. She makes no mention of the knife in her journal, where she describes how she spent a sleepless night and at seven o'clock in the morning made her way to Dostoyevsky's apartment.

> He was sleeping when I arrived. He let me in and then lay down and wrapped himself in the blankets. He was looking at me with fear and bewilderment. I was *absolutely* calm. I told him I wanted him to come to my apartment at once. I wanted to tell him everything and to ask him to be my judge. I did not want him to stay, because I was hoping Salv. would come when F. M. arrived, I was sitting up over my breakfast eating a piece of bread. "You can see I am quite calm," I said, laughing.
>
> "Yes," he said, "and I am glad, but who will ever be able to make you out?"
>
> After a few unimportant observations, I began to tell him about my love affair in detail right up to the encounter on the previous day, hiding nothing.
>
> F. M. said I should pay no attention to all this, because although everything was completely confused, still it was only a comparatively unimportant incident. Like all young men Salv. needed a mistress, and I had turned up, and he had simply made use of me; and why should he not, when a pretty young woman presented herself to him and he found her to his taste?
>
> F. M. was right. I understood all this perfectly, even though it made me look a fool.
>
> "I would not want to kill him," I said, "but I would like to torture him for a long time."
>
> "That's silly," he answered. "There's nothing to be gained by it, and he wouldn't understand anything. He is simply vermin who should be exterminated with insecticide. It would be stupid to ruin yourself over him."
>
> I agreed with him.[5]

She was now almost completely won over to Dostoyevsky, but to safeguard her pride she sent one last letter to Salvador,

[5] *Ibid.*, p. 55.

warning him to keep away from her. "I am an uncultured person (an absolute barbarian), and so incapable of understanding your artificial jokes," she wrote, adding: "I am saying this quite seriously."

They decided to go to Italy. Visas for Rome could only be obtained at the Legation of the Apostolic See, and there a curious incident occurred. Dostoyevsky's nerves were strained. He was in no mood to be kept waiting. The passports had been handed to a young priest, who disappeared into some office in the remote interior of the Legation so that they could be stamped by a Monsignore. After waiting a long time, Dostoyevsky exploded and asked what the devil the Monsignore was doing, to keep the passports so long. The priest answered that the Monsignore was drinking his coffee. Dostoyevsky's temper snapped completely. He shouted: *"Je veux cracher dans son café!"* and he rushed towards the Monsignore's room, with the priest and Polina hanging on his coattails and slithering on the parquet floor. Finally Dostoyevsky grew calm, and the passports were given to him. But before setting out for Italy, Dostoyevsky decided to make a fortune at the roulette tables in Baden, and accordingly they set out for Germany.

Polina describes in her journal how she tormented him by making him keep his promise to "live like a brother" with her. Here is her journal entry for September 6, the day after they arrived in Baden:

> Our journey with F. M. is quite amusing. While getting our visas, he got out of hand at the Papal Legation; and all the way here he spoke in verses, and now here, where we found two bedrooms only with some difficulty, and wrote down in the book *"Officer,"* and we both laughed over it a good deal.
>
> He is playing roulette all the time, and is very carefree. On the way he told me he was hopeful of winning, though previously he maintained he had no hope at all. I said nothing to him about all this, though I knew that

nothing would come of it. He said, too, that he approved of my determination to leave Paris. He had not expected it. One cannot, of course, build any hopes on such things —quite the contrary. Last night these aspirations of his were quite clear.

At ten o'clock we were drinking tea. I was tired during the day, and so when I finished I lay down on the bed, and I asked F. M. to come and sit close to me. I was in a good mood. I took his hand and for a long time held it in mine. He said it felt good to sit like that.

I told him I had been unfair and rude to him in Paris, and apparently I had thought only of myself, but I had really thought of him too, and I had said nothing, because I did not want to hurt his feelings. All at once he got up to go away, but he stumbled on my shoes which were lying close to the bed, and then he quickly turned back to me and sat down again.

"Where were you going?" I asked.

"I wanted to shut the window."

"Then shut it, if you want to."

"No, it is not necessary. You don't know what came over me just now," he said with a strange expression.

"What happened?" I looked at his face, which was quite agitated.

"I wanted to kiss your foot."

"Why?" I said in great embarrassment, and I was almost frightened by him, and I tucked my feet in.

"The idea came to me, and I decided to kiss them."

Then he asked me if I wanted to sleep, and I said: no, I wanted to sit with him. Thinking about going to sleep and undressing, I asked him whether the chambermaid was coming to remove the tea things. He was sure she wouldn't come. Then he looked at me in a way which made me feel uncomfortable, and I told him so.

"Yes, I too feel uncomfortable," he said with a strange smile.

I hid my face in the pillow. Then I asked him again whether the chambermaid was coming, and he again replied that she would not come.

"Then go to your room," I said. "I want to sleep."

"I'll go now," he said, but he remained there a little longer, kissing me ardently, and finally lighting his candle. Mine had burned out.

"You won't have any light," he said.

"No, I have a whole candle."

"But that's mine."

"I have another."

"You always find the right answers," he said, smiling, and left the room. He did not bolt his door, and soon came back into the room on the pretext of shutting my window. He came up to me and urged me to get undressed.

"I'm going to undress," I said, making believe I was only waiting for him to leave.

He went out, came back again on some excuse, and then he left and shut the door.

Today he mentioned last night and said he must have been drunk. Then he said he supposed it was disagreeable for me when he tormented me in this fashion. I answered that it was nothing to me, and did not dwell on the subject, so as to avoid giving him hope nor yet make him quite hopeless. He said I had a very mischievous smile, and no doubt I thought him stupid, and he was himself perfectly aware of his stupidity, but it was unconscious on his part.[6]

This artless and terrifying extract from Polina's journal is worth quoting at length because it shows Dostoyevsky at the mercy of a woman whose greatest pleasure lay in inflaming his desire and then denying him. He depended terribly upon her favors, and when she denied him he was reduced to quivering jelly. She had no love for him; he was simply a brother to whom she could always run for advice.

Sometimes she pitied him, and then it would occur to her that the rules she had elaborated were perhaps too strict. She was sorry when he lost 3,000 francs at the tables. "Partly I am sorry,"

[6] *Ibid.,* pp. 58–9.

she wrote, "because there is no way to repay him for his worries, but there's nothing very much I can do. Am I under an obligation —no, of course not!" Dostoyevsky gave up his effort to make a fortune from the tables when he had only 120 francs left. They made their way to Geneva, where he pawned his watch and Polina pawned a ring, and they waited in daily fear for the moment when the hotel keeper would present his bill. They had just enough money to reach Turin, where money from St. Petersburg awaited them.

> September 17, 1863. Turin.
> A feeling of tenderness again for F. M. I reproached him for something or other, and afterwards felt I was in the wrong. I wanted to smooth things over, and found myself being tender. He responded with such joy that I was deeply touched, and I became doubly tender. While I was sitting close to him and looking at him caressingly, he said: 'There's that familiar look; it's a long time since I have seen it.' I sank on his breast and began to cry.[7]

From Turin, too, she recorded one of those strange outbursts of Dostoyevsky, which might have been spoken by one of the characters of *The Devils:*

> While we were dining, he watched a little girl learning her lessons, and said: "There, just imagine a little girl like that with an old man, and suddenly some Napoleon or other says: 'Raze the whole town!' That's how it has always been in the world.[7]

This story is so characteristic that it provides a basis for believing that Polina recorded her impressions with reasonable accuracy. She made no attempt in her journal to conceal that she was deliberately taunting him, hoping that he would capitulate, divorce Maria, and marry her. She had also another purpose: to punish him because she had surrendered to him. "You cannot

[7] *Ibid.,* p. 60.

forgive me because you once gave yourself to me," he told her, "and now you are taking your revenge. That is a feminine trait." "She is a great egotist," he wrote to his sister afterward. "Her egotism and self-love are colossal. She demands everything from others, and denies that she has the slightest obligation to them." In her way she was a little like the Prince Valkonsky, who took the devil's part in *The Insulted and Injured*.

Polina seems to have driven him to the edge of madness. She was an expensive traveling companion, and he was continually writing to St. Petersburg for money to pay for their joint escapades. From Turin they traveled to Genoa, and then took ship for Rome. Polina amused herself by making eyes at handsome sailors, and she continued to invite Dostoyevsky to sit beside her bed, and she continued to rebuff his advances. She noted in her journal:

> F. M. again turned everything into a joke, and as he was leaving me, said it was humiliating to leave in this way (it was one o'clock in the morning, I was lying undressed on my bed). He said: "Russians never retreat." [8]

Neither Dostoyevsky nor Polina have left any impressions of their visit to Rome, where they stayed only a few days. They went on to Naples, and soon they were sailing back to Genoa. Alexander Herzen was on the same boat with his family. Polina was pleased with the attentions she received from the famous writer, and Herzen has recorded that he found her "very witty." Witty or not, she was still tempting Dostoyevsky with a dazzling display of her charms, and then repulsing him. Finally their quarrels became so violent that they decided to go their separate ways, Polina to Paris, Dostoyevsky to Homburg and the gambling tables. Five days after she arrived at her old apartment in Paris she received a letter from Dostoyevsky saying he had lost everything at roulette and begging for money to return home.

[8] *Ibid.*, p. 63.

Lack of generosity was not one of Polina's faults. She immediately borrowed money and sent it to him. By the end of October he was back in St. Petersburg, hurrying to join his dying wife who was now in the last stages of consumption.

In his novel *The Gambler,* Dostoyevsky later described his travels with Polina in a single sentence. "Everything," he wrote, "was fantastic, unsubstantial, and like nothing on earth."

As the years passed, he met her occasionally, and kept up a desultory correspondence with her. The days of enchantment were over even before he set out to meet her in Paris, but he still retained a curious affection for the woman who hurt his pride more deeply than any other. Polina felt no twinges of conscience. She returned to Paris, unsuccessfully sought to renew her affair with Salvador, and had passing affairs with a number of men whose names are recorded in the pages of her journal. There was an elderly Englishman, a young Georgian, a Dutchman, and many Frenchmen. Sometimes they would ask her about her celebrated affair with Dostoyevsky. "They talk to me about F. M.," she wrote. "Well, I hate him. He made me suffer so much when it was possible to do without suffering."

By all accounts she was a brilliant woman, but the journals rarely suggest that she possessed an acute intelligence. Yet among her papers there was found the rough outline of a letter which testifies to an acute understanding of Dostoyevsky. Though the letter is undated, she is evidently writing about their behavior during the tour. She wrote:

> You comported yourself like a serious man, preoccupied with your affairs, performing your duties according to your own fashion and not forgetting to enjoy your pleasures. On the contrary, you may have insisted on your pleasures, following the precept of some great doctor or philosopher who once declared that a hard drinker should get thoroughly drunk once a month.[9]

[9] *Ibid.,* p. 170.

Polina Suslova

It was not, however, the final taunt. There were more minor pinpricks to come. In the last years of his life, when his novels and *The Diary of a Writer* had made him very famous, an unknown visitor was announced. She was heavily veiled. Dostoyevsky stood up when she entered his study, and said: "Whom have I the honor of receiving?"

In answer she quickly removed her veil. Dostoyevsky still did not recognize her.

"Be kind enough to tell me your name," he said.

"You don't recognize me?"

"No."

The strange visitor allowed the veil to drop, and without a word marched out of the room.

Dostoyevsky described the incident to his wife. "She hasn't changed in the least," he said, "but she has disappeared from my life so completely that I failed to recognize her."

In the year of Dostoyevsky's death, Polina married the great critic V. V. Rozanov, who was then still an undergraduate. He was twenty-four, and she was over forty, but she was still beautiful, her fine imperious face unlined, her large eyes blazing with pride and self-assurance. In a photograph taken about that time she resembles the last Empress of China. Rozanov described her later as "a Russian Catherine de Medici," and he seems not to have been surprised when she left him for a shopkeeper.

She died in the Crimea in 1918, having survived her first lover by nearly forty years.

PITY AND LOVE

WHEN DOSTOYEVSKY returned to Russia, he was like a man making a rendezvous with disaster. Almost nothing happened as he hoped it would happen. He could not work; he could not find the money to finance the new magazine which was to replace *Time;* he was suffering from piles and had a series of severe epileptic attacks; and his wife was dying. He reached Vladimir, where she was staying, at the end of October 1863, and immediately decided to remove her to Moscow. She was in the last stages of consumption, with flushed cheeks and a fierce excitement coursing through her wasted body. All through the winter he remained by her bedside, watching over her as she lay dying.

Before they were married, he had loved her with the desperate love of a lonely man for a beautiful and cultivated woman. Within a few short years her beauty had perished, and her once cultivated mind had given way before the ravages of disease. Always quarrelsome and unpredictable, she had become irrational to the point of madness. She was continually winding up clocks until the springs broke. She complained that the sick-room was full of devils, and the doctor had to wave them out of the window with a handkerchief. She would go into hysterics if Pasha, the ugly son of her marriage with Alexander Issayev, came near her. Her husband watched her dying like a man obsessed with pity, and sometimes he was frozen with horror at the thought of the lonely old age which awaited him. She had never loved him, and he had long ceased to love her; yet he felt closest to her and to his brother Mikhail.

Maria knew her end was near, but sometimes there would come inexplicable moments when she felt a new strength in her veins and she would speak of spending the summer in Astrakhan or the Crimea. She had fits of sobbing. Her eyes were enormous; her skin was stretched tight over the bone; and sometimes her husband, struggling with a new story called *Notes from Underground* and with all the problems involved in launching the new magazine which was called *The Epoch,* could scarcely recognize her. Mercifully there were no financial problems; he had received a small inheritance, and the doctor's fees could always be postponed to some distant date in the future, for the doctor was a friend of the family.

More sorrow came in February. Varya, Mikhail's favorite daughter, died of scarlet fever, and Mikhail, who had been ill all winter, grew progressively worse, although he succeeded in publishing *The Epoch,* a skimpy magazine with a doubtful future. To drown his sorrows, Mikhail began drinking. His brother had better ways of drowning sorrow, working every morning on *Notes from Underground.*

On March 20, 1864, Dostoyevsky was wondering whether his wife would live to Easter; the doctor was saying she might die at any minute. All hope had gone. In despair he returned feverishly to the short story. He wrote to his brother:

> I went back to work on my story. I want to finish it as quickly as possible, and at the same time I want to do it as well as anything I have done. It's much more difficult to write than I thought. I must absolutely make a success of it for my own sake. It's written in a strange brutal style, very violent, and some people may hate it. That's why there must be poetry flowing through it, so making it bearable. I have hopes that it will improve.[1]

[1] *Letters:* 174. March 20, 1864.

The short story improved, but there was no improvement in Maria's health. "Under no circumstances can she last more than two weeks," he wrote to his brother a week later. "I will try to finish the story as quickly as possible, but it is hardly a propitious time." In April Maria's prolonged and fearful death agony began. Hourly they expected her death, but she lingered on. She possessed an unexpected strength. "Each day we expect her to die," he wrote to Mikhail on April 2nd. A week later she was still clinging to life. He wrote to his stepson Pasha on April 10th: "Your mother's condition grows progressively worse. The doctor has given up hope. Pray to God, Pasha."

On April 15th Maria vomited a great quantity of blood. There was so much blood that she was nearly choked to death by it. She lingered through the day, her small body, "as thin as a matchstick" shaking with violent tremors, her breathing raucous and labored. She died at seven o'clock in the evening after blessing all those who were gathered round the bed. The body was washed, and according to the fashion of the time it was laid out on the table, and later that night or on the next day Dostoyevsky wrote in his diary a strange, tortured sermon on his hopes of immortality and on the annihilation of the self into Christ. He wrote:

> April 16th. Maria is lying on the table. Shall I ever see Maria again? Can one love another as oneself according to the law of Christ? The law of the self attaches us to earth. The I is always in the way. Only Christ can help us to escape. The Christ after whom we strive is eternal, the very ideal of eternity, and it is a law of nature that man must strive. Meanwhile ever since the advent of Christ as the human ideal according to the flesh, it has become clear as day that the self must be annihilated (at the very moment of annihilation, at the moment when it is about to reach its aim), and at this moment man discovers himself and persuasively recognizes himself and vindicates the strength of his nature,

and so comes to his most important contribution of himself by way of the completeness of the annihilation of his self—the self so completely destroyed—and thereupon he is wholly delivered up, surrendering his undivided spirit wholly and indivisibly to all, and thus he enters the Paradise of Christ. . . .

The teaching of materialism—universal corruption and mechanical sciences mean death.

The teaching of history and philosophy—the annihilation of corruption leading to God and eternal life.[2]

There is a great deal more of it, and sometimes as he writes Dostoyevsky seems to be straining towards truths that were not completely stated until he composed *The Legend of the Grand Inquisitor*. The vision of eternal life weighs heavily on him. There will be no marrying or giving in marriage; only a peace beyond understanding. To achieve that peace there must first be the destruction of the self, that pathetic remnant of the earthly life which had bound him to Maria. Against the self he rages with a kind of helpless abandonment, seeing no hope for himself, and the vision of eternal life vanishes as he writes.

He suffered another blow a few weeks later, when his beloved brother Mikhail died. He was so crushed that for days he walked about like a man in a state of shock. Mikhail's estate amounted to 300 rubles; there were outstanding debts connected with *The Epoch* amounting to 33,000 rubles. Dostoyevsky regarded his brother's debts as his own, and assumed responsibility for them. He also assumed responsibility for his brother's family. Months later he wrote to Baron Wrangel a heartrending letter describing those two deaths which shook him as though he had been struck by a thunderbolt:

When my wife died, even though I had suffered to see her dying for a whole year, and even though I was sorrowfully aware of all that I was burying with her—

[2] *Sovremenniya Zapiski,* Paris, 1932. B. Ksheglavtsev: "Dostoyevsky: O lubvi i bessmertiy," page 50.

still I could never have imagined how empty and meaningless my life would become when the earth covered her. A year has passed, and my feelings have not changed. I buried her, and then I fled to my brother in St. Petersburg, for he alone remained to me. Three months later he died after a short illness, the acute stage lasting only three days.

So I was left alone, and very frightened. My whole life was broken in two. The first half of my life contained everything I had lived for. The second half, now beginning, was new and unfamiliar, and there was no one to replace those who had gone. Literally, I had no reason to live. Should I make new connections, invent a new existence? The very idea appalled me. Then I understood for the first time that no one would ever replace them, that these were the only ones I had loved in the world, and a new love was neither desirable nor possible. Around me there was only a cold emptiness.[3]

Notes from Underground was written in that prevailing mood of coldness and emptiness. It is a harsh, relentless story, saying at great length many things he had said before; but never had he said them with such icy passion, with such terrible lucidity. In the letter to himself he had written while Maria lay on the table, he celebrated the destruction of the self and the coming of the Kingdom of Heaven. *Notes from Underground* celebrates a world in which there is no hope of Heaven. In that world there are only maggot-like men imitating scorpions and stinging themselves to death with their own tails.

It is a book written without illusions, in the chill anterooms of the soul. The English translation of the title fails to convey the vehemence of the original. More accurately it should be "Notes from under the Floorboards." There is the suggestion of vermin breeding in the darkness of a fetid cellar and preparing destruction.

Though there is malice in the book, it is malice heightened and sharpened by genius, made tolerable by a desperate humility.

[3] *Letters:* 199, March 31, 1865.

Pity and Love

In this profoundly original work Dostoyevsky attacked all the accepted dogmas of his time. All dogmas were worthless, for they failed to take into account the human condition. They failed in particular to take into account man's ineffectiveness, his talent for bungling, his almost superhuman capacity to behave like an insect. "We are oppressed at being men," he cries. "We are stillborn, and for generations have not been begotten." Civilization is bankrupt, and if we must have proof we have only to look at soldiers—the most subtle shedders of blood are invariably the most civilized men.

> Civilization has made man, if not more bloodthirsty, then certainly more hideously and more contemptibly bloodthirsty. In the past he looked on bloodshed as an act of justice and exterminated those he thought necessary to exterminate with a clear conscience; but now we consider bloodshed an abomination, and accordingly we engage in this abomination more than ever.[4]

So he goes on, hammering at the current expressions of truth and goodness; reviling science, which has built stone walls around the imaginations of men, and which seems intent on reducing the world to a machine, and celebrating the crawling things "under the floorboards," who are at least more honest in their intentions than the men who pontificate about *la nature et la verité*. These gentlemen have forgotten the evil in the heart, the doom that hangs over mankind, man's fatal tendency to fantasy. They trumpet from the high places that 2 plus 2 equals 4, as though the statement possessed a supreme validity of its own, permitting them to commit any crime that enters their heads. Dostoyevsky's attack on civilization is put in the mouth of an insanely bad-tempered, retired civil servant, but is all the more effective for that. Half commentary, half story describing the civil servant's ineffectiveness, *Notes from Underground* is a work that can be put beside the more bitter pronouncements of Dean Swift.

[4] *Notes from Underground,* Part I, Chapter vii.

The explosive violence of the book is something to marvel at. It is not hate and intolerance and waspishness only; it is all these things raised to a universal level. The spirit cries out in agony of soul against the monstrous creations of men, and finds no solace anywhere. Like those Buddhist monks who deliberately allow themselves to be suspended head downward over an abyss, Dostoyevsky confronts the nothingness of life with his own horror, his own cries echoing back from the walls of nothingness.

There is so much controlled excitement in the early chapters that some scholars have been tempted to discover all kinds of obscure meanings in it. There are some who claim that the forty-year-old government clerk who writes the notes is only one more of those "doubles," whose presence in Dostoyevsky's works have sustained a multitude of Ph.D. theses. Thus Prince Myshkin is pitted against Rogozhin, and Dmitry Karamazov against his brother Alyosha, as though it were possible to write a dramatic novel without pitting opposites against one another. There are others who claim that the book is an undisguised and closely argued polemic against the philosopher Chernyshevsky who celebrated the coming of an anarchic paradise on earth in his novel *What Is to Be Done?* When Dostoyevsky was writing *Notes from Underground*, Chernyshevsky was a prisoner in the Peter and Paul Fortress, and the last man to deserve attack in Dostoyevsky's mind. Nothing is gained by refining the savage text.

Dostoyevsky wrote *Notes from Underground* when his whole world was falling apart. He was deeply in debt, his wife and his beloved brother were dying or already dead, and he had very little hope of survival. He had despaired many times, but never so helplessly. There was only one faint ray of light, only one solace—the exquisite joy which sometimes comes when a man recognizes at last his own helplessness and degradation. "Despair, too, has its moments of intense pleasure, intense delight," he wrote, and part of the purpose of these terrifying notes is to examine the pleasures of despair. In much the same way the European mystics have

chronicled "the dark night of the soul." Never again was Dostoyevsky to write with quite that sustained horror of the world
around him.

Perhaps the best commentary on *Notes from Underground*
was provided by Aristotle who wrote in a dialogue on philosophy
preserved by Cicero:

> Imagine a race of underground men living a civilized
> existence, provided with every necessity and luxury, but
> deprived of the light of day. And if one day the jaws of
> earth were opened, and they beheld for the first time the
> earth and the seas and the shining sun and the changing
> moon and the unchanging order of the heavens, such
> men would surely confess that the gods exist and these
> things are the works of the gods.

For Dostoyevsky, as for the underground men, divine despair
might be only an interlude before the coming of joy. And indeed,
shortly before his death, in *The Diary of a Writer,* he replied to the
accusations he had hurled against the world and against God in
Notes from Underground in a statement of the purest joy, saying:
"My hosanna has crossed the purgatory of doubt and is purified
in the chalice of temptation." There is a sense in which all his
major novels are the record of a man's progress through "the dark
night of the soul" until he comes into the presence of God.

His life, however, was not all bitterness. While editing *The
Epoch,* he found occasional moments of pleasure. One day during
the summer he received a letter from an unknown admirer, and
with the letter came a short story written with verve and imagination, called *The Dream,* about a young girl's hopeless love for a
poor student. Dostoyevsky was touched by the story which was
filled with a romantic despair, and he was perhaps even more
touched by the letter in which the young woman—for it was evidently a young woman—proclaimed her undying faith in his genius. He decided to publish the story, and he wrote a long letter
urging her to devote herself to writing. "Write, write," he wrote.

"It would truly rejoice me if you would tell me something about yourself—how old you are, in what surroundings you live. It is of importance to me to know all this, in order to judge your talents."

The mysterious correspondent did not write immediately. At intervals she sent him two more stories, and told him only enough about herself to whet his appetite for more information. One of the stories was called *The Novice,* a title which incurred the displeasure of the ecclesiastical censorship, and Dostoyevsky accordingly changed it to *Michael.* He also omitted a large section dealing with Michael's attitudes towards monks and monasteries. "The greatest mastery of an author," he wrote, "comes in knowing when to cut. He who knows and *has the courage* to cut—that man will go far." He was a little put out by her silence, her refusal to say anything about herself.

The writer of the stories was a tall, slender, long-legged woman of twenty, a descendant of Matthias Korvinus, the King of Hungary who fought the Turks to a standstill. Her name was Anyuta Korvin-Krukovskaya. She was a striking beauty with deep-set widely-spaced green eyes—"as green as a mermaid's"—and long silky blonde hair which she wore in two severe braids. She lived with her parents and young sister on an immense estate called Palibino in Vitebsk province: and there, in one of the towers of the great house, she had built a kind of hermitage for herself where she spent her days reading, writing and dreaming of being a nun, a recluse, or a world-famous writer, depending upon her moods. Her father was a retired general, who owned property all over the province. The family regarded itself as royal rather than aristocratic.

Anyuta was corresponding with Dostoyevsky through the housekeeper, but it so happened that on September 4, 1864 the housekeeper was busy superintending a party given for the neighbors in honor of Anyuta's mother's name day. On that day among the letters brought by the postman on his weekly visit to the estate was one from Dostoyevsky addressed to the housekeeper, and the envelope bore the name and address of *The Epoch.* The general was surprised, summoned the housekeeper, ordered her to open the letter, read it, and immediately fell ill. He suffered from gallstones and heart disease, and the doctors had urged him to avoid every kind of excitement.

General Vasily Korvin-Krukovsky was a gentlemen of the old school. He took to his bed, but ordered the festivities to continue. There was to be a banquet followed by a ball, attended by the officers of a regiment quartered nearby. Anyuta was dancing a quadrille when she saw her mother looking at her in a strange way.

"We know everything," her mother said. "Your father has read Dostoyevsky's letter, and he is dying of shame and anger."

Anyuta turned pale with horror.

"For God's sake compose yourself," her mother went on. "Remember the house is full of guests, and they would be only too pleased to have something to gossip about! Go back and dance as though nothing had happened!"

Anyuta did as she was told, but there came the inevitable confrontation with her father, who was more alarmed by the 300 rubles which Dostoyevsky had sent than by the thought that his daughter was corresponding with a noted êx-convict.

"What can one expect from a girl who corresponds with a complete stranger without her parent's knowledge, and even takes money from him?" he scolded her. "Today you are selling your work, and one day you will sell yourself!"

Anyuta was stung to the quick, but there was nothing she could do. She retired to her hermitage in the high tower, sulked, confided in her young sister, and waited. When her father ordered her to swear on the Bible that she would never correspond with Dostoyevsky again, she refused. As always, she was determined to have her own way.

In time the civil war within the family gave way to an uneasy truce and then to peace. The general in a forgiving mood asked her to read the story aloud to him, and when she had finished reading it, his eyes were full of tears. He got up and silently stalked from the room. A few days later he gave her permission to write to Dostoyevsky and even to see him during her forthcoming visit to St. Petersburg.

In January 1865 the entire family except for the general drove by sleigh and railway to the capital, staying with aunts and cousins who lived in a fashionable mansion on Vasilyevsky Island. On February 28 Anyuta sent Dostoyevsky an invitation to call on her. Two elderly German aunts acted as chaperones. Anyuta's mother and her sister Sonya, a bright-eyed child of fourteen, were also present. Dostoyevsky was ill-at-ease. He looked old and strained, and kept fingering his thin yellow beard and biting his lips. Anyuta was tongue-tied, and her mother tried unsuccessfully to keep the conversation going. Then they all fell into an awkward silence, and Dostoyevsky took his hat, bowed, and hurried away without shaking hands with anyone.

Anyuta thought she would never see him again. She was hurt by the behavior of her aunts, who had gazed with steely-eyed distaste at the middle-aged author, who was not at all the kind of man they expected. There were recriminations. For heaven's sake, why did you all look at him as though he were some wretched monkey suddenly descended upon us? Her mother wept, and Anyuta flung herself out of the room to find another hermitage.

Five days later Dostoyevsky arrived at the house, finding only the two sisters at home. Anyuta seems to have arranged the meeting. This time there was no wall between them. They sat on the sofa, held hands, and talked as though they had known one another for years. The ice was broken. He no longer looked like a middle-aged man; he was young, gay, passionately interested in the beautiful Anyuta and already half in love with her. Sonya showed him her poems, and he praised them eagerly. The mother returned from a shopping expedition to find Anyuta and Dostoyevsky sitting together on a sofa. She was out of breath and laden with parcels, and therefore at a disadvantage. Anyuta threw her arms around her mother's neck and begged her to let Dostoyevsky stay. He stayed for dinner, and soon he became the familiar friend of the family, visiting them three or four times a week.

Sonya adored him, Anyuta was falling in love with him, and the mother tolerated him. Sonya remembered afterward that he was especially captivating when he was allowed to talk in monologues; he was useless in any general conversation. So in the course of a few weeks they learned his entire history. He told them about the early days when he was writing *Poor Folk* and received the blessing of Belinsky, and about his arrest and imprisonment, and the long years in Siberia. He told them how one day on Easter Eve an old friend came to see him and they spent the night talking about everything under the sun—philosophy, literature, art, religion. He had hardly spoken to anyone all winter, and he was in that strange, exalted state which comes after long silence from the sheer pleasure of having someone to talk to. His friend was an atheist, and they discussed their differing views. Suddenly Dostoyevsky heard himself saying: "There is a God— there is!" and at that same moment the bells of the neighboring church rang the matins for Easter morning, the air trembling with the sound of their music. "I felt as though heaven descended to earth and completely absorbed me," Dostoyevsky told the two sisters. "I was inspired and penetrated by God's spirit. 'There is a God!' I cried, and then I knew nothing more."

He was telling them about his first attack of epilepsy which seems to have taken place during the last year of his imprisonment at Omsk.

"You strong people," he went on, "you simply have no idea of the bliss which epileptics experience in the moments preceding their attacks. Mahomet assures us in the Koran that he saw Paradise and even visited it, and all sensible people mocked at him and called him a liar and a deceiver. But he did not lie. He had quite truly been to Paradise during an attack of epilepsy.

"I do not know if his bliss lasted a second, an hour, or a month, but believe me, I would not exchange it for all the happiness that life could grant me!"

While he was talking, Sonya, who was watching him like a hawk, noticed his face was contorted and his mouth was working convulsively. Both sisters thought he was about to suffer another epileptic attack. He seemed to know what they were thinking, passed his hand over his face and smiled a little.

"Don't be afraid," he said. "I always know beforehand when it is coming over me."

He left almost immediately, but the next day when he returned he told them he had really suffered an attack during the night.

Towards the end of their stay in St. Petersburg the family gave a party for their relatives who were scattered all over the city. Some were prominent officials, others had fallen into obscurity and lived out their lives in remote corners of Vasilyevsky Island. It was a very large party. It included the wife of a minister, a ruined landowner from the Baltic provinces, and an ancient German of high position, who was continually reminding the two girls: "Your mother was a great beauty, and neither of you are as pretty as she was."

It was one of those dull parties which are endured with fanatical stoicism by the hosts, and with well-bred resolution by the guests. Dostoyevsky, the family favorite, arrived in an ill-fitting evening suit. He walked gracelessly at all times; now he walked still more gracelessly. He was in a state of confusion and irritation. He disliked many of the guests at sight, and when he was introduced to them, he behaved abominably, making low growls and turning his back on them. He monopolized Anyuta, leading her to a corner and devouring her with his attentions, continually holding her hand and whispering into her ear. Her duty was to entertain her guests, but when she tried to leave him, he said coolly: "Stay where you are, Anyuta Vasilyevna, I have not yet told you—" Her mother interrupted the one-sided idyll, spoke sharply, and carried off her daughter to meet the guests.

Dostoyevsky detested society, loathed parties, and was always infuriated in the presence of handsome young officers in uniform, perhaps because they reminded him of the officers who attended his execution on the Semyonov parade ground. He was incensed when a particularly handsome young officer of cuirassiers presumed to claim the attentions of Anyuta. The officer was well-bred, charming, the possessor of finely turned legs which were well-displayed by his fashionable tight-fitting trousers. Dostoyevsky saw him engaged in a *tête-à-tête* with her, and immediately came to the conclusion that the purpose of the party was to find an eligible husband for her. He imagined that Anyuta hated and despised the young fop, but was trapped by the remorseless conventions of high society, and he suddenly launched into an amazing speech, afterwards remembered in detail, for it shocked everyone who heard it.

"Were the Gospels written for the women of this world?" Dostoyevsky demanded in his hoarse, quavering voice. "It is written in one place: 'Male and female created He them,' and in another place: 'A man shall leave his father and mother, and cleave unto his wife.' This is what Christ says about marriage, but what can be said about those mothers whose only thought is to marry off their daughters as advantageously as possible?"

That extraordinary speech, spoken with great emphasis, so that he gave the impression of a gun discharging cannon balls at his frightened audience, was completely in character, for Dostoyevsky rarely succeeded in hiding his jealously and he was continually having recourse to biblical texts to defend whatever untenable position he had assumed in his private life. When he was excited he leaned forward in a crouching position, his shoulders narrowed, and his whole face seemed to be convulsed with emotion. His audience was a group of well-bred Germans. They understood every word; they were appalled and shocked, and after a few moments of dazed silence they did what all well-bred people do in similar emergencies: they all began talking at once to drown the memory of the terrible *contretemps*. Dostoyevsky glared at them savagely, withdrew into a corner and maintained a sullen, hurt silence throughout the rest of the evening.

The next time he came to the house he was treated coldly by the mother of the sisters, but she could not be angry with him for long, and he was soon admitted again into the bosom of the family.

The relationship between Anyuta and Dostoyevsky was changing. Anyuta was at the age when a young woman realizes her mastery over men, and she no longer worshipped him from a distance. She became contrary. She enjoyed teasing him. It amused her to poke fun at him. As she became more critical of him, so he in turn became increasingly critical of her, demanded a full accounting of her activities during the day, a list of all the people she met, and a verbatim account of what she said to them. The love affair was entering a critical stage. For Anyuta he was no longer the famous author, but a friend of the family who made intolerable demands on her, to be placated only if it amused her.

There were sudden flares of temper, followed by long silences. Anyuta would pick up her sewing and pretend to be immersed in her task. Dostoyevsky would snatch the sewing away. Anyuta would fold her hands resignedly, and refuse to speak.

"Well, what were you doing yesterday evening?" Dostoyevsky would ask irritably.

"At the ball," Anyuta would reply, shrugging her pretty shoulders.

"You danced, I suppose?"

"Naturally."

"With your cousin?"

"With him and with others."

"And all this pleases you?"

Pity and Love

"Yes, of course," Anyuta would say, taking up her needlework. "There isn't anything better to do."

"Then you are a light-minded, thoughtless nincompoop—that is what you are!"

So they quarreled, and the bright-eyed fourteen-year-old Sonya kept watch, delighted to see them quarreling and still more delighted to be in the presence of Dostoyevsky, whom she worshipped this side of idolatry. She, too, was beautiful, with her thick, curly hair and small, dark, serious face. She felt that she understood him perfectly. There existed no walls between them. She told herself she could read his thoughts, and in her dreams she was always beside him—on the Semyonov parade ground, in prison, in the frozen wastes of Siberia. Sometimes Dostoyevsky would take advantage of her adoration to taunt Anyuta. He said once to Anyuta: "You think you are beautiful, but your little sister will be much more beautiful. Her features are more expressive, and she has real gypsy eyes. You are only a pretty little German, that's all!"

At these taunts she smiled disdainfully; she knew her power over him, but she did not yet know what she would do with her power.

Sonya played the piano chiefly because she thought her playing pleased him, though he had no ear for music, and would listen to a street organ with the same rapture or the same air of boredom as he would listen to a Beethoven sonata. Because he praised her playing, she obtained permission to have an expensive tutor, practiced continually, and in three months made so much progress that she was able to play the *Sonate Pathétique* passably well. It was one of the few pieces which Dostoyevsky genuinely liked, because it always awoke in him a world of forgotten emotions.

One evening, when spring was coming and the whole family was about to depart for Palibino, Anyuta complained of a headache when her mother insisted that she attend a farewell dinner given by the wife of an ambassador. The young people remained at home, and as usual Dostoyevsky slipped into the house. He was in a strange, nervous mood, very gentle. He knew it might be the last time he would see them for many months.

Sonya sat at the piano, playing the *Sonate Pathétique,* her supreme offering to Dostoyevsky. She was still playing when she suddenly realized that she was alone in the room. Alarmed, she ran into the next room, but there was no one there. She found them at last in a little curtained alcove, sitting close together on a sofa, holding hands by the light of a lamp with a heavy shade. Dostoyevsky was in the light, but Anyuta was in shadow. He was pale and visibly excited, and he spoke in those passionate hoarse whispers which Sonya knew only too well.

"Believe me, dearest, I loved you from the very first moment when I set eyes on you!" Dostoyevsky was saying. "Even before that, when I read the letter you sent me, I had a presentiment about it. I do not love you merely as a friend, but with my whole being!"

Sonya had seen more than she wanted to see; she fled in panic, knocking over a chair. She heard her sister shouting, but she did not stop running until she had reached the safety of the bedroom which the sisters shared. She threw off her dress and petticoats, crawled into bed, and buried her face under the sheets. Her heart was pounding, and she knew that she was hopelessly in love with Dostoyevsky. After what seemed an eternity of weeping and apprehension she heard the quick ring of the doorbell; her mother and her aunts were returning from the ambassador's. There were voices in the hallway, and these voices were suddenly interrupted by the recognizable voice of Dostoyevsky. Sonya even thought she heard him pulling on his galoshes. Then he left, and the house grew silent, and some time later Anyuta came to the bedroom. Sonya was wide awake.

"Do you love him?" she asked pointblank.

Anyuta thought for a moment.

"No," she said slowly. "He is so good and noble, I thought at first I would really fall in love with him. But I am not the wife he needs. The woman he will marry must belong to him heart and soul, she must devote herself absolutely to him, surrender her whole life to him, think of him and only of him! I cannot do it! I must be true to myself! And then besides, he is so sensitive and *exigeant!* He wants to make me his prisoner and swallow me whole!"

Sonya recognized the truth of the statement and she understood perfectly what her sister was saying. She fell into a dreamless sleep.

A day or two later Dostoyevsky came to say good-bye. He stayed only for a few moments, behaved gently with Anyuta, and it was remembered that he was especially tender towards Sonya. He never saw her again, and seems to have been only vaguely aware that she became a famous mathematician under her married name of Sonya Kovalevsky. She held the chair of mathematics at the University of Stockholm and left an astonishing autobiography in which she described in minute detail her memories of Dostoyevsky when he was a constant visitor at their house. She remembered everything—his voice, his inflections, the way he held himself, and the innumerable stories he told. She saw him through the enchanted eyes of a fourteen-year-old child, and her entire account of him rings true.

Anyuta's autobiography, had she written it, might have been even more interesting. Dostoyevsky hinted that he was briefly engaged to her, but broke the engagement after learning that she would never change her political views. In the seventies, when he was staying at Staraya Russa, he found himself living only a few doors from her. By this time Anyuta had become a quiet matron living down her romantic past. In Paris she had married a young revolutionary, Victor Jaclard; together they were active during the Paris Commune, and Jaclard was arrested and sentenced to death.

Anyuta appealed to her father, who hurried to her side and, by bribing a guard with 20,000 francs at the fortress where her husband was imprisoned, succeeded in reuniting the couple.

Dostoyevsky never forgot Anyuta, and some traces of her appear in all the novels he wrote after the engagement was broken off. He was grateful for the affection lavished on him by those two highly-strung children. He needed them, for they entered his life at a period of profound discouragement, loving him and pitying him when he was downcast, reminding him that he was still young and capable of great achievements.

Very soon he was to launch the most classical and accomplished of all his novels, *Crime and Punishment*.

CRIME AND PUNISHMENT

THE POET Rainer Maria Rilke speaks of standing at a window by night and hearing a boy's cry and an old man's cough and a churchbell ringing, and gradually cough by cough, cry by cry, and bell by bell, the city would reveal itself to him in all its complexity. He believed that a city possessed a life of its own, and that it was perfectly possible to enter into its heart by a strenuous employment of patient imagination. The city—especially the city at night—could be assembled out of thousands of fragmentary impressions, and there would come a moment when the walls became diaphanous, revealing the lovers in their beds and the dying men coughing up their lungs in the hospitals as though they were present before his eyes.

The imagination of Rilke resembled thin beams of intensely colored light penetrating the darkness, going out, springing up again at a different angle and in a different place, always nervous and rarely at rest. Dostoyevsky's imagination was of another kind altogether. There is a thick yellowish light which does not penetrate very far, revealing little more than a face and the outline of a body. It is not strong enough to light up a house or a street, though it brilliantly illuminates small objects—a profile, a stair, a paperweight, a hand on a doorknob. Sometimes the light goes out, and the action proceeds in darkness. Dostoyevsky's beam is remarkably steady, and surprisingly resembles the floodlights used by the neo-romantic directors of Italian films after the second World War. In a night scene a single floodlight shines on a man running down a street. It is very bright, very dazzling, but we are to imagine the man is running in total darkness. Like the film director, Dostoyevsky sees no purpose in illuminating more than the essential features. All the rest of the world, the streets, the roofs, the factory chimneys, all these are invisible, or else they are diffused, out of focus, of no importance to his imagination.

With Dostoyevsky for the first time the light of the novelist is concentrated on the human face. There is a sense in which he invented the close-up, and all his novels consist of a series of close-ups glimpsed from a variety of angles. From a flicker of a brilliantly enlarged eyelid we deduce the movements of a soul.

Dostoyevsky's technique was a dangerous one, for sometimes his characters give the impression of living in a vacuum. We are told that they live in Moscow or St. Petersburg, but these are facts which we almost have to take on trust. They might be anywhere, or at least anywhere where there are tall houses with narrow, winding, dimly-lit stairways leading into complete silence and obscurity. A quite extraordinary amount of action takes place on those stairways or on landings in the presence of closed doors where the name plates have grown rusty and indecipherable. His figures emerge from buildings into lonely streets, and we are never permitted to see the jostling crowds and the sweating *droshky* drivers. There are only a few scenes which take place in full daylight. Dusk and darkness and the long white nights of St. Petersburg are his favorite setting. There are few colors, and only the most haphazard descriptions of people. We may be told that a character has "dark eyes and dark brown hair," but we do not know his height, his build, how he walks or how he carries himself. Almost his characters are anonymous, for even their names are very often the descriptions of a mood. Raskolnikov, for example, comes from *raskolnik,* meaning a "non-conformist" or a "dissenter." [1] Very rarely do his characters bear the names of ordinary, recognizable people. Very often his characters have the appearance of anonymous ghosts moving tragically and relentlessly through an anonymous city.

Here, for example, is Dostoyevsky's description of Rodion Raskolnikov as he wanders through St. Petersburg near the Kokushkin bridge:

> The heat in the street was terrible; and the stifling air, the crowds, the scaffolding, bricks, lime and dust, and the peculiar Petersburg stench so familiar to those who cannot afford a cottage in the country—all this worked painfully on the young man's overwrought nerves. There came from the pothouses, which are especially numerous in this part of the town, an intolerable stench, and the drunks he came upon every moment, although it was a working day, provided the finishing touches to a dismal and revolting picture. For a brief moment an expression of the profoundest disgust gleamed on the young man's refined face. Incidentally, he was an extraordinarily handsome young man, with beautiful dark eyes, dark brown hair, over the average in height, slim and well built. But he soon fell into a kind of deep reverie, or more accurately, into a kind of coma, and he went on his way without paying any attention to his surroundings and with no desire to observe them. From time to time he would mutter something to himself from the habit of indulging in soliloquies, a habit which he had just that moment confessed. At such moments he realized that his thoughts were hopelessly entangled, and

---

[1] A long list of names used by Dostoyevsky could be compiled, showing how he deliberately chose names which describe a mood or a character in broad terms. The following list could easily be extended: Devushkin, from *deva*, a maid; Golyadkin, from *goliy*, naked; Karamazov, from Tartar *kara*, black; Karmazinov, from French *cramoisi*, crimson; Lebyadkin, from *lebyed*, a swan; Shatov, from *shatkiy*, unsteady; Smerdyakov, from *smerdyet*, to stink; Stavrogin, from Greek *stauros*, a cross.

that he himself was very weak; for two days he had had hardly anything to eat.[2]

In this passage Dostoyevsky has merely sketched in the background. We do not see the crowds, the drunkards, the pothouses or the new buildings which are being erected; we are aware of them only as amorphous and hostile forces pressing down on Raskolnikov, like the walls of a prison. There is a cursory sketch of the hero: slim, well-built, hungry, with a fine face, empty of all expression except a momentary disgust. Characteristically Dostoyevsky speaks of the disgust *gleaming*—he uses the word *myelknut,* to flash for a moment and then vanish—and this word, set in the middle of the paragraph, is the kingpin round which the rest revolves. We are made aware of light, but it is the mysterious inner light of the human face.

Compare, for contrast, a passage from an unfinished novel by Lermontov, which also describes a young and handsome man walking in a state of extraordinary lassitude past the pothouses near the Kokushkin bridge:

> It was one of those humid November mornings in St. Petersburg, when the damp snow falls in flakes, and the houses look unwashed and somber, and the faces of the passers-by are all green. The drivers of the sleighs, waiting for people to climb into them, had fallen asleep under reddish-colored blankets. The long, wet hair of their poor nags was curled like lamb's wool. The mist gave distant objects a curious purple-mauve appearance.
>
> Over the sidewalk there came the occasional *clop-clop* of a policeman's rubber boots, and sometimes a burst of laughter from an underground pothouse when a drunk in a green plush overcoat and a waxed cloth cap was thrown out. Such scenes, you understand, are seen only in the suburbs such as the region around the Kokushkin bridge.
>
> At that moment a man was crossing the bridge. He was of middle height, neither thin nor fat, with heavy

[2] *Crime and Punishment,* Part I, Chapter i.

shoulders; he wore an overcoat and was dressed with taste. His varnished shoes, drenched with the mud and the snow, could hardly be seen. He gave the appearance of a man with no care in the world, his head lowered, his hands deep in his pockets, but there was something about his uneasy walk which suggested that he was afraid to come to the end of his journey or wished he was somewhere else. On the bridge he paused, looked up and gazed around him. It was Lugin. There were signs of weariness on his battered face, and there was a secret misery in his eyes.[3]

Here Lermontov is generously conveying a whole scene, describing all the salient objects in the neighborhood of his hero and convincingly arranging them so that the reader becomes intensely aware of the *ambiance* in which the hero walks. He gives you the atmosphere, the sights, the sounds, the colors. There is a kaleidoscope of colors—white snow, green faces, red blankets, purple objects in the distance, a green plush overcoat, glitter of black shoes. Everything is seen sharply with a wide-angle lens. Even Lugin, though he wears the uniform of a romantic hero, is a completely recognizable figure, sharply outlined. But there is no mystery in him. He is a self-portrait: the elegant Lermontov crosses the bridge, and when he pauses, it is to take out his notebook and jot down the important characteristics of the landscape. His shoes come from the best shoemakers, and his "secret misery" comes from Byron.

Dostoyevsky's picture of Raskolnikov is also a self-portrait: it is the face of Trutovsky's wonderfully expressive charcoal drawing done when the sitter was twenty-six, and the setting is the weather of his own soul. Dostoyevsky felt no need to describe the scenery; he would have regarded it as in the poorest taste if he surrounded Raskolnikov with the evidence of his powers of observation. Lermontov flings down his colors pell-mell; his aim

[3] M. Y. Lermontov: *Sobraniye Sochineniy* (Berlin: I. P. Ladizhnikov; 1921), Volume III, page 484.

is to startle you with his accurate observation and the lucidity of his mind. Dostoyevsky has no illusions about the mind's lucidity; he knows it is dark; and though a man may walk through it with a candle, he walks at his peril.

Dostoyevsky's St. Petersburg is a city of the mind ringed with towering and invisible walls, a river flowing through it, a police station, a few taverns, high stairways leading to rooms where there is almost no furniture. He was living at a time when the city was suffering from a vast industrial development with new factories coming up every day, but he seems to have been unaware of them. It is a city like a stage-set, made of painted cloth and cardboard, always unreal and strangely convincing only because the small handful of people who wander about the city are convincing. In the time of Peter the Great, when the city was rising with amazing rapidity on the edge of the Finnish lakes, the peasants were bewildered and said that Peter had drawn it down from the skies. Dostoyevsky sometimes wondered whether it would not return to the skies. The young Arkady Dolgoruky in *A Raw Youth* is haunted by the persistent fancy that when the fog rises, the whole city will rise with it, leaving only the famous statue of the bronze horseman. Everything will vanish like smoke, and the Finnish lakes will be exactly as they were before the coming of Peter the Great. "And often I am haunted by another question, which is utterly senseless: 'Here everything is flitting to and fro, but how can one tell, perhaps it is someone's dream, and there is not one real person here, nor one real action. Someone who is dreaming all this will suddenly wake up—and everything will suddenly disappear.' " So does Arkady Dolgoruky describe the insubstantial pageant of St. Petersburg, a city filled with the substantial presences of sin and guilt and the faces of solitary people working out the expiation of their crimes.

Occasionally, however, Dostoyevsky will permit the reader a tortured glimpse of his beloved city, which he never describes at length and always fleetingly. Here is another Arkady, in the story *The Faint Heart,* written before his exile in Siberia, as he returns to his home after realizing that his closest friend has gone mad:

> It was already dusk when Arkady returned home. As he approached the Neva he stood still for a minute and turned a keen glance down the river into the smoky distance hazy with frost, suddenly flushed with the last crimson glow of the blood-red sun slowly sinking on the misty horizon. Night lay over the city, and the vast expanse of the Neva—boundless, and swollen with frozen snow—shone in the last gleams of the sun with myriads of sparks from the silver needles of hoarfrost. The temperature had fallen to twenty below zero. Clouds of frozen steam rose from the hard-driven horses and pedestrians hurrying along the streets. The thin air quivered with the slightest sound, and columns of smoke rose up like giants from all the roofs on both sides of the river, and they streamed upwards into the cold sky, twining and untwining as they soared, so that it seemed that new buildings were rising above the old, and a new city was taking shape in the air. In this hour of twilight it seemed that all this world with all its inhabitants, the strong and the weak, with all their habitations, the hovels of the poor and the gilded palaces which are the solace of the powerful in this world, was like a phantasm, magical and illusory, a dream which vanishes in a moment and fades away like smoke in the dark blue sky.

This is the most graphic of all Dostoyevsky's rare descriptions of St. Petersburg, and characteristically he chose the moment of extinction before night descended on the city.

But though Dostoyevsky rarely describes the city, he never leaves us in doubt about where we are. He possessed a formidable sense of place. It is simply, as he indicated in one of his notes to *The Devils,* that he had more importang things to do than describe the colors of the sky, the appearance of buildings, and what it feels like to cross a bridge. "I do not have the time to paint

the details," he wrote. Nevertheless he is continually dropping
hints or making amazingly quick sketches of the scene. In his
wanderings Raskolnikov crosses another bridge. He notes the
cloudless sky, the bright blue waters of the Neva, and the glinting
cupola of the Cathedral," which is seen at its best about twenty
paces from the Chapel of St. Nicholas." Dostoyevsky delights in
these mathematical descriptions. He is always describing how far
his characters walk in feet or yards. His St. Petersburg is a kind
of abstraction imposed upon the St. Petersburg he knew, a thing
of straight lines, curiously silent, the shops closed or about to
close, and the air filled with a wheeling emptiness. He once described it as "the most abstract and premeditated city in the world."

When the novelist Pisemsky writes about St. Petersburg, it is
all noise and tumult, people rushing about, the whole city immersed in feverish activity. We see the washerwomen rinsing linen
from the rafts moored in the river; horses are being watered; the
water carriers are filling their great wooden tubs; the droshkies are
bowling down the long avenues; and the river is crowded with ships.
For him, St. Petersburg is alive and quivering. For Dostoyevsky, it
is a familiar and enchanted map.

There was one section of St. Petersburg especially familiar
to him. This was the Haymarket (*Sennaya Ploshchad*), a large
square reached by the Kokushkin Bridge and dominated by the
many towers of the Church of the Assumption. It was one of the
noisiest and most unpleasant places in the city during the day,
filled with the stalls of costermongers and vegetable sellers, and in
one corner meat was displayed on open barrows. Taverns surrounded it, stinking alleyways led off from it, and the horrible
smell of the place, carried by the wind, would sometimes reach as
far as the Winter Palace. Dostoyevsky lived very close to the
square, and, like Raskolnikov, he had a passion for wandering
aimlessly among the stalls and down the winding alleyways. Most
of the scenes in *Crime and Punishment* take place in the neighborhood of this square. But though Dostoyevsky was haunted by

the square, he never described as much as a single corner of it, and the only description he offers in the entire course of the novel consists of three or four lines to give an impression of the square emptying in the evening, the costermongers packing up their wares and joining their customers in the taverns.

But while St. Petersburg was largely a map to Dostoyevsky, a few incised streets where his heroes wandered, it was a map he had studied carefully and knew by heart. He knew exactly in what house the old pawnbroker and her sister were murdered; he knew where Raskolnikov lived, and where he hid the stolen money— it was under a stone in a dreary courtyard off Maximilianov Lane, not far from the Voznesensky Prospect, and Dostoyevsky pointed out the place to his second wife during the first weeks of their marriage. We know the exact site of the police station where Raskolnikov suffered his strange interrogations at the hands of the police inspector, Porfiry Petrovich, and we know the restaurant where Raskolnikov had his famous conversation with Svidrigailov. Dostoyevsky's imaginary map-like St. Petersburg included a few very real places, but these places are made real only because concentrations of spiritual energy took place in them. They were real only because it was in these places that the mind of Raskolnikov erupted with startling violence.

For him, St. Petersburg was always a wasteland, the dead end of the world. It was all the more exciting because it was flat and almost featureless and haunted by ghosts. Against that monochrome backdrop his characters seem to move like dark ungainly birds, flapping their wounded wings. Only when we finish reading the novels do we recognize that we ourselves are those mysterious birds.

When Dostoyevsky began to write *Crime and Punishment* he was afflicted with all the familiar hesitations and torments and sudden changes of direction which plagued him during the genesis of his works. Originally it was to be a novel called *The Drunkards,* concerned with the evils of drinking. It was to be a short novel, and he hoped to complete it in three or four months. He seems to have worked on this novel through the summer and autumn of 1865, and then abruptly abandoned it. Of this novel nothing has survived except a few fragments connected with the Marmeladov family in *Crime and Punishment.*

Some time in September 1865 Dostoyevsky wrote to his friend Katkov, the editor of *The Russian Messenger,* a long letter in which he outlined the novel later to become *Crime and Punishment.* The actual letter is lost; we have only the sketch for it which he wrote in his notebook. There were already more than a hundred pages of notes on the novel in existence, and the process of crystallization, if not completely accomplished, was very close to completion, with all the main ideas assembled in the proper order. He wrote:

> It is a psychological study of a crime. The action is contemporary, and takes place in the present year. A young man expelled from the University, bourgeois in origin, living in extreme poverty, decides to escape from his miserable situation in a single stroke, having allowed himself to be seduced by certain strange "incomplete" ideas which already exist in the air around him, and he does this because he suffers from lightness of mind (instability in his thought). He resolves to murder an old woman, the widow of a titular councillor, who is also a moneylender. The woman is stupid, deaf, ill, greedy (charges exorbitant interest), and evil. She is a bloodsucker, and wrecks the life of her younger sister who works for her. "She is useless." "What does she live for?" "Is there any living person who has some need of her?" etc.
>
> These questions prey on the mind of the young man. He decides to kill her, and rob her of all her possessions, and with the plunder he will bring happiness to his mother who lives in the provinces, and deliver his sister, who works as a companion among landowning gentry, from the lusts of the landowner which threaten to ruin her—then he will complete his studies, go abroad, and to

the end of his life he will remain sincere, honest and steadfast in fulfilling "the duty of humanity toward men," and so "expiate his crime," if indeed it is a crime to murder an old woman who is deaf, stupid, ill and evil, a woman who does not know what she is living for and who might conceivably die of natural causes within a month.

Although crimes of this kind are usually committed only with extreme difficulty and they are nearly always committed under circumstances of great vulgarity—I mean that the murderers always leave evidence behind, and luck plays a great role in causing their apprehension —it so happens that my criminal is blessed with good fortune and quickly and happily brings his task to fruition.

Then a whole month passes before the final catastrophe (no one suspects him, and it is impossible that there should be any suspicions). There follows the development of the psychological processus of the crime. Insoluble questions are raised in the mind of the murderer, his heart is torn by unsuspected and formerly inconceivable sentiments. The truth of God and the earthly law obtain their empire over him, and he ends by feeling compelled to denounce himself. He discovers the need to join his fellowmen, even if it has to be in prison. Having committed the crime, he becomes conscious of his isolation, of his withdrawal from ordinary humanity, and this makes him suffer too much. The laws of truth and of human nature triumph, and the criminal without any resistance at all decides to accept his punishment in expiation of his crime. In my novel I shall hint at the idea that the legal punishment inflicted on the criminal frightens him much less than one might think, because *he himself morally demands to be punished.*[4]

Such was the outline which Dostoyevsky followed to the letter. It is, however, no more than the barest outline, for he was to give the hero qualities of courage and remorse and warmth and

[4] *Letters:* 210, September 1865.

the most cold-blooded capacity to analyze the inmost feelings of a murderer. Raskolnikov is the murderer in all of us, but he is also a man endowed with a living mind of his own, capable of thinking out a vast variety of problems to their solution. Of all Dostoyevsky's creations he is perhaps the only one we would recognize if he entered a room.

When Dostoyevsky wrote to Katkov, he had found the essential thread of his novel, but he had not yet assembled the minor characters and he still did not know all the permutations and combinations of his hero's mind. He had to explore endlessly into his own character to discover the character of Raskolnikov. It was necessary to invent many situations to show the behavior of Raskolnikov under all possible conditions. Dostoyevsky had given himself the task of analyzing a murderer and at the same time giving him flesh. It was a task into which he put all his reserves of energy, and his inexhaustible patience.

It was not easy. He worked as he had never worked before, relentlessly and indefatigably, so immersed in the novel that he would sometimes be talking to friends and a moment later, in the midst of the conversation, he would turn away to his writing desk. A servant paid to sleep near him in case he should be overcome by an epileptic attack in the night reported that he must be a murderer planning some terrible murder, for all night he paced the floor, muttering to himself about the crime.

What was the chief characteristic of Raskolnikov? For a long time Dostoyevsky believed it was spiritual pride. He wrote in his notebook: "In his person will be expressed the idea of immeasurable pride, arrogance and scorn towards society. His idea: to obtain power over society. His chief feature is despotism." On another occasion he wrote: "N.B. To dominate society! He is revolted by all the ignominious circumstances surrounding him. Profound contempt for men. Pride. He tells Sonya about his contempt for men, his desire to escape from pride. He tells her: 'Oh, I cannot reconcile myself with them.' In the end he reconciles himself with all. Vision of Christ. He demands pardon publicly. Pride."

But pride is a bleak thing, and Dostoyevsky soon abandoned the conception of pride as the main motive force in the character of Raskolnikov. In fact, with all his astonishing powers of analysis, Raskolnikov never discovers why he murders. He argues with himself, presents all possible theories, and admits himself defeated. A great number of conflicting forces, some human, others inhuman, but all of them arising out of his character, have gone to form the murderer in him. Modern Soviet interpreters who see the murder as a protest against the social conditions of the age have fallen into the trap which Raskolnikov left open for them: the crime had no single purpose and arose from no single cause.

There are of course moments in the finished novel when pride obtrudes, when Raskolnikov permits himself a brief embrace of the demon of pride, as when he all but declares his complicity in the crime to his friend Zamyotov, but a moment later he disengages himself from the embrace. It is a terrifying scene. He teeters on the edge of a revelation. He smiles with the terrible smile of the self-defeated. He connives with himself. He is employing all his physical and spiritual strength in order to avoid confession, and at the same time he feels the compulsion to confess to someone worthy of the confession. But Zamyotov is not worthy, and so Raskolnikov draws back into that shell from which he will later emerge to fight his final battle with the demon and overcome it.

As the novel progressed, Dostoyevsky found himself more and more concerned with the theme of pride, the insensate desire to overcome God and man, but try as he would, he could not make Raskolnikov wear those royal robes with any assurance that they belonged to him. An entirely new character, Svidrigailov, was evolved to bear the weight of pride. He is a bankrupt noble who has been in prison, stealthy, feline, capable of committing extraordinary acts of corruption: he once raped a fifteen-year-old deaf and dumb girl, and was only mildly interested when she hanged herself. Dostoyevsky described him in his notes: "N.B. Very Important. Svidrigailov is aware of mysterious terrors within himself which he keeps secret, but he lets them slip out in conversation. He has convulsive, animal-like urges to rend and to kill; coldly passionate. A wild beast. A tiger."

Svidrigailov makes only brief appearances in the novel. He has no real place in the development of the story, and is present merely by an act of satanic grace. He had a strange face like a mask, white and red, with bright red lips, a light flaxen beard, and hair that was still thick and flaxen. His eyes were a little too blue, and his expression was heavy and immobile. There was something terribly repugnant about that handsome face, so young for his age. He has been in the cavalry, made a living as a cardsharper, and battened on the rich woman he married for her money. He is always well-dressed, and his gestures are those of an aristocrat. So Dostoyevsky describes him in a few quick, brief strokes, and because he has only a very small part to play in the novel he is all the more memorable, for wherever he passes, the air suddenly becomes filled with frenetic electricity.

Svidrigailov will betray because "it is amusing to betray." He poisons his wife, and destroys everyone who crosses his path. He is so amused, so self-assured, so wildly convinced of his own superiority over the human race that when Dounia, Raskolnikov's sister, finds a revolver and points it at him, he simply laughs in her face; and even when she shoots and wounds him, he is still laughing. He belongs to those cold regions of the earth where there is no difference between good and evil, and where all purposes and motives are reduced to nothingness by the presence of the destructive power of pride. On his last night on earth, after dividing his fortune among the women he had once loved and admired, he dreams of finding a five-year-old waif, wet through and shivering, and of carrying her back to his hotel room. He undresses her, puts her to bed, and watches over her as she slowly revives in the warmth of the bedroom. Then he sees that her long black eyelashes are fluttering, and suddenly it seems to him that she is winking at him lasciviously like a whore. "Then both eyes opened wide; they turned a blazing shameless glance at him; they laughed, invited him . . ." It is more than Svidrigailov can bear. He awakens from the nightmare and decides to kill himself.

It is almost the ultimate horror, but Dostoyevsky has one final horror in store.

Early in the morning Svidrigailov wanders through the dirty yellow fog of St. Petersburg on a winter day, making his way along the wooden pavements covered with slippery mud. He glances at the dark blue waters of the Neva, but this is not the fate he has reserved for himself. He has already written in his notebook his brief farewell to the world, saying only that he is dying in full possession of his mental faculties and blaming no one for his death. He decides to kill himself in the damp gardens of Petrovsky Park. Somewhere he will find a convenient bush where they will find him, and then it occurs to him that there is something to be said for killing himself outside a public building where at least there will be an official eyewitness—it is his last contemptuous bow to conformity. He comes to the fire-engine shed on Sezzhinskaya Street, and sees the young fireman on guard, wearing a grey coat and a copper Achilles helmet on his head. Svidrigailov and Achilles glare at one another.

"You've no business to be here," says Achilles.

"Well, good morning to you—that's true," says Svidrigailov.

"This is no place for you."

"I'm going abroad."

"Where to?"

"To America."

"To America, eh?"

Svidrigailov draws his revolver and cocks it. Achilles raises his eyebrows.

"What are you up to? This is no place for jokes!"

"What's wrong with the place?"

DOSTOYEVSKY

"It's all wrong—"

"Well, brother, it makes no difference to me. The place looks all right. If they ask you any questions, tell them I've gone to America."

Svidrigailov puts the revolver to his right temple.

"You can't do that!" Achilles protests. "It isn't the right place at all!"

Then Svidrigailov pulls the trigger.

Here the horror is piled on horror, but what is most especially astonishing is that somehow Dostoyevsky has succeeded in seeing horror accurately, in exact focus. The reader receives two blows coming one after another: the utmost corruption of sensuality is followed by the utmost corruption of reason. The suicide is not an *acte gratuit,* but a completely senseless and futile act. There is nothing in the least satanic about it. So might a man commit suicide because he is annoyed by a fly buzzing around his nose. In a few strokes Dostoyevsky has conveyed the vulgarity of the proud man as he wanders in search of his appropriate death.

There are many mysteries about the composition of *Crime and Punishment,* but one of the most mysterious concerns those concluding pages which describe the death of Svidrigailov and the repentance of Raskolnikov, who bows down to the earth before his beloved Sonya in the evil-smelling Haymarket and confesses that he bows down not to her, but to all suffering humanity. Dostoyevsky had not intended that Svidrigailov should die by his own hand; that fate was reserved for Raskolnikov. On the last page of his notes Dostoyevsky wrote:

The end of the novel.
Raskolnikov blows out his brains.

Svidrigailov: I am ready to go to America immediately, but no one really wants to.

Svidrig. to R. on the Haymarket: You will kill yourself, for it would be impossible to continue to live with your character, you have only two resources—either you kill yourself, or you confess.

Now we are corrupted, and we do not take account of our obligations, they smash into our faces and we hide, we have become so degraded—but there is more freedom in this. A kind of nihilism. For there are two nihilisms, and the two ends meet. On the eve of shooting out my brains, you may well imagine I will speak openly with you. Such a state is far higher, and more free, even though less happy.

This is what I want, and so I shall kill myself.

But I am burning with love for my country. . . .

Svidrigailov: the most cynical despair.
Sonya: the most unattainable hope.
(Raskolnikov himself says this.)
He is passionately attached to both of them.[5]

These are not the confused notes of a novelist who is undecided about the end of his novel. At this stage Dostoyevsky knew exactly how he would round out the long history of Raskolnikov's crime: Svidrigailov would vanish to America, and Raskolnikov would shoot himself after writing a long confession. It was not a particularly convincing ending, but it was the best he could manage.

The reasons behind the abrupt change in the ending can easily be discovered. They have a good deal to do with a change in Dostoyevsky's mood which came about when he suddenly found himself, at the beginning of October 1866, at the mercy of the unscrupulous publisher Stellovsky who, in the previous April, had advanced the sum of 3,000 rubles in payment for the right to publish all his previous works together with "a new novel, unpublished, containing at least 160 printed pages of large size." The new novel had to be in the hands of the publisher on or before November 1. If the manuscript was not delivered on time, the publisher would have the right to publish in book form everything

[5] *Iz arkhiva F. M. Dostoyevskovo,* Folio 150, page 216.

he wrote during the next nine years without payment. Dostoyevsky had been so engrossed in the composition of *Crime and Punishment* that he had forgotten or was incapable of paying attention to the clause in the contract which could so easily destroy him.

On October 1, with only a month to go before the new novel had to be finished, he discussed the contract with his friend Miliukov, who calmly suggested there was an easy way out of the difficulty—a group of Dostoyevsky's friends, Miliukov, Maikov, and some others, would write the novel for him. Dostoyevsky categorically refused, saying he would never sign the work of others. Miliukov suggested another solution: he should hire a secretary and dictate it quickly. Dostoyevsky was doubtful whether he could work with a secretary, but there was no other way out of the *impasse*. Miliukov found a secretary for him.

When the secretary arrived, Dostoyevsky had finished the first five parts of *Crime and Punishment,* and there remained only the final chapters. He began dictating on October 4th. Twenty-four days later the new novel, which he called *The Gambler,* was finished. *Crime and Punishment* was appearing in installments in the *Russian Messenger,* but there had been unforeseen delays in its publication. There was still time enough to complete the novel, and he set to work with the new secretary.

In the interval something of quite extraordinary importance to his life and work had happened—he had fallen in love with the secretary. The harsh ending to the novel gave way to another ending altogether. Raskolnikov, the suicide, vanished; in his place was the repentant sinner who finds in Sonya a woman who will accompany him to the wastes of Siberia, full of childlike tenderness and a haunting beauty. When he describes Sonya joining Raskolnikov in exile, he is speaking of the characters in the novel, but he is also celebrating the new life springing up between the ageing author and the young secretary.

Dostoyevsky never denied that his novels were autobiographical. He was—he could not help being—all his characters.

He identifies himself with Raskolnikov, giving him his own features when young, his own habits of thought, his own cynicism, his own generosity. Raskolnikov describes himself as "formerly a student, living in the house of Shill," which was the house where Dostoyevsky himself was arrested. Raskolnikov wanders through the streets muttering to himself, so that he is sometimes taken for a madman, and we know that this was characteristic of Dostoyevsky. In the Haymarket an old woman gives Raskolnikov a cross of cypress wood; this too happened to Dostoyevsky. The entire epilogue is filled with his memories of Siberia, and he even makes Raskolnikov an aristocrat regarded with mixed feelings by the other prisoners. A hundred details confirm that Raskolnikov is a projection of himself, and much of the strength of the novel comes from the deliberate gaze of the artist in the mirror. Later he would see himself in distorting mirrors; the single face would become many faces, and though all of them possessed a family resemblance, and were recognizably his own, they assumed infinitely complex contours. Like Rembrandt, Dostoyevsky was at his best when he painted himself.

The evil figure of Svidrigailov, the first completely rounded portrait of the evil man, was also Dostoyevsky. He too wears the features of his creator. He has the slyness, the capacity to summon up images of destruction, the knowledge of evil which Dostoyevsky found in the depths of his own soul. For him there is no God, man does not exist, and time is annihilated. There is an extraordinary passage in Dostoyevsky's notebook which reads:

> What is time? Time does not exist; time is a set of numbers; time is the relation of being to non-being.
> When Dounia shoots at him, Svidrigailov thinks:
> How very beautiful she is! [6]

With such miraculous confrontations of abstract and sensuous ideas Dostoyevsky prepared himself for the task of writing his novel.

[6] *Iz arkhiva F. M. Dostoyevskovo,* Folio 63, page 173.

Throughout the novel there is the awareness of the abstractions which dominate the phenomenal universe. Those huge abstract forces, beyond any manner of description, which can only be hinted at and suggested in legends and fables, receive from him the tribute of clear-eyed understanding. He knows the powers of darkness as he knows the powers of light. He speaks of them in legends which assume an appropriate place in his novels. Raskolnikov lies ill in Siberia, and suddenly there comes to him the vision of evil followed by the reign of blessedness:

He dreamed that the whole world was condemned by a terrible, new and unknown plague which swept across Europe from the depths of Asia. All except a few chosen ones were doomed to destruction. There appeared new trichinæ, microscopic beings penetrating the bodies of people. Yet these beings were spirits, endowed with a mind and a will. People who absorbed them immediately became mad and raved. But never, never had people considered themselves so understanding and unshakable in their knowledge of truth as the infected ones considered themselves; their verdicts, their scientific deductions, their moral convictions and beliefs—all were unshakeable. Whole towns, villages and people became infected and went mad. All were troubled, and did not understand one another. Each one thought he alone possessed the truth, and was tormented when he looked at others, and smote his breast, wept, and wrung his hands. They did not know how to judge, and could not agree upon matters of good and evil. They did not know how to accuse or how to release the prisoners. People killed one another in a kind of senseless spite. They raised whole armies against one another, but these armies, when already on the march, suddenly began to fight among themselves, their ranks broke, and the soldiers fell on one another, bit and clawed and murdered one another.

The tocsin was ringing all day long in the towns. They called everyone together, but why they were called and who was calling them no one knew. The most ordinary trades were abandoned, because everyone was propounding his own theories and offering his own solutions; and they could not agree among themselves. They abandoned their lands. Here and there men gathered in groups, vowed to remain together, and at once started doing things which had no relation to what they had planned. They accused one another, fought, and killed each other. Fires broke out; famine spread; wholesale destruction walked the earth. The plague spread and moved further and further. In the whole world only a few people could save themselves—these were the pure and the elect, destined to found a new race and a new life, to renew and purify the earth.[7]

Such legends, complete in themselves, yet flowing from the argument of the novel, appear in nearly all his later works, until in *The Brothers Karamazov* there is the danger that the legends will devour the whole work. Nearly all these legends give an impression of having been written quickly, in the full flood of excitement and inspiration. In most of them we hear the authentic voice of Dostoyevsky himself, no longer even pretending to link them except in the most arbitrary way to the characters who speak them, or imagine them, or write them down.

The dream of the plague is put in the mind of Raskolnikov; it would seem to be closer to the imagination of Svidrigailov. Here in contrast, from Dostoyevsky's notebooks, is the vision of the just God who embraces the proud and the humble alike:

We are all the children of God, living in the fire of the furnace. There is only Christ. He showered his mercy on all, and so they mocked him, and they mocked themselves, and insulted him, and he came and asked for his daughter who had been given into slavery by her drunken father, and he said: Come, come, all your sins are forgiven you, for you have loved much. And when he has judged all the world, he will say: Come, come all of you, even the drunken fathers who gave their daugh-

[7] *Crime and Punishment,* Epilogue.

ters away. And we shall all appear before him without shame, and he will spread open his crucified hands, and throw out his arms, and he will say: Come to me, all ye who are suffering and heavy-laden. You are despicable creatures of earth, but you have suffered. I have seen you and I have weighed you. I have seen the weakness in you, and I know you have suffered more than those you persecuted, and so come to me. And we shall all bow down before him and weep . . . Lord, may Thy kingdom come!

And the strong will say: Lord, we have committed these evils, and thou hast taken those we persecuted to thy bosom. They lived only to be unhappy and to cause unhappiness in others, and it was always their fault. All this I know, he will say, but they have been too deeply humiliated, beyond all measure, and they have become loathsome to themselves. They have suffered too much, and I shall take them to my bosom because none of them think themselves worthy of me.

So let them all come unto me. . . .[8]

There, if anywhere, is the heart of Dostoyevsky's belief, and it is strange that the words should have been hidden in the notebooks, not to be revealed until many years later.

In an early chapter of *Crime and Punishment,* the drunken Marmeladov says: "The true evil is when men no longer know where they are going." Marmeladov, too, belongs to the world of the nihilists, to those who see no blessedness on earth, and who go down to death like men exchanging one form of oblivion for another. Haunted by disbelief, Dostoyevsky yet held to the faith that men come to Christ in the end.

[8] *Iz arkhiva F. M. Dostoyevskovo,* Folio 12, pages 84, 85.

THE GAMBLER

O N THE EVENING of October 3, 1866, an obscure shorthand student, Anna Grigoryevna Snitkina, attended her classes, arranged her exercise books on the table in front of her, and waited for her teacher to begin the lesson. It never occurred to her that in a few moments the future life of a great writer would be decided. Dostoyevsky himself had no idea that great decisions were being made. At that precise moment he was suffering from an unusually severe epileptic attack.

The shorthand teacher did not take his customary place in the classroom. Instead he came and sat down beside Anna, and asked her whether she would like to do some shorthand work.

Anna was puzzled. She did not consider herself a proficient shorthand writer. She was slow and unsure of herself, and she was still in mourning for the death of her father, which had taken place earlier in the year. The teacher explained that she would not be expected to write more than a hundred words a minute.

"Who is it for?" Anna asked.

"Dostoyevsky, the writer. He is working on a new novel, and hopes to finish it with the help of shorthand. He thinks it will be about seven folios long, and he offers fifty rubles. If you want the job, be at his house at half past eleven tomorrow morning, and as he says himself, 'not earlier, not later.' I'm only afraid you won't like him very much; he is a grim and melancholy man."

"I don't have to like him, do I?" Anna said with an involuntary smile. "I'll do my work as well as I can—that's the important thing. As for Dostoyevsky the writer, I have so much respect for him that he frightens me already."

Anna spent the rest of the evening in a daze, listening to the teacher's lecture with a curious sense of unreality. She could hardly believe her good fortune. She knew Dostoyevsky's writings; she had wept over *The House of the Dead;* her father had been one of his fervent admirers. She could make no mental image of him. She was twenty, and she had very little experience of the world.

When Anna rang the bell at exactly half past eleven the next morning, armed with a fresh supply of pencils and a new portfolio, she was startled almost out of her wits by a series of extraordinary impressions. First, there was the middle-aged woman with the green checkered shawl thrown round her shoulders who threw open the door, and at once she remembered the checkered shawl worn by the Marmeladovs in *Crime and Punishment,* which she had read when it came out in installments, and she had the strange feeling of being about to enter a novel. A moment later she caught a glimpse of Pasha: the boy's chest was bare, and his hair was tousled. He saw her, screamed, and ran out of the room. Then Dostoyevsky appeared, looking very ill and drawn, with his reddish hair thickly greased and slicked down. He was wearing an old blue jacket, but she noticed that his shirt was snow-white. In his presence she felt acutely uncomfortable. She did not know he had had a severe epileptic attack the previous evening, and was incapable of concentrating for any long period. He was nervous and irritable, at the mercy of those fears which overwhelmed him for two or three days after an attack. His eyes especially frightened her, for one pupil was brown but she could not tell the color of the other because it was dilated; and because his eyes did not match, his face assumed a curiously distant expression. He was of middle height, and held himself erect.

But if Anna could make little of Dostoyevsky and was

frightened by him, Dostoyevsky could make little of her, and he was a little frightened by her.

She was unlike any of the women he had known—tall and thin, with a clear oval face and very fine deepset grey eyes. In her appearance there was nothing characteristically Russian. She took after her mother, who was a Swede of German extraction, and there was some English blood in her veins. She was one of those young women who can never disguise their feelings, whose innocent faces betray every passing thought. She was sweet-tempered and vulnerable.

Ill-at-ease, and looking more wretchedly ill every minute, Dostoyevsky tried to engage her in a desultory conversation. He offered her a cigarette, and seemed surprised when she refused. "You do not smoke out of politeness?" he suggested. She told him she did not like to see women smoking. They talked by fits and starts. Dostoyevsky was incapable of concentrating on any subject for more than a few moments. Suddenly he began to tell her he suffered from epilepsy; he was ill; he did not know what would happen to him. He spoke very vaguely about the work they would do together. "We'll see what we can do," he said. "We'll try. Perhaps something will come of it." He asked her name, forgot it, and then asked for it again. He smoked continually, and kept offering her cigarettes. At last he drew up a copy of the *Russian Messenger,* and dictated a paragraph to her at a vast speed. She was very slow in transcribing her shorthand, and he was visibly annoyed because she could not be hurried; and he sharply corrected her occasional faults in spelling and punctuation. At other times he would start talking and then wander restlessly around the room, leaving his sentences unfinished. Once he said: "I am glad they sent me a girl shorthand writer, not a man. Probably you regard this as a surprising statement?"

"Yes."

"Then I will tell you why I am glad. Because a man would drink a great deal, and you of course won't!"

Anna was so surprised by this outburst that she began to laugh.

"Of course I won't drink—you may depend on that," she said primly.

It was becoming clear that Dostoyevsky was in no state to work that morning. He asked her whether she could return at eight o'clock in the evening, when he would be, able to dictate to her at greater length. The request was inconvenient—she lived a long way away, and it would mean making both journeys in the dark—but she was determined to begin working, and she said she would be pleased to come. She was with him for nearly two and a half hours that morning, from half past eleven to two o'clock in the afternoon, and in all that time he offered her nothing but glasses of tea.

Everything about that first meeting was strange and terrifying. There were long pauses. Dostoyevsky fell into fits of abstraction, completely forgetting her presence, then recovering himself and suddenly asking some entirely meaningless question. She stayed with him not because she wanted the job or because she was fascinated by him, but because already in some obscure way she felt that he needed her. And in those terrible intervals of silence, she would look calmly round the room, taking note of everything there—the mirror framed in black walnut between the two windows, the beautiful Chinese vases on the windowsill, the couch covered with green morocco near the wall, and the portrait of a very thin old lady in a black dress and a black bonnet. She remembered afterward the extraordinary quality of stillness in the room. It was as though nothing had ever happened there.

When she returned in the evening, Dostoyevsky had recovered his good humor and no longer fell into fits of abstraction. He was in no hurry to work. As always after an epileptic attack his memory was impaired, and he again asked her name and sometimes repeated the same questions he had asked in the morning, but otherwise he was in full command of himself. He looked less tired. He listened carefully to everything she said, and he was pleased because she spoke simply and even a little sternly. She was quite unlike any young woman he had ever met. There were qualities of reserve and simplicity in her, and a great sympathy. He unburdened himself to her, telling her about the execution on the Semyonov parade ground. "I was happier that day than I ever was before," he told her. "When I was taken back to the Alexis Ravelin, I kept pacing the cell and I sang at the top of my voice, so happy that life was given back to me." He may have known even then that the quiet young woman with the deepset grey eyes and the thick black hair brushed straight back from her forehead was also to bring him back his life.

They talked. Fedosya the maidservant brought in glasses of hot tea with slices of lemon; from somewhere Dostoyevsky found two pears in a paper bag and silently offered one to her. Gradually she came to feel she had known him for many months, and their first meeting that morning seemed to belong to the distant and almost forgotten past.

It was already late in the evening when he began dictating the opening passages of his novel *The Gambler*. He had a habit of pacing rapidly across the room while dictating, going from the door to the fireplace and then back again, and never forgetting to knock twice on the fireplace. He smoked continually. He had not thought the novel out, he was still feeling his way, and his memory kept playing tricks on him. In the second sentence of the novel he mentioned the town "Roulettenburg." He asked her to read the sentence to him, and when she came to read the sentence, he was staggered. "Roulettenburg?" he gasped. "Did I really say Roulettenburg? It's quite impossible!" Anna said she had simply written what he dictated. "Well, it's a terrible muddle!" Dostoyevsky said, but he kept the name Roulettenburg, and never discussed the matter again.

So the days passed, with Anna coming every morning at twelve and staying until four in the afternoon. Dostoyevsky did not dictate all this time; usually he dictated for three half-hour periods, and spent the rest of the time telling her stories about his life. He lost his nervousness, and spoke to her about the most intimate things without fear of shocking her. Once he told her he had reached an impasse in his life, and there remained only three possible solutions. He could go to the East—to Constantinople and Jerusalem—and remain there for the rest of his life; or he could marry; or he could go abroad and become a gambler. He was trying to choose between the religious life, the human life, and the life of the sensation seeker. He asked her which she would choose for him, and she answered that he would be wise if he chose marriage.

"Yes, of course," he answered, "but who would marry me? And then, too, even if there were women disposed to marry me, should I choose an intelligent one or a warm and gentle soul?"

"You should choose an intelligent one," Anna replied, for she placed a high value on intelligence.

"No," he answered, "if I had to choose, I would choose a warm and gentle soul who would love and cherish me."

Then he asked her about her own prospects of marriage, and learned that she was being pursued by two suitors, but cared for neither of them. She respected them, but did not love them, and she felt that marriage without love was a meaningless imposition of the flesh—an opinion which he heartily shared.

In this way, over the weeks, they revealed themselves to one another. They shared their griefs and joys, and they both feared the time when the novel would come to an end.

Anna lived for Dostoyevsky. She no longer attended her shorthand school. Every day she spent four or five hours receiving dictation, and every night she spent the same number of hours transcribing from her notes. More and more he was attracted by her transparent honesty, her naivety, her sensitivity, and her astonishing good health. She had that shining healthy glow which is to be found often among young Swedish women.

Dostoyevsky would not have been Dostoyevsky if he had not occasionally played some sly tricks on her. There are passages in the novel which seem to be addressed to her; other passages which were perhaps designed to shock her; and much of the novel was a retelling of his love affair with Polina Suslova, with whom he still corresponded and whose image was still fresh in his mind. When Dostoyevsky asked her which characters she preferred, she answered truthfully that her sympathies lay with the grandmother and the strange young Englishman, Mr. Astley, and that she despised Polina and the hero of the novel who bows to her slightest caprice and surrenders to a mad passion for gambling. Inevitably Dostoyevsky's sympathies lay with the hero. It could hardly be otherwise, for the hero was himself.

Anna threw herself into the work to such an extent that she became almost his collaborator. Never before had he known such a willing and responsive assistant. Five days before the work came to an end Dostoyevsky was thunderstruck by the thought that he would have to live without her cheerful and benignant presence.

"We have got along so well," he told her, "and we have grown so accustomed to talking together, and soon the work will be over, and we shall never see each other again. I shall be sorry to miss you. How can we meet again?"

"But Fyodor Mikhailovich," Anna reminded him, "although two mountains never come together, two people can always come together."

"How?"

"In society, at the theatre, at concerts."

"As for that," Dostoyevsky said, "I go very rarely into society or to the theatre, and what is the good of meeting in society where we could hardly ever exchange a word in private? Now if you invited me to your house to meet your family—"

Anna knew as many feminine tricks as Polina. She invited him to meet her family, but deliberately kept on postponing the date. Meanwhile she was actively engaged in the conspiracy to defeat "the beast Stellovsky." It occurred to Dostoyevsky that the publisher might find some way to circumvent the contract. Stellovsky was perfectly capable of causing all kinds of trouble—he might even refuse to accept the manuscript and afterwards he would say it had not been delivered to him. Anna consulted her hardheaded mother, who in turn consulted the family lawyer, who advised that it was not at all necessary to deliver the manuscript to the publisher personally; it could be delivered instead either to a notary public or to the police inspector of the district where Stellovsky resided.

On October 30th, his birthday, Anna gave him the fair copy of the last pages of the novel. The whole novel had been completed in twenty-six days. Dostoyevsky was overjoyed and profoundly grateful to his assistant, who celebrated the occasion by appearing in a lilac-colored silk dress instead of the mourning clothes she had worn previously. In this bright dress she looked younger, taller, prettier. He complimented her, and she blushed happily. He gave her fifty rubles for her work, and asked when he could see her again. She suggested he should come to her house five days later, making various excuses for all the days in between. He had no power over her, and knew he must wait patiently against all reason for the opportunity of seeing her again.

"Such a long time to wait," he said sadly, and at that moment Anna knew she had won him for herself.

Left alone in the house, he put the finishing touches to the novel which amounted to seven folios or about 50,000 words. It was not among his greatest novels, but he was content with it. On November 1st he decided to take it to Stellovsky's house, for it occurred to him that the publisher might after all be a man of honor. At the house he was told that the publisher had left for his country estate and no one knew when he would return. Dostoyevsky understood perfectly well what this meant, but he went on to Stellovsky's office, determined to do whatever was right and proper, and to avoid complications, all the time telling himself that it was unthinkable that a publisher should deliberately plot to ruin him.

Stellovsky was in fact at his office. He still hoped to gain the entire copyright of Dostoyevsky's work for a mere pittance, and he had given orders that if a manuscript by Dostoyevsky arrived by messenger, then the messenger should be told that no one in the office had authority to accept it. Under no conditions was the manuscript to be allowed to remain in the office.

When he heard the news Dostoyevsky was alarmed. He was convinced that Stellovsky was a liar and a thief, capable of every kind of fraud. It was now afternoon, and he decided to follow Anna's advice and deliver the manuscript into the hands of a notary public. He called on the only notary public he knew, only to discover that the office was closed for the day. He still had one last line of defense. According to Anna a receipt from the police inspector of the district where Stellovsky resided would be a legal document proving that he had intended to place the manuscript in the publisher's hands. But it so happened that the inspector was absent. Dostoyevsky was panic-stricken. He seemed to be fighting a strange battle with shadows, and wherever he looked he was aware of the mocking invisible presence of Stellovsky.

He almost gave up in despair. One by one he had tried four different approaches, and all had failed. He knew that if he could not dispose of the manuscript by midnight, he would be at the mercy of the publisher.

At ten o'clock in the evening, when Dostoyevsky had almost lost hope, the inspector arrived. Within a few minutes Dostoyevsky walked out of the police station with a formal receipt in his pocket. At the last minute he had saved the most precious of his possessions—his ownership in the copyright of his works.

The Gambler is a disturbing book, which shows every sign of being composed hastily. It is shapeless, diffuse, and curiously unconvincing even when it deals with events which can be docu-

mented and even when Dostoyevsky simply describes the opera-
tions of the roulette table. Like nearly all the stories Dostoyevsky
wrote in the first person, it seems to lack a central focus. The "I"
of the novel is like water. He has no discernible character. He is
the antithesis of Raskolnikov, a man without conscience, without
thought, without energy. The water flows down the hillside, and
vanishes in the soft sands.

It is the story of a rake's progress, written in a state of
disenchantment, for the rake is evidently Dostoyevsky himself,
and the Polina Alexandrovna of the novel is only too evidently
Polina Suslova. "Polina," he writes, "always regarded me like that
Empress of ancient times who used to undress before her slave,
not regarding him as a man." Like the real Polina, the Polina of
the novel conquers her lover by alternately surrendering to him
and frightening him out of his wits. "I swear by all that is holy," he
says, "that if she had taken me to the Schlangenberg, and said,
'Leap into the abyss!' I would have jumped immediately, and felt
pleasure in doing so." At such moments the hero of *The Gambler*
comes to life, but those moments are rare.

For the most part the novel tells the story of the hero's
infatuation with Polina, who desperately needs 50,000 francs to
repay the advances of her former lover, a French adventurer. The
hero obligingly wins a fortune at roulette amounting altogether to
200,000 francs, and hurries to present her with the money she
needs. They sleep together. The next morning Polina climbs out
of bed, takes the money which has been lying on the night table,
and then flings the pile of gold coins at his face before rushing out
of the room. The hero consoles himself by hurrying off to Paris
with a French *coquette,* who helps him to squander his whole
fortune in three weeks. Inevitably, when the money runs out, she
abandons him. He returns to Roulettenberg, and he is still gambling hopefully when the novel ends.

Such are the bare bones of the novel, which Dostoyevsky
covered with strips of variegated flesh. There are long discussions

on the mechanics of gambling, brief thumbnail sketches of the gamblers, and some comic interludes involving an eccentric *grande dame* with the resounding name of Antonida Vasilyevna Tarasevicheva. This formidable lady storms into the casino in her wheelchair, takes charge of everything, loses all her money, and promptly falls asleep. She is human—all too human. The other characters resemble the little silver balls which are tossed into the roulette wheel, scurrying and slithering around the edge of disaster, of no particular importance to themselves or to anyone else, lighthearted even when they are behaving viciously.

The novel served its purpose: it prevented Stellovsky from holding Dostoyevsky in bondage. It is possible that there was another purpose. Dostoyevsky had fallen in love with Anna, and in the person of his wayward hero struck with the fever of gambling he was presenting one aspect of his own character. It is as though he were saying, as he paced the room and dictated to his neat and admiring secretary: "This is the kind of man I am! Think carefully before you decide to marry me! I shall lead you through all the gambling resorts of Europe, lose all my money, and drive you close to madness!"

On February 15, 1867, at seven o'clock in the evening, they were married at the Cathedral of the Holy Trinity in St. Petersburg. In April they set out for Germany, and for the next four years they wandered across Europe.

All through these years Anna was like an oasis of calm in the midst of tempests. From a shy girl she developed quickly into a remarkably astute and sensible woman. She possessed a brilliant capacity for affection; she loved him, cared for him, nursed him during his epileptic attacks and through his even more terrifying attacks of gambling fever, and she sedulously cultivated all that was best in him, while giving him the utmost freedom to carry on his work. She has been described as a simple-minded *bourgeoise* with neither beauty nor charm to commend her, but that is to misread both her character and appearance. She had a quick mind; she was intelligent; she had fine features and particularly fine eyes; and she had a voluptuous body. On the evidence of his letters to her, she was sexually mature and eager for every kind of sexual experience.

In the early months of her marriage this astonishing woman wrote a diary, which she kept in shorthand. In it she recorded their day-to-day activities, all the minor joys and major catastrophes. She recorded the price of bread rolls in Vilna and of chocolate éclairs in Dresden. She never indulges in fantasy; she describes things as they are with a quite extraordinary detachment. She notes the color of the glass buttons she bought, and where she bought them, and with exactly the same quiet matter-of-factness she notes the temperature of his moods and the curve of his fortunes. Once, when she was quietly jotting down her notes in shorthand, he leaned over and said: "I wonder what you are doing with all those hooks and wriggles?" She was writing a letter to posterity about her lover.

Dostoyevsky set out on his long honeymoon with many qualms. He was a little afraid of his young wife, and continued to be afraid for some months. He wrote to his friend Maikov in the summer:

> I went abroad with death in my soul. I even believed that these foreign countries would have a bad moral effect on me, and I had no faith in them. I was completely alone, without resources, with a young creature by my side, who had a naive joy in sharing my nomadic life. It occurred to me that her naive joy arose partly from inexperience and youthful fervor, and this depressed and tormented me. I was afraid she would be bored with me. So far we have been absolutely *alone*. I had no confidence in myself. I have a morbid character, and I was sure she would undergo many torments while she was by my side. It is true that Anna Grigoryevna has proved stronger and deeper than I ever thought or

guessed, and there have been many times when she acted as my guardian angel; but there is also much of the child and the twenty-year-old in her, which is charming and naturally *inevitable,* but I have scarcely the strength or the capacity to respond. All this haunted me when we left Russia; and although, as I said, she has turned out stronger and better than I thought, I am still not free from anxiety. Finally our modest means were always an embarrassment to me.[1]

He soon lost his fears; and indeed there is some reason for believing he was exaggerating them in his letter to Maikov. Anna was a tower of strength. She understood from the beginning his *physical* need to gamble at the roulette table: the excitement of gambling, by producing a very minor epileptic attack, had the effect of warding off the greater. She gave him her own money to stake at the tables, and comforted him when he lost, as he always did.

They stopped one day in Berlin, where he was irritated to the point of frenzy by the Berliners and took refuge in the Russian baths; and went on to Dresden, where he was irritated by the Russian exiles who were forever enlarging on the superior virtues of the Germans over the Russians. He fled to Baden where he lost so much money at roulette that he was forced to appeal to Turgenev for a loan. Turgenev had built a handsome house for himself and was living in great style. In a state of despair and nervous exhaustion Dostoyevsky called on him, and immediately forgot the reason why he had called. He was incensed by Turgenev's patronizing manner, the pomp and splendor of his house, and, like thousands of Russians, he was incensed by the strictures which Turgenev had directed against Russia in his latest novel, *Smoke.* Dostoyevsky forced a quarrel; and the two great Russian writers attacked one another like venomous children.

According to Dostoyevsky, who described the incident in another long letter to Maikov, he found Turgenev at an early

[1] *Letters:* 279, August 16, 1867.

lunch. It was not long before Turgenev began to make disparaging remarks about the critics who had damned his novel, saying the Russians "should crawl before the civilized Germans." Dostoyevsky told Turgenev to send to Paris for a telescope.

"Why?" asked Turgenev.

"So that you can look at Russia and see what is going on there," Dostoyevsky replied. "Otherwise you will find it hard to know anything about us."

It was a good quarrel, and they went at it hammer and tongs. Turgenev abused the Russians. Dostoyevsky abused the Germans, saying they were common thieves and swindlers, and completely stupid. Their civilization had added nothing to the world, and was in fact bankrupt. Turgenev seems to have taken this as a personal insult, and declared that he had settled permanently in Germany and now regarded himself as a German, not a Russian, and was proud of it. "In that case," said Dostoyevsky, "forgive me for having insulted you." There were ice-cold farewells, and Dostoyevsky left the house, promising himself he would never meet his rival again.

At ten o'clock the next morning Turgenev left his card with Dostoyevsky's landlady. It is possible that he hoped for a reconciliation, but it is just as likely that he intended to resume the quarrel. He had needled Dostoyevsky when he was a sick and struggling young writer in the salon of Madame Panayeva, and he was quite capable of needling him again when he was exhausted with epilepsy and gambling fever.

During the following seven weeks Dostoyevsky saw him only once more. It was at the railway station. They exchanged a brief glance, but there were no bows.

In *The Devils,* Dostoyevsky had his childish revenge, satirizing Turgenev in the character of "the great writer" Karmazinov. In the novel he is described as "a short prim old man, with a rather red little face, with thick grey locks of hair clustering under his chimney-pot hat, and curling round his clean little ears." It is a venomous and carefully considered portrait of a completely ineffectual intellectual.

Dostoyevsky hated Baden, and only stayed there because he was fatally attracted to the gambling tables. He loathed his lodging, which was above a smithy; and the sound of the hammers beating on the anvil nearly drove him mad. Children were continually screaming round the house. Destitute, he would borrow money from Goncharov or send emphatic appeals to his editor, promising that he would spend the money only on necessities; then he would go off to the gambling tables again.

Anna pawned her dresses, her rings, and the small treasures she had brought with her, while he pawned his clothes, his overcoat, and everything else he possessed. He had a theory that if a man remained completely calm, he was bound to win. Unhappily, he was rarely calm. He would suddenly think of Anna and all the sufferings she had undergone, or he would be disturbed by the pomade of an Englishman sitting beside him at the table. He was very calm after his interview with Turgenev, played magnificently, and returned with a small heap of gold coins. It amused him to pretend he had lost, and then to fling the coins in the air.

Anna surveyed their poverty with a mild eye. Once, to celebrate five months of marriage, she decided to have a celebration, although they were destitute again. She was quietly happy until she noticed that the heel of one of his boots had come loose; then the memory of all their miseries swelled into a fit of laughter, and through her tears she kept saying: "Good-bye, dear clothes, you are beyond saving now!"

Sometimes Dostoyevsky seemed to be beyond saving. It was not only that he habitually wore the look of a dying man, but the epileptic attacks increased in fury and grew more frequent. Anna left many careful accounts of these attacks, but none so terrible as the one she wrote shortly before they left Baden for Geneva:

> I was terrified to death, and tried to get him back
> on the bed, but I was too weak to do this, so I propped

him up against mine, and there he was, half-standing, half-sitting between the bed and the wall. He was in convulsions. His right foot, too, hurt him badly, for he had knocked it against the wall. After the cramps passed, he began to hurl himself about, and I could not hold him down. I threw two pillows on the floor and gradually managed to let him down on the floor, so that he could have room to stretch his legs, which was better for him. Then I undid his waistcoat and trousers, to let him breathe more freely. Then I saw for the first time that his lips were blue, and his face more scarlet than usual when suffering these attacks, and I was miserable.[2]

They left Baden for Geneva with a capital of 140 francs, but with the promise of an advance from Moscow. Anna was in good spirits, amused by everything she saw, delighted with Geneva, and hopeful that her husband had abandoned gambling for ever. He had not abandoned gambling. Soon he was traveling alone to Saxon-les-Bains, and there came the inevitable letters begging for a few francs; the crestfallen return; a week or two of penury until more money arrived from Anna's mother or from the publisher, and then he would be at the gambling tables again. Anna bore it all heroically, but she was glad when they went to live at Vevey, where there were no roulette wheels.

They spent a long summer at Vevey and then went off to Italy, pausing in Milan long enough to wander through the Cathedral. They settled in Florence in an apartment house facing the Palazzo Pitti. For once Dostoyevsky found a European city which pleased him. There were so many Russians living in Florence that a Russian library had come into existence; he could read Russian newspapers again, and borrow immense quantities of books. He liked wandering in the Boboli Gardens and sitting in the open-air cafes, and nearly every day he went to the Palazzo Pitti to examine his favorite Raphaels. That winter was unusually warm, with roses blooming in January; and the heat disturbed

2 *Diary of Mme Dostoyevskaya,* July 22, 1867.

him. He complained bitterly against the dryness of the weather, so unlike the weather of St. Petersburg. He was finishing *The Idiot,* that astonishing story of "a man who is completely good." He had indeed been writing it all through these feverish months which saw him spending his mornings alternately at the gambling table and the pawnshop.

When *The Idiot* was finished at last, he felt a great hunger to live in a Slavonic land and decided to establish himself in Prague. Anna enjoyed the journey, though she was pregnant. They went by way of Venice, Bologna, Trieste, and Vienna. Anna was "dumbfounded with joy" when she saw the Piazza of St. Mark's, and Dostoyevsky thought Vienna far more beautiful than Paris, but Prague was insufferable. They took the train for Dresden; and being weary of traveling they took root there, being as poor as cockroaches, but curiously content to be back in a known place.

In Dresden he suffered from the weather, and found himself dreaming of Florence, where he had had comparatively few attacks of epilepsy and the mildness of the air served to safeguard his health. Sometimes, too, the gambling fever struck him, and he would vanish for a few days to Baden, and once again, as so often before, there would come letters begging for the fare home, since he had lost everything. "My angel, read this letter carefully, keep calm, do not kill yourself . . ."

In April 1871 he suffered two terrifying shocks: he saw his father in a dream, warning him that there were evil things in store; and then he promptly gambled and lost all his money and felt himself going insane. He wrote an extraordinary letter to Anna, describing the experience and begging her to save him, for now unless he reformed there was no hope for him. He wrote like a man shuddering from pure terror, with one foot over the abyss and darkness everywhere:

> I saw my Father in a dream, with that terrible look which I have only seen twice in my life, warning me of some dreadful misfortune—and twice the dream came

true. (And now I remember my dream three days ago, when I saw your hair turn grey, and my heart grows numb! God be with you when you get this letter!)

I went back to the casino and began to think: Would I be able to guess correctly? And what do you think, Anna? I guessed right every time for ten minutes, and I even guessed the zero. I was so struck by this that I began to play and in five minutes I had won back 18 *thalers*. Then, Anna, I forgot myself. I told myself I would leave on the last train and spend the night at Frankfurt, but at least I would bring some money home! I was so ashamed of *robbing* you of those 30 *thalers!*

Believe me, my angel, I had always dreamed of buying you those earrings which I was never able to give you. You have pawned everything for me during these last four years and you have been wandering about with me with a fierce longing for home! Anna, Anna, do remember that I am not a scoundrel, but only a gambler in the toils of his passion . . .

By half past nine I had lost everything and left the tables stupefied. I was suffering so much that I ran to find a priest. While I was running to him in the dark, along unknown streets, I thought, "He is a minister of God, I will speak to him not as though I were speaking to a man, but as to a confessor." But I lost my way, and then I came to a church, and thought it was a Russian church, but they told me in a shop that it was not Russian, but a synagogue. It was like a cold shower. I ran to my hotel, and it is now midnight and I am writing to you . . .

Anna, save me for the last time, send me 30 (thirty) *thalers*. I will make it do, I will economize. Anna, I am at your feet, and I embrace you . . .

Do not think I have gone mad, Anna, my guardian angel! A great work is being accomplished in me, a hideous fantasy that *tortured* me for ten years has vanished. For ten years (or rather since the death of my brother, when I was suddenly loaded with debts) I always had this dream of winning. I dreamed this seriously, passionately. Not it is all over! Now it has happened for the very last time! Can you believe it, Anna, my hands are free at last. I was chained to the gambling table. From now on I shall think only of my work and will not dream of gambling all night as I used to do. Now my work will be better and God will bless me! [3]

This is the most frightening of all the letters from Dostoyevsky which have been preserved, for it shows him at war with the demon, and there are no webs of theories trailing the naked combat. He fights, and falls, and rises, and if there had been a sharp knife in his pocket, there might have been another issue.

After that day he never gambled again. The years of folly were over. Two months later he returned to St. Petersburg. He had finished *The Idiot,* and was working on *The Devils.* A week after they arrived, Anna gave birth to a son, who was christened Fyodor.

[3] *Letters:* 380, April 28, 1871.

THE FOOL OF CHRIST

THROUGHOUT the history of Christianity the Fool of Christ has had a special place. He is the one who goes counter to all normal existence; who neither toils nor spins, nor makes any preparations for the morrow; who laughs like a child, and like a child is immune to ordinary human laws. He is Perrenik the Fool, and also Parsifal. He is Francis of Assisi marching naked through the streets of the city and singing the praises of God, and Jacopone da Todi endlessly singing his simple love songs to the awful God who created the universe. Somewhere at the burning core of Christianity there is the flame of folly—the folly of old peasant women and of tumblers and of madmen. In Italy even today men will point to madmen and say: "Be kind to him, for there is Christ in him."

In Russia in the nineteenth century the flame of folly burned very brightly. The saintly *starets,* Serafim of Sarov, had shown the way. Like St. Francis he spoke to the birds, and enjoyed a strange power over wolves. The Queen of Heaven visited him in visions, and he overcame devils, and spent his nights in prayer and his days in performing miracles. In his sermons he spoke of the holy joy of children and fools as they stand before the gate of Heaven, and the gate opens for them. "It will open too for you," he would say, "if you are like a child or a fool." There was an astonishing simplicity in him. He wore a long white gown and a bright green shawl, and he had only to open wide his enormous eyes for people to feel that the Holy Spirit had descended on them. When he died on a winter day in 1833, it was as though some ancient patriarch of the early years of Christianity had died and left the people bereft of spiritual guidance.

The folly of Serafim of Sarov was directed to the glory of God, but Russians traditionally had a warm place for the simple-minded whose folly was directed at the world. The Russians have a special word for such saintly, simple, yet quick-witted men. They call them *yurodiviy,* and some of this same quality appears in the portrait of Yuri Zhivago in Pasternak's famous novel. Ivan-ushka the Simple-minded, who dared to go where less simple-minded people refused to tread, was the hero of a hundred fairy tales told in the villages to gaping children, who saw in him their own follies magnified.

When Dostoyevsky began to write *The Idiot* he had only the most sketchy idea of his theme. He wrote endless notes and outlines, and was continually scratching them out and beginning again. The theme eluded him. The character of the Idiot betrayed him by its inscrutability. He was saintly, certainly, but how much of the earth's dross was mixed up in him? In the end the Idiot became a curious amalgam made up of about one third Serafim of Sarov, one third Ivanushka the Simple-minded, and one third himself. It was a very odd mixture; and that it succeeded at all was due to the relentless pressure of Dostoyevsky's imagination, as he struggled through the many ambiguous meanings of folly to find the precise ingredients which went to make up the character of Prince Lyof Nikolayevich Myshkin. "Who is he?" Dostoyevsky wrote in his notes. "A fearful scoundrel or a mysterious ideal?" He never became a scoundrel, but all the other elements re-mained: he was fearful, mysterious, and belonged to the ideal world which has little relation to our own.

Month after month Dostoyevsky played with the idea of making him a scoundrel, constantly committing violent acts of revenge and pure wickedness—his folly was *la folie de grandeur,*

the knowledge that he was "superior to all creatures," and therefore capable of committing the most outrageous crimes without
remorse. So he is depicted in the early notes as a rapist, a wife-
murderer, a man whose chief desire is to become a banker or the
King of the Jews. Raskolnikov dreamed of being Napoleon; the
Idiot dreams of becoming a god, or at the very least a banker on
the scale of the Rothschilds. The early notes show the author
troubled by perspectives reaching out in all directions. Finally there
comes a note which shows the process of crystallization at work:

> The chief and fundamental idea of the novel is that
> the Idiot is so morbidly proud that he cannot avoid
> thinking of himself as a god, and at the same time he has
> so little respect for himself that he comes to despise him-
> self vigorously. He believes that his desire to take re-
> venge on everyone is vile, yet he goes on committing all
> kinds of wicked actions and revenges himself. He feels
> there is no reason why he should not behave in this fash-
> ion because he is exactly like everybody else and should
> therefore be content, but he suffers from an immeasura-
> ble pride and a passion for truth, and so he demands
> more from everyone.
> But none of this is enough for him, since he has ab-
> sorbed from his environment and upbringing all these
> poisons and abstract principles. A man who has always
> been injured and wronged usually possesses infinite
> generosity and love, but the Idiot does not possess them,
> and therefore takes revenge and commits evil on those
> he would like to love and for whom he would joyfully
> shed his blood. Instead of useful work—evildoing. His
> hopes for the future: I shall become a banker, a King of
> the Jews, and I shall trample them all under my feet and
> hold them in chains—either to be the tyrant and su-
> preme master of mankind or to die for everyone on the
> Cross.
> A man of my nature cannot act in any other way,
> for I have no desire to drag out a useless existence till
> I am old and decrepit.
> He is obsessed with the overwhelming desire to per-

238

form some heroic action, so distinguishing himself and becoming superior to everyone else. He rapes Olga Umetsky. It appears that Olga Umetsky has always been in love with him and always sacrificed herself for him and his wife. This vulgar rape was for her the greatest happiness, and also her death. His wife dies—signs of poisoning—the Idiot says he killed her, but it is Olga Umetsky who is guilty. He continues to insist that he killed her. His uncle leaves him the greater part of his fortune—the other son receives only a small part—but the Idiot refuses the legacy in favor of his brother. In Switzerland I often read the Gospels and the book by Renan. Account of the Holbein painting at Basle. The Idiot loves Olga Umetsky—a strange, childlike friendship between them. As a child he found himself thinking: I shall be superior to everyone. A Christian, and at the same time he does not believe in God.[1]

Nearly all of *The Idiot* is contained in this note, but not in the form indicated here. The single hero who suffered from "an immeasurable pride and a passion for truth" split into two and became two heroes—the ferocious Rogozhin and the saintly Prince Myshkin, the one determined to be master of the world and the other determined to die on the Cross. But since Prince Myshkin and Rogozhin were originally one person, their relationship in the novel remains equivocal. They are seen together in the train in the opening pages of the novel, and they are still together in the concluding pages. In the interval, of course, they have been transformed. Rogozhin has become a murderer, and Prince Myshkin has become a madman, having passed through folly to terror and that madness which is indistinguishable from a living death.

In the note the chief characters of *The Idiot* exist in a state of almost inextricable confusion; Dostoyevsky's problem was to disentangle them and to separate the incidents which belonged to the two adversaries. We can follow him, painfully making his way through the labyrinth, discarding one idea after another until he

[1] *Iz arkhiva F. M. Dostoyevskovo: Idiot*, p. 53.

triumphantly moves towards the final, unshakeable idea that the Prince is a man "drunk with humility," incapable of any action which was not intrinsically good to the point of being a defiance of evil. But there are many kinds of drunkenness and many kinds of evil, and perhaps even more kinds of humility. Dostoyevsky wrestles with the angel, and his notebooks are full of projected portraits of the Prince, which are all discarded except the last. Here is one quick thumbnail sketch:

> Principal elements in the Prince's character. He is cowed, fearful, humble, submissive, completely convinced that he is an idiot.[2]

This is a true portrait of the Prince, but it is not the whole truth. He was a little closer to the final portrait when he wrote: "N.B. The Prince—Christ." But this Christ had to be fleshed out and given the appropriate colors of his St. Petersburg setting. The details came slowly. At first he was a youth, aged nineteen, ungainly and without any history, coming from abroad and so unaccustomed to Russian habits that everyone laughs at him. He is somehow related to the general, but how? Dostoyevsky is not sure and imagines he must be the general's son by his first wife. So for many months Dostoyevsky worked on the portrait of the Prince like a sculptor working on resistant stone until finally there emerged the figure of the twenty-six-year-old exile with the large blue eyes, hollow cheeks, thick curly hair and beard so fair in color that it was almost white. He wears a cloak and a hood, and carries a small bundle wrapped in faded silk. He is one more of those pilgrims who used to wander across the Russian plains. His folly is that he believes in goodness, and will believe in it to the end.

Almost from the beginning Dostoyevsky weighted the scales against Prince Myshkin, depriving him of everything that will help him to succeed in life. He is penniless, an invalid, impotent,

[2] *Iz arkhiva F. M. Dostoyevskovo: Idiot,* p. 98.

inclined to cowardice, rarely capable of action, a gentle Don Quixote confronted by a murderous and tyrannical Iago; and indeed Dostoyevsky read *Don Quixote* and *Othello* while writing the novel and sometimes introduces them into his text with something of the effect of a distant chorus. Cervantes and Shakespeare presided over the birth of the obscure Russian prince, of whose early history before he arrived at the St. Petersburg railway station we learn almost nothing at all.

Dostoyevsky wrote *The Idiot* with more difficulty than any of his other novels. Four or five months were spent in attempting to break through the labyrinth. He was poverty-stricken, and his epileptic fits came at short intervals. Prodigiously restless, he kept wandering across central Europe, from one terrible hotel or apartment house to another. He worked best in Geneva where he spent altogether eight months, and in Florence, where he spent about seven months, completing the book in an apartment house facing the Palazzo Pitti; but there were many restless sojourns in other places. He spent two months in Dresden, six weeks in Baden-Baden, three months in Vevey, and as many in Milan. He was continually pulling up stakes and launching out into unknown territory in search of the composure he needed above everything else. The novel betrays his restlessness. It moves by fits and starts, with something of the jerkiness of early films, and many of the incidents give an impression of quite extraordinary artificiality, as though they were invented by sheer will-power on the spur of the moment to fill up the empty pages. Yet throughout the entire novel we are made aware of the hurricane, with the Prince standing at its still center. Surprisingly, Dostoyevsky himself did not know how the novel would end until he came to the last chapter.

Once again he was writing a morality. There are no characters, no scenery, no plot. Instead there are superhuman forces locked in merciless struggle. The Virtues confront the Seven Deadly Sins, only to be outnumbered and reduced to screaming impotence; yet the struggle is waged with such excitement and contempt for danger that we feel no sorrow over the defeat of goodness. We know from the beginning that evil will triumph; the best face death and madness in the end; but goodness also triumphs in its strange and foolish way.

During the writing of the novel, Dostoyevsky suffered more blows than many men suffer in a lifetime. For many months he was reduced to abject poverty; he gambled, and lost everything; and in May 1868 he lost his only child, Sonya, from pneumonia. The death of Sonya affected him deeply. "She loved to listen to my silly voice," he wrote to Maikov. "When I kissed her, she did not cry or pucker up her face; she would stop crying as soon as I came up to her cradle. Now there comes the doubtful consolation that I may have more children. But where is Sonya? Where is the little one for whom I declare in all honesty that I would rather have chosen a martyr's death in order to bring her back to life? . . ."

He could never forget the death of his daughter, and accused himself of being responsible. The child had never been strong, and that was his fault because he never gave Anna enough money to feed herself properly when the child was in the womb. He adored the child, and was completely shattered by her death. All his hopes had been placed in his daughter, who was buried in a white satin dress in a tiny coffin. Anna wept inconsolably, while he wondered how he could possibly endure living. Geneva, where he was staying, suddenly became intolerable, and at the same time he had to fight against the temptation to stay, to be near his beloved daughter. With a supreme effort he succeeded in taking Anna across the lake to the little town of Vevey. Grief held him prisoner, and although three more children were born to him he remained grief-stricken to the end of his life.

He was ill in Vevey, and work on the novel progressed fitfully. He hated it to the point of disgust, but he knew his only salvation lay in completing it. He disliked the people of Vevey, saying that the Kirghiz in their black tents were cleaner, more intelligent and more endurable than these "filthy and dishonest idiots." In his imagination he lived in a distant and unattainable Russia, purified of its excesses, made tolerable by the presence of a benevolent autocrat; his letters of the time breathe a confident faith in the future of his country as the generator of a new and hitherto unexpected blessedness which will embrace the whole world. He was never more rabidly Pan-Slav than when he was in Switzerland.

But while Dostoyevsky possessed implicit faith in the benevolent autocrat, the autocrat himself seems to have ordered a special watch on him. There had appeared in Russia a curious pamphlet called *The Mysteries of the Winter Palace,* purporting to document the scandals at court. The pamphlet was banned. The Tzar and the police believed that it had been issued by the revolutionaries, but it is more likely to have been published by an eccentric or a madman. The pamphlet is filled with inaccuracies, and most of these could easily have been corrected from available sources. It said, for example, that Dostoyevsky had been committed to the Peter and Paul Fortress on December 14, 1855, and his number on the police files was 7569—both statements were totally inaccurate, and so was the statement that Dostoyevsky's wife had appealed personally to the Tzar. Dostoyevsky was given a copy of the pamphlet, and he seems not to have been unduly alarmed, for he wrote a long attack on the authors and failed to send it, perhaps thinking that a rejoinder was unworthy of him.

If Dostoyevsky had known the consequences of failing to reply, he would have replied at once. As a result of the pamphlet he was held under secret police observation until the last days of his life. The police noted and sent to headquarters monthly reports on him. Long lists of visitors to his apartment were sent to St. Petersburg. Secret surveillance is rarely entirely secret, and he came to know the haunting fears which come to all men who are dogged and shadowed by the police.

The opening pages of *The Idiot* are as carefully wrought as the opening pages of *Crime and Punishment.* The chance meeting of Prince Myshkin with the merchant Rogozhin and the clerk Lebedev on the Warsaw-Petersburg train is described with extraordinary verve. The characters come alive at once. The reader has no time to remember that all the laws of probability have been broken by bringing together by chance three people whose lives are inextricably involved, and who will continue to be involved until the end of the novel. Dostoyevsky throws out his net, and we are all caught in it.

Myshkin is one of Dostoyevsky's supreme creations, comparable with Raskolnikov and Alyosha Karamazov. That we come to know him so well is due partly to a trick which the author had never employed before and was never to employ in quite the same fashion again; for when the Prince calls on his distant relative, the wife of General Epanchin and mother of three delightful daughters, she invites him to tell the story of his life. He does not tell the story. Instead he tells a number of disconnected stories and anecdotes so artfully woven together that we receive a fully rounded portrait of him. He tells the mother and her daughters about his attacks of epilepsy, about watching an execution, about the wronged and despised Marie, raped by a commercial traveler passing through the village, and derided by all the villagers. The Prince tells how he gradually taught the village children to love and cherish the girl who felt herself to be completely abandoned; and when she died, the children placed a wreath of blossoms round his head and heaped flowers over her coffin. Marie is perhaps the dead Sonya, and she is related to the Marya Timofeyevna of *The Devils,* a saintly woman with powers of prophecy, who derives her mysterious strength from the primitive earth. As the Prince describes the years he spent in Switzerland, the curtains seem about to part and we find ourselves on the verge of a revelation. It is a very strange revelation, unlike anything else in Dostoyevsky's works:

> There was a waterfall there, a very small one; it fell from high up in the mountains, like a thin thread, all

244

white and foaming. It fell from a great height, but seemed to be very near, and it was half a mile away, but you would have said it was only fifty yards. I loved to listen to its sound at night, and at such moments I would become terribly restless. Sometimes at noon I would walk in the mountains and stand there, half-way up the mountainside with the old resinous pines around me, so tall they were, and somewhere high up on the precipitous cliffs there was a medieval castle in ruins, far away, and the little village lay below, far away, almost invisible, and the sun shone, and the sky was so blue, and there was only this terrible silence all round me. I thought I heard a mysterious summons, and then it would come to me that if I went straight on and continued to walk for a long while, I would come to the line where earth and sky meet, and then I would find the key to the whole mystery and discover a new form of life richer and more splendid than ours. I dreamed of a great city as large as Naples full of palaces and tumult and exciting life, and then it struck me that life can be enjoyed just as magnificently in prison.[3]

As so often in the novels, we hear the authentic voice of Dostoyevsky himself, describing his own griefs and joys. He is not Prince Myshkin, but he is included within the circumference of the Prince. When he is describing an execution, he derives his knowledge from his own execution on Semyonov Square; and when he describes the torpor and loss of memory and intolerable agony of guilt which accompanies an attack of epilepsy, he is recounting his own experiences almost in the exact words of his letters and the notes about the disease he inserted among the preliminary drafts of *The Devils*. His own voice can be heard from the mouths of many of his characters. The drunkard Lebedev attacks the materialism of the age, in words that might have come from *The Diary of a Writer*. Much of the strange confession of Hippolyte could be inserted in *Notes from Underground* without anyone

[3] *The Idiot,* Part I, Chapter v.

detecting that it did not wholly belong to the earlier work. When Hippolyte describes Holbein's *Christus im Grabe,* we are aware that Dostoyevsky had seen the same picture at Basle. "He was completely carried away by it," his wife wrote. "In his desire to look at it more closely he got on a chair, with the result that I was in a terrible state of nerves fearing he would have to pay a fine."

The picture haunted Dostoyevsky. It was for him the most majestic and terrifying of all paintings of Christ. When he saw it for the first time he was spellbound, with the look of terror on his face which could be seen just before an epileptic attack. To Anna, who took refuge in another room and scarcely dared to look at the painting, he said afterward: "Such a painting can make one lose one's faith."

Christus im Grabe shows Christ enclosed in a kind of coffin, lying at full length, his head thrust back, every muscle of his tormented body proclaiming rebellion against the powers of corruption. He is stark and rigid, but he is also quivering with life; and an unearthly light shines on him. This is the Christ who will not rise again, or if he does, it is only by a miracle so great that in the process the entire earth will be shattered and reformed. It is a painting to be placed beside Grünewald's *Crucifixion* in the Isenheim altarpiece for the terror it inspires.

Dostoyevsky gazed at the painting steadily, and placed in the mouth of Hippolyte his own conclusions:

> There is still a look of suffering on his face, as though the agony were still present, and nothing has been spared. It is altogether natural, and any dead body— one who has died in great suffering—might look like this.
>
> I know that the early Church laid it down that Christ suffered actually and not symbolically. His body on the Cross suffered according to the laws of nature. In the painting the face is terribly mangled and swollen, with bruises which are bleeding, the eyes wide open and squinting, the whites having a dead and glassy appear-

ance. But what is strange above all is that when one gazes upon the dead and tortured body, one finds oneself asking a peculiar question: If this dead body were seen by the disciples, by the future apostles, by the women who followed Him and stood by the Cross, by all those who believed in Him and worshipped Him, how could they have believed as they gazed upon Him that He would rise again?

And so we are gripped by the thought, whether we like it or not, that there is no way to overcome the laws of nature or the horror of death. If He could not overcome them, how can they ever be overcome? During His lifetime He overcame nature, and nature obeyed Him, and he said *Talitha cumi,* and the maid rose from the dead, and He said *Lazarus, come forth,* and the dead man rose from the grave at His summons. But when we look at the painting we see nature as some enormous, implacable and dumb beast or, to put it even more correctly, however strange it may seem, as some huge mechanical engine of modern days which has senselessly seized and crushed and swallowed up a great and precious Being, a Being worth all of nature and her laws, worth the entire earth, which was perhaps created merely for the sake of His coming.

There is in that painting an expression of blind, dumb, eternal unreasoning power, and all men and everything in the world is subordinate to that power. No one who gazes at the painting can escape the knowledge of this power.[4]

This is a sermon of despair written like a lawyer's brief, and all the more effective because Dostoyevsky has striven towards a kind of devilish logic. He had found his vision of Paradise in Claude Lorrain's *Acis and Galatea;* he found his vision of Hell in Holbein's *Christus im Grabe;* and between those two visions, as he had indicated long before in his letter to Natalya Fonvizina, he was to swing like a pendulum throughout his life.

But all through *The Idiot* we are made aware of Paradise in

[4] *The Idiot,* Part III, Chapter vi.

the shape of the tall, slender man with the pointed yellow beard and the enormous eyes, who in the notes is sometimes called Prince Christ. The Prince carries Paradise with him. It is not only that he is devoid of malice and sensuality and the knowledge of evil, but he moves among the vultures with the air of a man who cannot conceive that they are evil; they too are God's creatures. He comes from another world. "I have never been in love," he says, "but I have been happy in another way." And it is clear that his happiness comes from holiness, and against such holiness the vultures cry in vain.

The character of the Prince is complex, very warm and at the same time strangely detached. He is a master of the arts of goodness, and watches for every crack in the armor of his enemies and then insinuates goodness wherever he can find a point of vantage. Speaking of the portrait of the fierily destructive Nastasya Philipovna, one of the Epanchin sisters exclaims: "With such beauty one might overthrow the world!" The words might have been addressed to the Prince, whose beauty is also destructive. He too has the power to overthrow the world, but not for the pleasure of destruction. His purpose is to remake the world in the image of Christ.

He is Paradise walking through Hell. Arraigned against him are a galaxy of devils, mountebanks, perjurors, procurers, parasites, and degenerates; like Christian in *Pilgrim's Progress* he moves among them with dispassionate unworldliness. For all of them he has only one word—a word of blessing. He even blesses Nastasya Philipovna, though she has done her best to destroy him; and when at last she collapses under the weight of her anguished pride and outraged jealousy, he takes her in his arms and consoles her in the belief that consolation is the only gift worthy of suffering humanity:

> The Prince sat beside her, gazing steadily into her eyes, stroking her face and hair with both hands, as though she were a child. He laughed when she laughed,

and he was ready to cry when she cried. He said nothing, but listened closely to her quick excited babble, hardly understanding a single word, but all the time smiling gently. As soon as he detected the slightest appearance of complaining or weeping or reproaching, he began to stroke her hair again and passed his hands gently over her cheeks, soothing and consoling her as he would a child.[5]

It is almost the only gesture he possesses: the gesture of consolation and compassion. Yet it is a gesture conveying innumerable subtleties of meaning and many different kinds of love. With that same gesture the Prince asks Nastasya Philipovna to be his wife, for only in this way can he save her from her enemies and most of all from the unscrupulous and merciless merchant Parfen Rogozhin.

In the stupendous last chapter of the novel, at once the most dramatic and the most completely realized scene in all Dostoyevsky's works up to this time, Rogozhin murders Nastasya Philipovna, and the Prince comes to the house where the dead girl lies under a sheet. A heap of lace lies at the foot of the bed, and through the lace there can be seen a small foot which seems to have been chiseled out of marble. All round the bed is the evidence of the murder: her discarded clothes and jewels, the jars of disinfectant, bits of lace, ribbons and flowers. A knife had penetrated two inches just under her left breast, and she had died instantly.

Through the night the murderer and the saint keep their long vigil. The Prince asks questions about the events leading up to the murder, but he is not an accuser: he asks only because it is natural to him to form an exact account of events. Sometimes Rogozhin bursts into wild laughter, and the Prince calms him. For the most part they speak in whispers, aware of Nastasya Philipovna as of a brooding presence concealed beneath the bedsheet. The winds of madness disturb the air, but for long intervals there is a terrible quietness.

[5] *The Idiot,* Part IV, Chapter viii.

The Prince watched and waited; time was passing, and soon it began to grow light.

Rogozhin's mind began to wander, and sometimes he would burst out in loud incoherent speech, or he laughed aloud, or uttered little screams. At such moments the Prince would stretch out his trembling hand, and gently stroke his companion's hair and cheeks, hoping to soothe him and quieten him—he could do nothing more. His legs trembled again, and he seemed to have lost the power to use them. A new sensation oppressed him, filling his heart with infinite anguish.

Meanwhile it was growing light, and at last he lay down on a cushion in utter weariness and exhaustion, and he laid his face against the pale, motionless face of Rogozhin. Tears flowed from his eyes on Rogozhin's cheeks, and perhaps he was no longer aware of his own tears and knew nothing about them.[6]

Dostoyevsky never wrote with greater intensity, nor with greater insight. There is a perfection in this last scene which goes beyond the art of storytelling: he is creating a legend. He knew very well that he had accomplished his purpose. He wrote to Maikov: "There may be some people who will be a little surprised by the ending to *The Idiot,* but on the whole the ending is one of the most successful pieces I have written, I mean, simply as an ending." He was pleased that the work was done, and the many months of bafflement and despair over the creatures of his imagination were over.

He knew as well as anyone that the novel was full of faults. It was written too hastily, under too many pressures, and there were too many characters. There were many grotesque inventions in the novel which could scarcely be expected to meet the favor of readers, and he wondered sometimes whether the grotesque had a proper place in literature, and concluded that everything depended upon a valid conception of reality. "Reality," he wrote in his notes, "is the most important thing of all. It is true

[6] *The Idiot,* Part IV, Chapter xi.

that my idea of reality may differ from the ideas of others. Perhaps in *The Idiot* man is more real. They may say to me, even though this is true, you did not succeed, you were never able to justify your facts, you are a bad artist. But that, of course, is another pair of shoes altogether."

There was a kind of somber secret underlying the entire theme of *The Idiot:* Prince Myshkin was not an idiot, nor very foolish: he is nothing less than Christ walking through the wasteland of the modern world, and Dostoyevsky speaks too often of 'Prince Christ' in his notebooks to permit any other interpretation.

In *The Idiot* he portrayed Christ and the highest good. In his next novel he portrayed the Devil and the most diabolical evil.

THE DIABOLIC PRINCIPLE

O N NOVEMBER 26, 1869, there occurred in the Petrovsky
Park in the northwest of Moscow a strange murder. An
agricultural student called Ivanov, belonging to a small conspiratorial group, was invited into one of the grottoes which honeycomb
the park, and he went willingly, believing that a small printing
press had been hidden there and he was to be asked for his advice
about the management of the press. Waiting for him inside the
grotto were five or six young revolutionaries, dedicated to the destruction of the Russian state, headed by a short, well-built young
man of twenty-two, Sergey Nechayev, who was their leader. He
was waiting for Ivanov. He was hoping to kill him with the knife he
had slipped inside his heavy boots.

At all other times in his life Nechayev displayed an uncon-
querable calm. He had organized cells under the noses of the
police. He had planned and was about to execute an attack on the
Imperial Armaments Factory at Tula, an important center for the
production of weapons. He had conceived vast and complicated
plans for the overthrow of the monarchy, and was quietly preparing to carry them out. He had composed a spine-chilling document
called *The Revolutionary Catechism,* superbly directed towards
the subversion of the state by revolutionaries as dedicated as Jesuits. He had outlined with the help of Bakunin a comprehensive
philosophy of revolution. He was a man devoid of ordinary human
sympathy, who declared calmly: "Our task is total, terrible, uni-

versal, and merciless destruction." But when it came to the destruction of the student Ivanov, he very nearly panicked.

No one knows exactly what happened in the grotto: we can only piece together the evidence the conspirators furnished at the trial. We know that Nechayev was on edge, wildly excited, muttering to himself. Ivanov had refused to obey his orders and even hinted that the vast conspiratorial organization which Nechayev claimed to control was a figment of his imagination, a statement which was not true, although there was sufficient truth in it to make Nechayev wonder whether his secret had been discovered. He was determined to kill Ivanov if only to demonstrate his power over the conspirators.

There came a moment when Nechayev, gazing into the half-darkness of the grotto, thought he recognized Ivanov. He sprang forward, put his hands round the neck of a young man called Nikolayev, and would have throttled him if others had not come to his rescue. At the time Ivanov was in fact in the grotto. There were whispers, shouts, scuffling sounds. He knew something was wrong, and hurled himself out of the grotto, closely followed by Nechayev who had at last recognized him. They grappled together. Nechayev succeeded in pulling Ivanov down to the ground. He forgot the knife in his boots, or perhaps he was squeamish, for he was heard shouting: "Bring me the revolver!" Ivanov was still fighting, and he succeeded in biting Nechayev's thumb to the bone, but he did no more damage. Suddenly there was a shot, and he was dead, and Nechayev was busily going through his pockets, but no one knows what he was searching for. Nechayev called out to the others to bring heavy stones. He had decided to dump the body in a pond. Afraid that Ivanov was not dead, he fired another shot into the student's head. The other conspirators were milling aimlessly around, whispering and running in the dark and getting in each other's way. Nechayev was calling upon volunteers to help carry the body to the pond, but at first none came. They were desperately frightened. Nikolayev helped to carry the body, and when they came to the pond, Nechayev seems to have pushed Nikolayev into the water. Then at last the body of a perfectly innocent youth, weighted with stones, was dropped into the pond, and the conspirators fled.

Five days later the newspapers announced the discovery of the body, which had risen to the surface. Nechayev had taken the train for St. Petersburg, and was not at first connected with the crime. But gradually, as the weeks passed, students who had known the conspirators began to talk. Quite suddenly the police were aware that a vast conspiratorial network, headed by Nechayev, with ramifications in all the universities, existed. They learned, too, that an attack on the Tula Armaments Factory had been planned and was about to be executed. In their excitement the police tended to magnify the dimensions of the conspiracy. There was a hue and cry for Nechayev, who slipped out of the country in disguise at the beginning of January. He made his way to Locarno, where Bakunin was staying, and contemplated the organization of the revolution from abroad. The police rounded up eighty-four of Nechayev's followers, who were put on trial in July 1871. A year later, with the complicity of the Swiss police, Nechayev also was arrested. He was brought back to Russia and placed in solitary confinement in the Alexis Ravelin of the Peter and Paul Fortress, where he died nine years later. Even in solitary confinement Nechayev fought against the Tzar, and he very nearly succeeded in escaping from prison. He was as merciless to his guards as he had been to his fellow conspirators.

Nechayev's chief claim to fame lies in *The Revolutionary Catechism,* and in his wholehearted defiance of the Tzar even when he was shackled with irons to the walls of his cell. No one ever wrote with such concentrated and cold-blooded venom against the Tzarist regime, nor did anyone ever describe the mind of the pure revolutionary in such pitiless and accurate detail. Here are some of the clauses of *The Revolutionary Catechism:*

The Diabolic Principle

The revolutionary is a dedicated man. Everything in him is subordinated towards a single exclusive attachment, a single thought and a single passion—the revolution.

In the very depths of his being, not only in words but in deeds, the revolutionary has torn himself from the bonds which tie him to society and the cultivated world, with all its laws, moralities and customs, and with all its generally accepted conventions. He is their implacable enemy, and if he continues to live with them it is only in order to destroy them more quickly.

The revolutionary despises and hates the existing social order in all its manifestations. For him, morality is everything that contributes to the triumph of the revolution. Immoral and criminal is everything that stands in his way.

Tyrannical toward himself, he must be tyrannical toward others. All the soft and tender affections arising from kinship, friendship and love, all gratitude and even all honor must be obliterated, and in their place there must be the cold and single-minded passion for the work of revolution. For him there exists only one pleasure, one consolation, one reward, one satisfaction —the success of the revolution.

By a popular revolution the society does not mean a revolution tailored to the classic western pattern, which is fundamentally restrained by the existence of property and the traditional social orders. The only salutary form of revolution is one which destroys the entire state to its roots and exterminates all imperial traditions, the entire social order and the existing classes in Russia.

The society refuses to impose an organization from above. Any future organization will doubtless arise as an expression of the movement and life of the people, but this is a matter for future generations to decide. Our task is total, terrible, universal, and merciless destruction.[1]

Throughout the carefully considered clauses of *The Revolutinary Catechism* there is implicit a new and hitherto unexplored philosophy of destruction. For the first time in modern history a revolutionary had appeared equipped with a valid theoretical basis for the destruction of the state. Lenin found much to admire in Nechayev's thesis, and Hitler indirectly learned from it. When during the trial of the followers of Nechayev *The Revolutionary Catechism* was published in the government newspapers, there were many Russians who realized that the very boldness of Nechayev's plans might crown them with success. At the time of the trial Nechayev was still in Switzerland, out of reach of the Tzar's police.

Dostoyevsky was at work on a novel devoted to a group of conspirators when he learned about the murder of Ivanov. He had begun the novel towards the end of 1869, and the opening chapters were published in the conservative monthly *The Russian Messenger* in February 1870. He hoped to finish the novel in about six months and then return to his long-cherished plan of writing a vast epic which would examine the history of a Russian family through thirty or forty years; the epic was to be called "The Life of a Great Sinner." In the end this epic suffered many transformations, and a truncated version of the original plan appeared as *The Brothers Karamazov*.

Meanwhile he was having difficulties with his new novel. He had little sympathy with the revolutionaries, but a deep and perplexing understanding of them. He worked slowly, tore up whole sections, remodeled his characters, and found himself continually at odds with them. The general plan of the novel escaped him, and was revised at least six times. At one time one of the major characters was to be a Bishop whose task was the reform of the diabol-

[1] *The Terrorists,* pages 21–7.

ical Nikolay Stavrogin, who in the preliminary drafts was known simply as the Prince. An astonishingly varied gallery of revolutionary portraits is contained in the novel. Petrashevsky was vividly remembered even to the details of his dress. Belinsky, too, was remembered, and some of his trenchant arguments are echoed in the long discussions between the revolutionaries. A certain Professor Granovsky, who taught history at Moscow University, and who possessed an overwhelming affection for the history of the Spanish empire, became the model for the old liberal Stepan Trofimovich Verkhovensky, who stands at the threshold of the novel like an old faded emperor. There were also far more surprising influences, which Dostoyevsky made no attempt to conceal, and the most surprising of all was perhaps Prince Hal from Shakespeare's *Henry IV,* who became one of the many prototypes of the most terrifying character he ever invented, for in some of the preliminary drafts of the novel Nickolay Stavrogin was given the name of "Prince Harry." But of all the influences which worked on the novel the greatest was Sergey Nechayev.

The first intimation of Nechayev's influence comes in a letter of Dostoyevsky to his friend Katkov from Dresden on October 8, 1870, after he had been at work on the novel for nearly a year. He wrote:

> One of the most important events in my novel will be the well-known Moscow murder of Ivanov by Nechayev. I hasten to add that except from the newspapers I never knew either Nechayev nor Ivanov, nor the circumstances of the murder, nor do I know them now. And if I did know, I would not copy. I only take the accomplished fact. My imagination may differ in the highest degree from the actual event, and my Pyotr Verkhovensky may not in the least resemble Nechayev; but it seems to me in my astonished mind that there has been created by my imagination a person, a type which corresponds to that murder.
>
> No doubt there are some advantages in presenting such a person, but he alone would not have tempted

me. I feel that these pathetic monstrosities are unworthy of literature. To my surprise he appears in the novel as a half comical figure. Therefore, notwithstanding the fact that the event occupies an important place in the novel, it is nevertheless only an accessory and setting for the acts of another character, who may well be regarded as the central character of the novel. That character is also sinister, essentially evil. It seems to me that this other character belongs to tragedy, though no doubt there will be people reading the novel who will ask: "What does it all mean?"

I sat down to compose this character because I had long wished to draw him. I believe him to be both Russian and typical. I shall be very hurt if I do not succeed with him, and I shall be still more hurt if he is regarded as pompous and inflated. He comes from my heart. Certainly he is a character who rarely appears in all his essential form: he is a Russian character belonging to a certain stratum of society. But please defer your judgment of me until the novel is completed. Something in me tells me that I shall manage that character. I dare not characterize him in greater detail; I am afraid of saying the wrong thing. I say only this—I have described his character in scenes, in action, and not in discussion; therefore there is hope that he will become a real person.

For a long time I could not manage the opening of the novel. I rewrote it several times. In fact something happened to me which has never happened before— for weeks I stopped working on the opening and concentrated on the end. I am afraid this may be the reason why the opening is not livelier. With the five and a half folios, which I am sending, I have hardly set the plot going. Still, I am sure the plot and the action will expand and develop unexpectedly. I can vouch that the novel will continue to be interesting.[2]

It is an important letter, for we see Dostoyevsky grappling with his conceptions of Stavrogin and the young Verkhovensky

[2] *Letters:* 356, October 8, 1870.

(Nechayev), pausing in mid-passage, gazing at them afresh, still debating with himself what direction they would take, uncertain of himself, certain only that he had the energy and knowledge to complete the portraits of the revolutionaries on many planes and in many fields of experience.

When he spoke of knowing nothing about Nechayev or Ivanov "except from the newspapers," he may have been a little ingenuous. His mother's name was Nechayev, and though it was a fairly common name, there is some reason for believing that he was distantly related to the revolutionary; and it is more than likely that he paid particular attention to every scrap of information about him, not only from newspapers. His connection with Ivanov was perhaps closer, for his wife's brother was a student at the same agricultural college in Moscow and an intimate friend of Ivanov. When Dostoyevsky returned to St. Petersburg in July 1871, he was in time to attend the trial of Nechayev's followers and he made inquiries through Anna's brother about all the circumstances of the murder.

In later years he felt a strange compulsion to identify himself with Nechayev. He wrote in *The Diary of a Writer:* "I myself am an old Nechayev, or else—perhaps—might have been a follower of Nechayev, I am not sure. In the days of my youth it might certainly have happened." For him the Nechayev conspiracy was the inevitable corollary of the tensions produced by the time, and he was profoundly aware that the followers of Petrashevsky might have followed "the way of Nechayev," and were in fact very close to following it. In his notes for the novel he sometimes wrote "Nechayev" when he meant "Verkhovensky."

In the novel Dostoyevsky was free to change the circumstances of the murder at his pleasure, but chose to make only a few small significant variations. Oddly enough, though Dostoyevsky mentions the grotto, he makes no use of it. Three conspirators jump on Shatov (Ivanov) in the light of three lanterns, and almost at once Pyotr Verkhovensky shoots at Shatov's forehead. A moment later he is going through Shatov's pockets—he finds only some scraps of paper, the title of a book, and an old bill from a restaurant—and soon he is giving instructions for getting the stones and tying them to Shatov's neck and legs; and then the conspirators, awed, argumentative, and giving way to sudden senseless screams, carry the body to a pond. Dostoyevsky made his conspirators far more hysterical than they were on the night of the murder. They scream, they indulge in fights among themselves, and the swinging lanterns light up a scene of madmen dancing wildly in circles, some with handkerchiefs stuffed in their mouths to prevent them from shouting, others crowding round the dead body and still others running around in a wild panic. In fact, when Ivanov was killed, the conspirators appear to have been remarkably quiet and undemonstrative, and though there was some purposeless running about, most of them stood quite still, regarding the murder with considerable detachment. It was Nechayev's responsibility, and they felt little responsibility of their own.

In *The Devils* Dostoyevsky used Nechayev with extraordinary effect. Verkhovensky is not a madman, or the possessor, like Stavrogin, of diabolic gifts. He is calm, rational, intensely aware of everything that is happening outside him, a student of the logic of revolution. There is a sense in which he can even be regarded as a good man, and in *The Diary of a Writer* Dostoyevsky, in reviewing the arguments caused by the novel, carefully underscored the meaning he intended to convey:

> In my novel *The Devils* I attempted to depict the complex and heterogeneous motives which may prompt even the purest of heart and the most naive people to take part in an absolutely monstrous crime. *The horror lies precisely in the fact that the most vicious and terrible crime may be committed by someone who is not a villain at all.*[3]

[3] *The Diary of a Writer*, 1873, No. 50.

The Diabolic Principle

This is not, of course, the premise with which he started. It evolved after long and painful consideration of the nature of crime in general rather than the particular crime which took place just outside the grotto; and it is as true of Raskolnikov as of Verkhovensky. Dostoyevsky's conception of a crime committed by an innocent man is counterbalanced by his conception of "the diabolic crimes" committed by Nikolay Stavrogin, who is capable of the most absolute evil, and who represents the burning satanic core at the heart of things. He is the Fallen Angel who wanders disconsolately through the world, making evil everything he touches.

Stavrogin is perhaps the greatest single creation of Dostoyevsky, but he is also one of the most puzzling. Quite deliberately he is never sharply outlined. He appears as a presence, as a shadow, almost as a breath of corruption. "Thou art proud and beautiful as a god," Pyotr Verkhovensky says of him, and calls him Ivan the Tzarevich to his face. He is a man of superb and overwhelming pride, capable of the most audacious feats of seduction, "a traitor in the sight of Christ, who is also treacherous to Satan." He is not the Prince of Darkness only, but the one who would destroy the Prince of Darkness if he could, only because destruction should be carried to its utmost possible extent.

In all his life Nechayev, the archnihilist, succeeded in destroying only one man. In all his life Stavrogin succeeded in corrupting only one child. But for Dostoyevsky's purposes this was enough.

Curiously, the power of Dostoyevsky's conception of Stavrogin comes from the author's strange indecision in portraying him. There are signs of fumbling. There are many Stavrogins, and it is only at the very end of the novel that they come together in a single person. In the first drafts the Prince is clearly intended to find regeneration in the bosom of the Church. "The principal idea, i.e., the pathos of the novel," Dostoyevsky wrote in an early note, "is that the Prince and the foster daughter are *new people,* who have undergone temptation and are resolved to begin a *new* restored life." But this conception was quickly abandoned. Gradually, all hope of redemption fell away, and as the notes progress, we see a starker, more terrible, more unregenerate Stavrogin. In a later note Dostoyevsky says: "The Prince speaks to Shatov of the Apocalypse, of the name of the Beast, of the bruised head." The Prince is of course speaking about himself; he is himself the serpent with the bruised head, and the chapter of the novel which describes him at length is called *The Wise Serpent*. But the crucial entry in the notebook, showing Stavrogin for the first time at his full stature, is the following:

> The Prince and the Bishop. The *idea*. The Bishop argues that there is no need for a leap, but one must first restore the man in oneself (by means of long labor, and only then making the leap.)
> *The Prince:* "And if it should suddenly prove to be impossible?"
> *The Bishop:* "Impossible? Then instead of the work of angels, it will be the work of devils."
> *The Prince:* "Exactly as I thought." [4]

We see him gradually turning into a man with a knowledge of evil, impatient of goodness, surprised by nothing that happens to him, accepting evil without fervor because for him evil is something as inevitable as sunrise and sunset. He wears a mask. A faint smile hovers perpetually at the corners of his lips. He walks with royal self-assurance, but there is always something indefinably strange about his appearance. He is in fact the Stranger, the man who has come to the earth from some foreign world, and so he calls himself in the celebrated scene in which Marya Timofeyevna asks whether she may kneel before him. "No, you mustn't," he answers in the voice one uses in speaking to a child. "Remember that though I am your devoted friend, I'm a stranger." Strangeness hovers over him to the very end.

[4] *Iz arkhiva F. M. Dostoyevskovo: Byesi,* Folio 26.

The Diabolic Principle

That strangeness, that sense of a man inhabiting other worlds, was never more brilliantly displayed than in the chapter generally known as "Stavrogin's Confession," which was omitted in the published text. This chapter is not only about Stavrogin's culminating act of evil; it is also about his dreams of unattainable blessedness. It includes a final brilliant portrait of the diabolic principle when it wears the appearance of a mortal man.

In this chapter we see Stavrogin for the first time confronting a man worthy of him, a certain Bishop Tikhon living in retirement in a monastery. Significantly Tikhon means "quiet" or "peacefulness," and the brief sketch of the Bishop is a preliminary portrait which was later to be enlarged and given a quite extraordinary profundity in the figure of Father Zossima in *The Brothers Karamazov*. Stavrogin visits the Bishop and engages him in a discussion on atheism. "It is written that a man with faith can move a mountain," Stavrogin says. "Of course, that's nothing but nonsense. Still, it would interest me to know if you could move a mountain." The Bishop in his slow, restrained voice replies: "If God commands, I can move mountains." Stavrogin extracts from him the confession that even with God's command, he might fail to move a mountain, and laughs in his face. But the Bishop has already taken his measure. According to the Bishop, Stavrogin belongs to "the indifferent ones," those who are neither hot nor cold, those who do not care, and for them there can be no salvation on earth or in heaven, for they are the ones whom God has rejected. Like Father Zossima, the Bishop possesses the gift of prophecy and he can read what is written in minds. He asks Stavrogin whether he has come with the intention of confessing, and Stavrogin replies by giving him the famous three sheets of ordinary notepaper sewn together which contain "Stavrogin's Confession." Significantly the confession is printed, probably on one of the secret printing presses used by revolutionaries abroad, and resembles a revolutionary leaflet. It is entitled simply: "From Stavrogin."

The whole of this confession has a compulsive hallucinatory

263

character. Stavrogin tells how, while intending to play a stupid trick on his mistress, he takes lodgings in St. Petersburg with a working-class couple. They have one child, Matryosha, a little girl of eleven. One day he is left alone with her, and violates her. She falls a victim to the delusion of Lucretia, and believing that she has herself committed a crime, though in fact she is only the victim, she hangs herself. For the few remaining weeks of his life Stavrogin is haunted by the sight of the little girl as he last saw her, standing on the threshold of his room, silent, shaking her little fist at him.

That is all, but Dostoyevsky describes the incident with so much detail and with such terrifying dramatic effect that we seem to be physically present in the room with Stavrogin and the little girl. The actual rape is not described, perhaps for the same reason that we never see the murders on the Attic stage. In her delirium before she decides to hang herself the little girl keeps saying: "I killed God," and this is the only palpably forced note in the chapter. The words belong more properly to Stavrogin himself.

"Stavrogin's Confession" is an essential part of the plan of the novel; its omission in many published editions is a disservice to the author, for with that confession Stavrogin at last declares himself and throws aside the veil of mystery which he has carefully wrapped around him. In that confession, too, we are permitted for the first time a glimpse into the strange career of this man who repudiated both Christ and the Devil. We hear of his travels in the Orient, and his voyages to Egypt and Iceland. We learn that he attended the University of Göttingen, leaving after a single academic year. We hear of extensive travels in Germany, Switzerland and France. He is the wanderer restlessly searching for something which will put an end to his restlessness: in the end he finds it in a hammer, a piece of soap, and a large nail. The rope is heavily smeared with soap, so that the hanging is over more quickly.

But before he dies Stavrogin is vouchsafed a vision of the Paradise which is forever denied him. The vision disintegrated into a red spider crawling on a geranium leaf, but while it lasted it filled him with an extraordinary sense of exaltation. The vision was conveyed by a painting in the Dresden gallery by Claude Lorrain or, as modern critics believe, by Filippo Lauri. This painting is described in a catalogue of Dostoyevsky's time as "a scene on the coast of Sicily. On a rock Polyphemus sits among his flock. In the foreground Acis and Galatea." This is of course only the merest outline of the painting, which does suggest in a quite convincing way a sense of primitive earth-bound peace. The sun is rising in glory over a wooded headland. Ships sail across the seas. Bathers are floating in the calm waters. In the foreground, under a tent made by throwing a cloth over the stumps of trees, Acis and Galatea are embracing one another, while their child plays at their feet. Not far away Polyphemus, with his curiously mask-like face, lying on the ground and resembling one of those drawings composed by Henry Moore in the London Underground during the bombing of London, rests among his sheep. Behind him mountain upon mountain rise into the distance.

Stavrogin is entranced by the painting. Characteristically he believes he is seeing a sunset rather than a sunrise. Perhaps too he sees in the face of Polyphemus a portrait of himself. He has come to Dresden for no other purpose than to stand before the picture. In his confession he describes the effect of the painting on him:

> I saw a remote corner of the Greek archipelago as it was three thousand years ago, the caressing blue waves, rocks, islands, the flowering shore, and far off lay a fantastic panorama, the beckoning sunset—words fail me. In the West, men remember this place as the cradle of the race, and the thought of such a cradle filled my soul with the love that comes from kinship. Here was man's earthly Paradise, the gods descended from heaven and united with mortals, and here too was the beginning of mythology. Beautiful men and women lived here! In blessedness and innocence they awoke, they went to sleep, and the woods rang with their happy songs, and a huge overflowing of unspent energy

poured itself into love-making and simple joys, and I was aware of all this, and at the same time I was aware as though with second sight of the future that awaited them—the great future, the three thousand years of life which lay unknown and unguessed before them, and my heart was shattered by these thoughts.

Oh how happy I was that my heart was shattered in this way, and that at last I was aware of love! The sun poured its rays on these islands and on the sea, rejoicing in its fair children. Oh marvelous dream, lofty illusion! The most improbable of visions, to which mankind throughout its long existence has offered its best energies, for which everything has been sacrificed, the origin of so much yearning and torment, the deaths of so many prophets killed and crucified, the vision without which no nation can afford to live or even to die.

I lived through all these sensations like someone in a dream. I repeat, do not know exactly what I dreamed about, for my dream was only of sensations, and when I woke up I still seemed to see the cliffs and the sea and the slanting rays of the setting sun, and then for the first time in my life my eyes were wet with tears. I remember those tears, and how happy they made me, and I was not ashamed of them. There came to me such a feeling of happiness such as I had never known, which pierced my heart until it ached. Evening had come, and a spear of sunlight pierced the green leaves of the window boxes of my little room and flooded me with light. I closed my eyes quickly, hoping to recapture the vanished dream, and then I noticed a small dark spot in the center of the formidably bright light. I am now speaking very exactly and carefully, for that is how it began. Suddenly this spot assumed a shape of its own, becoming a small red spider.[5]

In putting the vision of Greece into the confession of Stavrogin, Dostoyevsky is not quite playing fair. He was himself deeply impressed by the painting, which he always examined carefully

[5] *The Devils,* Part III, Chapter **v.**

whenever he was in Dresden, and with significant alterations he repeated his lengthy description of the painting on two more occasions, once in *A Raw Youth* and again in *The Dream of a Ridiculous Man*. In his notes for *The Devils* he wrote: *"Götter Griechenlands,* and what God says to man." It would seem that at one time he intended the conspirators to debate on the subject of the Greek gods, setting them up against the God of Christianity, but no such discussion occurs in the finished novel. On the rare occasions when his mind turned towards Greece, the painting of *Acis and Galatea* always occurred to him. In the same gallery he found the *Sistine Madonna* of Raphael, and to this painting also he paid the tribute to devoted admiration. A photograph of the painting, presented to him by Countess Tolstoy, was hanging in his study in the last years of his life.

How profoundly Dostoyevsky was affected by the painting of *Acis and Galatea* appears when we discover it again, subtly disguised and transformed, in the strange and very beautiful utterances of the poor madwoman Marya Timofeyevna, who plays the role of a primitive chorus possessed of an innocence beyond the dreams of the nihilists. She enters the world of the nihilists like a visitation from an unknown and more blessed world than theirs, and while they are telling cards, she suddenly launches into a long rambling speech about the saintly Lizaveta who lived in a cage seven feet long and five feet high let into the wall of the nunnery, and she had been sitting behind these iron bars for seventeen years, wearing only a hempen cloth, hated by the Mother Superior who thinks she has immured herself out of spite or obstinacy. Marya Timofeyevna is sympathetic to Lizaveta. It seems to her that in some mysterious way Lizaveta is fulfilling the proper function of someone dedicated to God. From contemplation of Lizaveta she goes on to contemplate the Mother of God, and she remembers the words spoken by an old woman living in the nunnery in penance for prophesying the future. "The Mother of God is the Great Mother," she says. "She is the damp earth, and therein lies a great joy for men. Every earthly sorrow and evey earthly tear is a joy for us, and when you have watered the earth with your tears a foot deep, you will rejoice at everything at once, and your sorrow will be no more, for so it has been prophesied."

This invocation of the pagan Magna Mater who is also the Mother of God is only the introduction to Marya Timofeyevna's own memories. She remembers a luminous scene on the shores of a lake:

> "I used to go off to the shores of the lake: on one side was our convent and on the other our hill with its pointed top, they called it the Crest. I used to go up that mountain, turn my face to the east, fall to the ground, and weep and weep, and I don't know how long I wept, and I didn't remember anything about it, and I don't remember anything now. Then I would get up and go on my way back when the sun was setting— oh, so big, so splendid, so lovely—do you like looking at the sun, my dear? It's ever so beautiful, but it's ter- ribly sad, too! I would turn to the east again, and then the shadow—oh, the shadow of our mountain was fly- ing like an arrow over our lake, long and narrow, nearly a mile long, as far as the island on the lake, and it would cut that rocky island right in two, and when the island was cut in two, the sun would set altogether and suddenly everything would be dark. And then I used to be so miserable, and then my memories would come back. I'm afraid of the dark, my dear. But what I wept for most was my baby . . ." [6]

Nowhere else in the works of Dostoyevsky is there a land- scape painted so poetically, fraught with so many mysterious terrors. It seems to have spring unbidden into his imagination, pushing up through many layers of the mind. The mountain called the Crest is many things: it is Golgotha, but it is also recognizably the mountain disappearing into the clouds in Claude Lorrain's painting, which also describes a quiet shore bathed in an antique

[6] *The Devils*, Part III, Chapter v.

light. Faintly discernible in the distance the painting shows an island, not unlike Capri, split in two by the sun's rays. While Dostoyevsky was writing the scene, the painting seems to have been hovering in his imagination, summoning him towards the Golden Age when the Great Mother ruled over the damp and fruitful earth.

The vision of Marya Timofeyevna is pagan and Christian: the components are ineluctably bound together. But when she goes on a little later to describe even more mysteriously the cause of her weeping, in a passage of quite extraordinary poetry, we are aware that she is hinting at things too deep for words. Shatov, the revolutionary, amuses himself by asking about the baby. Did she really have one? Marya Timofeyevna replies:

> "Yes, of course, I had a baby! It was a little rosy one with tiny little nails, and my only grief is that I cannot remember whether it was a boy or a girl. Sometimes I remember it was a boy, sometimes a girl. When it was born, I wrapped it in cambric and lace, and tied pink ribbons round it, and strewed flowers round it, and made it ready, and said my prayers, and then I took it away, unchristened as it was, and carried it into the woods; and I was afraid of the woods, and frightened, and what I wept for more than anything else is that I had a baby, but couldn't remember whether I had a husband."
>
> "Perhaps you did have one," Shatov said cautiously.
>
> "That's silly, my dear! You shouldn't talk like that! Perhaps I had one, but what's the use if having one is the same as not having one? There's an easy riddle—can you guess the answer?"
>
> "Where did you take the baby?"
>
> "I took it to a pond," she said, sighing.
>
> Shatov was nudging me with his elbow again.
>
> "But what if you never had the baby, and just imagined it all?"
>
> "You're asking a hard question," she said dreamily, without showing any surprise at the question. "I can't

tell you anything about it. Perhaps there wasn't a baby. I think it is only your curiosity. I'll never stop crying for him anyway, and I couldn't have dreamed about it, could I?" And the big tears glittered in her eyes.[7]

This is sheer poetry, but it is also very much more, for it includes many legends, many hopes, many despairs. Dostoyevsky is despairing over the death of his own child, but at the same time he is vividly remembering one of the oldest of European legends—the legend of Korê, the Great Mother, who came to Eleusis in search of her lost child Persephone and sat on the Laughless Stone and her child was given back to her, but only for half the year, and therefore she could never claim that it was entirely her own.

Dostoyevsky was perfectly aware of the Eleusinian mysteries, if only through his familiarity with Schiller's poem on them. What Marya Timofeyevna calls "an easy riddle" is easy only for her; it is profoundly difficult for the revolutionaries who scorn her because she is lame and half-mad and believes so helplessly in her own visions. Stavrogin marries her in an act of self-betrayal, and he too never comes to understand her riddles, for they are all beyond the understanding of the human intelligence. They are the truths possessed only by the innocent, those who in the words of Shatov "bear God within themselves, and to whom are given the keys of life and the coming world."

There is a sense in which Marya Timofeyevna's story stands at the burning heart of *The Devils*. Hers is the ultimate truth shining like a wavering candle over the huddled groups of revolutionaries, who weave blindly like somnambulists in the darkness, betrayed by the contradictions of the nihilism which they espouse without ever understanding it. In her eyes they are all shopkeepers, blind owls, bad actors and Judases—words which she flings into the teeth of Stavrogin after one of her visions.

Dostoyevsky has of course weighted the scales in her favor.

[7] *The Devils,* Part III, Chapter v.

The Diabolic Principle

This lame epileptic, whom Stavrogin married after a drunken dinner for a bet, is another of "the fools of Christ" who proclaim the coming of the kingdom of God. The revolutionaries proclaim the coming of the kingdom of man, or else they proclaim the final destruction of the world.

The Devils is a vast novel, with many facets, but it includes among its major purposes a catalogue of the many forms which nihilism can take. "There are two forms of nihilism, and their ends meet," Dostoyevsky wrote in his notes for *Crime and Punishment*. By the time he came to write *The Devils* he discovered that the forms of nihilism were legion. There was not only the terrible and weirdly empty Prince of Darkness represented by Stavrogin, and the clean-sighted agent of deliberate destruction represented by Pyotr Verkhovensky (Nechayev), but there were many more, colored in varying shades of darkness. Ranged against Marya Timofeyevna is a motley crowd of intellectual assassins, cutthroats, braggarts, and nincompoops. There are men driven by strange inner compulsions, and others who are outwardly honest with themselves, but incapable of seeing that their plans are self-defeating. There are revolutionaries modeled on Petrashevsky and Durov and on Dostoyevsky himself in his early years, and there are others modeled on the revolutionaries of the seventies. Hence a curious ambivalence in the work. The reader who is informed about the history of Russia in the nineteenth century finds himself confronted by perpetual anachronisms. Incidents happen which simply could not take place in the seventies: they belong to the time of the Petrashevsky conspiracy. So it is throughout the novel, as Dostoyevsky jumps from one period to another, and back again. Yet there was an underlying method in Dostoyevsky's confusion. In the end he assembled so many nihilistic characters that we find ourselves presented with an exhaustive catalogue of them, and this catalogue has been so accurately prepared that we can recognize in the characters of *The Devils* many of the revolutionary leaders who came to power in our own age.

271

Manuscript page of notes for "The Devils."

Dostoyevsky ranges the whole gamut of nihilism, from the quiet Shigalov who announces calmly that he is perplexed by his own data: "My conclusion is in direct contradiction with my original idea—starting with unlimited freedom, I end with unlimited despotism," to the bumbling Lyamshin who believes that the only solution is to destroy nine-tenths of mankind, leaving a handful of people who are educated, to live happily ever after on scientific principles. At some point in between stands the noble compassionate Kirillov, always ready to help others even to the extent of killing himself for a cause he does not believe, a complex character who sometimes speaks in the authentic tones of Dostoyevsky himself. Included among the nihilists is Karmazinov, who belongs to the older generation and "clings to honor only from habit." The portrait of Karmazinov is a cruelly etched study of Turgenev written at a time when the two authors had fallen out, and it is a measure of Dostoyevsky's skill that it proves to be a completely successful portrait—not of Turgenev, but on a certain type of exile from Russia who assists the revolutionaries simply because it amuses him to see the downfall of the motherland. A host of minor nihilists are categorized and placed in their appropriate niches. They are "the swine feeding on the mountain" who ran headlong into the Gadarene lake. "It's a good thing, too," says Stepan Verkhovensky, "for that's all we are good for, and afterwards the sick man will be healed and sit at the feet of Jesus and all will look at him with astonishment."

In this sense the novel is quite deliberately a Christian tract written to show that all the forces of destruction are powerless before the armies of Christ, represented by the peasants. Yet the references to Christian belief are curiously perfunctory. We cannot believe in Stepan Verkhovensky's conversion, and Marya Timofeyevna, who dies tragically at the hands of thieves, seems to stand on the threshold of the novel rather than to have any real place in it. Though she speaks like an angel, she never raises her voice which is drowned by the brilliant roaring and ranting of the assembled devils.

Inevitably the Devil has the best speeches, and what speeches they are! A wild poetry surges through them. The ecstasy and the thudding beat of Marlowe's *Tamburlaine* and *Faustus* run through the proclamations of the revolutionaries. Here is Pyotr Verkhovensky celebrating the chaos he will bring down on Russia:

> One or two generations of debauchery are essential now: unparalleled debauchery, when man turns into a filthy, cowardly, cruel, vicious reptile. That's what we need! And what's more, a little 'fresh blood' that we may grow accustomed to it . . . We will proclaim destruction! . . . Why, why has this idea such a fascination? But we must get a little exercise; we must . . . We'll set fires. We'll set legends going . . . Every 'mangy' group will be used by us! I'll find keen fellows in each of the groups who will be happy to fire a gun, and will be grateful for the honor. And then the uprising! There's going to be such an upheaval as the world has never seen before! Russia will be plunged into darkness, and the earth will weep for the old gods! [8]

This is not the voice of Nechayev, who spoke of destruction with a kind of cold and conniving brilliance; this is a man from the provinces suddenly fired with the ferocious poetry of destruction, his brain teetering as he walks on the rim of the abyss. It was said of Verkhovensky that "when he was excited, he preferred to risk everything rather than remain in uncertainty"; and of all things that excited him destruction was the greatest.

There is nothing new about the poetry of destruction. Again and again through the centuries we come upon those sudden poisonous explosions which fill the air with shuddering. Before Marlowe there was Seneca, and before Seneca there was Aeschylus. Nor is this poetry uniquely European. There are passages in the Koran which breathe the same fire, and there is a famous speech by the Arab leader Hajjaj ibn-Yusuf to the people of Kufah which makes the hair stand on end with its determined threat to destroy the whole city inch by inch, until nothing is left but powder.

[8] *The Devils,* Part II, Chapter viii.

The Diabolic Principle

The famous Ming dynasty general Chang Hsien-chung, who decimated the province of Szechuan and cut off the feet of his officers' wives to make a mound on which he placed the feet of his favorite concubine, was also a poet, and in three spine-chilling lines he described the nature of the nihilist mind:

Heaven brought forth innumerable things to support man:
Man has not one thing with which to recompense heaven.
Kill. Kill. Kill. Kill. Kill. Kill. Kill.

This indeed is the argument of Verkhovensky. Since there is no God, then everything is permissible, morality is bankrupt, and only expediency rules; and it is always expedient to kill. Verkhovensky, Hajjaj and Chang Hsien-chung share the same contempt for the human race. Since men are unworthy, nothing is to be gained by preserving them, and the pure vacuum is to be preferred over the teeming ant nest.

Not all the revolutionaries assumed this high moral standard. While Verkhovensky raves, Kirillov applies himself to wrestling with his intellectual angel. He has Ivan Karamazov's sharpness of perception. He is an engineer, and possesses an engineer's power to deduce absolute laws from a set of relative facts; and if the absolute laws he discovers have a maddening habit of equating all things with zero, it is hardly his fault; he is one of those men doomed to suicide by the disease of atheism. "I cannot understand," he says, "how an atheist could know there is no God and not kill himself at once."

Kirillov is painted in broad strokes. He is wonderfully and poignantly credible as he argues with his angel. He states the case for the divinity of man endowed with self-will. If he were presented with the argument that "man has not one thing with which to recompense heaven," he would answer: "man is the possessor of vast intellectual gifts, capable of storming heaven by a supreme act of self-sacrifice." For him suicide is the sacrifice he offers to the world. By this act he makes himself a god. He says:

Terror is the curse of man, but I will exert my will. I am bound to believe what I don't believe. I will begin, and make an end of it, and open the door, and save. Only in this way will mankind be saved and transformed physically in the next generation; for with his present physical nature man cannot get on with God, I believe. For three years I have been seeking the attribute of my Godhead, and I've found it! The attribute of my Godhead is my own self-will! So suicide is the most I can do to prove my defiance and my new terrible freedom. For it is very terrible. I shall kill myself to prove my defiance and my new terrible freedom! [9]

But the categories are not so easily or so brilliantly assailed. That freedom, which Kirillov desires above all things, is not given for the asking: doubts and hesitations occur to him: he is like a man on the brink of a revelation who suddenly remembers he has duties nearer home. He does not really know whether this freedom will be given to him; he knows only that it was given to one man, and never since that time has freedom of this kind been given to anybody, or even to God.

So he pauses, not to reconsider, but to find more arguments to feed his pride. In all this he is like Dmitry Karamazov who was accused by the prosecutor at his trial of "trying to leap over two precipices simultaneously." He is sure of his pride, but not sure it will sustain him in the leap across the abysses. Kirillov suffers from epilepsy. He knows what it is like to be granted momentary visions, even visions which last only a few minutes of terrestial time; but if he flings himself into eternity, what then? Will the vision endure through eternity, and will the world be renewed?

Kirillov follows his own argument to its logical end. He must annihilate God—this is the last, the most important of the tasks to be performed by man. Since he is perfectly prepared to annihilate God, he sees himself standing at the turning point of history, which must henceforth be divided into two parts—"from the gorilla to the

[9] *The Devils,* Part III, Chapter vi.

The Diabolic Principle

annihilation of God, and from the annihilation of God to the trans-
formation of earth and man physically." But an overwhelming
doubt occurs to him. *What if God has already been annihilated?*

At this point in the argument his ecstasy gives way to despair,
for if God is annihilated there is no meaning to life, and therefore
no meaning to suicide. His suicide will bring about the new age
only if there is a living God who can be toppled from his throne,
only if he, Kirillov, can snatch the fire from the heavens and in
some mysterious way bring it down to earth. The name Kirillov
means "the king," but he wonders whether he possesses the kingly
power. Perhaps after all there is no God, and the whole world is
completely meaningless, and suicide for the sake of mankind is an
act of complete inconsequence. Confronted by despair, the engineer speaks in a kind of desperate poetry:

> Listen to a great idea. There was a day on earth, and
> in the midst of earth there stood three crosses. One on
> the cross had such faith that he said to another: "Today
> thou shalt be with me in Paradise." The day ended,
> and both died and were taken hence, but they found
> neither Paradise nor resurrection. His words did not
> come true. Listen: that man was the highest above
> everything on earth. He it was who gave meaning to
> everything on earth, and the whole planet with every-
> thing in it is sheer madness without him. There has
> never been anyone like him before or since, and there
> never will be, not even if a miracle takes place. For
> this is the miracle, that there never was and never will
> be another like him. And if this is so, if the laws of
> nature are powerless to spare even him, and have not
> spared even their miracle, then the whole planet is a lie,
> and based on a lie, and they have even made him live
> in a lie and die for a lie, and it is all lies and the most
> senseless mockery. Then the very laws of the planet are
> lies, and a charade of devils. What is there to live for?
> Answer, if you are a man! [1]

[1] *The Devils,* Part III, Chapter vi.

So Kirillov twists and turns, caught in a trap from which there is no possibility of escape. Neither his noble-mindedness nor his logic can help him. He recoils, advances, hints at improvisations, makes a baffled retreat, lunges forward, and when he is safest he shouts in alarm to put his antagonist off the track. It is an extraordinary argument, but he plays it well, with a terrifying sense of the urgency of his cause. In the daring and terrible syllogisms of Kirillov we occasionally hear the authentic voice of Dostoyevsky, as he wrestles with his own demons.

The Devils is not a finished work of art like *Crime and Punishment* and *The Brothers Karamazov*. There are too many characters—there are more than thirty—and they keep nudging one another off the stage. There is little organization, and very little development in the characters. Though *Crime and Punishment* was written under great strain, under conditions of appalling poverty and despair, it gives an impression of quiet mastery, with the author in permanent control. In *The Devils* we sometimes have the impression that the characters are hurrying ahead, with the author panting after them. From the beginning to the end there is a sense of incompleteness and distortion, the characters are out of focus, the incidents curiously foreshortened, the plot bent according to prevailing winds. It must be counted among the four major novels, but it is as shapeless as *A Raw Youth* and *The Insulted and Injured*.

Dostoyevsky wrote it with more difficulty than his other novels, against the grain, with many pauses and long periods of sterility. The plan of the novel kept constantly changing. "I could not cope with it, and burst," he wrote at one period. "My work progressed drowsily, and I felt there was an essential defect somewhere, but what the defect was, I could not guess." While writing the novel he suffered one of his most alarming series of epileptic fits, and for a whole month the work had to be abandoned. When he returned to it, an entirely new plan for the novel occurred to him, and he threw away everything he had written and began afresh. Exaggerating only a little, he wrote that a whole year's work was gone, and he would inevitably end up by spoiling it, because he would be forced to write against the clock. "If only I could write for two or three years without worry, secure in my work like Turgenev, Goncharov and Tolstoy, then I assure you I would write such a work as would be talked of a hundred years hence."

Yet he seems to have known that the novel would endure, and until he wrote *The Brothers Karamazov* it was the novel for which he had the most affection. There, if anywhere, he had come closest to the secrets of the human heart. "The idea of the novel," he wrote, "is so fine and so significant that I myself bow to it."

He had good reason to bow to it. In spite of all its defects, and perhaps because of them, he was able to speak "from the heart to the heart."

THE GREAT SINNER

CAROLINE FLAUBERT tells the story of her brother walking across a field near the banks of the Seine on one of the last days of his life and coming at last to the house of a woman who was surrounded by her children. For a long time he gazed at them, lost in dreams. It seemed to him that he was witnessing something very strange and desirable, something which was for ever denied to him. He gazed at them with an expression of unappeasable longing, and then he murmured gravely: *"Ils sont dans le vrai."*

Gustave Flaubert was not the only artist to sacrifice himself to his art and to discover late in life that a family may possess a truth greater than any other truth known to man. The man who spends his life relentlessly searching for perfection in his art may find the walls closing in on him. He is always in danger of suffocating in the rarefied air and of losing his human roots.

Dostoyevsky was perfectly conscious of that danger. He lived for his art, but increasingly his mind turned to the time when he could live for his family. His letters to his wife are filled with self-accusations. He curses himself for wasting his time over the novel instead of being with her. His thoughts turn continually to her: her warmth, her gentleness, her body which filled him with wonder. In his notes for *The Devils* he wrote: "Shatov paces the little chamber where his wife lies in bed, saying: 'How good it is to live quietly, to love, to have children,' "and it is clear that Dostoyevsky has put his own thoughts onto Shatov's lips. But to be able to live quietly, to love, and to have children there must be a modicum of security. The peasant may have security; the artist has none.

Dostoyevsky was physically exhausted by his work on *The Devils*. He wanted a rest, a very long rest. He thought of making a long journey to the Holy Land, partly as an act of penance for the ferocious display of atheism in the novel, partly to find the material for a projected life of Christ. Most of all he felt the need to discover new roots in Jerusalem, Constantinople, and Greece—Jerusalem because it would give him a deeper understanding of Christ, Constantinople because it was the ancient capital of the Byzantine empire and the ancestral home of the Russian Orthodox Church, and Greece because he hoped to discover there some vestiges of the Golden Age. But he knew he could not afford to make such a journey, and even if he could afford it, it would mean leaving Anna for a whole year. He abandoned the journey to the East, but from time to time he talked about it as something he would certainly do before he died.

He had no immediate plans for writing another novel. The miraculous years which saw the creation of *Notes from Underground, Crime and Punishment, The Gambler, The Idiot, The Eternal Husband* and *The Devils* had come to an end; the seven fat years were to be followed by the seven lean years, which produced only one novel, and this one the least of his works. For all those seven years his genius lay fallow. Then in a sudden prolonged blaze of activity during the last years of his life he produced the greatest of all.

There are authors whose individual works receive little acclaim until quite unexpectedly the sheer mass of their work imposes itself on the public imagination. After years of obscurity, they are suddenly propelled into the limelight. So it was with Dostoyevsky. Once more, as in the days after the publication of *Poor Folk,* it began to be a point of honor to make his acquaintance, to meet him at literary salons, and to gossip about his clothes, his behavior, and the words which he spoke in a strange hoarse voice.

Dostoyevsky was pleased with these attentions, and easily seduced by men in high positions who saw in him a defender of the autocracy and an unregenerate enemy of nihilism. He attended the Wednesday gatherings at the house of Prince Vladimir Meshchersky. He fell under the spell of that handsome and beetle-browed young man, who claimed to have the ear of the Emperor. On his mother's side the Prince was descended from the historian Karamzin, the idol of Dostoyevsky's childhood. He was only thirty-two, but he wielded considerable power behind the scenes. He was cynical, corrupt, and wholly mercenary. He edited a magazine, *Grazhdanin* (The Citizen), which in spite of its republican title was in fact an organ of the autocracy subsidized out of state funds. So successful was the Prince in weathering all storms that he was still editing the magazine and receiving a state subsidy more than forty years later. He became a close friend of Rasputin, and died in the odor of sanctity at the age of seventy-five in 1914.

Through Prince Meshchersky, Dostoyevsky was introduced to a still more powerful figure, Konstantin Pobedonostsev, who became his friend and adviser. Pobedonostsev (the name means "bearer of victory") was far more reactionary than Meshchersky, and far more dangerous. He was a cold ascetic scholar, the translator of *The Imitation of Christ,* deeply religious, and in love with power. Tolstoy is said to have modelled Anna Karenina's husband on him, portraying him as "a gaunt old man with protruding ears, orders strung across his starched shirt front, and fingers crackling audibly at the knuckles." He was a Senator, six years younger than Dostoyevsky, and clearly headed for important positions. In time he became Procurator of the Holy Synod, and the power behind the throne.

Dostoyevsky was the willing captive of the reactionaries. He had depicted a young nihilist in *Crime and Punishment* with affection and understanding; but the times had changed. In *The Devils* he depicted them with understanding and a kind of brood-

The Great Sinner

ing hate. More and more he came to fear the nihilists; more and more he came to believe that the autocracy provided a bastion against the disastrous consequences of revolutionary upheaval. In nearly all matters he found himself in intellectual agreement with Pobedonostsev, who proclaimed the virtues of the Russian peasantry and the divine right of kings. But intellectual agreement was tempered by a curious hesitation concerning dogma. He would agree, but there was always a hint of reserve, a suggestion of mocking laughter. The ex-convict was never comfortable in the presence of the princes of this world.

Dostoyevsky also attracted the notice of Tretyakov, the millionaire merchant who had built up a great art gallery in his palace. Tretyakov wanted a portrait of Dostoyevsky to add to the other portraits of contemporary authors in the gallery, and commissioned the famous artist Vasily Perov to do it. Perov went about the work carefully, determined to paint his sitter in a characteristic mood. For a week he went to the apartment, talked, watched, sketched. Dostoyevsky spoke freely, took an immense liking to the painter, and became interested in the painter's art. Finally Perov painted him in a heavy brown coat, his hands clasped over his knees, his broad shoulders hunched a little, on his face an expression of intense absorption as he gazes into the far distance. It is a brilliant portrait. When seen in color, it suggests rude health and a settled composure. There is no shadow of grey on the orange-yellow beard. There is a suggestion of strain in the hands with their long fingers, but it is only a suggestion. The fingers are slender, and so are the wrists. The temples are hollowed, but the brow is unfurrowed, with the skin drawn smooth to the bone. It is the face of a man who has suffered deeply, but is at peace with himself, at peace with the ideas teeming through his brain.

His wife was startled when she saw the portrait. She thought she was the only person who had detected that peculiar air of absorption, of withdrawal from the world. She would see that expression when she entered his study at night, when he was unconscious of her presence. In her eyes Perov was a miracle-worker, who had caught Dostoyevsky in the moment of creation.

With *The Devils* completed at last, Dostoyevsky was in no hurry to create new characters. His chief desire was to return to the world, to study people, to observe at his leisure; and Prince Meshchersky fulfilled all these desires by making him assistant editor of *Grazhdanin* at a salary of 3,000 rubles a year with additional payments amounting to about 2,000 rubles for the articles he wrote under his own name. He liked editing, and he especially liked to write the articles later collected together under the title *The Diary of a Writer,* in which he discussed anything that occurred to him. He wrote reviews, criticisms, stories, reminiscences, interpretations of crimes, political essays, obituaries. He wrote like a man obsessed with the desire to communicate his experiences to others; and perhaps one tenth of these short articles make rewarding reading today, but nine-tenths belong to the facile journalism of the time. Too often he descends into banality and triviality, and much of the writing betrays a sense of exhaustion.

But the flame of genius never quite died down. Occasionally, as though to prove himself, he wrote a story or a few paragraphs of reminiscences which showed him in full command of his powers. One of the earliest numbers of *Grazhdanin* under his editorship contains the story *Bobok,* which forms a kind of sequel to *Notes from Underground. Bobok* describes the conversations of the dead in a cemetery as they recount their former glories and pass judgment on the newcomers. Their chief pleasure lies in needling each other, and planning complicated graveyard debaucheries, while occasionally discussing the philosophical implications of death. Platon Nikolayevich, scientist and Master of Arts, mutters his portentous theories of consciousness. Someone else, almost completely decomposed, arouses himself sufficiently once every six weeks to utter the meaningless word *"bobok,"* so demonstrating that there is an imperceptible speck of life still warm in him. Avdotya Ignatyevna screams: "Let's undress!" and a moment later reminds herself that she can do anything she pleases, for no human laws operate beyond the grave; then she realizes that no human hands will ever caress her. In a sense it is Kirillov's problem: she has found perfect freedom in death, but this freedom involves a perfect tyranny.

Dostoyevsky pursues the dead into their hiding places. The grotesque conversations are reported with a terrifying air of verisimilitude. We are no longer "under the floor boards," but further down: some five or six feet further down. There are no ghostly voices: instead, there are screams, titters, sudden ejaculations, explosions of sudden laughter, spasms of hysterical anguish. It is a graveyard bedlam seen with uncanny clarity, and Dostoyevsky is keen to point the intolerable lesson—"Such are the dead of our time!"

If Prince Meshchersky had read *Bobok* carefully, he would have realized that Dostoyevsky was displaying an intellectual nihilism as savage as the nihilism of the revolutionaries. Dostoyevsky might believe in the divine principles of Russian autocracy, but he possessed singularly sharp reservations about the officials who supported the autocracy, for he pilloried them unmercifully. He also had reservations about the Prince's capabilities as editor-in-chief and lost no opportunity to edit and re-edit the pompous editorials of his employer.

In March 1874, when Dostoyevsky had been editor for only a few months, Prince Meshchersky sent him an article which included some quotations from the speech of the Emperor to a deputation of Kirghiz tribesmen. Dostoyevsky apparently did not know that the Emperor's words could never be reproduced in direct quotation without the permission of the minister of the court, or he assumed that permission had been granted. He printed the article and was immediately arrested, fined twenty-five rubles, and given a three-day prison sentence. He was lodged in a fairly clean room, and on the whole enjoyed the experience. His friends came to visit him, and they found him sitting at a table, sipping tea and reading

Les Misérables, which he immensely enjoyed. Meshchersky had the good grace to write him an abject note of apology. Dostoyevsky regarded the experience as only one more of the pinpricks he had received at the hands of the Prince, and as the year advanced, he found himself more and more out of sympathy with the magazine, his employer, and life in St. Petersburg. In December 1874 he resigned, and soon afterward he rented a small country house in Staraya Russa, where he had spent the summer of 1872. There he began to write *A Raw Youth.*

Staraya Russa was a small watering-town about 150 miles from St. Petersburg in Novgorod province. Though small, it had nineteen churches and a considerable theater, and people flocked from all over Russia to take the saline waters. Apartments were cheap and could be rented at eighty rubles for the season "except for laundry." The town stood at the confluence of three rivers, and the air of the place was balmy and restful.

Dostoyevsky, his wife, and the two children, Luba and Fyodor, occupied a small comfortable house embellished with *chinoiserie.* In later years Luba remembered it: "Everything in the house was in miniature. The tiny, low-ceilinged, narrow rooms were furnished with old empire pieces. The mirrors were green, and they distorted the reflections of all who gazed into them. Instead of the usual painted walls there were false walls made of canvas on which wallpaper was pasted; our young, amazed eyes saw enormous Chinese women with fingernails several inches long and tiny feet inserted in baby shoes. Our greatest joy was a verandah with many-colored panes of glass. There was also a tiny billiard table which was Chinese and equipped with glass balls and little bells, and this kept us amused during the long rainy nights of our northern summer. Behind the house was a garden with miniature flowerbeds."

In this miniature setting Dostoyevsky thrived. He led a life of tranquil activity, regulated by the clock. His house—it was really a long, low cottage, with the bath house, where he steamed himself, set in a small garden-orchard—was on the outskirts of the town,

Chris Ethin
English

4/30/84

For minutes I would not
be able to pay or do anything.
I would be standing there dum-
swaying (mean my knees), or the
verge of fainting.

so providing him with an excuse for an afternoon walk to the center of the town, and in this he behaved exactly like countless other visitors. He still worked at night. He woke at eleven, took his first meal at noon, and spent part of the afternoon with Anna in the locked study, dictating the work of the previous night. Then he went out for his afternoon walk, the same walk day after day. Beggars knew the exact minute when he would be passing along the road, and since he was usually deep in thought and in any case had no memory for faces, they took advantage of his coming by lying in wait for him; and day after day he gave the same beggars money. According to Luba, Anna knew this and decided to put a stop to it. She threw a shawl round her head, and stood by the roadside with her small daughter beside her, and when Dostoyevsky came down the road, she stretched out her hand and whined: "Dear gentleman, have pity on me! I have a sick husband and two children to support." Dostoyevsky gave her money and would have passed on, but she burst out laughing. Like many men who like to play practical jokes, he hated to have practical jokes played on him. He shouted at her that it was a stupid trick, and she should have known better than to hold him up to ridicule in front of his own daughter.

Day after day he followed the same routine, calling at a sweetshop to buy sweets for the children, and then going on to the newsstand for the St. Petersburg papers. He was like an elderly bourgeois, content, tranquil, with no shadows disturbing the quiet round of his work and leisure.

The epileptic attacks became less frequent. Some of the very worst of them had taken place while he was writing *The Devils,* and his notes on the novel are interspersed with detailed summaries of the attacks. He noted that many of these attacks took place in the early morning, shortly after he had gone to bed. Generally they came about every three weeks, although on occasion there might be an interval of only ten days. Many of these attacks occurred on rainy nights, at the time of the full moon; and they al-

ways left him weak and unable to concentrate on writing for a period of three to five days. Here he is describing an attack in February 1870:

> The attack came while I was asleep. I had gone to
> bed at ten past five in the morning, before dawn. I
> knew nothing, and it was only when I woke up at
> eleven in the morning that I realized there had been an
> attack. They say it was a very small attack, and so I
> suppose it was, though the consequences—heaviness,
> headaches, jangled nerves, nervous laughter and mysti-
> cal sadness—lasted just as long as they did in the past.
> For five days or even a week these things endure, and
> the head is not clear. Absolutely no moon: much
> warmer, haze in the air, but during the day the sun
> came through. I am writing this on February 27, Sun-
> day. One might truly say this is the first day of Spring.
> But on the moral plane—innumerable worries, no
> news, Luba has fallen ill (may God preserve her!) [1]

Most of the attacks seem to have been precipitated by emo-
tional disturbances. Often they came unexpectedly during sleep,
but sometimes they were preceded by terrible shivering fits. There
was nothing he could do to ward off these blows; he could only
suffer them and prepare himself as best he could for the moment
when he recovered consciousness and saw Anna looking at him—
an almost unrecognizable Anna, for she could never hide her horror at the sight of his pale, tortured face after an attack, and it hurt
him that she should suffer so.

But with increasing security the attacks began to taper off. In
1874, when he worked as editor of *Grazhdanin,* there were only
twelve attacks, and it pleased him that they were widely spaced,
thus giving him an opportunity to recover during the intervals. The
horror lay in the knowledge that the next attack might kill him;
that he had never sufficient money to make financial provisions for
Anna and the children; that each attack had the effect of confusing

---

[1] *Iz arkhiva F. M. Dostoyevskovo: Byesi,* Folio 62.

him about the characters of his novels and it needed a prodigious effort of will to resume work on them; that there was always a period of "mystical sadness" following the attack, when the world seemed remote and unreal and hardly worth the effort of making peace with it, and the winged clouds of darkness settled on him. At such times he was like a man wandering through darkness without hope of seeing the light.

In his novels and letters he described the oncoming of these attacks many times and nearly always he spoke of the overwhelming sense of guilt which followed them. He spoke of a "mystical horror" or a "mystical sadness," filled with sensations of grief and the knowledge of some forgotten crime committed long ago. Such experiences were well-known to the mystics who journeyed through "the dark night of the soul," and there is no reason to suppose that he was grief-stricken over some real crime committed in his youth. The melancholy came from the knowledge of evil in the world, which he shared with all human creatures; only he knew evil more clearly and more desolately by virtue of these attacks.

At such times he saw himself as "a great sinner," and the phrase lingered in his mind until it became the title of a long projected novel which in the manner of projected novels exfoliated in a number of separate novels. Parts of "The Life of a Great Sinner" were included in *The Devils*. At least one chapter of *A Raw Youth* derives from this source, and *The Idiot* betrays the influence of some of the notes he wrote on this theme, while *The Brothers Karamazov* is perhaps the same novel seen in the light of an apocalyptic judgment, where the great sinner is the innocent Alyosha, whose sins were to be recorded in the sequel that was never written. In the last years of his life the theme of the great sinner seems to have haunted Dostoyevsky continually.

The phrase however was not new. He had used it years before in *Crime and Punishment,* where Raskolnikov says to Sonya: "You are a great sinner, and your worst sin is that you have destroyed and betrayed yourself for nothing." But the projected novel implied another kind of sin altogether, one so great that it would shake the foundations of heaven.

The notes for "The Life of a Great Sinner" are to be found in the notebooks of *The Devils*. They are scattered over many pages, and it is not always easy to distinguish them in the mass of disjointed material. Here and there we hear the authentic tone of the new novel:

> I myself am God, and he makes Katya worship him. God knows what he is doing with her. "I shall love you when you can accomplish everything."
> In the vagaries of his imagination there are infinite dreams reaching to the overthrow of God and the putting of himself in His place.

> After the monastery and Tikhon, the Great Sinner returns to the world to become *the greatest of men*. He is sure he will be the greatest of men, and he behaves accordingly: he is the proudest of the proud, and conducts himself toward men with the greatest arrogance. He is vague as to the form his future greatness will take, and this accords perfectly with his youth. But (and this is important) he has acquired from Tikhon the idea (conviction) that in order to conquer the whole world it is enough to conquer oneself. Conquer thyself and thou shalt conquer the world. No career is chosen for him, but neither has he the time: he begins to observe profoundly within himself. . . .

> Sudden adolescence and debauchery. Atrocious sins. Abnegation. Insane pride. By pride—

> He becomes an ascetic and a pilgrim. He travels across Russia (love story. Thirst for humility) etc.
> Fall and recovery.
> An extraordinary man—but what has he accomplished?
> *Characteristics*. Through pride and immeasurable arrogance towards people he becomes meek and humble to all, precisely because he is already superior to all.

N.B. He wants to blow out his brains (a small child left outside his door).

In the end he establishes a school for foundlings in his house and becomes someone like Haas.[2] More and more serene.

Dies confessing his crime.[3]

There are eight or nine pages of notes which can with some certainty be attributed to "The Life of a Great Sinner": most of these pages detail incidents and scraps of conversation which assume no recognizable pattern. The intelligible portions are those quoted here, and they too suffer from having only a rudimentary pattern. There is a nameless hero burning in a ferocious flame of pride until the fire cleanses him; a prolonged visit to a monastery; a love story; a journey through Russia; a foundling; a school. These are the bare facts of the novel, but more important is the mood, the particular glow and trajectory of pride as it flares across the heavens and illuminates him. This is another Kirillov, wrestling with God, girding himself with the weapon of pride, the most deadly of the seven deadly sins, until the weapon turns in on him and destroys him as a protagonist in the drama, leaving him with no recourse but to become a man of charity. But the outlines are never clear. *An extraordinary man—but what has he accomplished?* We can only guess the kind of adventures he would experience. We do not need to guess that the pride was satanic.

From hints here and there in his letters and especially from a long letter to Maikov it is possible to fill out some of the details of the projected novel, which was originally called *Atheism,* and went through many successive phases. Writing to Maikov in December 1868, Dostoyevsky spoke of it as a very long novel which would take two years to complete, and he would need a whole library of books on atheism, and on Catholic and Orthodox churchmen. He wrote:

[2] Fyodor Haas (1780–1853) was the chief medical officer of the Moscow prisons and a well-known philanthropist.
[3] *Iz arkhiva F. M. Dostoyevskovo: Byesi,* Folio 12, 19.

The chief character is a Russian of our own class, mature, and not very well educated, but not without an education or without rank—*suddenly*, in his maturity, he loses his faith in God. He has spent his life wholly absorbed in his work, following an unchanging routine, and in all his forty-five years he has done nothing extraordinary. (The psychological solution—deep feelings, a man, and a Russian.) When he loses faith in God he is absolutely shattered. (The action of the novel and the environment are exhaustively treated.) He makes fun of the new generation and studies them—atheists, Slavs, Europeans, Russian fanatics, hermits, priests. Also, he is thoroughly captured by a Jesuit, and then by a propagandist, and then by a Pole: so he falls to the utmost depths of self-degradation, and in the end he returns to discover Christ and the Russian earth: the Russian God and the Russian Christ. (For God's sake don't tell anyone about this: I am going to write this last novel even if it kills me, and whatever happens I shall say what I have to say.) [4]

But though he had a complete picture in his mind of the direction he was going, the novel's characters obstinately resisted him. He tried to flesh them out, but they remained hollow. He thought there would be a Catholic priest, a good priest, someone like St. Francis Xavier, but the character never materialized, and the only Catholic priest he ever created in his own works was the Grand Inquisitor of *The Brothers Karamazov*.

There were other problems which confronted him as he girded himself to write "The Life of a Great Sinner." It would have to be a work of vast complexity, covering a huge area of Russia, involving complicated family relationships, many saints and many sinners: for such a work an author might reasonably prepare himself with a number of minor supporting works acting like cruisers escorting a battleship. He had no doubt in his mind that "The Life of a Great Sinner" would be the culmination of his career. He would put into

[4] *Letters:* 318, December 11, 1868.

it everything of himself, and everything he knew. But the more he looked on the work, the more he dreaded it, and before his eyes it began to disintegrate. Instead of the great novel which would weave together all the varied strands of Russian life, he found himself contemplating a series of five shorter novels each of which would deal with some characteristic aspect of Russian life in the fifties, those years which Dostoyevsky spent largely in Siberia and which were therefore all the more precious to him. These five novels would be quite independent of one another. He went so far as to give them titles—"Early Years," "The Monastery," "Before Exile," "Satan and the Female," and "Great Deeds." "Early Years" seems to have been designed as an autobiographical fragment with one difference—the hero would resemble Dostoyevsky in all particulars except that he would be dedicated to crime. He would steal, lie, murder, commit blasphemy, steal the jewels from a holy icon, and torment a poor crippled girl. He would see his own father killed by serfs and detect his stepmother in an act of adultery. The novel would describe the development of the criminal instinct in a youth who was recognizably Dostoyevsky, not as he was, but as he might have been, and as he sometimes saw himself—the Great Sinner, the man with a load of murderous mischief on his back.

In the second novel, "The Monastery," we see the boy sitting at the feet of a saintly old priest. Dostoyevsky put great hopes on this novel, for it delighted him to show crime and sanctity confronting one another. Another Rogozhin would confront another Myshkin. The boy, who is never named, would take the priest's words to heart, but finally in a mood of disillusionment with all the affairs of the monastery he would return to the world and resume his life of debauchery, join the nihilists, and suffer exile. The fourth volume would presumably deal with his adventures with women, and in the final volume, having achieved some high position in the government, he would commit a terrible crime which would have a widespread effect throughout Russia. Pardoned by the Tzar, the hero would commit acts of penance and make his peace with the world by founding an orphanage.

"The Life of a Great Sinner" was never written, for a very good reason. It was not a novel, but an autobiographical fantasy, and it could never be written because the portentous character of the sinner belonged to day-dreams and was circumscribed by Dostoyevsky's consummate inexperience. He was not, and never could be, a Great Sinner, although he could assume the guilt of all sinners everywhere and imagine himself inhabiting their flesh. He could not make himself the central character of a novel, as Job is the central character of *The Book of Job,* for he lacked the power to project his whole self on paper. In his novels he divides himself into many parts: he is Myshkin and Rogozhin, and there is something in him too of the temper of Nastasya Philipovna, Hippolyte and Lebedev. He was all these, and he gloried in his power to assume their characters; but it was beyond him to be one person involved in a senseless orgy of crime and an equally senseless repentance. If "The Life of a Great Sinner" had ever been written, it would almost certainly have been a tragic failure.

But though the novel was never written, the cumulative sketches and outlines which he wrote to prepare himself for the task had a profound interest for him and an equally profound influence on him. The next two novels derive from it. *A Raw Youth* is clearly a variation on the preliminary sketches for "Early Years," while *The Brothers Karamazov* describes in the person of the saintly Alyosha the youth who might one day escape from the monastery and wage war against the world.

For Dostoyevsky "The Life of a Great Sinner" was a reservoir from which he could draw inexhaustible reserves of power. Without that all-encompassing and impractical design, he would never have accomplished the great work of his maturity. From his notes on the unwritten novel he derived the philosophy which gave meaning and significance to his characters: they were all part of that design, even if the design was never explicitly stated. From these notes, too, we can deduce the central elements of his philosophy as a novelist. It was a home-made philosophy, hammered out of experience, and it spoke of a man's determination to force his way back to God while suffering in himself the crimes committed in his own time. Dostoyevsky saw himself as another Pushkin, one of those who incarnate their age, who look steadily to the future and are not afraid, because all the forces of the age are working through them.

For him there was one central fact: that life was meaningless without God. Against that fact he struggled with all his strength, pitting himself against the world and against Heaven, hoping to take Heaven by storm and the world by conquest, resolute in the examination of his despair whenever he fell back, and taking courage from despair whenever he had strength enough to attack. He showed incredible audacity. He had the theologian's temper, and the theologian's determination to penetrate all the disguises of God. He made a profound study of crime, because crime was the visible sign of God's absence; and since crime was ever-present, and seemed indeed to be endemic, threatening the entire social structure, he determined to follow it to its hidden roots even if it meant following it through labyrinthine darkness. No one ever understood crime so clearly, with such a frightening clairvoyance. There exist whole territories of crime which remained unmapped until he surveyed them. He was among those rare men who dare to enter uncharted regions of the spirit, and in this sense he was the forerunner, for his own dilemmas proved to be the dilemmas of subsequent generations. He was the first modern man.

"The Life of a Great Sinner" gathered force within him, and never left him. Though he was never to write it, he knew he would write some part of it, a work intimately related to it. He wrote *A Raw Youth,* which resembles the sound of an orchestra tuning up before the performance. Afterward in *The Brothers Karamazov* there came the massive voice of the full orchestra.

THE BREATH
OF CORRUPTION

WHEN DOSTOYEVSKY set about writing *A Raw Youth* he intended it to be a full-scale study of the corruption of his time. He would bring the youth to St. Petersburg and introduce him to a great variety of corrupt officials, merchants and revolutionaries; and the story would describe the youth's journey through a corrupt landscape where all values were in jeopardy and God lay hidden behind clouds. It was to be a study of the "underground man" as he emerges into the light, helpless and a little dazzled as he travels through the unfamiliar landscape. The hero of the morality play was to be a young man walking the tightrope between innocence and corruption, succumbing at last to the temptations of the great city.

Dostoyevsky had planned the novel on a large scale. In his own mind his purpose was clear. He regarded the novel as a "poem" about the raw youth, "the story of his strivings, hopes, disillusionments, griefs, regeneration, whatever he learned from life— the story of a very precious and sympathetic creature." In the end, like the Great Sinner, the youth would enter a new life, and the novel would conclude with "a hymn to every blade of grass and to the sun." The novel then was to be a study of corruption in society and in the family, and of regeneration through tragedy. The hero was to possess three distinct characteristics—a charming gawkiness in his appearance, an intense thirst and passion for life, and a deadly seriousness in debate. He was to be a heroic figure provided with heroic trappings, but there were to cling to him many elements of the "underground man." In Dostoyevsky's eyes he was writing a book of quite extraordinary contemporary interest. The hero was to be typical of his time.

Dostoyevsky was perfectly serious in his desire to invent a "typical" character, emerging from "the underground" and confronting the corruptions of his time. He regarded the "underground man" as the most truthful of his creations; and he made out a special claim to be the discoverer of this hitherto unknown territory. He proclaimed in his notes for *A Raw Youth:*

> I alone have evoked the tragic condition of the underground man, the tragedy of his sufferings, of his self-humiliation, of his aspirations towards an ideal world, and of his incapacity to reach it. I alone have evoked the lucid insight with which these wretched creatures penetrate into the fatality of their beliefs and conditions; a fatality so great that it is impossible for them to avoid it.[1]

The drama of the callow youth rising out of the lower depths was to be played against the scenes that Dostoyevsky knew well—the houses of princes and merchants, and the tenements with their cheerless apartments filled with the misery of chipped washstands, screened beds, and sofas from the secondhand markets with the stuffing pouring out. Like Raskolnikov, the hero would find himself daydreaming of great wealth, and like Prince Myshkin he would possess a natural attraction for danger. The theme was magnificent, and well within Dostoyevsky's grasp.

A Raw Youth was the first novel to be written by Dostoyevsky when he was comparatively free from financial worries. He had saved some money from the time when he was editing *Grazhdanin,*

---

[1] Quoted in Gorge Steiner: *Tolstoy or Dostoevsky* (New York: Alfred A. Knopf; 1959), p. 215.

and he had received a handsome advance from Nekrasov, who intended to publish the book in serial form in his magazine *Fatherland Notes.* For the first time in his life Dostoyevsky was enjoying considerable affluence. Except for a lonely visit to Ems to take the cure, he was living quietly and happily with his family at Staraya Russa.

Perhaps it was the very quietness and security of his life which made for the looseness in the novel's structure, and the curious diffuseness of the characters. Julius Meier-Graefe spoke of the novel progressing "like the shattering bumps of a badly sprung carriage on an interminable journey," and there is some truth in the statement. The novel fails to grip. We never quite believe in the hero, Arkady Dolgoruky, who is empty, vain, rather childish, at the mercy of whatever winds are blowing. He has no muscle. He very rarely exerts himself. He suffers, but his suffering lacks grandeur. There is nothing about him corresponding to the furious electricity which plays about the features of Raskolnikov, Pyotr Verkhovensky and Prince Myshkin. He never wages war against the surrounding corruption, but accepts it willingly. From the beginning he gives the appearance of a man too timid and too exhausted to cope with life, and he is still timid and exhausted at the end.

Dostoyevsky was perfectly aware of the book's faults, but was incapable of correcting them. He wrote to his wife that there are four novels in *A Raw Youth,* but this is an underestimate—there are at least six themes which are continually getting in each other's way. The major fault however lies in his curious detachment from the hero. It is as though he is hardly interested in the fate of his hero, and quite cheerfully uses him as a peg for his own sermons, his own prejudices, and his own daydreams.

In January 1876, some months after the publication of the novel, Dostoyevsky made an attempt in *The Diary of a Writer* to describe the characteristics of his hero. He wrote:

> *A Raw Youth* was the first trial flight of my new ideas. I was writing about a child who had already out-

lived his childhood, and appeared now as an unfledged youth, timidly and then boldly seeking to take his first steps in life. I took an innocent soul already touched with the possibilities of corruption, with an early hate derived from his own nothingness and "accidentalness," and possessed of that largeness of spirit with which a pure soul will often entertain vice in his thoughts and nourish it in his heart, and shyly give way to daring and tempestuous dreams—all this is left to his own innate strength, his powers of reason, and even more truthfully to the will of God. These are all the abortions of society, the "accidental" members of "accidental" families.[2]

What Dostoyevsky means by "the accidental" is never quite clear. Arkady Dolgoruky is the illegitimate son of the wealthy Versilov by a serf woman, and for no particular reason he has been given the princely name of Dolgoruky. His name therefore is a ridiculous one. "Whoever," he asks, "has heard of a Dolgoruky who is not a Prince?" He comes to St. Petersburg with a secret document sewn into the lining of his coat pocket, and very soon the document, which concerns the inheritance of a huge fortune, is eagerly sought by a host of relatives, cutthroats and assorted revolutionaries who want to put the money to the service of the revolution. Young Arkady and the document are the two thin threads which give a sense of direction to the novel. Neither the document nor Arkady himself, who writes the novel in the first person, are particularly credible. Credibility is reserved for the aristocratic Versilov and for Arkady's real father, the saintly and disingenuous Makar Ivanovich. Neither of them is touched to any remarkable extent by the sense of corruption which Dostoyevsky described in his notes as the principal theme of the novel:

> *Chief idea.* The concept of disintegration in everything. Disintegration is the most important and obvious conception of the novel. Everything is falling apart—

[2] *The Diary of a Writer,* January 1876, I, ii.

even the children are alone. Society is chemically disintegrated.[3]

Versilov is an aristocrat, and a defender of aristocrats. He believes like Dostoyevsky that God has reserved a special place for the Russian aristocrat, the custodian of Russia's future. "There are perhaps only a thousand of us in Russia," Versilov says. "Perhaps a few more, perhaps a few less, but so far Russia has existed only to produce that thousand. I may be told that the result is poor, if so many hundreds of years and so many millions of people have produced only that thousand. Myself, I don't think it is poor!"

Versilov is not being pompous. He is simply repeating a statement of faith not unlike the statements made by Dostoyevsky himself in *The House of the Dead*.

Though not a self-portrait, Versilov reflects many of Dostoyevsky's opinions, It was one of Dostoyevsky's most cherished ideas, stated most dramatically in his famous speech in honor of Pushkin in 1880, that the Russian in Europe had more understanding of European culture than the Europeans themselves. The Russians alone were the true cosmopolitans. The Europeans were decadent, frail, weighed down by materialism, without religion. They were doomed to destruction, while the Russians were dedicated to the task of regenerating the world. "Yes, indeed," says Versilov, "only Russia lives for an idea, and you must agree that for the last hundred years Russia has demonstrated that she is not living for herself, but for all the other states of Europe! And what will happen to those countries? Well, they are doomed to pass through a period of frightful tribulation before they enter the Kingdom of God!"

At one time Versilov appears to have been intended as the central character of the story, playing a part like Stavrogin in *The Devils,* and indeed he has some resemblance to Stavrogin. He has wandered through Europe. He has suffered many adventures in many countries, visited many museums, and lived through a period of religious asceticism. He was one of those proud men who

[3] Quoted in V. Ermilov, *F. M. Dostoyevsky,* p. 221.

"turn to God to avoid doing homage to men." He is perfectly capable of evil, but his instinct is to do good, and he calls himself a philosophical deist, a believer inclined to add to the Gospel story the uncanonical vision of "Christ on the Baltic Sea" by the poet Heine. Into the mouth of Versilov there is placed the dream of the Golden Age which had previously appeared in the banned chapter of *The Devils*, now known as "Stavrogin's Confession." But where Stavrogin saw the painting by Claude Lorrain as a portrait of the legendary past, rich with intimations of a way of life which has for ever departed, Versilov characteristically suggests that it represents the sunset on the last day of civilization: for him the painting portrays the apocalypse of our time. Suddenly, and very curiously, he speaks in tones a little like those of Marya Timofeyevna, as he describes the day when civilization died:

> "I imagine the time when all wars have come to an end," he said with a dreamy smile, "and there is no more strife in the world. After the curses and the hisses and the pelting with mud there comes a lull, and men are left alone, according to their desire. The great ideas of the past have abandoned them. They no longer possess those great sources of strength which nourished them in the past—all this had faded away like the majestic sun setting in Claude Lorrain's painting. The last day of humanity has come, and men suddenly realize that they are altogether alone, and they are gripped by a terrible fear.
>
> "Of course, my dear boy, it has never occurred to me that men are completely stupid and lacking in gratitude. It seems to me that when men are faced with such a situation, they will draw more closely and more lovingly together, and they will take each other by the hand, because they know this is all that is left to them. The great idea of immortality will have vanished, and in some way they will have to put something in its stead; and I believe that all the wealth of love lavished upon Him, who was immortal, in ancient days will now

be lavished on the whole of nature, on the world, on men, on every blade of grass!

"The time will come when they will inevitably come to love the earth and life itself as they begin to realize their own transient and finite natures, and they will do this with a special love quite unlike the old love. They will begin to observe the secrets in nature which they never observed before, and they will see nature through new eyes, as a lover looks upon the beloved. When they wake up they will be quick to kiss one another, knowing that their days are short, and this is all that is left to them. They will work for each other, and each will surrender his possessions to the community, and only in this way will they be happy. And every child will know and feel that all the people on earth are his fathers and mothers.

"Gazing at the setting sun, they will say: 'Tomorrow may be my last day, but even though I should die, the others will remain and so will their children.' And the thought that the others will remain to take care of each other will replace the thought of meeting after death.

"Oh, they will be quick to love, to put an end to the sorrow in their hearts. For themselves they will be proud and brave, but they will be fearful for one another, and everyone will tremble for the happiness of others, and they will grow tender, and not ashamed as they are now, and they will offer caresses as children do. When they meet they will gaze upon one another with deep and thoughtful eyes, and in their eyes there will be love and sorrow. . . ." [4]

According to the notes these words were to form the coda of the novel, and Dostoyevsky's original intention seems to have been to give the words to Arkady Dolgoruky after his long excursion in the world. They come oddly from the lips of Versilov, the aristocrat, and would be more appropriate from the lips of the old house serf, Makar Ivanovich, who is Arkady's father. Indeed, Makar Ivanovich could make a reasonable claim for plagiarism,

[4] *A Raw Youth,* Part III, Chapter vii.

since he had said these words, or others very much like them, in conversations earlier in the novel. "Everything is a mystery— God's mystery," says Makar Ivanovich. "In every tree, in every blade of grass there is the same mystery, and whether the small birds of the air are singing, or the stars in their multitudes shine in the nightly heavens, it is all one mystery. And the greatest mystery of all is what awaiteth the soul of man in the world beyond!"

Versilov's Legend of the Last Day is one of the most poignant things written by Dostoyevsky, for it suggests that he had abandoned, if only for a while, the belief that the world without God is unendurable. The legend describes the day when God finally abandons the earth, leaving men to their own resources. And suddenly it occurs to Dostoyevsky that the world without God, but with all men assisting each other in love and compassion, might be perfectly endurable, and perhaps even more endurable than the present world where God is present, but hidden from the eyes of men. Like Marya Timofeyevna he seems to be following some ancient and primitive pathway into remote regions of the pagan spirit. In that shadowless world he is at home.

Versilov is a complex figure, larger than life, contemptuous of men, living by a continual process of self-invention as he creates roles for himself in a world which rarely grants the seal of its approval to actors. He dresses elegantly. He has the careless smile of those who are supremely sure of themselves. He despises society, lives on his mistress, and abandons his children to relatives. He suffers from the disease of *sluchainost,* which may be translated as "accidentalness." He will never think a thought to its conclusion. Like the liberals of the forties, like Herzen and Belinsky and Chaadaev, he is continually playing with his ideas, tossing them in the air and admiring his own prodigious feats of prestidigitation. He lacks Stavrogin's authority and power, and exists in the vacuum of his own inactivity. He is not a character for a novel, and Dostoyevsky succeeds in pouring a little life in him only with the greatest difficulty.

Makar Ivanovich is a man of a different temper, and far more credible. He is a peasant, but as Versilov points out he is a real peasant utterly unlike the peasants found in novels and on the stage. He is serene and even-tempered, with an inner gaiety, and in his younger days there was an extraordinary stateliness about him, and an almost godlike beauty. He has wandered all over Russia on foot. He knows men, not in the ordinary way but with the benefit of spiritual insight, and he speaks in a language deeply influenced by biblical texts. He likes to talk of the hermits going into the desert. "At first when you enter the desert, then you are full of sorrow," he says," but with every passing day the joy becomes greater, and at last you look upon the face of God." And when Arkady Dolgoruky points out that doctors and men of science serve humanity better than hermits, Makar Ivanovich answers gently: "Yes, my dear, that's true! God bless you, for your thoughts are full of truth!"

Makar Ivanovich represents the primordial wisdom of the Russian peasant. He will assent to modern scientific inventions, but he knows in his heart that they offer no comfort. He has the cunning of a peasant, but he also has the peasant's capacity to talk in well-embroidered sermons; and sometimes he seems to have stepped out of a previous century. There is always some peasant adage on his lips, and he likes to talk in apocalyptic riddles. "Take a grain of sand and sow it on a stone," he says, and then delivers himself of a sermon which might have been spoken by Christ to the Grand Inquisitor:

> Take a grain of sand and sow it on a stone; and when the yellow sand springs up on the stone, then your dream will come true in the world. . . . Thou wilt be a thousand times richer than before; for not by bread alone, nor by rich garments, nor by pride, nor by envy wilt thou be happy, but only by the infinite multiplication of love. Thou wilt not gain a small gift of riches, nor wilt thou gain a great gift amounting to a hundred

thousand or a million—instead, thou shalt gain the whole world. . . . Thou shalt gain wisdom, which cometh not from books alone, and thou shalt come face to face with God, and the earth will shine brighter than the sun, and there shall be no more sorrow nor sighing, and there shall be only a precious Paradise.[5]

Here we are still close to the world of Marya Timofeyevna, the sense of the earth's veils dropping away, the Easter of the heart, and the knowledge of Paradise, not in some remote region of the heavens, but on earth, and therefore enjoyable in an earthly way.

It is strange that there are so few of these sermons, for the tone in which they were written shows that they were very close to Dostoyevsky's deepest beliefs, deriving perhaps from his childhood and the stories and legends told him by the peasant women in his father's house.

Makar Ivanovich plays only a small role in the novel, although he is evidently the hero, the only person untouched by corruption of any kind, the possessor of a natural nobility. Versilov will change his point of view like a weathercock, but Makar Ivanovich is stable as rock. Arkady Dolgoruky, too, is continually changing his point of view. When it pleases him he is "a man from underground," with the soul of a spider, desperate for the sunlight, capable of extremes of self-humiliation and self-surrender as he wanders disconsolately "under the floorboards." But there are times when he appears as a charming disingenuous youth, affectionate to his two fathers, alert and intelligent. He is especially alert when he falls in with a band of revolutionaries and asks them searching questions. "Tell me," he asks the revolutionaries, "what inducement do you hold out that I should follow you? How do you prove you will make things better? How will you deal with my individual protest in your common mess halls? You will have barracks, community houses, *strict necessaire*, atheism—those are your ideals. I know all about that. And just for all this, for these mediocre ad-

[5] *A Raw Youth,* Part III, Chapter iii.

305

vantages, for a bit of bread and a warm corner, you will take away my personal liberty?"

Dostoyevsky seems to have written *A Raw Youth* as though it were a substitute for *The Diary of a Writer*. His own ideas are continually breaking through. He will interrupt the story to introduce long essays on subjects close to his heart—there are essays on photography and the nature of laughter—and then resume the thread of the story as though there had been no interruptions at all. The novel has an anarchic looseness of structure, and Dostoyevsky seems to have lost the reins very early in its composition. In the third part a long short story, quite independent of the novel, is introduced for no particular reason. And since Dolgoruky speaks in the first person throughout, and since he is by definition a youth of very few talents, the novel meanders disconcertingly, with a kind of grotesque loping gait, to a conclusion which is as jejune as anything written by the third-rate novelists of the time. At the end of the novel Dolgoruky remains unchanged. Experience has left no mark on him. The mysterious "idea," which he conceals in his breast at the beginning of the novel, is still mysterious at the end.

What then of the breath of corruption which Dostoyevsky had announced as the theme of the novel? No doubt it is present as a very faint and distant perfume, sickly sweet and evanescent. It is as though Dostoyevsky had stepped away from the terrible and haunting corpses of Shatov, Svidrigailov and Nastasya Philipovna, and was determined for a brief while to enjoy a leisurely holiday in the ordinary world of the living. There is nothing in the novel as fiercely dramatic and pregnant with meaning as the single entry in the notebook: "Undoubtedly Christ does not love us as we are. He tolerated and forgave us, but of course He despised us."

While Dostoyevsky was poring over his notebooks it sometimes happened that he would outline a phrase or sketch an epigram or the conclusion of some long chain of thought. Among descriptions of characters and scattered fragments of dialogue there come intensely personal statements of uncommon power and sometimes of frightening simplicity. Here are a few of these state-ments taken at random from the notebooks:

> The demons have faith, but they tremble.

> All comes from my not knowing what is better: pins under the fingernails, or Christ.

> The holy spirit is the immediate comprehension of beauty, the prophetic consciousness of harmony, and therefore the unalterable aspiration towards it.

> Shakespeare was a prophet sent by God to proclaim the mystery of man and the human soul.

> Nihilism—this is the slavery of thought. A nihilist is the slave of thought.

> All nihilists love terribly to profit.

> All great men are happy, their sorrows are joys to them, and so are their sufferings. They cannot help being happy, and it is impossible for them to be miser-able. And if they are crucified, it is a matter of no im-portance.[6]

So he wrote during those long hours of the night when he paused from the composition of his novels and wrestled with the angel. But while he was writing *A Raw Youth* he was like a man treading water, preserving his strength for the final struggle ahead. In his own good time he would write the great novel about the cor-ruption of his age, and of all ages. Then at last, in *The Brothers Karamazov,* he would find himself in full control of a magnificently equipped orchestra. Then at last he would say what he had always wanted to say.

[6] The first sentence is taken from the notebook of *The Idiot.* The remaining sentences are taken in order from the notebooks of *The Devils* except for the fifth and seventh which come from the ncte-books of *Crime and Punishment.*

THE PROPHET

IN THE SEVENTIES a remarkable change appeared on Dostoyevsky's face. Nearly all his life he had been ill, but his face had not registered his illnesses, and even his sufferings were left unrecorded. A photograph taken at Semipalatinsk, not many years after his prison experiences, shows him sitting crosslegged and at ease, and the heavy mustache does nothing to conceal the blandness of the face. It might be the face of a young aristocrat with no thought in his head except the pleasures of the moment. He is still handsome and bland in photographs taken in the sixties. He has grown a beard, which is carefully trimmed, and he wears a patterned waistcoat. He has an air of conscious superiority, and might be a successful novelist or a junior minister in the government.

In the seventies the air of conscious superiority vanishes, and in its place there is the suggestion of unconscious power. The face becomes craggy, remote, elemental, more and more resembling an abstract portrait of a thought. Those who met him were struck by the brooding eyes, the settled sadness of his expression, a curious diffidence. He held himself like a man of a former age with the politeness and deliberately assumed timidity fashionable in the time of Pushkin. The Vicomte Melchior de Vogüé, who met him in St. Petersburg, spoke of him as "a small slender man, all nerves, his long beard and hair still blond, and all the time he breathes 'the vivacity of a cat.' It is the face of a Russian peasant, a real *moujik* from Moscow, with his broken nose and little eyes twinkling now tenderly, now with a somber fire. His forehead is high and heavy with folds and protuberances, his temples have been hollowed out as with a hammer."

Dostoyevsky would not have approved of this portrait, for he would have been astonished to find himself described as a *moujik,* but the photographs bear out the general truth of the description. As his hair receded, and age began to mark the face, he seemed to become all forehead and nervous energy. The flesh seemed to be only a light covering for the bone. With his hollow cheeks and smoldering eyes and look of profound abstraction he came to resemble one of those wandering monks who traveled across Russia with only a knapsack on their backs; and since his eyes were weak and he was continually being given drops of atropine which dilated the pupils, there was always a kind of strangeness in his appearance. He wore spectacles in private, but never in public.

Quite suddenly he was growing old, and like many men who retain an air of youth through middle age, he began to age quickly. His body had been wasted by innumerable attacks of epilepsy; he suffered excruciatingly from throat catarrh, and there were inexplicable fits of dizziness. At fifty-five he looked like a man of seventy.

He was living quietly, preserving his strength. He was more and more in love with Anna. He doted on his two children, and behaved towards them like a proud and exacting father, consciously or unconsciously imitating the habits of his own father, giving them Karamzin's *History* to read and reading aloud to them Schiller's *The Robbers,* which had the effect of sending them to sleep. He made them recite poetry, and when he took them for walks he gave them lessons. Characteristically, when the children were taken to the theater, and when Dostoyevsky discovered that a comic opera had been substituted for the serious opera he intended to show them, he told them they would have to leave the theater. They pleaded to be allowed to remain, and at last he relented. It annoyed him that they preferred comedy to tragedy.

Still, he was gentle with them. He was always buying them sweets and reading to them the captions on the drawings of comic books. He took his fatherhood seriously, and read books about the treatment and behavior of children, and worried over their future. He loved them more because they were the children of Anna than for their own sake.

He was becoming a permanent visitor in Staraya Russa, leaving the small watering-place only for occasional visits to St. Petersburg. He intensely enjoyed the life of the small town, his daily walks, the knowledge that his family was gathered under one roof, and he even enjoyed the occasional visits of Pasha, the son of Marya Dmitrievna, who was also raising a family of his own. Pasha was continually trying to borrow money. In Anna's eyes he was a nuisance who told lies and behaved with the irresponsibility he had inherited from his parents—he was uncouth, and ugly, and not very clean, but he amused the children, who roared with laughter whenever Pasha pulled faces and displayed his talent for mimicry. Dostoyevsky loved his stepson to distraction, and was rarely able to refuse him anything.

So the months passed until *A Raw Youth* was published, and on the whole Dostoyevsky was pleased with its critical acclaim. Nekrasov found merit in it, pointing especially to the description of a girl's suicide by hanging as a master stroke, though to modern eyes it remains a dreary repetition of an incident which Dostoyevsky had depicted with greater sympathy and tenderness in previous works. Turgenev damned the work as "psychological twaddle." Most reviews were guardedly favorable, and the book sold well. Dostoyevsky was especially pleased to find himself in the good graces of Nekrasov, whom he had always venerated.

But though he could live comfortably and quietly in Staraya Russa there were still debts to be paid off, and he suffered as usual from the knowledge that he could never save up enough money to provide for his wife and children if he died. He decided to resume

The Prophet

The Diary of a Writer, publishing it not in the columns of *Grazh-danin* but in monthly installments, each the size of a pamphlet, and he hoped to make enough money to support him through the lean years until he could write "The Life of a Great Sinner," the master-piece which would crown his literary activity.

Dostoyevsky's private purpose in producing *The Diary of a Writer* was to record the social changes; his public purpose was very different. He had long ago regarded himself as a man pos-sessed of a deep knowledge of the forces which sway the people, and he hoped to influence them in his articles and criticisms. There was something of the politician in him. Writing like a visitor from another planet he would judge the times and prophesy the future.

These monthly articles repay careful reading, but they very rarely show him exerting his full powers. He is *en pantoufles,* tak-ing his ease. He is like a loquacious clubman holding court. He will discuss anything under the sun, repetitively and at enormous length, undisturbed by the murmurs of applause or the snores of the other clubmen. He will discuss spiritualistic séances, court cases, murders, robberies, the behavior of Russian generals abroad, the proper behavior of Russians in German watering places, the peculiar ambivalence of the Russian character. He makes solemn prophecies—the English are bound to take Constantinople, the Catholics and the Socialists will join together in a vast conspiracy to overthrow the bourgeois states of Europe! He made these proph-ecies in perfect seriousness. Prophecy indeed had always attracted him, and he was deeply moved when he learned from a book called *Prognosticationes* by Johann Lichtenberger, published in Latin in 1528, that "the great eagle which sleepeth many a year shall arise and compel the sea-girt people of the Land of the Virgin to trem-ble, and he shall fly southward to retrieve the lost lands." It seemed to him that "the great eagle" must be Russia, and "the sea-girt people of the Land of the Virgin" must be the English, but he was not too happy with his interpretation; perhaps some other

meaning was indicated; perhaps after all there were mysteries concealed in the prophecy which were beyond interpretation altogether.

He was on safer ground when he spoke of the conspiracy of the
Socialists and Catholics to rule the world, for it was an idea widely
current in Russia, and particularly encouraged by the Masons. The
alliance between the Pope and the International founded by Karl
Marx implied a devastating shift of power. Writing in *The Diary of
a Writer* for May, 1877, two years to the month before he wrote
The Legend of the Grand Inquisitor, Dostoyevsky described how
the Pope would bring about the revolution which would alter the
face of the world:

> On foot and barefoot the Pope will go among the
> beggars, and he will tell them that everything the social-
> ists teach is contained in the Gospels, but that up to
> this time it was not found necessary to reveal this to the
> people. But now at last the time of revelation is at
> hand, and the Pope willingly surrenders Christ to them
> and believes in the anthill.
>
> Roman Catholicism has no need of Christ. (This is
> transparently clear.) It strives for universal sover-
> eignty. The Church will say: "You need to unite against
> the enemy! Therefore unite behind me, for among all
> the principalities and powers of the earth I alone am
> universal. And let us march forward together!" [1]

That strange little legend, embedded in a discussion on the politics of Prince Bismarck, is the kernel of *The Legend of The Grand
Inquisitor,* a story which Dostoyevsky regarded as the summit of
his literary career. Many other influences went to feed the finished
story, but not the least of the influences was Dostoyevsky's curious
belief, repeated many times in *The Diary of a Writer,* that the
"black" army of the Jesuits would ally itself with the Socialists to
overthrow all established governments.

When Sergey Nechayev, the famous author of *The Revolu-*

[1] *The Diary of a Writer,* May 1877, III, iii.

tionary Catechism, set about defining the true revolutionary, he emphasized the need of the revolutionary to imitate the ascetic self-abnegation of the Jesuit who submits himself wholly to the propagation of the faith, and permits no other thought to enter his mind. Dostoyevsky believed, or professed to believe, that not even the most bloodthirsty socialist revolutionary possessed the sense of dedication of the Jesuit revolutionary. The Jesuits were to be feared far more than the socialists. He wrote:

> When they have succeeded in bringing about a coup d'état, even the most rabid and bloodstained revolutionaries may be expected to accept certain forms of the previous established order. But the Jesuit revolutionaries cannot act lawfully—they can only act extra-legally. This black army stands outside the boundaries of ordinary humanity and civic responsibility. It has its habitat outside civilization, and emanates exclusively from within itself. It is the Pope's army, a state within a state. It seeks only the triumph of its own idea, and is perfectly content if everything standing in its way perishes. Let all its enemies wither on the stem! Let everything in disagreement with it perish! Let there be an end to civilization, society, science! [2]

There is no doubt that Dostoyevsky quite seriously believed in the menace of Jesuit power. He was not alone; innumerable articles in the newspapers and magazines of the time pointed to the growing political power of the Jesuits, especially in France. France, indeed, was the culprit, for had not the French Revolution brought about the desire for universal equality, and had not the French revolutionaries turned their backs on Christian ethics in order to bring this about? Like the Jesuits "they resorted to all possible means, and refused to stop at anything."

Dostoyevsky's prophecy of the marriage of the Pope and the International proved to be false, but his prophetical powers were amply demonstrated in his novel *The Devils,* where he showed that

[2] *The Diary of a Writer,* May 1877, III, iv.

the revolutions of the future would become religious, even if they began by repudiating religion. He deduced a theory of revolution which proved to be amazingly correct. He foresaw that the revolutionaries would emerge, not from the working classes but from the middle classes, the rootless aristocrats, the minor clerks, the discontented mechanics and engineers. He foresaw, as Nechayev had foreseen before him, that the revolutionaries would be ruled by ruthless inner cliques consisting of men who possessed no loyalty to one another and would inevitably fall apart and murder each other. He knew, as we have learned to know, that "the cement of revolution" would be the compulsion to share in the bloodshed. He knew that the revolutionaries would rewrite history in order to glorify their own legends, and that the inevitable fruit of absolute liberty was absolute slavery.

In *The Diary of a Writer,* Dostoyevsky is at his best when he discusses tragedy. Almost any commonplace tragedy found in a newspaper might be the occasion for a sermon or an extraordinary attempt to enter into the mind of the victim. A boy is punished by his schoolmaster and kept late in school after all the other schoolboys have left. Alone in a deserted room, the boy sees a rope and pulley, and hangs himself. Why did he do it? What was he trying to say at the moment when the rope choked him? The boy was twelve or thirteen, and yet he had calmly and confidently killed himself for no reason that is intelligible. Why do these things happen?

Dostoyevsky knew only one way in which he could explain such strange events. He imagined himself into the mind of the victim, employing all the resources of the novelist's art in order to *become* the victim, suffering with him up to the last moment. Suicides always affected him deeply. At one time according to his notes Raskolnikov was destined for suicide, and there is a sense in which nearly all the characters of *The Devils* meet death by suicide. But what shall one say about an intelligent twenty-five-year-old woman who comes from a rich family and goes to work as a midwife in a peasant community. Suddenly she feels very tired and decides to poison herself, because "the grave is the best place to rest in." She leaves a curious little note, which begins:

> For heaven's sake don't get excited. Pull yourself together, and read this to the end, and then decide on the best course to take. Don't frighten Petrova. Perhaps nothing will come of all this except laughter. My passport is in the cover of the trunk.[3]

Perhaps nothing will come of all this except laughter . . . Dostoyevsky examines the letter, annotates it, worries some meaning out of its most extraordinary and unexpected passages, and like a classical scholar annotating a passage from a long-forgotten Greek author, he attempts to define the weight of each word, each sentence, each turn of thought. What did she mean by "laughter"? Why did she give such exact and scrupulous attention to the small bequests to her friends? Why was she in such a hurry? Dostoyevsky concluded characteristically that she was a socialist weighed down with the tedium of living in her material world, her only belief being "that these stones be made bread," and this belief was not enough to carry her through a period of depression. "She had lost faith," he said, "in the magnificence of being alive."

He showed greater understanding in the case of a young seamstress whose death was reported in small print in the Petersburg newspapers. She had thrown herself from a fourth floor window "because she could find no work to keep herself alive." As she fell, it was observed that *she was clasping an icon in her hands.*

Dostoyevsky devoted an entire issue of *The Diary of a Writer* to a long commentary on the suicide of the seamstress, which took the form of a short story called *A Gentle Creature.* It is one of the most powerful stories he ever wrote, filled with a kind of desperate and unavailing tenderness for the young woman married to a shiftless and ill-tempered pawnbroker whose chief amusement lies in tormenting her. She rebels against him and tries to kill him; and

[3] *The Diary of a Writer,* May 1876, II, ii.

the description of her as she comes up to his bed and presses a revolver against his temple is spine-chilling. Having failed to kill him,
she is wholly at his mercy. She falls ill, and when she recovers they
have all the appearance of being quietly and miserably reconciled
to one another. He promises to take her to France for a holiday,
and while he is getting the passports she kills herself. The maid
Lukerya describes what happened:

> She was standing near the wall, quite close to the
> window, and she was leaning her arm against the wall,
> and her head was pressed against her arm. She was
> standing there thinking. She was so deep in thought that
> she did not hear me open the door, and she did not see
> me standing there and watching her. Then I saw her
> smile. She was standing there, thinking and smiling. I
> looked at her, turned round quietly, and went back to
> my kitchen. Presently I heard the window being opened,
> and I went back and said: 'It's quite cold outside, and
> you'll catch your death of cold—' But she was already
> climbing on the windowsill, and she was standing there
> with her back turned to me, and she was holding the
> icon in her hands. I called out: "Madam, madam!" and
> I think she heard me, for she made a movement to turn
> round, and then she took a step forward, still pressing
> the icon to her breast, and she leaped down.[4]

It is an extraordinary passage, so lyrical and tender and filled
with a kind of quiet joy, and suddenly we realize that we are no
longer in the world of the pawnbroker, "the underground man,"
with his snivelling contempt and his incessant desire to justify himself; we are in the world of Marya Timofeyevna, with the waterfall
and the blade of grass. The poor waif who married the pawnbroker
only from poverty has become the votary of a temple performing
an act of sacrifice. A perfectly commonplace suicide on a winter
day in St. Petersburg takes place at high noon in ancient Greece.

[4] *The Diary of a Writer,* November 1876, II, iii.

The Prophet

Throughout his life Dostoyevsky seems to have been quietly obsessed by the vision of the Golden Age which exists, not in the remote past, but in a curtained corner of the heart. In one of the notes for the first draft of *Crime and Punishment* he puts into the mouth of Raskolnikov the words: "Oh, why doesn't everything come to happiness in the end? The painting of the Golden Age. It is implanted in men's minds and hearts. But why does it never come?" And in another of those anticipatory phrases which were never used in the novel, he has Raskolnikov saying: "I never saw Venice nor the Golden Horn, but I believe life must be long extinct there. Flew to another planet." But this curtained corner of the heart, this other planet *n'importe où hors de ce monde* is in fact very close to him, and perhaps it is closer to him than anything else. We have seen that it is both pagan and Christian, or rather it is essentially pagan, being Christian only when the rituals of Christ can be identified with pagan origins. It is a vision which seems to owe much to the stories told to him in his childhood by the peasants who came to the doctor's apartment.

In *The Diary of a Writer* for April 1877, he wrote about the Golden Age for the last time in a story called "The Dream of a Ridiculous Man." Of all his stories it is the most effortless, the most limpid, the most acutely personal. Into this story he seems to be pouring all the experiences of his life.

"The Dream of a Ridiculous Man" describes the nightmare of a man who tried to kill himself one night after he had rudely brushed away the appeals for help of one of the street waifs who haunted St. Petersburg. She was about eight years old, soaked to the skin, her teeth chattering. She tugged at his coat, but he paid no attention to her. He had long ago decided that his life was useless; now it seemed more useless than ever. In disgust with himself, he shot himself through the heart, not long after he reached his apartment.

After his death he finds himself lying in a waterlogged coffin—

it is the world of *Bobok* again—and suddenly the coffin bursts open and he is being transported through the skies towards a familiar star. The star resembles the earth, but is not the earth:

Oh, everything was just as it is on our earth, except that everything seemed to be bathed in the radiance of a festival, the splendor of some great and holy triumph attained at last. The gentle emerald sea softly lapped the shore and kissed it with manifest, visible, almost conscious love. Tall, beautiful trees stood in all the luxury of their green foliage, and their countless leaves —I am sure of it—welcomed me with soft, tender rustling, seeming to speak words of love. The grass blazed with bright and fragrant flowers. Birds were flying in flocks through the air, and showing no fear of me they perched on my shoulders and hands, and they joyfully beat against me with their dear fluttering wings.

At last I came to know the people of this blessed land. They came to me of themselves. They surrounded me and kissed me. Children of the sun, children of their sun—how beautiful they were! Never on earth have I beheld such beauty in man. Only perhaps in our children in their earliest years one might find some remote faint reflection of this beauty. The eyes of these blessed people shone with a clear brightness. Their faces radiated intelligence and a serenity which had reached the height of fulfillment. Gaiety shone from them, and in their words and voices there was a childlike joy.

Oh, then at once, at the first glance of their faces, I understood everything, everything! This was an earth unstained by the Fall, and people who had never sinned lived on it. They were living in that Paradise which, according to all the legends of mankind, was the place of our first parents before they sinned; the only difference being that all this earth was the same Paradise. These people, laughing joyfully, thronged round me and caressed me. They took me to their homes, and they were always trying to reassure me. Oh, they asked me no questions, but I fancy they knew everything already, and they longed to remove the signs of suffering from my face.[5]

So he comes to live among these people who worship the stars and the trees, and seem to be in communion with all living creatures, and with the dead, and even with inanimate things, until the time comes when corruption sets in. It begins innocently, with a jest, with the desire to show off, but soon the children of the sun are behaving like the children of earth. They learn to know evil, make war, form political parties, produce social programs, and set up a guillotine. They have forgotten the days of innocence, and would not return to them if they could. Instead of songs of joy, they sing songs of destruction. The narrator, who is evidently speaking with the authentic voice of Dostoyevsky, says: "I loved the earth they had polluted even more than when it was Paradise, only because sorrow had made its appearance among them." The dream ends after the narrator has begged to be crucified by the people he has corrupted, only to be told that he must be a madman to have such a desire.

The Dream of a Ridiculous Man is in fact two dreams confronting one another: the dream of Paradise and the dream of the earth given up to a permanent orgy of corruption. When Dostoyevsky admitted that he loved the face of sorrow, he was admitting to an incontestable truth. But for him it was also incontestably true that he yearned for Paradise.

Sometimes, as he wrote his diary, it would occur to him that Paradise might be in the gift of the Russian people. There were no people so deeply religious as the Russians. "The lost image of Christ in all the light of its purity is preserved in Orthodoxy," he wrote. "From the East there will come the new word which will save Europe from Socialism." So he wrote in November 1877, and two years later only a few weeks before his death he wrote: "The Socialism of the Russian people is not expressed in Communism,

[5] *The Dream of a Ridiculous Man*, Part III.

or in any kind of mechanical program. They believe they will be finally saved *through the universal communion in the name of Christ.*"

In those last years it was noted that he became more deeply religious. He was often ill, and knew he would have to husband his strength. In November 1877 Nekrasov died, after a lingering illness which reduced him to a shambling imitation of himself; and Dostoyevsky attended the funeral. A month later he wrote a memorandum to himself about his future work, which has survived. He hoped for ten more years: he was given only a little more than two years. He wrote:

24 December /77.   Memento for my Whole Life.
1. To write a Russian *Candide.*
2. To write a book about Jesus Christ.
3. To write my memoirs.
4. To write a poem, *The Commemoration of the the Dead.*
NB. All this, in addition to the last novel, and the proposed publication of the Diary, will require at least 10 years of full activity, and I am now 56.

During that same month he abandoned the publication of *The Diary of a Writer,* explaining to subscribers that he hoped to finish during the following year "a work which has imperceptibly and involuntarily molded itself during the two years which saw the publication of the *Diary*." This work, which he hoped to complete in so short a time, was *The Brothers Karamazov*.

Such was the first public announcement of the project, which had been his private concern for many months of protracted pondering. He hoped to produce occasional numbers of *The Diary of a Writer* while writing this long novel, which he had mentioned long before in his letters under a variety of titles—it was "The Life of a Great Sinner," but it was also "Fathers and Sons," and there seem to have been many more provisional titles. At long last he felt he had the strength to begin the work, and he probably outlined the book during the autumn or early winter of 1877. By December 17, 1877, he was writing to his friend Dr. Yanovsky: "I have a novel in my heart and head which demands to be written." By the spring of the following year he was making preliminary studies for the novel, and by June most of the problems concerned with the novel had been worked out. There remained the task of putting his white-hot vision onto paper.

Only a few of the preliminary notes and sketches have survived in the opening pages of the notebooks; the later pages of the notebooks show him in full command of the developed material. Here and there he provides clues enabling us to determine the genesis of the novel. From the beginning it was to be about a parricide —a peculiarly outrageous parricide. Among the prisoners he met in Siberia was a young nobleman called Iliynsky who was reputed to have murdered his father and to have stuffed the body in an open sewer, with the head lying beside the trunk. In prison Iliynsky gave the impression of being curiously insensitive, and once he was heard saying: "My father, you know, never complained of his health to the very day of his death." At another time he was overheard shouting in a nightmare: "Cut off the head! Cut off the head!" The details of the murder were widely known, and it was especially remembered among the curious details of the parricide that the murderer laid the dead man's head carefully on a pillow.

Some years later it was discovered that the young nobleman was completely innocent. He was thereupon freed, and the real criminals, who had confessed, were given long prison sentences.

Dostoyevsky's habit was to use the names of real people in his notes, and accordingly he wrote in his notebook:

> Iliynsky in his cell declares that he refuses to let any-one deliver sermons at him in a loud voice . . .

> Iliynsky hopes to obtain a part of the inheritance. He needs 3,000 as quickly as possible, because he kept the money of his fiancée. The same evening (first part of novel), after the scene in the cell. Iliynsky comes to his father with the Idiot to arrange about the 3,000. Since you already have it. The brawl . . .

> The resurrection of ancestors. The landowner concerning Iliynsky: he will not only be unable to resurrect them, but he will succeed in driving them even further away. Iliynsky rises: a shameful comedy.

> Everything is permissible.[6]

No one seeing those apparently innocuous phrases for the first time would suspect that they include a brief description of a major event in the life of Dmitry Karamazov, a judgment of Alyosha Karamazov, and at least two of the principal themes of *The Brothers Karamazov;* but all these are in fact included within Dostoyevsky's shorthand notes. Iliynsky is a preliminary sketch of Dmitry Karamazov, the Idiot is his brother Alyosha, and the scene in which Dmitry, already close to madness, discusses borrowing 3,000 rubles from his father with Alyosha's help occurs in the novel in the chapters called *The Confessions of a Passionate Heart.* "Everything is permissible" is Dostoyevsky's shortened form of the often repeated theme: "If there is no God, then everything is

[6] *Materiali.* Folio 6, page 88.

permissible." "The resurrection of ancestors" derives from the remarkable letters of Nikolay Fyodorovich Fyodorov, then an obscure library assistant in Moscow. About the time that *The Diary of a Writer* was being temporarily abandoned, Dostoyevsky received the first of his communications from Fyodorov which proclaimed that the time had come for "the true, literal and individual resurrection of the body." Fyodorov meant precisely what he said. He believed that by an act of unparalleled love it would be possible to resurrect the dead, all the dead, and so put an end to childbearing, which would then no longer be necessary. According to Fyodorov the task of bringing about "the first Resurrection" mentioned in the Gospels and *Revelation* was to be accomplished by the Russian people, and this was the most important of the tasks set before them. Far from being appalled, Dostoyevsky enthusiastically agreed, and showed the letter to his young friend, the philosopher Vladimir Solovyov, who came to share his enthusiasm, though he was to write later: "Shatter this goblet; there is poison in it." Dostoyevsky absorbed Fyodorov's ideas within himself. "I have so thoroughly absorbed them," he wrote, "that they seem to be my own."

Many of the preliminary notes for *The Brothers Karamazov* are lost, and we do not know the stages in the development of his characters. Old Fyodor Karamazov, corrupted by carnal sensuality, derives perhaps from the drunkard Marmeladov in *Crime and Punishment,* but where Marmeladov cringes and suffers agonies of self-pity, Fyodor Karamazov possesses a devouring lust for life, and when he cringes and pities himself, it is only because his desires exceed his capabilities. Grushenka and Katerina Ivanovna are perhaps both portraits of Polina Suslova in her different aspects. But all the major characters of *The Brothers Karamazov* possess a fierce and intimidating grandeur which removes them altogether from the ordinary world of mortals. They are cast in heroic size like figures on the Brocken mist. None of the commonplace motives of human beings affect them; they thirst after absolutes. Because they are all so filled with the sap of life, they seem about to burst through their skins.

While he was preparing preliminary drafts for the novel, Dostoyevsky visited the family property at Darovoye, where his father had been murdered. It was an uncomfortable journey, for though Darovoye is only a little more than a hundred miles from Moscow, he was continually being forced to change trains, and at one station had to wait three hours until the train arrived. It took him ten hours to cover the distance, and he complained bitterly about the railroad company. For forty years he had thought of returning to the scene of so many of his childhood adventures. He spent only a day there, but the entire setting of *The Brothers Karamazov* takes place in a town which has much in common with that obscure village; and in the course of the novel he mentions Chermashnya as a place nearby, as though to remind himself that he was writing about his own native soil.

The novel grew slowly. Though he hoped to finish it in a year, by October he had finished only the first two books, amounting to rather less than a hundred pages. It was a year of delays, interruptions and tragedy. In March came the trial of Vera Zasulich for the attempted murder of General Trepov, the Chief of Gendarmerie in St. Petersburg. Dostoyevsky attended the trial in the public gallery, notebook in hand. The young terrorist was defended by a brilliant lawyer, who went over to the offensive and attacked all the arguments of the prosecution, with the result that she was acquitted. A strange scene occurred while she was being mobbed outside the courtroom. General Trepov, incensed by the verdict, had issued a warrant for her re-arrest, but the crowds refused to let the police reach her. She was being lifted up into a carriage driven by a young artillery officer when a shot rang out. The officer was killed, but Vera Zasulich succeeded in escaping to Switzerland.

Dostoyevsky attended the trial largely to acquaint himself with court procedure and to make notes for the trial of Dmitry

Karamazov. His sympathies seem to have been with the government, for about this time he was constantly visiting Konstantin Pobedonostsev, the "grey eminence" behind the throne, and he was seen in the palaces of the Grand Dukes Paul and Sergey. Tzar Alexander II was showing a commendable interest in the ageing novelist, whose writings were being regarded with high approval among the aristocracy.

In May came tragedy, with the death of his three-year-old son Alexey. The child had been born with a misshapen skull, but was bright and intelligent. He died after a violent epileptic fit which lasted more than three hours. Dostoyevsky was heartbroken, believing himself responsible for the boy's death: It was perhaps inevitable that the hero of his next novel should bear the name of his dead son. In this way he would resurrect the dead.

Grief-stricken, he accompanied Vladimir Solovyov to the famous Optina Pustyn monastery at Kozelsk in the province of Kalouga. This monastery was dedicated to the discipline of the spirit—a harsh discipline especially salutary for those who needed consolation. The authorities had revived the medieval custom of permitting holy men to live in hermitages on the outskirts of the monastery; and in fact it was these holy men, deeply venerated by the thousands of pilgrims who came each year, who had given the monastery its present fame. Dostoyevsky was granted two private interviews with the *starets* Amvrosi, and the young priests willingly answered his innumerable questions about the workings of the monastery. The two short days spent in the monastery in June 1878 provided Dostoyevsky with the material for all the scenes which take place in the monastery in *The Brothers Karamazov*. The saintly Amvrosi deeply affected him. He was also curiously moved by a note he found in the magazine *New Times* and entered into his notebook, about an archimandrite who wrote in his will that he wanted his body thrown to the dogs in punishment for his habitual drunkenness. Sanctity, the corruption of the flesh, drunkenness of every kind—these are the principal themes of the novel, which he began to write in earnest after returning from the monastery.

It was slow work, chipped off his breastbone. The third book, which is entitled *The Sensualists,* pleased him. It is full of long earnest discussions about women and God and the nature of faith, but where previously he would permit these arguments to run riot, here they are all anchored to their appropriate setting and to the development of the novel. The half-lunatic Smerdyakov proves to have something of Ivan's Jesuitical temper; he argues that it is perfectly right for a soldier captured by the Moslems to abjure his faith if his life depends upon it, for God will forgive him, or if God does not forgive him, then there is no hope for God. "There are perhaps two hermits in the Egyptian desert who still have the faith to move mountains, but as for the rest of us . . ." Smerdyakov shrugs his shoulders. He has discovered the measure of man. Thereafter, though appearing rarely, he sometimes gives the impression of subtly dominating the novel.

The Sensualists was sent off to *The Russian Messenger,* which had contracted to print the novel, in January 1879. Dostoyevsky went on working slowly and steadily. The novel became his whole life for the next twenty months. He was like a man who has found a rich ore in his mine, but finds difficulty in transporting it to the railhead. In February he suffered an attack of pulmonary emphysema, and complained of weariness; gave some readings of *The Brothers Karamazov* and *Crime and Punishment* in public; received from the archimandrite Simeon a detailed account of a funeral service in a monastery, which proved useful when he came to write an account of the funeral of Father Zossima; and kept working. When spring came, he wrote the terrible and beautiful story called *The Legend of the Grand Inquisitor.* He remained at Staraya Russa with his family around him through the spring and summer, and when his throat began to show alarming symptoms he hurried off to Ems to take the cure. From Germany he wrote to Anna, complaining that he could only work for a few hours a day. He missed her terribly. Those hours in the afternoon when he dictated to her had become a part of the ritual of his life; and he was a man who loved ritual.

So very slowly and patiently he continued to write, spending the winters in St. Petersburg and the summers in the remote quietness of Staraya Russa. He tried to live wholly in the imagination, but sometimes the outer world erupted within him. It was the time when the Nihilists were making concerted efforts to destroy the Tzar and the state.

On February 5, 1880, a cabinetmaker of peasant stock, Stepan Khalturin, lit a fuse attached to a packet of dynamite in one of the basement rooms of the Winter Palace, and calmly walked out of the palace. It was nearly half-past six in the evening, the city already dark. At that hour the Tzar was preparing to have dinner in the great Yellow Hall, but being detained by a reception given for the Grand Duke of Hesse and for Alexander, Prince of Bulgaria, he was some distance from the dining room when the dynamite exploded, smashing a thousand windowpanes and killing eleven of the servants and guards attached to the palace. Of the many terrorist attacks on the Tzar, this was the most frightening, the one closest to fulfillment.

Like everyone else in St. Petersburg, Dostoyevsky heard the explosion. He was profoundly disturbed. He had little sympathy for the nihilists, though he seems to have admired their courage; and he viewed the war between the court and the students with a kind of sardonic detachment. What he feared above all was the descent into anarchy, the rule of chaotic unreason by a handful of dedicated revolutionaries without any sense of responsibility towards the Church or the continuing traditions of Russia.

Two weeks after the explosion in the Winter Palace, a visitor, Alexey Suvorin, appeared at Dostoyevsky's apartment. He was a handsome, well-dressed man, very rich. He had been a serf, later a teacher, and at the age of forty-one he became editor of *The New Times,* the most influential newspaper in St. Petersburg.

Lenin hated Suvorin sufficiently to call him "that shameless, self-willed millionaire supporter of the bourgeoisie." Chekhov, who loved the man, said: "No one ever helped our Russian writers so much; there is no one to whom we should be more grateful." Dostoyevsky trusted Suvorin so much that he exchanged his most secret thoughts with him.

Dostoyevsky was at work when Suvorin was announced. He came out of his study and met Suvorin in the living room. He was sweating heavily, Suvorin observed, and looked like a man who has just come out of a Turkish bath.

They greeted one another, sat down at a small table, and talked about business matters. Dostoyevsky was thinking of reviving *The Diary of a Writer,* and since these journals had been printed on the presses of *The New Times,* the two men had much to discuss. Dostoyevsky kept rolling cigarettes on the table top. For a while he seemed lost in dreams. Suddenly he looked up and said: "Tell me, Alexey Sergeyevich, what would you do if you were looking at the pictures in Daziaro's shopwindow, and there was someone else standing beside you pretending to be looking at the pictures, and suddenly someone came running up to him and said: 'The Winter Palace will blow up soon! I've just placed a bomb there!' What would you do, eh?" [7]

Suvorin smiled. He had heard such things from Dostoyevsky before; and he knew that no answer was expected of him.

"Listen," Dostoyevsky continued, "there are those two men, and they are so excited that they pay no attention to us, not even lowering their voices. But please tell me—how should we act? Should we run to the Winter Palace and warn them, or tell the

[7] Daziaro's was a photographer's shop at the corner of the Nevsky Prospect and Admiralty Square. We know that Stepan Khalturin met Zhelyabov, the leader of the conspirators, shortly after the fuse was lit. Khalturin, usually stolid, was nervous and excitable when he met Zhelyabov, and might conceivably have divulged the secret outside the photographer's shop. It is just possible that Dostoyevsky did overhear the conversation between them.

police? Imagine there is a policeman standing not far away.
Should we go up to him and tell him to arrest those two men?
Would you?"

"No."

"Nor would I. But I keep asking myself, why not? Surely
it is a terrible thing! There is going to be a terrible crime! Surely
we should do something! I was rolling cigarettes as you came in,
and all the time I was thinking about this, and I thought of all the
reasons which would lead me to prevent such a crime—weighty
substantial reasons—and then I thought of all the reasons why I
would do nothing at all. And really, it is because if you do anything at such a time, you make yourself ridiculous. Why? Simply
because I would be afraid to be called an informer. Imagine! I
am on my way to the Winter Palace, they look at me, they
question me, they cross-examine me, they offer me a reward, and
they wonder whether or not I have an accomplice. Then it is in all
the newspapers—'Dostoyevsky informed against the terrorists.'
How absurd! It is a matter for the police. After all, they are paid
to do these things. The liberals would never forgive me; they would
drive me to despair and hound me to death! Everything in this
country is abnormal; that is why these things happen, and no one
knows how to behave any more, not only when circumstances are
very difficult, but even in the simplest things. I would like to write
about this. I could say a great many things both pleasant and
unpleasant, about society and the government, but of course I
shall do nothing of the sort! In Russia one is not allowed to
speak of the most important things!"

The talk drifted to *The Brothers Karamazov*. Dostoyevsky
hinted that Alyosha would join the revolutionaries, but went into
no details. Suvorin had the unpleasant feeling that Dostoyevsky
had actually seen the revolutionaries who planned the explosion
at the Winter Palace. On the other hand, as he knew only too well,
Dostoyevsky invented scenes on the spur of the moment and
introduced them into his conversation as though they had actually

happened. Also, he was stating a moral conundrum, and his novels were full of such conundrums. Suvorin did not press him for an answer.

Dostoyevsky was shaken by the attack on the Winter Palace and the attempt to assassinate the liberal Minister, Count Mikhail Loris-Melikov, which occurred a little later. He was filled with a brooding sense of fatality, as Russia seemed to move closer to the abyss; and some of the more terrifying passages in the tenth book of *The Brothers Karamazov* reflect his uneasiness.

Towards the end of May he left for Moscow to deliver a speech before the Society of Friends of Russian Literature. He had prepared the speech carefully, and some of the main ideas had already been discussed in *The Diary of a Writer* during the previous year. The ostensible subject of the speech was Pushkin, who had died forty-three years before; in fact he spoke about the future greatness of Russia, about peace, about the thirst of men for God, and for the brotherhood of men on earth. Pushkin was simply the peg for a wild, torrential flow of prophetical utterances.

Dostoyevsky's speech came on the second day of the celebrations. The novelist Ivan Aksakov was scheduled to speak first, but at the last moment Dostoyevsky was asked to take his place. It was very hot. The great hall of the Nobles' Club was crowded to capacity when he mounted the platform, a small bent figure in a tight dress coat, a sheaf of papers in his hands. There was a tremendous roar of applause as he shuffled across the stage, facing the audience sideways. His body, shrunken with age, was like an appendage to the deeply scarred and familiar face. The applause was deafening. He smiled nervously, waved his hands to silence the audience, and the applause was renewed.

They were applauding him as the author of the unfinished novel which everyone was reading in the pages of *The Russian Messenger*.

He began to speak in a low, hoarse, urgent voice. He began calmly by reminding his audience that Russia possessed in Pushkin a universal genius who came to maturity at the time when Russia herself emerged into full self-consciousness. Pushkin was not Russian only; he possessed the sensibilities belonging to other countries. Dostoyevsky quoted from Pushkin's poem *The Gypsies,* which describes a young Russian joining a band of gypsies, marrying a gypsy girl, and murdering her when she proves unfaithful to him. The gypsies drive him away from their camp with the words:

> *Depart from us, thou haughty man:*
> *We're wild, we have no binding laws,*
> *We neither punish nor torment.*

On this text Dostoyevsky delivered a sermon against the uses of violence and the errors of pride, directing his shafts equally at the aristocracy and the revolutionaries. In ecstatic language he extolled the humble, the seekers after truth, those who serve the people:

> Humble thyself, proud man! Above all, break down thy haughtiness! Humble thyself, ye idlers, and learn to labor in our sacred earth!
> Truth is within thee; it is not to be found without. Therefore find thyself within! It is not thy task to overwhelm others. Subdue thyself! Be master of thyself! Thus shalt thou perceive truth!
> Not in things, nor without thee, nor in distant lands lies the truth. It lies in thine own seeking for self-improvement. If thou conquerest thyself, if thou humblest thyself, then shalt thou be free beyond thy dreams. Thou shalt labor at a worthy task. Thou shalt make others free, and therein shalt thou find happiness, since thy life will be fulfilled, and thou shalt discover at last an understanding of thine own people and their sacred truth.[8]

He spoke in those measured liturgical tones, like another Zossima speaking to another Alyosha; and perhaps like Zossima

---

[8] This and the following quotation are from *The Diary of a Writer,* August, 1880.

he knew he was dying. From time to time he would drop his prophetic robes and discuss briefly some aspect of Pushkin's genius. He would quote long-familiar lines of Pushkin, and somehow transform them into prophetic utterances. Finally he made an impassioned plea for the brotherhood of man:

> Oh, the peoples of Europe have no idea how dear they are to us. I believe that we Russians—I am speaking of those who will come after us—will learn to understand that a true Russian is one who has reconciled in himself all European conflicts, one who resolves all the agonies of Europe in his humanitarian and all-embracing Russian soul. He will hold out his arms with brotherly love toward our brethren, and there will come from him in time the word of universal harmony and the brotherhood of all nations under the law of the Gospel according to Christ.

In English we miss the great rolling periods, the ecstatic gestures, the appearance of an ageing prophet. We are only too familiar with "the all-embracing Russian soul." But even in English we can glimpse some of the passion with which Dostoyevsky held his audience spellbound.

At the end the audience rose to its feet and burst into fanatical applause. People wept and cried for joy; and some embraced their neighbors and swore to behave better in the future and to love their fellow men. Dostoyevsky stepped into the wings, off the platform, but he was called back. His beard was drenched with sweat, his eyes were swollen, his face was pale with exhaustion, but he came out onto the platform and smiled and bowed and made little gestures with his hands. "You are a saint and a prophet!" people shouted at him; and his friend Ivan Aksakov rushed onto the platform and announced through his tears that they had all witnessed a historical event of great magnitude, for this day marked the birth of the brotherhood of man. "Yes, yes!" they cried, and there was more weeping, more embracing. Everyone was trying to touch him or to kiss his hand, and some ladies mounted the platform with a huge wreath of flowers which they held behind his head to form a halo. A group of students rushed into the hall, and one of them appropriately fell unconscious at his feet.

At last it was Aksakov's turn to deliver a speech on Pushkin. He came on the platform and pointed out that any speech by him would be an anticlimax after the speech of Dostoyevsky, yet they insisted that he should read his prepared paper. Later Dostoyevsky was summoned back to read Pushkin's poem *The Prophet,* and there was another prolonged outburst of wild acclamation when he came to the concluding words:

> *Then God called unto me and said:*
> *"Arise, and let My Voice be heard;*
> *Charged with My Will go forth and spread*
> *In every land My holy Word!*
> *Lay waste with fire the hearts of men!"*

That night when he returned to his hotel he was too exhausted to sleep, too confused by the incidents of the day to rest, and too excited to read. He lay for a while in his bed, but at last when he could bear the mounting fever no longer, he dressed, went out of the hotel and took a *droshky* to Spasskaya Square, where there stood and still stands a statue of Pushkin on a bronze and granite column. With him he carried the heavy laurel wreath which had been presented to him.

It was a calm silent evening, with a warm wind blowing. With a great effort, for he was suddenly very weak, he laid the wreath at the foot of the monument, and then he bowed very low to the earth.

Two days later he returned to St. Petersburg to resume work on *The Brothers Karamazov.* Seven months later he was dead.

THE KARAMAZOVS

W HEN DOSTOYEVSKY came to write *The Brothers Karama-zov,* the last and greatest of his novels, he was perfectly conscious that he was writing a book for the ages. He was not writing a novel only. He was making a statement of his most intimate beliefs, a record of his spiritual adventures. The book was to be a summary of the human heart. Everything he knew, every-thing he had guessed at, all the dark landscapes he had traversed in his imagination—all these were to be included in a work to which he proposed to give every last ounce of his talent and genius. If all his other works perished, he hoped to be remembered by this book which he regarded as the culmination of everything that had gone before.

From the beginning he seems to have found the form which the novel would take. There were hesitations, sudden alterations of direction, curious dissonances which were never resolved, but none of these were important. The novel possessed a momentum of its own, and carried him with it. In *The Devils* and *The Idiot* he sometimes gives the impression of a man shadowboxing: he has no sooner struck out at an imaginary enemy when another appears from some altogether unsuspected direction; the shadows are everywhere, and even the narrator seems sometimes to belong to the shadow-world. In *Crime and Punishment* we are made aware of a real battle fought with all the weapons of the imagination. So it is in *The Brothers Karamazov,* where the reality of the characters is never in doubt. Fyodor lusts; Smerdyakov kills; Dmitry broods; Ivan wrestles with the angel; Alyosha smiles tenderly and compassionately. These people live in the intense supercharged atmosphere of an enclosed world so rich and credible, so filled with human passion and spiritual thunder, that it staggers the mind. Only two other men have created worlds comparable with the world of the Karamazovs. They are Aeschylus and Shakespeare.

There is no record that Dostoyevsky ever read Aeschylus, or showed the least interest in Greek tragedy, or ever contemplated the theories of Aristotle, but *The Brothers Karamazov* moves with the same impassioned tread towards inevitable tragedy as the *Agamemnon* of Aeschylus, and there is the same tremendous burden of thought, and the same grandeur of conception. The war is waged on earth, but it is a battle between giants. There is never a moment when the speed slackens, when the eye of the spectator is allowed to rest. The war which is being fought is no small skirmish involving a few thousand or even a million soldiers. It is the war within the human heart in which we are all implicated. Dostoyevsky wrote about an obscure family in an obscure town in southern Russia. Aeschylus wrote about the family of the conqueror of Troy, an emperor returning to his own palace after a ten-year siege against his enemies. But it is the same war.

All of Dostoyevsky's novels are dramas; we call them novels only because there is no other word by which we can describe those vast and turbulent theatrical displays where the action moves forward by means of the thrust and counterthrust of speeches. There is a minimum of stage direction. Everything takes place in the minds of the characters, and is instantaneously translated into speech. There is no holding back of motives. The words are challenges, and the course of the drama moves from challenge to challenge as the characters deploy their forces, seek for advantage, and finally grapple in a death struggle. So had Corneille patterned his dramas, borrowing from Aeschylus, and Dostoyevsky followed the well-worn path, but with one difference.

335

His vision of the characters was at once so fresh and so loaded with his own sense of responsibility that he saw them with an immediacy denied to all the successors of Aeschylus except Shakespeare. It is as though in some mysterious way Dostoyevsky was able to tap the ancient springs.

In theory, the events described in *The Brothers Karamazov* took place in the sixties of the last century. In fact,they belong to our own time, and to all time. The story is rooted in legends so ancient that we no longer know their beginnings, and in thoughts so modern that we marvel at their freshness.

Essentially *The Brothers Karamazov* is a long, complex and brilliantly conceived morality play concerning man's search for God and his fatal addiction to crime which prevents him from seeing God face to face. Man is depicted as a being of heroic size, caught up in his own disastrous passions, hot for certainty, tormented by doubts, at the mercy of his lusts and his beliefs, possessing a strange grandeur and an even stranger insignificance. Man is seen under many aspects: he is a creature who simultaneously moves through time and eternity, through earthly law and sacred morality. All the characters of the novel are supremely conscious of the roles they are called upon to play, and even when they are silent, they exert themselves to the uttermost. There is a sense in which, like Versilov in *A Raw Youth,* they can be regarded as people "who have invented themselves." They are all in their different ways spiritual *virtuosi.*

They come on the stage fully developed, blazing with contradictions, affronting one another with their rhetoric and sudden bursts of paralyzing activity, and from the beginning they know they are doomed. The curse on the House of Atreus was the nemesis which inevitably falls on the proud. The Karamazovs also are proud, but each is proud in his own way. All are betrayed by their own lusts—those spiritual and earthly lusts which are the common lot of men, though among the Karamazovs they are sharper and more clearly defined than among most men. We fall under the spell of the novel because we see ourselves in that extraordinary family. Alyosha, Dmitry, Ivan, Smerdyakov and Fyodor Karamazov are in all of us; and we can no more escape from them than we can escape from ourselves.

For the first time in *The Brothers Karamazov* Dostoyevsky showed himself as the complete master of a complex situation. In *Crime and Punishment,* the only novel which showed a comparable control, the problem of resolving the fate of a single hero was almost absurdly simple compared with the problem of resolving the fates of five heroes, who are all murderers in different ways. They are men of flesh, but they are also allegorical characters. They are inextricably involved in one another's fate, and at the same time they are separate individuals leading their own lives. The complexities and contradictions are everywhere, but Dostoyevsky magically succeeds in resolving them. After the failure of *A Raw Youth* and the formlessness of *The Idiot* and *The Devils* this achievement of Dostoyevsky is all the more surprising. *The Brothers Karamazov* possesses a deliberate and inevitable form, and though Dostoyevsky sometimes falters, as all novelists do when they attempt large novels embracing vast areas of human experiences, for the greater length of the book he marches forward imperiously, uncommonly aware of his own strength and complete mastery of his material.

But in order to write *The Brothers Karamazov,* Dostoyevsky found himself compelled to jettison many of his favorite techniques. Formerly he had reveled in long sustained chapters filled with talk, with a minimum of incident, and with only the most casual attempt to convey the atmosphere of his scenes. His characters move about a darkened stage, climb staircases, pause to deliver long monologues, and suddenly vanish. We are permitted only the briefest glimpse of their faces. Everything is in the tone of voice, the way they walk across the stage, the shock of seeing them as they come down to the footlights and explain their dilemmas to the audience. But in *The Brothers Karamazov* Dostoyevsky quite deliberately followed the technique used by Tolstoy. The chapters are short, rounded, controlled. The action is described, sometimes almost too minutely described. There is no longer an ill-lit stage. The characters walk in the sunlight, observe the surrounding scene, and find themselves a little to their surprise bathed in the attendant air. They are not drawn white ghosts with hollow eyes; they have color on their cheeks.

For the first time Dostoyevsky permitted himself the luxury of describing the physical appearance of his characters. He went to great lengths to describe them accurately, and he filled his notebook with ink sketches of them. We recognize his portraits of Alyosha, Dmitry, Ivan, and Smerdyakov. There are often two or three portraits on a page, and he seems to have been determined to stamp their images on his own mind. We know very little about the appearance of Raskolnikov—we are told that he is unusually handsome, with beautiful dark eyes, dark brown hair, that he is over medium height, slim and well-built—and we are given only brief details of his childhood. Dostoyevsky deliberately fills many pages with an account of Alyosha's childhood and then describes him in terms not unlike the description of Raskolnikov, but the grey pencil sketch is filled out with palpable color. He is recognizably of the family of Raskolnikov:

> Some of my readers may imagine that my young man was a sickly, ecstatic, poorly developed creature, a pale dreamer, a weak and emaciated little fellow. On the contrary, Alyosha was at this time a well-built, red-cheeked, clear-eyed boy of nineteen, radiant with health. He was very handsome, too, slim, and of medium height, with dark brown hair, with a regular and rather long oval face, a pair of widely set sparkling eyes between grey and black; he was very thoughtful and apparently very self-composed. If the question is raised that red cheeks are incompatible with fanaticism and mysticism, then I would answer that Alyosha was more of a realist than anyone.[1]

[1] *The Brothers Karamazov*, Part I, Book i, Chapter 5.

So we have the hero presented as a young man possessing the rude health of a farm boy, who looked younger than his years, intelligent, sympathetic, deeply religious and practical. He is such a youth as any girl would yearn for.

Dmitry, his eldest brother, has a character and appearance which in nearly every respect are the direct opposite. Alyosha appears in his cassock, Dmitry in a frock coat with black gloves and a top hat. Alyosha carries with him the indisputable air of innocence, Dmitry has inherited from his father a sickly and stubborn lust for any woman he can get his hands on. There is something earthy in him, and Dostoyevsky hints at his earthiness in giving him the name Dmitry, which is derived from Demeter, the Goddess Mother of the Earth. Dostoyevsky describes him with the same exact care with which he describes Alyosha:

> He was a young man of twenty-eight, of medium height and pleasant appearance, looking much older than his years. He was muscular, and one could see that he possessed considerable physical strength, but there was something quite unhealthy about his face. His face was thin, his cheeks hollow, his complexion a sickly yellow. His rather large protruding dark eyes had an expression of determination, but there was also something evasive in them. Even when he was excited and talking irritably, his eyes seemed somehow un- affected by his mood and expressed something else, and sometimes they seemed to express complete indiffer- ence to whatever was happening at the moment. "It is hard to know what he is thinking about," people who talked to him would say. And those who saw something pensive and sullen in his eyes were startled by his sudden outbursts of laughter, which showed that his thoughts were amusing and playful just at the time when he looked so melancholy.[2]

There is something, then, of Pan, with his goatlike lusts and ferocious laughter in Dmitry. When Pan laughs, according to the

[2] *The Brothers Karamazov*, Part I, Book ii, Chapter 6.

339

Greek legends, everyone is thrown into a panic. Dmitry has sources of knowledge denied to his brothers: he is closer to the earth and the ancient past than any of them.

Significantly, there are no detailed portraits of Ivan, who is Alyosha's elder brother by old Fyodor's second wife, or of Smerdyakov, the illegitimate son "who grew out of the mildew in the bath-house." They are the same age; both are proud and conceited, but there is a vast difference in their attitudes to the world. Ivan is a brilliant intellectual, trained in the sciences, the author of a widely known pamphlet on the question of the functions of the ecclesiastical courts. He has a clear-cut intelligence colored a little by Dostoyevsky's own beliefs and prejudices: it is almost a self-portrait. Smerdyakov is unsociable and taciturn, a kind of growling Caliban, a slave in his master's house. He is "a man from the underground," and it is possible that Dostoyevsky intended him as a portrait of that wild, impulsive and bitterly resentful part of himself which lay just below the surface of consciousness. Smerdyakov murders his father.

The faces and appearances of Ivan and Smerdyakov are veiled, perhaps deliberately. We come to know them well, for we recognize their tones of voice, their behavior, and their motives. But we never see them in the warm light that bathes their brothers.

The father, too, is described with minute and loving care. He does not in the least resemble Dostoyevsky's own father. He is a buffoon who claims to have made his living as a youth as a court jester in the houses of noblemen. He is a congenital liar, a sot, the owner of bordellos. With his repulsive features and terrible shrill cackling laughter, he only just avoids being grotesque. Dostoyevsky's description of him is one of the most wonderful things in a book which is filled with wonders:

> I mentioned before that he looked bloated. By this time his face bore the unmistakable traces of the kind of life he was living. Beside the long fleshy bags under those little eyes of his, which were always insolent,

suspicious and ironical; beside the multitude of wrinkles on his fat little face, there hung under his sharp chin a large Adam's apple, fleshy and heavy like a goitre, and this somehow gave him a revolting sensual appearance. In addition he had a long, rapacious and sensual mouth with full lips, and between these could be seen the stumps of little black teeth decayed almost to the gums. He slobbered every time he began to speak. However, he loved to make fun of his own face, though apparently he was well satisfied with it, and he specially liked to point to his nose, which was not very large, but very thin and conspicuously aquiline. "A real Roman one," he liked to say, "and with that Adam's apple of mine it's exactly like the face of a Roman patrician of the decadent period." He seemed proud of it.[3]

In such ways do painters build up the portraits of their sitters, filling in the essential details and then joining them with solid planes of color. We shall not easily forget that swollen Adam's apple and the grinning black teeth. Fyodor Karamazov has introduced himself shamelessly and unforgettably into the story.

Father Zossima, who plays a dominant role in the early part of the novel, is sketched in more cursorily. Like Dmitry, he looks older than his years. Like Dmitry, too, he has a strange earthiness; he might be the brother of Marya Timofeyevna. He is a short, bent little man with weak legs, and his thin face is covered with a network of fine wrinkles. His eyes are small, light-colored, quick, and they gleam like two points. There are only a few grey hairs over his temples; he wears a small scanty beard which comes to a point. His lips are thin as strings, his nose sharp as a bird's beak, and his smile has the effect of putting all except the corrupt and the sinners at their ease. He is evidently modeled on a much older Prince Myshkin.

Dostoyevsky's deliberate attempt to give color and substance to his characters is worth pausing over, for it implies a quite

[3] *The Brothers Karamazov,* Part I, Book i, Chapter 4.

extraordinary change in his attitude towards the world. For the first time souls are enclosed in flesh. For the first time, too, Dostoyevsky is looking at a palpable and richly colored world, a world which does not consist of lines of force or lines of explosive violence. Abstractions are tossed aside; instead there is an attempt to suggest living and breathing people. He takes careful note of furniture, rooms, houses. We are given their shapes. An icon on a wall will suddenly attract his attention, and he will describe it minutely. We are never left in doubt where the characters are, what clothes they are wearing, and how they hold themselves. After a prolonged and feverish contemplation of the inner man, Dostoyevsky arrives during the last years of his life to the contemplation of the whole man.

This is not to suggest that there is any slackening of intensity. The fears, the threats, the sense of menace are still present, and perhaps all the more present because he has given so much life to that doomed family. The brothers, the father and the monk are perilously involved with each other. They hurtle against each other with demonic force. In their different ways they are all capable of torturing one another; and sometimes even Father Zossima's lips will curl with saintly disdain, and the angelic Alyosha, with some seemingly innocent phrase, will twist a knife in a wound.

Where did Dostoyevsky find his characters? We can only guess at an answer, suggest possible derivations. Alyosha is clearly related to the Mohammedan boy Alei, who slept on the plank bed beside Dostoyevsky in the prison at Omsk; there is something in him, too, of Dostoyevsky's boyhood friend, Ivan Shidlovsky, who once wrote in a letter: "God is good, or He would not be God, and the universe is the palpable beauty of His goodness." Shidlovsky's gentle persuasiveness and vivid idealism were remembered by Dostoyevsky throughout his life. Alei and Shidlovsky are strange companions, but they are not alone. Prince Myshkin, too, helped to form the character of Alyosha; and sometimes in his notebooks Dostoyevsky will write 'the Idiot' when he means the young seminarist. Then there is the young monk Alexis, who is the central character of George Sand's novel *Spiridion*. Finally there was the young philosopher Vladimir Solovyov, the handsome and brilliant son of a famous historian, to whom Dostoyevsky was deeply attached. With Solovyov, Dostoyevsky made a journey to the monastery of Optina Pustyn to meet Father Amvrosi, who became the model for Father Zossima.

All these influences, and perhaps many others, went to make the portrait of Alyosha. With astonishing success, Dostoyevsky was able to fuse them into a single, completely credible portrait of a modern saint.

Ivan, of course, is very largely Dostoyevsky himself in his younger days, when he was still attached to Fourierist socialism. He wears his brilliance lightly, and does his best to conceal the burden of an alarming conscience. Like Dostoyevsky himself, he was continually being confronted with the dark question: "If there is no God, surely everything is permissible?"

Dmitry's origins are harder to grasp, but he is clearly related to the world of Marya Timofeyevna, the half-pagan, half Chris tian world filled with ghostly demons and strange intimations of the Golden Age, before the angel came and troubled the waters. Dmitry has tapped the ancient veins in the earth, and possesses a passionate love of the Russian land. "Beauty," he confesses to Alyosha, "is a terrible and awful thing! It is terrible because it has not been fathomed, for God sets us nothing but riddles. Here the boundaries meet, and all contradictions exist side by side." He is like a plant being choked to death by weeds, but there is purity in him. In a great and famous scene in the opening of the novel, Father Zossima bows low to Dmitry, touching the earth with his forehead. He bows because he has recognized the potential murderer, though in fact Dmitry does not commit the murder; but this is not the only reason why Father Zossima bows.

Father Zossima himself has mined that ancient wisdom: he is not wholly Christian. Again and again in his speeches he takes

343

wing and veers towards those mysterious and poetic regions where Marya Timofeyevna and the dying Hippolyte found themselves at home. Prince Myshkin had glimpses of it when he came upon a white and smouldering waterfall among the pines of Switzerland. Makar Ivanovich saw it in the blades of grass, and Versilov saw it in that strange vision of civilization dying away, leaving only the lovers on the sacred earth. Father Zossima sees it in his last days, as he writes those nine sermons, which cost Dostoyevsky so much labor that he complained that it took him two months to write them.

Father Zossima speaks in the authentic voice of Makar Ivanovich when he says: "Love all God's creation, the whole of it, and every grain of sand! Love every leaf, every ray of God's light! Love animals, love plants, love everything! Loving everything, you will perceive the divine mystery in things, and once you have perceived it you will begin to comprehend it ceaselessly more and more every day, and you will come at last to love the whole world with an entire and universal love. Love animals . . ."

Though a dying priest speaks, he is giving utterance to a pagan joy. Father Zossima is singing his *Hymne an die Freude,* or rather that strange medley of hymns derived from Schiller's verses on the Eleusinian mysteries which are sung by Dmitry during his ecstatic meeting with Alyosha in a garden house much earlier in the novel. A fierce joy surges through him. He speaks as though everything in the world were blessed, and there was no sin, and no Crucifixion. There is no fall from grace; no flight from the garden. Instead there is the promise of the waterfall and the blade of grass.

Into that mysterious region one walks at one's peril, for though the mysteries of Eleusis (*"The water falls, and the seed flowers"*) have their place in it, Dostoyevsky is not bound by the ancient mystery, but gives it a peculiarly Russian amplitude. He is not at ease in this landscape, but trembles on the edge of revelation. In the sermons of Father Zossima we catch fleeting glimpses of the Golden Age, but in the end they fade into darkness. Like the Karamazovs, the saintly monk dies into corruption.

The monk represents the purest good; Fyodor Karamazov represents the purest evil. This lecherous old man has seduced Lizaveta Smerdyashchaya, Stinking Lizaveta, the mad girl who wanders homeless through the town, sleeping wherever she lays her head, and he has produced a mad son, Pavl Fyodorovich Smerdyakov. There is nothing to be said in favor of Fyodor except that he remains human; only too human. Dostoyevsky's daughter Luba declared that he was modelled on her grandfather, the doctor who after the death of his wife surrendered to his grief and went mad and was murdered; but since Luba has been proved to be the least responsible of Dostoyevsky's biographers, we can afford to dismiss her testimony.

Many abstruse pages have been written on the relationship between Dostoyevsky's father and Fyodor Karamazov. Freud, for example, claimed that Dostoyevsky's attacks of epilepsy began when he heard of his father's murder, a statement which can be easily disproved, and that Dostoyevsky showed himself possessed by an unconscious desire to assume responsibility for the murder, a statement which can be neither proved nor disproved. It is certain, however, that throughout his life Dostoyevsky was haunted by his father's death. Grief can endure over long periods; a man may suffer agonies of grief over the death of someone who died thirty or forty years ago. Grief can feed on itself; it does not wear out. In all the surviving letters and documents of Dostoyevsky there are only the briefest references to his father's death, suggesting that he deliberately concealed in his heart the most terrible event in the family history, spoke about it rarely, and never permitted himself the luxury of dwelling on it. He was like a man carrying a time bomb. In the end, when he wrote about sons murdering their father, the energy of his grief may have exploded within him.

Between Fyodor Karamazov and the doctor there is no

physical resemblance, nor any common ground of experience. The stern precise doctor who moved like clockwork is the antithesis of the garrulous old reprobate who kept innumerable mistresses, mocked at everything under the sun, and showed a devilish cunning. If Dostoyevsky had his own father in mind he would have left some revealing traces. There is evidence and to spare that Ivan is partly a self-portrait: that Alyosha portrays his dearest friends; that Katerina Ivanovna is modeled on Polina Suslova. But never by the least gesture does he suggest that he was thinking of his own father when he depicted the murder of Fyodor Karamazov.

Dostoyevsky had many models, but the principal model was the one closest to him—himself. He entered his characters so fully that he became them, suffered and died with them. There is a sense in which Fyodor Karamazov is Fyodor Dostoyevsky.[4]

Again and again in the novel Dostoyevsky puts into the mouths of his minor characters his own very personal visions and nightmares. When Liza Khokhlakova dreams of a child crucified against a wall and of herself eating pineapple compote while listening patiently to the groans, Dostoyevsky is clearly recounting a nightmare of his own, one, moreover, which is very close to the heart of the novel, for the novel is concerned as much with the reason why God permits the suffering of children as with the search for God the Father. When Dmitry describes himself as an

---

[4] The puzzling and wonderfully effective Karamazov name has never been fully explained. No families of that name have been traced. It would seem to derive from a fusion of three quite separate ideas— the Turkish *kara* meaning "black," a word which Dostoyevsky knew well from his stay in Semipalatinsk; the figure of the historian and story writer Karamzin who dominated his childhood; and the medieval Jewish sect of the Karaites, known in Russia as *Karaimi,* who demanded a return to primitive Judaism. The sect was founded by Anan ben David in Baghdad. There was a small colony of them at Semipalatinsk, and there were large numbers of them in south and central Asiatic Russia. The primitive patriarchal character of Fyodor Karamazov, and the peculiarly un-Russian cast of his features, has suggested to some scholars that Dostoyevsky was aware of Karaite influence on his portrait of that extraordinary man.

insect—"I am that insect, brother, and it is said of me specially" —he is merely repeating an argument which has already been discussed at length in *Notes from Underground*. Everywhere we look we find echoes of the authentic Dostoyevsky; he makes no attempt to hide his voice, which can be heard like a groundswell below the voices of his creations.

In the sermons of Father Zossima, on which Dostoyevsky expended so much energy, he has attempted to distill the wisdom acquired during a long life; and indeed Zossima, the former soldier, the saint whose body falls into corruption, is perilously close to a self-portrait. Significantly, Zossima is no monk dedicated to lifelong contemplation: he has known the world and engaged in its traffic. He, too, is an insect, a sinner, and at the same time he is an angel, the most majestic of God's creatures. He is a saint who has embraced the whole gamut of God's creatures and known all human experience, because this too belongs to human dignity.

In those brief sermons composed during the last days of his life, Zossima speaks his most intimate thoughts. They are not essentially Christian sermons, though they might have been spoken by St. Francis of Assisi. Beyond God, beyond Christ, there is the Earth Mother, the joy of the earth. He speaks in simple parables, but they are parables which are closer to the ancient Greeks and the mysteries of Eleusis than to the preoccupations of the Orthodox Church. He points not to the crucifix but to the Golden Age. In the end he always comes back to the mystery of earth and all earth's joys.

The Earth Mother herself is present in the novel. She is in fact only too abundantly present, in all her vigor and ripeness, in the person of Grushenka, "the young pear tree." Dostoyevsky lavished great care on her portrait, and nowhere else in his works is there to be found such a detailed description of a woman. He was so much in love with her that he described her twice over, and continually elaborated on her beauty. She was a creature of instinct, and therefore could commit no evil, but she was also a child, with a child's contempt for the world of grown men. There is a childlike innocence in her eyes. Her body is soft and voluptuous. She moves gracefully and silently like a cat, and she has the heaviness, the broad shoulders and ample bosom of the Venus de Milo. An air of mystery attaches to her: it is the mystery of the animal world, of the earth and the ancient goddesses. When Alyosha meets her, he is thunderstruck. He expected to see a common harlot and confronts a goddess:

> Her face was pale, with a pale pink tint on her cheeks. The modeling of her face seemed rather broad, and the lower jaw even protruded a little. Her upper lip was thin, her slightly prominent lower lip was at least twice as full, so that she seemed to be pouting. But her magnificent, abundant dark brown hair, her sable-colored eyebrows, and her exquisite grey-blue eyes with their long eyelashes would have made the most indifferent and absentminded person, meeting her in a crowded street, pause suddenly at the sight of her, and he would remember her long afterwards.
>
> What struck Alyosha most in her face was the childish, goodnatured expression. There was a childlike look in her eyes, she expressed delight like a child. She came up to the table evidently filled with delight, as though she were expecting, with childish, impatient and confiding curiosity, something pleasant to happen. The light in her eyes gladdened the soul—Alyosha felt that. There was also something about her which he could not understand or was unable to put into words, and which unconsciously affected him—this was her softness, the voluptuousness of her bodily movements, her catlike silence. And yet hers was a powerful and well-developed body. Beneath her shawl there could be discerned full broad shoulders, and a high, still girlish bosom.[5]

Alyosha trembles before the spectacle of her beauty, of her fatal opulence. Himself possessing "the highest beauty," which is a moral beauty, he confronts "the highest beauty" in its physical

[5] *The Brothers Karamazov,* Part I, Book iii, Chapter 10.

presence; and in the original version of the novel as outlined in the notebooks he very nearly succumbs to her charms. Grushenka even resembles him in her generosity. "Everyone in the world is good," she says during a drunken orgy with Dmitry. "Everyone— even the worst of them. Tell me, there is something I want to know, why am I so good?" She wishes she were God, and then she would forgive everyone. Drunk, but very wise, she speaks of the time when she will be close to the earth, digging with her own hands. She will go with Dmitry to Siberia, to be close to him and to the earth. Katerina Ivanovna calls her "the tigress," and she admits to having a fierce heart, but in reality she is passive.

Dmitry, too, is passive, with the passivity of a farm laborer who waits hopefully for the autumn rains. There is no resource-fulness in him. He too is moved by mysterious forces beyond the bounds of logic. Arrested and brought before the prosecutor he denies his guilt, for he is in fact innocent of the crime of murdering his father. Later he has a dream of a burnt-out village in the snow, and women standing beside the road, one of them with a weeping babe in her arms. The women too are weeping. Dmitry cannot understand why they are all weeping, and asks the coach-man.

"It is because of the babe," the coachman replies. "The weeping babe."

"Why is it crying?" Dmitry asks. "Why are its little arms bare? Why don't they wrap it up? Why is the steppe barren? Why don't they sing songs of joy?"

At that moment, in his dream, his fate is decided. Repeatedly he is heard saying: "I will go to Siberia for the sake of the babe," and in the chapter *A Hymn and a Secret* he relates to Alyosha his joy at the thought of suffering penance for the sake of the child he had seen in his dreams. This starving child is related to the lost child of Marya Timofeyevna. In one of the strangest and most lyrical of all the passages written by Dostoyevsky, Dmitry affirms his faith in the earth, and in God, and in the darkness beneath the earth, in the terrible world of "the underground" where God is perhaps more present than he is in the sunlight:

A new man has risen in me. He was hidden inside me, but he would never have appeared if it had not been for this bolt from heaven. It's terrible! But what does it matter if I spend twenty years in the mines, breaking off the ore with a hammer? I'm not afraid of that—it is something else I'm afraid of—what happens if this new man departs from me? Even there in the mines, under the ground, you may come upon a human heart. It will be there beside you in another convict or another murderer, and you can make friends with it. Even there you can live and love and suffer! You can revive the frozen heart of such a convict. You may wait for years and years, but one day you will bring up from the dark depths a lofty soul, a soul that has suffered and become conscious of its humanity; one may restore an angel to life, or bring forth a hero! There are so many of them, hundreds of them, and we are all responsible for them. Why did I dream of the "babe" at that moment? "Why is the babe so poor?" That was a sign for me! It's for the "babe" I'm going, for we are all responsible for all—for all the "babes," since there are little children and big children. All of us are "babes." I'll go for all, because someone has to go for all! I didn't kill my father, but I have to go. I accept! It all came to me here, within these peeling walls. There are so many of them, hundreds of them, all working underground with hammers in their hands. Oh yes, we shall be in chains and there will be no freedom, but then, in our great sorrow, we shall arise again in joy, without which man cannot live nor God exist, for God gives joy. It's his privilege, his great privilege . . . O Lord, man should be dissolved in prayer! What would happen to me there in the underground without God? If they drive God from the earth, then we shall shelter him under the earth! A convict cannot exist without God! It is even more impossible for him to exist without God than a free man! And we shall be the men under the earth, singing from the bowels of the earth our tragic hymn to God, in whom there is joy! Hail to God and his joy! I love him!"

Mitya was almost gasping for breath as he uttered his wild speech. He turned pale, his lips twitched, and tears rolled down his cheeks.

"No," he began again, "life is full, there is life even under the ground. You wouldn't believe, Alexey, how much I want to live now, what a burning desire to think and to be alive has arisen in me inside these peeling walls . . . And I seem to have such strength in me now that I shall overcome all things, all sufferings, so that I may say at every moment: I exist! In thousands of agonies—I exist! Tortured on the rack—I exist! I see the sun, and if I don't see the sun, I know it is there! And there's a whole life in that, in knowing that the sun is there! [6]

There is nothing in all Dostoyevsky's work to be compared with that cry of triumph, which he wrote in the last months of his life. It was as though he were concentrating all his thought and feeling in one last symphonic celebration. Dmitry exults in the grace of life, yet he is perfectly aware of its tragedy. He knows the darkness where the lost babe dwells; he knows the terror of working underground; he knows that if God is banished from the earth, he can still live like Persephone beneath the earth, and return into the sunlight. "Beware of your dream, old man," says Dmitry to his father earlier in the novel, "for I have my dream, too." And now at last Dmitry has revealed his dream.

Ivan, too, has his dreams. He dreams of the Devil, who wears "a tortoise-shell lorgnette on a black ribbon," and his hallucinatory conversations with the Devil are wonderfully conveyed. But Ivan, a man of subtle intellect, has more important dreams to worry about. In particular there is his dream of the Second Coming, which we know as *The Legend of the Grand Inquisitor*.

[6] *The Brothers Karamazov,* Part IV, Book xi, Chapter 4.

Manuscript page of notes for "The Brothers Karamazov."

Ivan prefaces the story with a description of the sufferings of innocent children, to prove that God is evil. Children are raped and beaten to death, and wild dogs are set on them; there is no end to the horrors practiced on innocent children. The agony of children proves to Ivan the absurdity of the divinely created order of things. Must they suffer so that "eternal harmony" will be established? Ivan is presenting the same argument as Dmitry: the babe weeps, the stones cry out, and Dmitry sees in the weeping babe the need for repentance. For him, the babe weeps, and all humanity shudders at the weeping, but there is always the hope of a miracle brought about by the repentance of the evildoers in the world. Ivan will have none of this. Because children are torn from their mothers' breasts and savaged by dogs, "I shall have no share of it, and most respectfully return God his ticket." He denies God. He refuses to take comfort in God's law, for His law is no longer operative.

At this point Ivan relates the story of Christ's coming "in the most terrible time of the Inquisition, when fires were lit every day to the glory of God."

Christ comes very humbly, alone and unheralded, but he is immediately recognized. A blind man cries out, and the scales fall from his eyes. On the steps of Seville Cathedral a child lies in a small white coffin heaped with flowers, and the child's mother appeals to Christ to return the child to life, and the child sits up in her coffin. The Grand Inquisitor appears in his cardinal's robes and orders the arrest of Christ, and that night he enters the prison cell and interrogates the prisoner. The rest of *The Legend of the Grand Inquisitor* consists of the Inquisitor's carefully reasoned speech, accusing Christ of spoiling the work of the Church. He threatens to have Christ burned at the stake.

A single lamp burns in the prison cell. Christ stands there in all the beauty of His young manhood, confronting the ninety-year-old Inquisitor who is close to death.

The Inquisitor speaks on many levels and in many voices, and he has many weapons. He can burn Christ, or destroy Him with irony, or reduce Him to madness and despair by proving that men no longer have need of Him, for His work has been corrected and mankind has been granted the happiness it has always desired *without Him*. Christ's law has been reversed. Instead of love and freedom, there is Miracle, Mystery, and Authority; and the greatest of these is Authority. The Inquisitor offers a sermon on the text: "And the devil said unto him, If thou be the Son of God, command this stone that it be made bread." With remarkable force he points out that the Inquisitors of the new age have succeeded in turning the stones into the bread, and the people are filled with gratitude and worship for their masters. They are weak and submissive before the power of their rulers, trembling impotently before their wrath, turning from tears to laughter at a signal, incapable of any decisions of their own because all decisions are made for them; and they are happy as children are happy, with a childlike happiness "which is the sweetest of all."

The Inquisitor paints a picture of the Golden Age as enjoyed by mechanical marionettes. A small handful of men endowed with great wisdom dominate the world by virtue of the authority vested in them by Christ. There has been an act of treason, but centuries of conformity have sanctified the treason, and there is no longer anything that Christ can do to alter the established pattern:

> We have corrected your great work and have based it on *Miracle, Mystery,* and *Authority.* And men rejoiced to be led once more like sheep and because the terrible gift which brought them so much suffering has been removed from their hearts. Were we justified in doing this and teaching this? Speak! Did we not love mankind when we humbly acknowledged man's impotence and lovingly lightened his burdens, and we even permitted man in his wickedness to sin, granting him our permission. Why then hast thou come to meddle with us now? And why dost thou look so silently and searchingly at me with thy mild eyes? Be angry! I do not desire thy love, for I have no love for thee! And what have I to hide from thee? Since it is all known to thee already, is it for me to conceal our mystery from thee? Perhaps thou hast desired to hear these words from my lips? [7]

So, as he spins his treacherous web, involving Christ in the massacre, making him responsible for the crimes committed by

[7] *The Brothers Karamazov,* Part II, Book ii, Chapter 5.

354

the Inquisitor, we are led to the terrifying vision of the people enslaved by authority, with no hope of ever extricating themselves from its toils, for they welcome it with open arms:

> Yes, we shall force them to work, but in their leisure hours we shall make their life like a child's game, and they will sing children's songs in chorus and dance innocent dances. Oh, we shall allow them even to sin, for they are weak and helpless, and they will love us like children because we permitted them to sin. We shall tell them that every sin can be expiated on condition that it is done with our permission. We shall tell them that we permit them to sin out of our love for them, and as for the punishment of their sins—this we shall take upon ourselves. And we shall take it upon ourselves, and they will adore us as their saviors who have assumed the burden of their sins before God. And they will have no secrets from us. We shall allow or forbid them to live with wives or mistresses, to have or not to have children—according to the measure of their obedience —and they will submit themselves to us gladly and joyfully. The most painful secrets of their conscience— everything, everything without exception they will bring to us, and we shall answer for all. And they will be glad to believe our answer, for it will save them from great anxieties and the terrible torments of coming to decisions for themselves. All will be happy, all the millions of creatures except the hundred thousand who rule over them. For we alone, we who guard the mystery, only we shall be unhappy.[8]

It is, of course, a vision of the authoritarian state such as the world came to know long after Dostoyevsky had foreseen its coming; and the vision, as it was written, gains a terrible force because it is stated in the silent presence of Christ. As Ivan tells the story, the Grand Inquisitor has a change of heart. Instead of burning Christ, he dismisses him from the prison, saying: "Go, and

[8] *Ibid.*

come no more." But before this happens Christ kisses the Inquisitor on the lips, as he had kissed Judas, or as he would kiss a child.

Ivan tells the story with such ruthlessness that he is himself astonished. *The Legend of the Grand Inquisitor* is a poem, but it is also a terrifying attack on the Church, whether Orthodox or Catholic, for it points to Christ's example betrayed by the spiritual lords of our time.

Dostoyevsky spoke of the legend as "the culminating work of his literary activity." Into it he poured all his powers of description and analysis. He was on the side of Christ against the Grand Inquisitor, but the diabolical argument is stated with tremendous force. Against this argument Alyosha can say only: "The sticky little leaves, the precious tombs, the blue sky, the women you love? How will you live? How will you love them? With such a hell in your heart and head, how is it possible?"

The Grand Inquisitor's portrait of the world ruled by Miracle, Mystery, and Authority did not emerge fully fledged; it had a long history. We can trace its beginning in *The House of the Dead,* where Dostoyevsky describes the prisoners as "men who hate liberty." "In prison," he wrote, "a man eats as much as he wants to eat, and sometimes better than he could have hoped to eat, had he remained outside. On holidays he will have meat, and fine people will give him alms, and he will be paid for his evening's work. He will consider himself in the best company possible." The world of the Grand Inquisitor is not very far removed from a prison ruled by a dictatorship of priests.

On many occasions Dostoyevsky wrote as though the dictatorship of the priests was already in existence in the Roman Catholic Church. There is a strange passage in *The Idiot* where Prince Myshkin, emerging from a period of fever and delirium, gives vent to a ferocious attack on the Catholic Church. He says:

> In my opinion Roman Catholicism is worse than Atheism. Yes, I truly believe it. Atheism only preaches the negative, but the Catholics go further—they preach

a disfigured, distorted Christ—they preach Anti-Christ
—I am sure of it, I swear it is so! The Roman Catholics
believe that the Church on earth cannot exist without
universal temporal power. They cry: "Non possumus!"
In my opinion Roman Catholicism is not really a faith
at all: it is just the continuation of the Roman Empire,
and everything is subordinated to this idea, beginning
with faith. The Pope has seized territories and an
earthly throne, and he holds onto them with the sword.
And so it has gone on, only to the sword there have
been added lying, deceit, intrigue, fanaticism, superstition . . .[9]

Prince Myshkin goes on to declare that socialism is the
progeny of Roman Catholicism and the romantic spirit—*Fraternité ou la Mort.* He never quite makes clear how he comes to
this extraordinary conclusion, but it is one he shared with Dostoyevsky, who feared the alliance of the socialists with the
Church, even when it was demonstrable that such an alliance
could never take place. What could, and did, take place was the
emergence of a form of socialism led by men possessed by the
complete devotion and self-dedication of the Jesuits. Against
dedicated socialists and all their works Dostoyevsky raged with all
his strength.

There were other sources of *The Legend of the Grand
Inquisitor.* All through his life he was an admirer of Schiller. He
was nineteen when he wrote to his brother Mikhail: "You say in
your letter that I know nothing about Schiller. How wrong you
are! I have been completely absorbed in him, I talk and dream
of him, and believe that fate has never done anything more
wonderful for me than to introduce me to him."

He read Schiller's drama *Don Carlos* again and again during
his life, and returned to it when he began writing *The Brothers
Karamazov.* The drama recounts the betrayal of Don Carlos of
Spain, heir to the throne of Philip II. With a reckless disregard for

[9] *The Idiot,* Part IV, Chapter vii.

history, Schiller invents his own Don Carlos, whose struggle to obtain the crown was equalled only by his determination to refuse any disguises. He lives for his ideals: virtue, freedom, gentleness. "A strange chimera has caught his imagination," says the King's confessor. "He honors mankind—how then can he be fit for a king?" Because he passionately espouses liberty, he is doomed, and in the last act the King summons the Grand Inquisitor and demands that his son be handed over to the arm of the Inquisition, for he dare not put his son to death with his own hands.

In a scene of extraordinary power the blind Inquisitor comes into the presence of the King, demanding that the King should bow to the will of the Church, while the King, who has ruled half Europe for sixty years, demands that the guilt for what he is about to do to his only son be taken from him.

KING
My son is plotting treason!

GRAND INQUISITOR
Have you decided—?

KING
I have decided it shall be all or nothing!

GRAND INQUISITOR
And "all" means—?

KING
It means I shall let him escape
Unless I can bring myself to let him die.

GRAND INQUISITOR
Well, then—?

KING
Canst thou not invent a new religion
To sanction the murder of my only son?

GRAND INQUISITOR
For the redemption of eternal justice
God's only son was sacrificed upon the Cross.

358

The Karamazovs

KING
This idea—wilt thou sow the seed
Through all the lands of Europe?

GRAND INQUISITOR
                    It shall grow
Wherever the Cross is worshipped.

KING
If I should outrage Nature
Couldst thou silence her mighty voice as well?

GRAND INQUISITOR
The Creed affords no recognition of that voice.

KING
Then I resign my office as the highest judge.
Shall I withdraw myself entirely?

GRAND INQUISITOR
Give him to me!

KING
He is my only son. For whom
Was all my wealth assembled?

GRAND INQUISITOR
Detter for corruption than for freedom.

KING
Then we are in agreement. Come with me.

GRAND INQUISITOR
Where to?

KING
Where I myself shall hand the victim to you.[1]

Such is the dénouement of the play, with the dark forces represented by the blind and infirm Inquisitor in the ascendant, though Don Carlos's pleas for freedom among the people are still ringing in our ears. Catastrophe overtakes the human protagonists, but their efforts are not completely vain, for we know—or rather, Schiller believes—that in some far-distant age, after many travails and many more bloodbaths, the cause of human dignity will

[1] Friedrich Schiller: *Don Carlos,* Act V, Scene 8.

prevail; without this hope the play would simply be the narration of a long list of vain endeavors and futile sacrifices.

The Grand Inquisitor appears only once in the play, but every word he speaks is filled with significance. He questions, he instructs, he dominates. To him all things are possible when sanctified by God's will, and he is in the happy position of being able to pronounce that God's will supports the monarch against the prince, and that to kill, and therefore to be corrupted by bloodshed, is as nothing compared with permitting the young prince to defy God and the King. "Better for corruption than for freedom"—*der Verwesung lieber als der Freiheit*—such is his final argument, and in its own terms it is incontrovertible. A good part of Dostoyevsky's life was devoted to shaking some meaning out of these words and attempting to destroy the argument, which he first encountered when he was very young.

Though *Don Carlos* is the principal literary source of *The Legend of the Grand Inquisitor,* it was not the only source. That brilliant and penetrating story has many origins. Many legends are hidden within it, and many strands of meaning have entered into it. There are memories of Christ before Caiaphas, of the raising of the daughter of Jairus, of Dostoyevsky's own arrest and imprisonment, and of his lifelong argument with Belinsky, whose shadow falls over the story. Belinsky indeed had once hinted that he was against the Inquisitor. He wrote in a famous letter to his friend Vasily Botkin in 1841:

> Let me inform you, with all respect to your philosophical philistinism, that if I ever happen to attain the highest rung on the ladder of evolution, I would there demand that an account be rendered to me of all the martyrs of life and history, of all the victims of hazard, of superstition, of the Inquisition, of Philip II etc., otherwise I will throw myself headlong from the top rung. I will not have happiness even if it is delivered to me gratis, unless I am reassured by every one of my

brothers, who are bone of my bone and flesh of my flesh.[2]

Belinsky was continually changing his mind—he admitted in the same letter that his views had been diametrically opposite only a year before—and by the time he wrote the letter which Dostoyevsky read to the Petrashevsky conspirators he had moved a long way from this position. For Dostoyevsky there was no possibility of moving beyond this position, because for him the human condition demanded sympathy for all men as the price of existence.

There has survived among Dostoyevsky's notebooks a rough draft of *The Legend of the Grand Inquisitor,* which seems to have been written only a short while before he composed the story. Often the expression is raw, shot out from the brain, incomplete, as though jotted down on a scratch pad at his elbow. These notes begin with the Grand Inquisitor's solemn appraisal of his own humanity:

> THE INQUISITOR: What need have we of "over there"? We are more human than you. We love the earth. Schiller sings to joy, John Damascene. What price we pay for this joy? What torrents of blood, tortures, ignominies and almost unendurable brutalities. About this we shall not speak. Oh, the Crucifix is a terrible argument.
> THE INQUISITOR: *God like a merchant.* I love humanity better than you.
> where the serpent breaks his fang
> The kiss burns his heart, but he does not change his ideas.
> CHRIST: the whole world is not worth this thought —invented God.
> So holy, and so tender, and so reasonable! And it is all absurd—an insane attempt.
> The trial balloon has gone up.

[2] Letter to V. P. Botkin, March 1, 1841.

Believe in the words of the heart.

The Inquisitor is then just, but, even though he is just, I refuse to accept him.

The secret—that there is no truth, no God, that is the God you are teaching.

Despair not tragic, but comic.

He laughed when they led the wretched creature away, the abject rabble of an abject parliament

Alyosha rose and embraced him (he is silent)

Ivan—The Inquisitor! The Inquisitor! . . .

Oh, He gave His Son and sent Him to be crucified—tortured. Oh, this is an argument of terrible power, an eternal argument.

Why have you come to trouble our work? I shall burn you.

INQUISITOR: From love of humanity I tell you—I speak to you who loved humanity more than yourself. You alone can understand me, and that is why I can reveal to you our secret. I shall burn you at dawn . . .

The angels will sing. If the mother embraces, pardons, the torturer of her son, then there occurs something so great that it is truly worth all these miseries—but I do not desire—for this revolt . . .

We shall have to wait a long time before we organize the Kingdom.

A swarm of locusts will arise from the earth crying out that we reduce men to bondage, that we corrupt virgins—but these wretched creatures shall submit, and the greatest among them will join with us and they will know that we assume our suffering for the sake of power. . . . But they, the damned, do not know what burdens we are undertaking—the burdens of knowledge—and suffering.[3]

At such moments we seem to be peering into the crucible of Dostoyevsky's mind. The arguments follow one another in rapid succession. The Mother of God, the angels, and the Kingdom are followed by the swarms of locusts, the damnation which hangs

---

[3] *Materiali,* Folio 36, p. 129.

over the Grand Inquisitor, and the fearful burden of his knowledge, from which he can no longer escape, for all avenues of escape have been closed to him. "Of late the world has proclaimed the reign of freedom," says Father Zossima, "but what do we see? Nothing but slavery and self-destruction." The Grand Inquisitor is the mechanism by which slavery and self-destruction are brought about. His name is legion.

In the somber conclusion of the story Dostoyevsky worked his greatest miracle. The silent Christ moves away, but whether it is to Heaven or Galilee no one knows. We watch him as he wanders through the dark alleys of the town, and then he vanishes.

All through *The Brothers Karamazov* there is this urgency, this terror, this sense of the darkness falling upon the earth and the heavens opening. The human soul, caught in the massive toils of its own making, contrives to justify itself in the sight of God and man, and succeeds only because it wrestles with the angel. It wrestles nakedly, having thrown all its weapons away, and we watch the combat with mounting horror, because Dostoyevsky has expressed the most dangerous perturbations of modern man. We are the brothers Karamazov. There is a Smerdyakov in every one of us, and a saintly Alyosha, and a coldly intellectual Ivan, and a Dmitry in love with the teeming earth.

Perhaps it was for this reason that T. E. Lawrence called the novel quite simply "the fifth Gospel."

THE LAST DAYS

As the writing of *The Brothers Karamazov* came to an end, Dostoyevsky knew that weariness which comes to nearly all authors as they approach the end of a long task. It was not, of course, that he was tiring of his characters; it was simply that the long months of unremitting attention to the development of their lives—those lives which were so fraught with danger and excitement—had exhausted him. For more than two years he had been steadily writing the book: writing at night, against the clock, for the messenger from *The Russian Messenger* came only too regularly. He was ill, and the doctors had begged him to take a rest, but even if he had wanted to rest, he knew it would have been impossible. In *The Brothers Karamazov* he was pouring out his whole life, all his experiences, everything he had ever known about himself and the Russian people; and mostly the work was autobiographical. He no longer controlled the brothers, for he was possessed by them, and each of them was a reflection of one side of his character. And so the war between them had to be fought to a conclusion, and he hurried on, writing in a state of extraordinary excitement, as eager as his readers to know how the story would end.

Sometimes it occurred to him that the story would have no end, as it had no beginning. There would be more volumes—many more volumes. He would tell the story not only of a whole generation, but of a whole epoch. When he asked himself how the story had begun, he would say it had been part of him from the very beginning. It was the story of a murder, a very simple murder. His father had been choked to death under an oak tree by serfs who were never brought to trial, and therefore the responsibility for the murder had never been fixed. In a sense *The Brothers Karamazov* was about the guilt which everyone brings into the world, but it was also indirectly and obscurely the story of a father's murder: an attempt to fill the gaping holes of responsibility, with Dostoyevsky playing all the roles—the murdered man, the plotters, the actual murderer, the witnesses, the judge, the prosecutor. He was writing a novel while at the peak of his creative ability, but he was also quietly tormenting himself with his guilt, surrendering to that small dark blood-red core where all horror is concentrated. Murder fascinated him; he had lived in prison with murderers and all kinds of rootless criminals, and felt an imaginative sympathy for them. He was a man who had committed innumerable crimes, blasphemed with extraordinary violence, and shaken the pillars of government. He had done all this in his novels.

He was haunted by a conception of man possessed of the highest dignity, closer even to God than the angels; and so inevitably *The Brothers Karamazov* dealt with devils as well as with angels. The novel was a nightmare compounded out of his own dreams, his own flesh, those who were nearest and dearest to him, and sometimes—and this happens when we least expect it—we see behind the masks of old Fyodor and Dmitry and Alyosha and Ivan and Smerdyakov the familiar face of Dostoyevsky himself.

In the fall of 1880, when the novel was coming to an end, this familiar face was worn and ravaged. He was fifty-nine, but looked many years older. Epilepsy had wasted him. As he sat at his desk and the night's work went on, he would grow pale and gaunt until in the early hours of the morning when he went to bed he looked like a skeleton, with heavy rings under his deepset grey eyes. His large forehead, once smooth, had grown lumpy and withered and wrinkled, and his temples were hollowed out as though a fist had struck deep in them. There was on him that look of frailty which comes to men in the last weeks of their lives.

Most of his life he had looked younger than his age; now time caught up with him. His skin was paper-thin, his cheekbones jutted, his finely carved lips sometimes trembled inexplicably. He had a strange old-young appearance, for his orange-beard had not a touch of grey, nor had his thinning hair. Old he was certainly: old and exhausted and very tired. But an observer seeing him casually in the street, walking rapidly, his shoulders hunched in a slight stoop, might take him for a much younger man. In all the time he had been writing *The Brothers Karamazov* he had not suffered a single epileptic fit.

He had, of course, suffered other ailments—colds, fevers, terrible bouts of asthma, periods of nervous prostration when it was impossible for him to write, impossible to put his ideas in order. At such times he would glare mournfully at the pile of manuscripts on his table and wonder whether he would ever be able to finish the novel. To help his asthma he sucked cough lozenges called Ems pastilles. During his periods of nervous prostration only his wife Anna was allowed to come near him; she massaged him, saw that he ate regularly, made everyone walk about on tiptoes, and saw to it that unwelcome visitors like the ugly stepson Pasha were kept away from him. She was selfish in her devotions, but she had to be. To the very end she gave her husband her stern and unyielding devotion.

Night after night he worked on the manuscript, writing hurriedly in a vigorous cramped knotty hand which had replaced the bold and ample handwriting of earlier days. He still doodled, drew endless gothic spires and windows and profiles on the margins. He wrote by candlelight: there were always two candles on his desk. Usually there was a glass of sweetened tea, which he sipped at intervals—one glass of this sirupy tea would last through the whole night. In a drawer there were raisins, nuts, a box of Turkish delight, and the inevitable pastilles. When the inspiration flowed, he would write uninterruptedly for two or three hours on end, and then the only sound was the splutter of the pen in the inkwell.

His workroom was a large room with a window overlooking the street: it had striped wallpaper, and an air of faded gentility. The heavy mahogany desk stood against the wall, immediately beneath a framed photograph of the Sistine Madonna, a present from Countess Sophia Tolstoy. The table was usually cluttered, piled high with books. In front of the desk, beside his chair, stood a smaller desk, where Anna took dictation in the afternoon or early evening; and just behind him stood a heavy wardrobe in which he kept some of his clothes, including the light summer overcoat he wore on cold nights rather than a dressing-gown. There were small photographs of himself and his wife above the desk. Against another wall stood a long Turkish sofa. There were heavy curtains over the window, a faded carpet on the floor—nothing else. It was so forbidding a room that he rarely received visitors in it. He received them instead in the adjoining living room.

Dostoyevsky at the height of his fame was living in an apartment which a moderately successful druggist would have rejected. This apartment was on the first floor at No. 5 Kuznechny Pereulok, in an unfashionable part of St. Petersburg; everything was old, tawdry, or bought cheaply. Except for the chapters written during the summer holidays at Staraya Russa and some pages written during a brief visit to Ems, he wrote all of *The Brothers Karamazov* in this room, as bleak as any described in his novels. He was indifferent to creature comforts: for him there was only the endless study of the Karamazovs, the pen, the white paper, the two candles on the table and the knowledge that Anna was somewhere near.

In August he had nearly finished, but he was still far from the end. At white heat he was revising, collating, editing, changing whole scenes, pondering the development of an almost unmanageable subplot, considering a number of alternative endings. At the end of August he wrote to his friend Ivan Aksakov:

> No one can possibly imagine how busy I am. I work hard all day and all night. I am finishing the Karamazovs, and continually reviewing in my mind the pages I have written, which for me, at any rate, are very precious, for there is a good deal of myself in them. I find myself very tense while I am working, for the book causes me much pain and sorrow. Working hard, I become physically ill. But now at last I feel I can strike a balance of all those pages which have absorbed me for three years, redrafting it and writing it down. It must be done well, at least as well as I can.[1]

He was fighting for time, fighting for his life, with only one thought—to finish the novel. Deputations of students came and begged to be permitted to speak to him, and were turned away. He tried to write as few letters as possible. "Writing letters is a torture to me," he wrote, but it had always been a torture to him, and there was nothing unusual in this. On October 15 he wrote a revealing letter to Pelageya Guseva, a little-known poetess he had met during one of his visits to Ems:

> I was in Siberia, in prison, for four years, but my life and work are now far more difficult than they were then. From 15th June to 1st October I have written 20 folios of my novel and 3 folios of *The Diary of a Writer*. I dare not write freely, I must produce a work of art. I am under obligation to God, to poetry, to the success of what I have already written, and to all the Russians who read my work and who await the end of my novel. So I sit and write literally day and night . . . Will you believe me when I say I have not had the time to read a single book or even the newspapers? I haven't even the time to talk to my children. I haven't the time to talk. My health, too, is so bad that you could hardly imagine it . . .

[1] *Letters:* 769, August 28, 1880.

The Last Days

> I have literally not had a moment to fulfill my most sacred and pressing duties. I have neglected everything, not to speak of myself. It is 6 o'clock in the morning. The city is awakening, but I have not yet gone to bed, and the doctors tell me I must not wear myself out with work sitting over my desk for ten or twelve hours a day uninterruptedly.[2]

By this time the book was nearly finished, and there remained only the final stages of the trial, Dmitry's plans of escape and "the speech at the stone." For three more weeks he worked on, exhausting himself with constant revisions. There is a sense in which all that had gone before is merely a preparation for the great scene in which Dmitry, Katerina Ivanovna, and Grushenka confront one another; but this scene gives the impression of having been written recklessly, quickly, with too many echoes of similar scenes written long before. The fire was dying out. It blazed for a moment with Dmitry's great cry of innocence at the end of the trial: "I swear by God and the dreadful Day of Judgment I am not guilty of my father's death!" and it blazes again in the last ecstatic cry: "Hurrah for Karamazov!", but in the interval between the cries there are long, arid passages where Dostoyevsky seems to be in doubt of his own purposes. A good deal of the trial is simply journalism; worse still, it is journalism at second hand, for much of it is based on newspaper reports, references to law books, and inquiries among his lawyer friends. He took unusual care that the description of the trial should be accurate in all particulars. He was determined to follow exact protocol. He had never been concerned with these matters before. Three quarters of the novel is written with the fierce and probing light of a relentless imagination which could search into the most remote crannies of the human soul. Now the light was failing, the journalist in him took over, and his imagination was growing careless.

He was also much more ill than he suspected. He had strange

[2] *Letters:* 772, October 15, 1880.

fevers and sudden outbursts of inexplicable excitement. He was not exaggerating when he said he was working ten or twelve hours a day, driving himself at a backbreaking pace. Even Anna, who rarely attempted to take him away from his desk, complained that he was looking unusually haggard, and begged him to rest. He refused to rest. He must finish the novel, whatever the cost. Finally on November 8 the last chapter was sent to the printer. With the manuscript went a message to the editor, saying that he felt better than he had felt for a long time, and expected to go on writing for the next twenty years. He told Anna he would take a brief rest, devote himself for the next two years to *The Diary of a Writer,* that *potpourri* of reflections and recollections which he wrote whenever the novels were lying fallow, and at the end of that period he would begin the second volume of *The Brothers Kara-mazov.* The first volume dealt with the middle years of the sixties, the second would bring them into contemporary times.

Dostoyevsky had worked out his program with an admirable sense of the realities of the situation. He was at the height of his fame and influence. He was still in debt, but the publication of the book, which had so far appeared only in monthly installments in *The Russian Messenger,* was likely to bring him enough money to allow him to rest for a while. He had important connections in court circles, where the religious chapters of the novel had been greeted with enthusiasm; some fashionable ladies had even made a cult of the saintly Alyosha. Konstantin Pobedonostsev, the Proc-urator of the Holy Synod, had even hinted that he had accom-plished a great work on behalf of the Church and the Government, and his talents would be rewarded "in high places." From the publication of *The Diary of a Writer* alone he expected to receive a competence. Before him there stretched two years of leisure and the company of enlightened aristocrats, for he was worshipped as much by the aristocracy, who saw him as the defender of their privileges, as by the students, who saw him as a figure of protest, the intellectual leader of "the conspiracy against the Tzar." Dostoyevsky saw himself as neither of these things. He was above the aristocracy and above the students, or rather he was committed to neither. His task was to be a novelist: to probe the human soul and illuminate it fearlessly, and from his knowledge of the human soul to act as a sensitive barometer foretelling the weather of the soul in the days to come. He saw himself as a prophet, leading both aristocrats and students a little way to the Kingdom of Heaven. There was in him a fierce religious thirst. After his triumph during the Pushkin celebrations in Moscow, he was heard saying sadly: "They don't understand the chief thing about me. They heap tribute on me for being satisfied with the present political condition of the country, but they cannot see I am showing them the way to the Church."

They could not see it, because he had never completely expressed it. To the end Father Zossima remains an ambiguous figure; he is a saint, but he belongs to an order which could have no existence outside Dostoyevsky's imagination. Here and there we come upon hints that the saintly Alyosha will not always behave compassionately. There was iron in his soul, and in the second volume Dostoyevsky proposed to have Alyosha turn against the world in savage retribution for some nameless sin it had committed against him or his brothers.

Dostoyevsky seems to have spent a good deal of the early days of his freedom after completing the novel in contemplating the themes he would take up in its successor. He spoke about this novel with Anna, going into considerable detail. In her reminiscences she mentions how he discussed it "with great eagerness," but of the plan he was forming in his mind she says only that "the characters would appear again twenty years later, almost in our own time, and during the interval they would have managed to achieve and go through great things." To Pobedonostsev, Dostoyevsky wrote that the second volume would deal with "a Christ not crucified." Suvorin reports an extraordinary conversation with Dostoyevsky during the last month of his life. They had been discussing business matters, and the conversation turned to the sequel of *The Brothers Karamazov*. The publisher suggested that the novel foreshadowed many things to come; it was full of a special sense of clairvoyance, an eerie doom in store for the whole country.

"You are right," Dostoyevsky exclaimed. "If you think there is a good deal of clairvoyance in my latest novel, wait till you read its sequel. I am working on it now. I am taking Alyosha Karamazov out of his holy retreat in the monastery and I am making him join the Nihilists. My pure Alyosha shall kill the Tzar!"

Suvorin has told us no more about the interview, and Dostoyevsky himself was disconcertingly reluctant to put any of his thoughts about the sequel into writing. Among the mass of papers he left behind there are no notes or sketches for the second volume. All we have is the evidence of his letters and casual conversations during his last year. His brief statement to Anna, a conversation with Suvorin, a letter to Pobedonostsev—these are the only clues to the shape the second volume would have taken, apart from some hints which are to be found in the prophetic passages of *The Brothers Karamazov*. Deliberately prophetic passages describing the fate of all three brothers exist, and it is reasonably certain that Dostoyevsky intended the prophecies to come true.

In the second volume Alyosha was clearly intended to be the central figure. Alyosha was a saint, but he was also a sensualist like his father and brothers. At one of their last meetings, Father Zossima had prophesied the form his life would take:

> There is still a long road before you. You'll have to take a wife, too, and you'll have to go through it all, before you come back here again. There will be much for you to do. But I have no doubts about you, and that is why I am sending you into the world. Christ is with you. Do not abandon him, and he will not abandon you. This

is my last message to you: in sorrow seek happiness. Work, work unceasingly.[3]

At the very last meeting Father Zossima turns to the embarrassed Alyosha and explains why he is moved whenever he sees the boy's face—Alyosha reminds him of his brother, who died at seventeen. Once more Father Zossima speaks in prophecies:

> You will go forth from this monastery, Alyosha, but you will live like a monk in the world. You will have many enemies, but even your enemies will love you. Life will bring you many misfortunes, but you will find your happiness in them, and will bless life, and make others bless it—this is what matters most. Well, as I say, this is your character.[4]

All this suggests that Alyosha was destined to be the leading character in a vast epic related to "The Life of a Great Sinner," of which only a few rough jottings remain, though there is enough sense of direction in those jottings to enable us to guess that Alyosha would suffer from the deadly sin of pride, like Father Zossima, and that he would be involved in a murder. We can guess that Alyosha would marry Lise and have affairs with many women, but in the end he would return to the monastery, where he would end his days surrounded by a flock of children. Suvorin thought that Alyosha would be a revolutionary, who would be brought to the scaffold for his crimes; Pobedonostsev thought he would suffer the torments of Christ, but afterwards he would lead a saintly life showering his beneficence all round him. It is possible that both were partly right. It is also possible that Dostoyevsky had not yet reached any conclusions about the development of the novel.

Of the unwritten sequel to *The Brothers Karamazov* we observe only the faintly discernible skeleton. We are left with hints,

[3] *The Brothers Karamazov*, I, ii, 7.
[4] *The Brothers Karamazov*, II, vi, 1.

brief illuminations, the sense of a continuing tragedy, the resolution unknown to us. We shall never know what happened to the brothers after the solemn moment when Alyosha stands among the children listening to their joyful cries. Perhaps, after all, it is better that we should not know. Sequels are notoriously dangerous, and the few chapters of the second volume of Gogol's *Dead Souls* that have survived suggest that Dostoyevsky too might have fallen into the trap of continuing a novel after the original enthusiasm has vanished. We have his *Oedipus Rex;* somewhere among his papers there may still be a sketch for his *Oedipus Colonus.*

For the moment Dostoyevsky was busy with plans for bringing out a new issue of *The Diary of a Writer,* and enjoying his fame. That winter he was lionized as never before. He was at once the greatest novelist of his time, and the prophet pointing the way towards the future with his vision of the community of all men living together in an era of brotherhood and peace. And now, whenever he appeared in public, he would be asked to recite *The Prophet.* He would begin the recitation in a low hoarse voice, gradually gaining strength, until with the last line: "Lay waste with fire the hearts of men!" the voice rose with the effect of thunder, shaking the room, astounding everyone with its power and vehemence. He looked like a prophet; he was a prophet; and in his presence people were aware that no one quite like him would ever appear again.

He recited *The Prophet* at the soirées of Countess Sophia Tolstoy, a cultivated woman with a flair for amateur theatricals. He agreed to play the part of the saintly ascetic in a production of her husband's play, *The Death of Ivan the Terrible.* He was passionately devoted to drama, and had only recently planned to dramatize *The Brothers Karamazov,* though nothing came of the plan. His role in the play about the death of Ivan the Terrible was a very small one; the ascetic appears only once. When Ivan the Terrible is close to death, after having killed off nearly all his friends and supporters, he remembers that thirty years before he had thrown this ascetic into prison for prophesying about his fate. The ascetic is still in prison. Ivan orders him to be brought into his presence. In despair, Ivan asks whether anything can be done to save the throne. The ascetic answers: "Summon your friends," and the Tzar replies: "I have no friends—they are all dead, or in exile, or they have gone over to the enemy. How is it that you do not know these things?" The ascetic replies:

> *How should I know? My cell was like a closed*
> *Door against the world, where only silence*
> *Penetrated through those dim and ghostly walls.*
> *I heard the roaring of the storm of God,*
> *And the faint tolling of the temple bells.*

Dostoyevsky was well chosen for the part: he had heard the storm of God and the tolling of the temple bells, and for many years he had lived obscurely in his cell. He attended rehearsals for the play, which was to be performed on the first Sunday of February.

On December 16th, Dostoyevsky was received by the Tzarevich, to whom he gave a copy of *The Brothers Karamazov*. He had already met the Tzarevich informally at soirées, but this was his first formal introduction to the huge, broad-shouldered, red-cheeked man who was soon to come to the throne. The Tzarevich was affable. He complimented Dostoyevsky on the success of the novel, and made some discreet inquiries about whether Dostoyevsky would be a suitable tutor to his children. Nothing came of these inquiries, but Pobedonostsev prevailed upon the Tzarevich to attend a reading which Dostoyevsky gave a week later. The Tzarevich was bored, and left early. A more welcome connection with the imperial family came through the Grand Duke Konstantin Konstantinovich, the Tzar's nephew, who was exceptionally gifted and wrote admirable poetry. Except for Catherine the Great, the young Grand Duke was the only member of the imperial family to show any literary talent. Dostoyevsky had known him for at least a year, and had in fact often dined at his palace. Now that *The Brothers Karamazov* was completed, these invitations to dinner were renewed. He was moving in exalted circles. Every Saturday night he met Pobedonostsev to discuss religion and politics, and every Sunday evening there were theatricals in the house of Countess Sophia Tolstoy.

There were of course less exalted visitors, among them the young poet Dmitry Merezhkovsky, who came to visit Dostoyevsky a few days after the meeting with the Tzarevich. Merezhkovsky was at the beginning of his literary career, and asked for advice. "I can give you no advice," Dostoyevsky said, "except this—to write, you must learn to suffer." Merezhkovsky was deeply moved by these words. At any ordinary time he would have felt insulted by them, but they came with added strength from a man who was evidently very ill, his face etched with lines of suffering: so gaunt and ravaged a face that it somehow resembled a map of all the suffering endured by Russia. In his reminiscences Merezhkovsky speaks vividly of the impression Dostoyevsky produced on him— the gnarled and riven forehead, the wart on the right cheek, the smoky grey eyes "which gazed out dimly and with an inexpressible heaviness." "What was most painful in this face," Merezhkovsky said, "was a sort of immobility in the midst of movement, an endeavor arrested and turned to stone at the height of effort." At one point in the conversation Merezhkovsky asked him whether he wrote easily. "Not easily," Dostoyevsky answered in a shaking voice. "Recently I assure you it has become inexpressibly difficult."

Merezhkovsky left the house with the feeling that the end was in sight. Others, too, were appalled by the look of strain on Dostoyevsky's features. Nikolay Strakhov, a close friend, later his biographer, encountered him at one of the aristocratic soirées. "He looked unusually thin and wasted," Strakhov wrote. "He tired easily, and was clearly living on his nerves. His body had reached such a state of frailty we all thought he would be laid low by a single blow, even a very small blow."

Nevertheless Dostoyevsky behaved as though he were in perfect health. He was in no pain. Occasionally there would come those periods of inexplicable weariness, and then he would pull out the drawer beneath the Turkish sofa, remove pillows and blankets, make a bed and lie down until the weariness left him. While working on the final chapters of *The Brothers Karamazov,* he found no time to play with his children, Luba and Fyodor. Now he made up for lost time, and he especially enjoyed reading to them the comic strips which appeared in the magazine called *Dragonfly.* There was an understanding with Anna that neither of them should discuss the state of his health at any length.

So December passed, and in January he was still in good heart. For a long time he had been jotting down notes for *The Diary of a Writer,* and now he began to assemble them in order. *The Brothers Karamazov* had at last been published in book form and had done surprisingly well—fifteen hundred copies were sold in a few days, and subscriptions for *The Diary* were coming in with pleasant frequency. He gave himself a deadline. He told himself he would have *The Diary* off the presses by the end of the month.

As usual he permitted himself the widest freedom, discussing any subject that entered his head. For some reason he was unusually concerned to produce a memorable number. He wrote to a friend: "I decided to reissue *The Diary,* and many times since then I have fallen to my knees and prayed God for a pure heart, a truthful sinless word uttered without envy or any irritability of soul." But, alas, there were many irritable words in the curious, ecstatic hodge-podge which he wrote in the last month of his life.

He wrote about economics, politics, military strategy, the relations between Russia and Europe, his own battle to retain his faith, his visions of the future. He had lost none of his vitality in writing; he wrote vigorously and trenchantly about matters close to his heart. He attacked the bureaucracy. He called upon the governing classes to realize their deficiencies. There were too many bureaucrats—four could do the work of forty, and what savings there would be! The peasants needed help. Had the government truly looked into their own hearts and understood the nature of the peasantry, which alone provides food and sustenance, and possesses an immense treasure of spirituality? Peter the Great had turned Russia towards the West, but the Europeans always despised the Russians. Well, that was the fault of the Europeans, who never sufficiently recognized the spirituality of the Russian peasantry. And then, too, the Russians themselves were rarely aware of their own achievements. General Skobolev had won a resounding battle against the Turkomen in Central Asia: the news reaching St. Petersburg in December had created only a mild excitement. How wrong the Russians were! This victory should have been regarded as a sign from heaven, a great prophecy. Did not the future of Russia lie in Asia? As for the Europeans:

> They realize of course that our scientists have produced some remarkable work, even some work which has served the cause of European science. Though they admit we have several talented scientists, they will never permit themselves to believe we are able to produce men of genius and leaders of mankind to be ranked with Bacon, Kant, and Aristotle. They refuse to believe this, because they refuse to believe in the validity of our civilization, and they know nothing of our future flowering.
>
> And they are perfectly right in this, for we shall have no Bacons, no Newtons, no Aristotles until we have ourselves marked out the path of our progress, and are spiritually independent; and this is true also of our arts and industries. Europe is always ready to praise us, but she will never recognize that we belong to her, for she despises us, openly or secretly, considering us to belong to an inferior race. She especially despises us when we throw out our arms in a brotherly embrace.
>
> Yet it is immensely difficult to turn away from "the

window to Europe," and this is our fate. Meanwhile Asia beckons to us! If only we could realize how important Asia is to us! Asia, our Asiatic Russia—a sick plant, all ready to be refreshed and resurrected and transformed! We need above all a new principle, a new vision! [5]

So, dreaming of the immense spaces of Russia bordering on Persia and China, he wrote steadily through the night, and sometimes he would pause and wonder what the censors would do to those disorganized and passionate pages in which he attacked the bureaucrats and defended Europe, "our second mother," against the Slavophils, and went on to defend the Slavophils against the rest of the world.

One evening, while he was writing, his old friend Orest Miller came to the apartment. Dostoyevsky rushed out of the study to meet his friend in the living room, his pen in his hand. Miller had come to ask him to attend a memorial meeting to be held in St. Petersburg on the anniversary of Pushkin's death, the 29th January. Dostoyevsky was in no mood to discuss the meeting. He had written his attack on the bureaucracy, and he was afraid that a passage which he wanted to develop would be cut out by the censor. He was shaking with indignation. "If they cut it out, then everything is lost!" he declared. He talked for a while about the censorship, shaking his head. Miller tried to comfort him, and offered to use his good offices at the censorship. Still raging against the censors, Dostoyevsky returned to his study.

He was still trying to complete *The Diary of a Writer* in time for publication at the end of the month. Outside the snow was falling, and once again he returned to the old rhythm of working by night and sleeping until late in the morning. He would rise about eleven, sing merrily in his croaking voice in the bathroom while he was at his toilet, drink a glass of hot tea, and then make his way to the study to look over the pages written during the night.

[5] *The Diary of a Writer,* January 1881, II, 3.

379

There would be dictation early in the afternoon, and the inevitable walk which took him to Ballet's, the confectioner's shop at the corner of the Ekaterininskaya. Sometimes, to the annoyance of Anna, he would drop into the house of Countess Tolstoy, and remain there for several hours. Then he would return a little shame-faced, to tell Anna everything that had happened. She rarely accompanied him on these visits, for there were two young children in the house.

On Sunday, January 25, Dostoyevsky was in an unusually good mood. *The Diary of a Writer* was finished and in the hands of the printer, and through the intervention of Countess Tolstoy and Orest Miller there was no more trouble with the censorship. The house was full of guests, among them his younger sister Vera, a rather stern and matronly woman who had come to St. Petersburg expressly to discuss the matter of the Kumanin inheritance, a sum of money left by the rich sister of their mother. Rightly or wrongly, Vera felt that her brother had received more than his fair share of the estate, and was determined to force a redistribution of the money.

Dostoyevsky sat down to dinner in good humor. He was pleased to see his sister, and spoke at some length about their childhood days in the Maryinsky Hospital, about the games they played at Darovoye and the endless talks he had enjoyed with his brother Mikhail. He joked and laughed, and he seems not to have been aware that his sister was acutely embarrassed. Suddenly she broke out in a violent tirade against her brother, accusing him of taking the lion's share of the inheritance for himself. She spoke of his cruelty and the dishonor he was bringing on the family, and burst into tears. Dostoyevsky was shaken, and seemed to be on the verge of an epileptic attack. Anna saved the situation by accompanying Vera to the door, while her husband took refuge in his study. Later Anna went to bed, and the house was silent.

Dostoyevsky went on working in his study. He smoked incessantly, making up his cigarettes by hand. It was his custom to roll the cigarette paper round a penholder. He had done this thousands of times before. It was a purely mechanical operation. His hands were shaking, and the penholder fell to the floor, and rolled under the heavy mahogany wardrobe which stood near his desk. He tried to reach the penholder; could not reach it; and attempted to lift the wardrobe, which was very heavy. Suddenly he was spitting blood. It was only a small trickle of blood, and he decided not to awaken Anna. Instead he opened the drawer of the Turkish sofa, pulled out the bedsheets and blankets, and went to sleep.

The next morning he told Anna what had happened. He was visibly shaken, though he seemed to make light of it. Anna was terrified, and sent the houseboy Peter in search of the family doctor, Jacob von Bretzel. Peter returned to say that Von Bretzel was out and not expected to return until five o'clock.

To Anna's astonishment Dostoyevsky was behaving as though it were any ordinary day. He drank his glass of hot tea, opened the morning newspaper, talked and played with the children. Early in the afternoon, his two close friends Apollon Maikov and Nikolay Strakhov came to call on him. Later Orest Miller came to remind him of his appointment to address a meeting in honor of Pushkin, and Miller suggested that it would be an excellent thing if Dostoyevsky recited some verses from *Evgeniy Onyegin*. It was no more than a suggestion, but Dostoyevsky flew into a rage.

"I don't need to be told what to recite!" he shouted. "I know exactly what to do!"

Miller was annoyed by the outburst. Anna heard the sounds of quarreling, rushed into the room and warned Miller, who was highly excitable, against shouting at a man who was obviously unwell. Peace was restored. The announcement that Dostoyevsky would recite from *Evgeny Onyegin* had already been made, but Miller offered to publish a correction. About five o'clock the visitors left.

Just before six o'clock, the usual hour for dinner, Anna went into the study to find her husband sitting on the Turkish sofa and staring straight in front of him. There was a trickle of blood on his beard and chin. Anna screamed at the top of her voice: "Fetch the doctor!" The children—Luba was eleven, and Fyodor nine —grew panic-stricken, and Dostoyevsky calmed them by showing them the comic magazine, *Dragonfly,* which had just come in. There was a cartoon showing two fishermen struggling in a net, and he read out the verses underneath. The children seemed relieved, and there were no more panic-stricken shrieks. Around seven o'clock Dr. Von Bretzel arrived and began to examine the patient. He was sounding Dostoyevsky's chest when there was another hemorrhage. This time it was so violent that the patient lost consciousness. As soon as he recovered, he asked Anna to send for a priest.

"I must make my confession and receive the last sacrament," he said, and there was an unusual authority in his voice.

The apartment on the Kuznechny Pereulok was only a stone's throw away from the Vladimirsky Church. Father Megorsky arrived half an hour later. Dostoyevsky made his confession, received holy communion and remained closeted with the priest for some time. He was very calm, very much in control of himself. Afterward his wife and children entered the study to receive his blessing. He commanded the children to live in peace, to love one another, and to honor their mother; and when the children were gone, he spoke quietly to Anna, telling her that he loved her, thanking her for the happiness she had given him, and asking for forgiveness if he had ever caused her pain. At this point the doctor broke in, saying there must be no further conversation, for the least movement, the least excitement was dangerous. Later a certain Dr. Koshlakov was called in, and the two doctors discussed the health of the patient. They agreed he was not fatally ill—he had lost only a little blood, and the burst artery in the lung might be expected to heal. Dr. Von Bretzel remained by Dostoyevsky's bedside, and Anna went to bed.

The Last Days

On Tuesday, January 27, the patient had recovered his spirits and no longer talked of dying. He was cheerful, spoke gently with the children, and inquired about the galley proofs of the *The Diary of a Writer*. In the course of the afternoon the proofs arrived from Suvorin's printing house, and Dostoyevsky spent some time going over them. There were seven lines too many on the last page, and Anna offered to make the necessary changes. Skobolev had gone on from one victory to another, and Dostoyevsky's last public utterance remains, as he had intended, a great shout of praise for the conquering Russian army. "In Europe we were slaves; in Asia we shall be masters!"

Meanwhile news of his illness had spread all over St. Petersburg; a stream of visitors came to inquire about him. None were allowed to enter his study, but Dostoyevsky was told about them, and he was pleased at their coming. Anna was usually the messenger who slipped out of the study and told them about his progress. Dr. Koshlakov thought he saw definite signs of improvement, and announced that the patient would probably recover in two weeks. That night Anna slept on a mattress at the foot of the Turkish sofa. At seven o'clock in the morning she awoke to see her husband gazing sorrowfully at her.

"I've been awake for three hours," he whispered hoarsely, "and all the time I have been thinking. But just this moment I realized I shall die today."

In a state of terrible anxiety Anna heard herself saying: "Dear one, you should not say such things. You are better now, and there is no hemorrhage, and probably all is going well, as Dr. Koshlakov says. For the love of Christ, do not torment yourself with doubts! I'm sure you will live for many more years."

"No, I shall die today! Light the candle, Anna, and give me the New Testament."

She went to his desk and brought out the New Testament, bound in black leather, which had been given to him when a prisoner in Siberia. He opened it at random, and asked her to read

383

the first words she saw on the page. She began to read from the third chapter of the Gospel of St. Matthew, and the first words at the top of the page were: "But John would have hindered him, saying, I have need to be baptized of thee, and comest thou to me instead? But Jesus, answering, said unto him: "Suffer it now, for thus it becometh us to fulfill all righteousness."

"You see, Anna," he said. "Suffer it now—that means I am going to die."

He spoke very quietly of his love for her, telling her about the happiness they had enjoyed together, and he even assured her that in the fourteen years of their married life he had not been unfaithful to her even in thought, forgetting that he had thought often of Polina Suslova. He seemed to be in no pain, but there was growing weakness. At ten o'clock in the morning he fell asleep, only to awaken an hour later with another hemorrhage from the mouth. During the afternoon his stepson Pasha, that strange swarthy yellow-complexioned youth, arrived at the apartment and tried to force his way into the study. He kept shouting that his stepfather was dying without leaving a will, and it was time a lawyer was summoned. The stepson was removed, and the day passed quietly with Anna and the children kneeling beside the Turkish sofa. From time to time Dostoyevsky whispered to Anna: "It will be so hard for you . . ."

At half past six he gave his New Testament to his son, and blessed him. Apollon Maikov entered the study, to whisper briefly with his friend. A few other visitors were allowed to see the dying man. Suddenly around eight o'clock he gave a little shiver and coughed up more blood, and lay unconscious. His breathing became more labored, and his pulse weaker. He died at exactly 8:38 p.m.

About an hour later Anna's brother, who had received no news of Dostoyevsky's illness, arrived at the house. He saw people milling up and down the stairs, and on all of them there was a strange look as though something momentous had happened, and they were still a little dazed. He was pushing his way upstairs when someone plucked at his sleeve.

"Sir, be good enough, sir, to give us the order," the man said.

"What order? What are you talking about?"

"We are undertakers' men, sir. We have come about the coffin."

"Who is dead?"

"Some writer, sir—I forget the name. The concierge told us . . ."

In this way Anna's brother, the friend of the murdered Ivanov, heard the news.

That night Dostoyevsky's body was washed and dressed in his best clothes, and laid on the table which stood in the living room. From the Vladimirsky Church came tall gilded candlesticks and a golden cloth to lay over the body; and the priest recited the *panikhida,* the service for the dead. His head lay on a pillow, the golden cloth reached from his feet to his waist, and his hands lay crossed over his breast. So many people came to pay tribute to him that there was not enough air in the room to keep the candles burning; and they went out.

Anna was beside herself with grief. She wandered from one room to another, wringing her hands, as though she were perpetually looking for something she had lost. She hated the strangers who flocked round the table. In her lucid moments she made arrangements for the burial. She remembered that Dostoyevsky had once said he wanted to be buried close to Nekrasov in the cemetery of Novo-Devichiy, a convent for nuns close to the Arch of Narva on the outskirts of the city. She sent her brother to the convent with the children. It was a bright day, with hard snow on the ground, and the children enjoyed the drive on the sleigh. But the Mother Superior had never heard of the writer Dostoyevsky, demanded an enormous sum for a burial plot and declared that all men were equal under God, and a writer was no better than anyone else.

Unknown to Anna, Pobedonostsev, the Procurator of the Holy Synod, was actively working behind the scenes. He had decided that Dostoyevsky should be buried in the grounds of the great Alexander Nevsky monastery where Karamzin, Glinka, Zhukovsky and many other Russian poets, writers and musicians were buried; and through his influence there came a delegation of monks to the house. They offered to bury "the jealous guardian of the true Orthodox faith" at their own expense and to pay the costs of a funeral mass in his honor. Once long ago Anna had said jokingly: "They ought to bury you in the Alexander Nevsky cemetery."

"Among all those writers who hated me?" Dostoyevsky answered. "Besides, the place is full of generals."

"That is why you should be buried there, because you are a general of literature."

Behind all the plans for the funeral, which was unlike any funeral seen in Russia, we can discern the all-powerful hands of the Procurator. He took it upon himself to write to the Tzarevich the day after Dostoyevsky's death:

> Last night there died in this city Fyodor Mikhailo-vich Dostoyevsky. He was a very close friend, and I am stricken with grief at his passing.
> Russia too is grief-stricken. Among writers he was almost alone as the fiery preacher of the fundamental principles of religion, nationalism, and patriotism. Our unhappy younger generation have gone astray like sheep without a shepherd, but they cherished a deep faith in him, and his influence was very great and for the best. There is no one now to take his place.
> He was poor and left nothing except his books. His family is in dire poverty. I am writing to Count Loris-Melikov, asking him to petition the Tzar. It is my earnest wish that the Tzar should take an interest.
> Will not Your Highness support the application? You knew and valued the deceased for his good works,

which will for ever remain a memorial to a great Russian spirit.[6]

Pobedonostsev never failed in anything he attempted. The Tzar graciously consented to grant the widow a pension equal to that of the widow of a Major-General, amounting to two thousand rubles a year. The steward of the imperial household delivered the message to Anna, who ran into the study to tell her husband, and then nearly collapsed with shock.

All day the living room was crowded with visitors. Grand Dukes, society ladies, scholars and students passed the body, and sometimes in the Russian fashion they bent over to kiss his hands. The painter Kramskoy, who had been Dostoyevsky's favorite among living painters—one of Kramskoy's paintings of a birch forest in winter with a peasant in ragged clothes standing in absolute solitude is described in *The Brothers Karamazov*—painted him as he lay dead, a look of extraordinary peace on his face. All the lines of suffering have been erased. The lips are pursed, but not in pain. He looks younger than sixty years and completely at peace.

On Saturday, January 31st, a crowd of thirty thousand people accompanied the body to the Alexander Nevsky monastery. There was a garland of flowers and laurels sixty feet long; there were sixty-seven large floral crowns, and fifteen choirs took part in the procession. Deputations representing innumerable organizations followed the coffin, and the monks came through the gates to welcome Dostoyevsky, a privilege reserved previously only to Tzars. That night the coffin was laid in the Church of the Holy Spirit, and the students kept their nightlong vigil.

The next morning at ten o'clock the burial service began. Flowers were heaped on the grave, and speeches were made in Dostoyevsky's honor. The first speaker was the elderly novelist

[6] Dostoevsky, *Letters and Reminiscences,* tr. S. S. Koteliansky and J. Middleton Murry. (London: Chatto and Windus; 1923), p. 264.

Palm, one of the few survivors of those who had stood beside Dostoyevsky on the Semyonov Square; there followed Grigorovich, the friend of his youth, now old and bent, and the young Vladimir Solovyov, who was tall and so alarmingly handsome that he was called "the angel," and many other speakers. Orest Miller and Apollon Maikov both made speeches. At four o'clock in the afternoon, while the writers, the students and the professors were still making speeches or reciting poems, Anna stole away with her children, unable to bear the strain any longer. By that time it was already growing dark, and cold sharp wind from the Neva was tossing the flowers hither and thither.

A month later students threw a bomb at the Tzar as he was returning to to the Winter Palace after a review. The long night of Russian had begun.

THE LEGEND

As soon as Dostoyevsky was safely dead, the processes of legend and mystification which always attend the fame of great men began their strange and insidious work. The slender man with a quizzical smile, an orange beard and the open gaze which often goes with a reddish tint in the hair became transformed into a dark and brooding monster. Perov's famous painting, reproduced in black and white, suggested a man glowering into space with an expression of fanaticism; and that portrait, and others resembling it, were reproduced in hundreds of magazines to illustrate his texts. The original painting shows a man in the prime of life with a fine color on his cheeks, and an expression of quite astonishing calm. Only the eyes are strange; they seem to be looking into different worlds. It is the face of a scholar or a poet, compact with energy, with no heaviness, no hint of brooding. Such a man would have chosen his goal early in life, and succeeded in all the purposes he set out to accomplish.

So it was with nearly all the contemporary accounts of him. He was a dark, brooding presence, a kind of avenging angel sent to punish and excite the world, a stranger to ordinary human emotions. The Vicomte Melchior de Vogüé spoke of him as "an apparition from another world," meaning that he possessed satanic gifts. Others spoke of his relentless pursuit of evil, and of how he plumbed the loathsome recesses of the human spirit because he felt an obscure impulse towards self-degradation. The real Dostoyevsky was lost in mythology. It was forgotten that when he died the students of St. Petersburg came from all directions to join the funeral procession and silently offered to an arch-reactionary the homage which can only be paid by young revolutionaries, who had no reason to admire his principles and every reason to love his genius and his humanity. In their eyes he was one of those rare divinely gifted men who open the paths of the future.

The legend of the evil Dostoyevsky, the great sinner, the man given over to a remorseless traffic with the evil in the human soul, persisted. His own words were remembered against him. His closest friends turned against his memory. His sins were counted. He was an inveterate gambler, a sensualist, a man who had consciously or unconconsciously desired to murder his father. Worse still, he had raped a young child and gloried in it.

Shortly after Dostoyevsky's death, his friend and enthusiastic biographer, Nikolay Strakhov, wrote to Tolstoy a long letter describing the funeral and the grief that had settled over St. Petersburg. "It is as though half the city has sunk into the earth," he wrote, "or as though half of literature had perished. How melancholy it is! For myself, I have no desire to do anything, and the grave where I shall find my repose seems to be very close to me, and waiting. All is vanity!" He spoke, too, of the very real greatness of Dostoyevsky who had spoken boldly on subjects hitherto considered *temptation* and *madness,* while surrounded on every side by hostile critics. Shortly afterward Strakhov, with the assistance of Orest Miller, wrote the first comprehensive life of Dostoyevsky. It was an admiring document, passionately defending him from his critics.

In November 1883, when the biography was completed, Strakhov wrote another letter to Tolstoy. The tone had oddly changed. The admirable friend had suddenly become a monster of depravity. In this venomous letter Strakhov poured out his griefs, relating events which had occurred twenty years before, setting himself up as the prosecuting attorney where previously he had

acted for the defense. He told Tolstoy that while writing the book
he had deliberately suppressed the evil side of Dostoyevsky's character, but for the sake of truth and honesty he felt bound to admit
his error. All through the writing of the book he had struggled
against mounting disgust, but now he could struggle no longer. He
wrote:

> I cannot regard Dostoyevsky either as a good men or
> a happy one, for generally these two things coincide.
> He was wicked, envious, vicious, and all his life was
> spent in violent agitations which would have made him
> pitiable and ridiculous if he had not been so spiteful
> and so clever. Like Rousseau he considered himself the
> best of men and the happiest. While I was writing his
> life I vividly remembered all these traits in his charac-
> ter. One day in Switzerland in my presence he har-
> rassed a waiter until the poor man rebelled and ex-
> claimed: "Surely I too am a man!" I remember how
> astonished I was to hear these words spoken to the
> apostle of *humanity*. It seemed to me that these words
> expressed the idea of free Switzerland about the *rights
> of man*.
>   Such scenes were always happening, for he could not
> control his spitefulness. Many times I had to disregard
> these outbursts which would come quite suddenly and
> for no explicable reason, like the spiteful utterances of
> some wretched old woman. On one or two occasions I
> found myself compelled to give him some home truths.
> But of course, in as far as giving pain to others was con-
> cerned, he had advantages of his own. The worst of it
> was that he delighted in all his mean actions, and never
> repented of them. He was drawn to abominations, and
> boasted of them.
>   Viskovatov told me one day that Dostoyevsky
> boasted that he [had intercourse] in a bath with a little
> girl brought to him by the governess. For all his animal
> sensuality, he had no understanding, no feeling whatever,
> for the beauty and charm of woman. This is quite evi-
> dent in his novels. The characters most resembling him

are the hero of *Notes from Underground,* Svidrigailov in *Crime and Punishment,* and Stavrogin in *The Devils.* One scene from Stavrogin (rape, etc.) Katkov refused to publish, but Dostoyevsky read it to many people.

With such a nature he was of course prone to sweetly sentimental longings, to lofty and pious dreams; and these dreams were his *forte,* his literary muse and his chosen path. All his novels are in fact merely a self-justification. They show that a man may possess, together with nobility of spirit, all kinds of abominations . . .

He was a thoroughly unhappy and wicked man who imagined he was happy and heroic, but the only person he ever loved tenderly was himself.[1]

Tolstoy, who had previously spoken of his abounding love for Dostoyevsky and of how he had wept over *The Insulted and Injured* and regarded *The House of the Dead* as the greatest of modern works, now reversed his opinion. In his view Dostoyevsky suffered from a fatal quirk. There was something impure and obscene about him; and in this he differed from Turgenev, who possessed an essential purity. According to Tolstoy, Dostoyevsky was an occasionally interesting writer, devoid of any real substance, and it was absurd that people should put him on a pedestal. "All Dostoyevsky's wisdom and emotion were wasted," Tolstoy wrote, adding that he was sure Turgenev would be remembered long after Dostoyevsky was forgotten.

This pathetic correspondence was not published until October 1913, and did not reach the attention of Dostoyevsky's widow until the summer of the following year. She was understandably overwhelmed and exasperated. She had always trusted Strakhov, and she had always possessed a warm feeling toward Tolstoy, who had so often praised her husband's work. Why this sudden change?

Patiently and without rancor she went about the task of refuting Strakhov's allegations. She admitted that the incident with the

[1] *Dostoyevsky Portrayed by his Wife,* tr. S. S. Koteliansky. (London: George Routledge and Sons; 1926), pp. 232–3.

waiter in Switzerland was entirely probable; her husband's irascibility was famous, and she would be the last person to deny it. But was it a crime to shout at a waiter?

She was especially hurt by the statement that Dostoyevsky loved only himself. Genius is selfish, but she knew in her heart that her husband was selfish only for his work, and showed throughout his long career as a magazine editor a generosity to young writers which had become proverbial. He was always helping the poor and the aged. He answered letters for advice and help at once, as though he had a duty to perform. Especially during the last years of his life, when he was famous, he was constantly sought by people who regarded him as a father confessor. The man who loved only himself possessed an abundance of love for his fellowmen.

Strakhov said Dostoyevsky was spiteful, envious, vicious, and he was perhaps all of these in moments of bafflement, when reduced to extreme poverty, when riding one of his hobbyhorses, or when suffering from exhaustion; but it was not typical of him to show envy or spite or viciousness. He was generous in his praise of Turgenev, until the final break between them. He wrote about Turgenev to his brother: "What a wonderful fellow he is! I have almost fallen in love with him. A poet, a man of talent, an aristocrat, rich, handsome, highly educated, twenty-five years old—nature has denied him nothing! Finally, his character is absolutely straightforward, splendid and well trained." So it was in innumerable letters filled with the praises of his contemporaries. His impulse was to praise, and he praised endlessly.

But the gravamen of Strakhov's charge lay elsewhere, in the widespread belief that Dostoyevsky had experienced the vices which he sometimes described with amazing psychological penetration in his novels. The incident known as "Stavrogin's Confession," was widely believed to be a disguised account of an incident which had happened to Dostoyevsky himself. There were many different versions, but in the main they agreed that at some time in his life, probably in the 1860's, he had raped a child. The child's age was variously stated as six, ten, or twelve. The rape was described as taking place in a bathhouse, in a house of prostitution, or a school for juvenile delinquents, or in his own apartment. Sometimes a governess or a procurer were present, but more often he was alone with the child. He is supposed to have recounted the episode many times in many different places to many people. Strakhov said the incident was vouched for by a certain Viskovatov, who is known to have been a professor of Russian Literature at the University of Dorpat, who met Dostoyevsky briefly and made no lasting impression on him. If the case against Dostoyevsky rested on the evidence of Viskovatov, it would be thrown out of court. Unfortunately it did not rest entirely on the evidence of the obscure professor. The gossips and the rumor-mongers had been at work, and there were many *littérateurs* in St. Petersburg who were prepared to relate in detail exactly how the rape had taken place or exactly how Dostoyevsky himself, with curious bravado, related it.

Anna remembered that Dostoyevsky had read the chapter aloud to his friends Maikov, Strakhov and Pobedonostsev, and they had all agreed that the chapter was "too realistic," even though the nature of the novel demanded that Stavrogin should commit some unpardonable crime. Accordingly, Dostoyevsky wrote several variants, but none of them met with the approval of the publisher, and in the end the whole chapter was omitted from the novel with the result that it reads very curiously at the point where the confession should have been inserted. What particularly puzzled her was the idea that he should have practiced the vices he described. He had not committed murder in order to understand the mind of Raskolnikov. Why should he commit rape in order to understand the mind of Stavrogin?

So she wrote in her measured prose, like a lawyer with a brief for the defense, a rebuttal of the accusations which hurt her more deeply than any of the sufferings she had undergone during her husband's lifetime. She concluded her defense of her husband with

the words of Strakhov: "A man may possess, together with nobility of spirit, all kinds of abominations."

No one paid very much attention to her brief for the defense.
The First World War came, and the question whether Dostoyevsky had or had not committed a crime assumed very little importance while greater crimes were becoming the commonplaces of
daily life. "Stavrogin's Confession" is still widely believed to be the
literal account of a crime committed by Dostoyevsky himself.

The issue is a grave one, of fundamental importance for the
understanding of Dostoyevsky's character and the motives which
lay behind his life's work. If he committed the crime, he was one
kind of man. If he did not, he was another kind of man. He was
essentially a moralist, and a moralist who rapes or murders places
himself outside the human family and all his verdicts are cancelled. He cannot repent, for the crimes he has committed are
skandala, beyond the power of divine forgiveness.

"The heart of man is desperately wicked, yea, who can know
it" might serve as the epigraph of all Dostoyevsky's later novels.
As few other men, he knew the depths of depravity in the human
heart. He deliberately set himself to explore those uncharted regions of evil which are the common property of the human race.
He knew that in their imaginations all men are murderers, and all
or nearly all have raped children, and this is only the beginning of
their depravity and corruption. "We are all guilty, for all of us and
for everything," he wrote in *The Brothers Karamazov.*

He was one of those rare men who possess the gift of "seeing"
ideas. He moved restlessly through life, at ease only among those
categories of the imagination which Wordsworth called "modes of
being." He saw the world as the battlefield of the spirit; and he
shared with St. Paul, St. Augustine and Pascal a peculiarly exact
knowledge of the powers of corruption. In the minds of men there
are many abysses: some we know and have charted, but others
are hidden by mists which only the bravest and most incorruptible
have dared to penetrate. Dostoyevsky walked through the darkness

and the mists with an uncanny surefootedness. He seems to have possessed some sixth sense which enabled him to walk unharmed in lands where other men have walked to their peril.

He was not of course the only man to have wandered into these desolate and terrible regions. Occasionally the Church Fathers explored this territory, and returned with accounts of strange animals lurking in caves and sudden descents into unfathomable depths. Job, too, had explored this landscape; the young Schiller had penetrated a little way through the rim of darkness. There were obscure religious pamphlets, once widely current in Russia, which spoke of the pilgrimage through the dead lands of the soul and the presence of evil. Dostoyevsky knew Bunyan's *Pilgrim's Progress* well in the Russian translation, and in his famous Pushkin speech he even suggested that Pushkin was indebted to it; and there, too, he would find a sketch map showing the unending roads through the dark landscapes of the soul. He belonged to those who have mapped the spirit.

To find his equal one would need to go back to a time when men were beginning to make a concerted attack on the unknown and unsuspected landscapes which lay behind the veils of human understanding. To the Greeks of the fifth century B.C. there was given the privilege of tearing those veils apart for the first time in recorded history. Quite suddenly, apparently without any preparation at all, they discovered that the human mind could be sharpened to penetrate all, or nearly all the surrounding mysteries. With clear eyes they prepared themselves to look at the most awful possibilities which presented themselves to men, to plumb all depths, to raise themselves to any imaginable height. For the first time man assumed responsibility for his own existence. In their statues and in their tragic dramas they showed men as fearless explorers of the mind's farthest reaches. They discovered that an entire world lay within each man, and that everything was far more complex, more beautiful, and more weighty with tragedy than it had seemed. In the sculptures of Alcamenes and in the tragic dramas of Aeschylus

we are presented with the spectacle of man doomed and triumphant. In *Prometheus Bound,* in the *Oresteia,* and especially in the
majestic *Seven against Thebes,* we enter a world where the phan-
toms of the mind are allowed free rein, where the human spirit is
pitted against elemental forces, and where the end is not defeat at
the hands of alien forces, but the triumph of the spirit of man over
himself.

Dostoyevsky is closer to Aeschylus than to anyone else. He
has the same quick desire to battle against the encompassing forces
of evil, the same abrupt tenderness, the same determination to
hold the balance even. Like Aeschylus, he must use a dramatic
form, though patently at odds with it. The theme they share in
common is heroic suffering and tormenting pity, and man's effort
to accomplish his destiny against all odds. Aeschylus saw the world
in the light of an ancient mythology which had already reached the
stage of crystallization: it was a mythology which provided a perfectly valid framework for observable phenomena. In Christianity
Dostoyevsky possessed a still more mysterious but equally valid
framework for the understanding of the world. Their aims were
similar: to portray the soul in its journeys through the unknown
and evil lands which fatally attracted it, and to point the paths to
blessedness.

Without danger one can push the comparison farther. Both
were men who took part in the political crises of the time. Aeschylus fought at Marathon and Salamis; Dostoyevsky fought the Tzar
in the Petrashevsky rebellion. Beginning as a "liberal," celebrating
the democracy of Athens, Aeschylus became a confirmed believer
in tyranny and entered the court of Hieron of Syracuse. Beginning
as a revolutionary, Dostoyevsky became a reactionary, beloved by
the Russian court and under the special favor of the Procurator
of the Holy Synod, the arch-reactionary who was the real ruler of
Russia. But it is in their methods and in the peculiar attitudes they
possessed towards their heroes that they are most astonishingly
similar, for they possessed the faculty of seeing the chosen crea-

tions of their imagination simultaneously *sub specie aeternitatis* and *sub specie temporis,* in the light of religion and in the light of politics. Their use of the dramatic form—for all Dostoyevsky's major novels are dramas—is equally comparable. Both enjoyed the use of abrupt transitions, and introduced immensely long choruses, and were obsessed with guilt and atonement, and were only too intimately aware of the presence of the wrath of God. One can even find similarities in their styles, for Aeschylus wrote a verse that was at once heavy and maddeningly fast, diffuse and with only a modicum of grace, reminding one of a farmwagon covered with precious tapestries and lurching forward at full speed. Dostoyevsky's style, quick, vivid, relentless, curiously heavy, and only rarely ornate, has the same faults and the same virtues.

Where they differed was in their attitude towards the central heart of the mystery. For Aeschylus the gods were real and potent vehicles of divinity: for Dostoyevsky there were no gods, only the one God, who walked on earth and was crucified. Dostoyevsky profoundly believed in the fact of Christ, and his belief was quickened by raging doubts and anchored in penitence. He believed, and did not believe; but his belief was greater than his unbelief. So he became the greatest Christian novelist of modern times. How great he was we realize when we set him against Graham Greene and François Mauriac, and realize how much they resemble small plants growing in the shade of an enormous oak.

Dostoyevsky's Christianity was not orthodox, though he belonged to the Orthodox Church. It was something he hammered out on his own mind and flesh. There was in him a fearful impatience. He was ruthlessly determined to discover the truth, and thought he had discovered it, but it nearly always escaped him. In his novels the rhythm of belief and unbelief is continual: one wave follows the other, and they move in majestic progression as though obedient to some spiritual law which ordains that every victory shall be followed by a defeat. Something of the same phenomenon can be seen in the plays of Aeschylus.

The Legend

Dostoyevsky was continually wrestling with his angel and displaying an almost incredible spiritual and physical energy. To portray him as a restless neurotic is to forget how much order and deliberation were present in his life. Physically, he possessed extraordinary stamina. He survived countless epileptic attacks, and was usually back at his desk before the effects of the attack had worn off. He husbanded his health, and lived modestly and carefully. His greatest vice was that he smoked too much, and his occasional bouts of gambling fever may be explained as the product of his epilepsy. His was no broken tormented life: it was rounded to its close, and he lived his life to the uttermost. Yet he was a scholar of ideas, and possessed a scholar's patience and a scholar's devotion to his task.

The clue to Dostoyevsky lies in his notebooks, which show him engrossed in the patient exploration of those ideas which he was the first to express. No one ever plumbed so deeply into the recesses of the human soul, or faced with such composure so many terrifying discoveries. He remains one of the most significant and ominous figures in the history of the human mind because he dared to enter the dark places of the spirit. He entered; and walked out again; and showed that though they are terrible beyond belief, yet a man armed with his human dignity may confront them unharmed. "Man is a mystery," he wrote when he was very young. "This mystery must be solved, and even if you pass your entire life solving it, do not say you have wasted your time. I occupy myself with this mystery, since I want to be a man." To this belief he remained faithful to the end of his life.

His strength lay in his single-minded determination to solve a mystery which no one before or since has ever solved. He failed, as all must fail; but his failure was a triumph. With extraordinary daring he tore down the veils of the temple until there remained only the last veil of all. Beyond this no man may go.

So he became the prophet of our time and a figure of compelling power, warning and prophesying like one of the patriarchs of old. His shadow grows larger with each passing year, and still today he rebukes the evil and comforts the innocent. He comes to those who will receive him with open hands, blessing the works of men and setting the tasks which must be fulfilled in our age. Sometimes the saint vanishes, and there is revealed, for all to wonder at, the Angel of Terrible Aspect, robed in fire, wielding his defiant sword and searching us with his steady gaze.

BIBLIOGRAPHY

W ITH THE PUBLICATION of the final volume of Dostoyevsky's
collected letters in 1959, nearly all the documents for a
study of Dostoyevsky's life are now available for scholars. There
remain to be published only the brief diary which he kept in
Semipalatinsk, some of the working notes for his minor novels, and
a few occasional articles written in magazines and never reprinted.
His Bible, preserved among the archives of the Dostoyevsky Museum in Moscow, may contain a number of important annotations
which would throw light on his religious life, but if so, they remain
unpublished. A few more letters may be found, but it is doubtful
whether they will add materially to the more than 900 collected
over many years and brilliantly edited by A. S. Dolinin. Eighty
years have passed since Dostoyevsky's death, and it is now unlikely that any documents of major importance remain to be discovered.

This is not to suggest that there is any finality in the work of
understanding Dostoyevsky. For a long time to come there will be
the need for a continual comprehensive re-examination of his
books. Many special studies remain to be written, especially on the
details of his daily life and on the influences he suffered. A careful
scrutiny of the texts of his four major novels is long overdue. There
has been so far no scholarly exploration of Dostoyevsky's attitude
to the Orthodox Church. Scholars are still debating the most ele-
mentary aspects of his life; and while for example the Soviet

scholar Belchikov asserts on the plain evidence of the testimonies of the defendants that the Petrashevsky conspiracy might have assumed formidable proportions, the *emigré* scholar Mochulsky in the best book on Dostoyevsky to appear in this generation asserts flatly that there was no conspiracy at all. It is unlikely that Mochulsky is right—the detailed testimonies are overwhelmingly convincing—but some of the difficulty of interpreting Dostoyevsky is significantly emphasized by the disagreement between these two authorities.

Although nearly all of Dostoyevsky's published works and all the more important letters have appeared in English, very few of the essential studies by Russian scholars have been translated; it is to be hoped that these will appear in due course. The recent spate of new translations of Dostoyevsky's work is not altogether an unmixed blessing, for they tend to add a peculiarly modern crispness to the deliberate and carefully contrived vagueness of the originals. Constance Garnett wrote in the idiom of the nineteenth century, which was also the idiom of Dostoyevsky; and little is gained by presenting him as an author writing in the idiom of the modern age.

I have not attempted an exhaustive bibliography: it would cover too many pages and be of very little help to the reader. An excellent checklist of critical works and translations into English appeared in the Dostoyevsky special number of *Modern Fiction Studies* in the autumn of 1958. It covers twenty closely-printed pages. An even more exhaustive bibliography of Russian studies on Dostoyevsky appears in Dr. Vladimir Seduro's *Dostoyevski in Russian Literary Criticism 1846–1956* (Columbia University Press, 1957), where the checklist of Russian works extends to more than fifty closely-printed pages.

I have included here only the more important works I consulted during the writing of this book. I have added an asterisk to those books which seemed to have permanent value.

Bibliography

IN ENGLISH

*Baring, Maurice: *An Outline of Russian Literature.* New York: Home University Library, n.d.

Belinsky, V. G.: *Selected Philosophical Works.* Moscow: Foreign Languages Publishing House, 1956.

*Berdyaev, Nicholas: *Dostoevsky.* New York: Meridian Books; 1957.

*Carr, E. H.: *Dostoevsky, 1821–1881: A New Biography.* London: Allen and Unwin, 1949.

Dostoevsky, Anna: *Dostoevsky Portrayed by His Wife: The Diary and Reminescences of Mme Dostoevsky,* tr. S. S. Koteliansky. New York: Dutton, 1926.

————: *The Diary of Dostoevsky's Wife,* ed. René Fülöp-Miller and Friedrich Eckstein. New York: Macmillan; 1928.

Dostoevsky, Fyodor: *The Diary of a Writer,* tr. Boris Brasol. New York: Scribners; 1949.

————: *Letters and Reminiscences,* tr. S. S. Koteliansky and J. Middleton Murry. New York: Alfred A. Knopf; 1923.

————: *Letters of Fyodor Mickailovich Dostoevsky to his Family and Friends,* tr. Ethel Colburn Mayne. London: Chatto & Windus; 1914.

————: *The Letters of Dostoevsky to his Wife,* tr. Elizabeth Hill and D. Mudie. New York: Richard R. Smith; 1930.

————: *Pages from the Journal of an Author,* tr. S. S. Koteliansky and J. Middleton Murry. London: Maunsel & Co.; 1916.

————: *Winter Notes on Summer Impressions,* tr. Richard Lee Renfield. New York: Criterion Books; 1955.

Fülöp-Miller, René: *Fyodor Dostoevsky: Insight, Faith and Prophecy,* tr. Richard and Clara Winston. New York: Scribners; 1950.

Gide, André: *Dostoevsky.* New York: Alfred A. Knopf; 1926.

*Ivanov, Vyacheslav: *Freedom and the Tragic Life. A Study in Dostoevsky.* New York: The Noonday Press; 1952.

Lednicki, Waslaw: *Russia, Poland and the West.* New York: Roy Publishers; 1954.

Leffler, Anna Carlotta: *Sonya Kovalevsky.* London: T. Fisher Unwin; 1895.

Lloyd, J. A. T.: *Fyodor Dostoevsky.* New York: Scribners; 1947.

Mackiewicz, Stanislaw: *Dostoyevsky.* London: Orbis; 1947.

Payne, Robert: *The Terrorists.* New York: Funk and Wagnall; 1957.

Roe, Ivan: *The Breath of Corruption: An Interpretation of Dostoevsky.* London: Hutchinson; 1946.

Seduro, Vladimir: *Dostoyevski in Russian Literary Criticism, 1846–1956.* New York: Columbia University Press; 1957.

*Simmons, Ernest J.: *Dostoevsky: The Making of a Novelist.* London: John Lehmann; 1952.

Yarmolinsky, Avrahm: *Dostoevsky. His Life and Art.* New York: Criterion Books; 1957.

IN RUSSIAN

Antonii, Metropolitan of Kiev: *Slovar i tvoreniyam Dostoyevskovo.* Sophia: Rossisko-Bolgarskoe knigoizdatelstvo; 1920.

*Belchikov, N. F.: *Dostoyevsky i protsesse petrashevtsev.* Leningrad: Gusudarstvennoe izdatelstvo; 1936.

Belchikov, N. F. and P. N. Sakulin: *Iz arkhiva F. M. Dostoyevskovo. Idiot. Neizdannyi materiali.* Moscow: Gosudarstvennoe izdatelstvo; 1931.

Dolinin, A. S.: *Statii i materialy.* Leningrad: Izdatelstvo Akademii Nauk SSSR; 1935.

————: *V tvorcheskoi laboratorii Dostoyevskovo.* Moscow: Sovietskii Pisatel; 1947.

Dostoyevsky, F. M.: *Sobraniye Sochinenii.* 10 vols. Moscow: Khudozhestvennoi Literaturi; 1957.

*————: *Pisma* I, II, III, IV. ed. A. S. Dolinin. Moscow-Leningrad: Akademia, Khudozhestvennoi Literaturi; 1928–59.

Bibliography

————: *Pisma. F. M. Dostoyevskovo k zhene.* Moscow: Gosudarstvennoe izdatelstvo; 1926.

Ermilov, V.: *F. M. Dostoyevsky.* Moscow: Khudozhestvennoi Literaturi; 1956.

Glivenko, I. M.: *Iz arkhiva F. M. Dostoyevskovo. Prestupleniye i nakazaniye.* Moscow: Neizdannyi materiali, GIKhL; 1931.

*Grossman, Leonid: *Dostoyevsky na zhiznennom puti.* Moscow: Nikitinskiye subbotniki; 1928.

*————: *Put Dostoyevskovo.* Moscow: N. A. Stollar; 1928.

*————: *Tvorchestvo Dostoyevskovo.* Odessa: Vseukrainskoye gosudarstvennoye izdatelstvo; 1921.

Komarovich, L.: "Yunost Dostoyevskovo," in *Byloe,* No. 23, Leningrad; 1924.

Konshina, Y. N.: *Zapisnye tetradi F. M. Dostoyevskovo.* Moscow: Akademia; 1935.

Lyaskovsky, A. L.: *F. M. Dostoyevsky.* Petropolis; n.d.

Mikulich, V.: *Vstrechi s pisatelyami.* Leningrad: Izdatelstvo pisatelei; 1929.

Miller, Orest F. and N. N. Strakhov: *Biografiya, pisma, zametki iz zapisnoi knizhki F. M. Dostoyevskovo.* St. Petersburg: Suvorin; 1883.

*Mochulsky, K.: *Dostoyevsky: zhizn i tvorchestvo.* Paris: 1947.

Nechayeva, V. S.: *V semye i usadbe Dostoyevskikh.* Gosudar stvennoye sotsialno-ekonomicheskoye izdatelstvo; 1939.

*Rozanov, V. V.: *O Velikom Inkvizitore F. M. Dostoyevskovo.* St. Petersburg: Pirozhkov; 1906.

*Suslova, A. P.: *Gody blizosti s Dostoyevskim.* Moscow: Izdanie Sabashnikov; 1928.

*Vrangel, Baron A. Y.: *Vospominaniya o F. M. Dostoyevskom v Sibiri (1854–1856).* St. Petersburg: Suvorin; 1912.

*Yanovsky, S. D.: *Vospominaniya o Dostoyevskom.* Moscow: Ruskii Vestnik; 1885.

INDEX

A NOTE ABOUT THE AUTHOR

ROBERT PAYNE, born in Cornwall, England, in 1911, was educated at St. Paul's School, London, and subsequently at the Universities of Capetown, Liverpool, Munich, and the Sorbonne. He has worked as a shipwright, an armaments officer, and war correspondent; has lived all over Europe, in Africa, and in Asia, before he came to New York, where he now makes his home.

He studied Russian language and literature under Dr. Bruce Boswell at Liverpool University, and he had already translated the short stories of Boris Pasternak by 1937, printing them in Singapore, just before the outbreak of the Pacific war. His first published work was a translation of Yuri Olyesha's *Envy* (1937), published by Virginia and Leonard Woolf in London, and he has also translated Olyesha's short stories. His book *The Terrorists* was a study of Russian political movements in the last years of the nineteenth century.

Robert Payne has also written *Forever China* (1945), *The White Pony* (1947), *The Three Worlds of Albert Schweitzer* (1957), *The Holy Fire* (1957), *The Gold of Troy* (1958), *The Shepherd* (1959), *The Three Worlds of Boris Pasternak* (1963), *The Rise and Fall of Stalin* (1965), *Mao Tse-Tung* (third edition, 1969), and *Ancient Rome* (revised, 1970).

A NOTE ON THE TYPE

THE TEXT of this book was set on the Linotype in TIMES ROMAN, designed by *Stanley Morison* for *The Times* (LONDON), and first introduced by that newspaper in 1932. Among typographers and designers of the twentieth century, Stanley Morison has been a strong influence, as typographical adviser to the English Monotype Corporation, as a director of two distinguished English publishing houses, and as a writer of sensibility, erudition, and keen practical sense.

Composed, printed and bound by KINGSPORT PRESS, INC., Kingsport, Tennessee. Paper manufactured by S. D. WARREN Co., Boston. Typography and binding design by WARREN CHAPPELL.